AF528810

Interventions and Tribal Development
Challenges before Tribes in India in the era of Globalisation

Interventions and Tribal Development

Challenges before Tribes in India in the era of Globalisation

M.C. Behera
Jumyir Basar

SERIALS PUBLICATIONS
NEW DELHI (INDIA)

First Published – 2010

ISBN: 978-81-8387-389-5

Published by

SERIALS PUBLICATIONS
4830/24, 1st Floor, Ansari Road
Darya Ganj, New Delhi-110002 (India)
Phone : 23245225. Fax : 91-11-23272135
E-mail: serials@satyam.net.in

CONTENTS

Section – II
Stunted Transformation

Section – III
Specious Dynamics

Section – IV
Innovation as Intervention

Section – V
Intervention Perspectives

Section – VI
Untended Context: Challenges in Tradition

ACKNOWLEDGEMENTS

Some of the papers included in this volume were presented in the national seminar on *Encountering Globalisation and Tribal Communities in India* held on February 27-29, 2009. The papers selected from the presentations in the seminar were reviewed and sent to the respective authors with comments, observations and suggestions for improvement. The editors are grateful to the authors for their timely cooperation. Other papers were invited subsequently from the scholars of tribal studies. The papers were reviewed and edited in the light of comments. The seminar was funded by ICSSR, New Delhi. The editors take this opportunity to put on records their gratitude to ICSSR also. The authors also express their sincere gratitude to Prof.Tamo Mibang, Director, Arunachal Institute of Tribal Studies, Prof. K.C.Belliappa, Vice Chancellor, Rajiv Gandhi University and faculty members of AITS for their help, cooperation, guidance and encouragement to make the seminar successful.

Finally, the editors acknowledge their deep sense of gratitude to S.K. Jha of Serials Publications for undertaking the publishing responsibility of this volume.

LIST OF CONTRIBUTORS

A. Wati Walling, M.A, M.Phil (Sociology) is a Research Scholar in the Department of Humanities & Social Sciences, IIT, Bombay, Powai Mumbai-400 076. His present research interest included environmental sociology, natural resource conflicts, social stratification in rural India, cultural and ecological studies, Tribals studies and issues of livelihood in contemporary Nagaland. el: +91-22-2576-7351/52 Fax: +91-22-2572-3480; Cell:+91-9930-437-887 E-mail-samuelwati@ gmail.com; watiwalling@iitb.ac.in

Ajay Kumar is a Research Scholar, Department of Public Administration, Himachal Pradesh University, Summer Hill, Shimla, Himachal Pradesh.

Alok Chantia, M.A., Ph.D (Anthropology), UGC–JRF an ICSSR Fellowship in 2003, is a Lecturer, Dept. of Anthropology, Sri J.N.P.G. College, Lucknow. His paper on "Ideology, Conflict and Tolerance" was awarded by ICPR, in Goa Session, 1991, A Manuscript "Pehala Kadam" (in Hindi) was awarded by State Government., U.P. in 1995, a story, "Sandeh" (in Hindi) awarded by the then Prime minister Shri Atal Bihari Vajpayee in Kadamani Mahotsava in Lucknow, 1995 and "Fate of a book" by Mahatama Gandhi International University, New Delhi, 2003. He has a book entitled *Vikalp Ka Samaj* (in Hindi) to his credit. Presently his areas of Academic interests are HIV/AIDS, Human Rights, Functional errors of culture and developmental sociology. Email: alok chantia@rediffmail.com

Bina Saklani, M.Sc. D.Phil (Anthropology), is an Associate Professor, Department of Anthropology, HNB Gahwal University, Srinagar,(Garhwal),Uttarskhand,245174. Her current research interest lies in Medical Anthropology, Reproductive Anthropology, Women Anthropology, Food and culture and Tribal Studies. She is a member of many professional bodies like Medical Anthropological Association (India), Nepal Study Centre, New Maxico (USA), South Western Association on Asian Studies, Austin (USA). Her important work includes *Base line survey of PTG Bhoxa tribe of Garhwal division* and *Mother and Child in Himalayas*.Ph. No. 09411357440, E-mail: binasaklani@hotmail.com

C. Lalrozami, M.A (Communication) is an awardee of Rajiv Gandhi National Fellowship (Senior Research Fellow) and Ph.D Research Scholar in S.N School, University of Hyderabad, Hyderabad. Her present research interest is Media and Culture.

Daisy Nath, M.A (Political Science), is a Research Asso-ciate in North Eastern Social Research Centre, 110 Kharghuli Road, Guwahati-4, Assam. Her current research interest includes children and women issues.

Debojyoti Das is a Graduate Research Scholar, Department of Anthropology and Sociology, School of Oriental and African Studies (SOAS), University of London, Ph. No. 09436700838, debojyoti.das@gmail.com

Felix Padel, M.A, M.Phil (Sociology), D.Phil (Social Anthropology) is Freelance Social Anthropologist. His current research interest is Tribes, Mining & Displacement issues, Historical Anthropology, and 'Reverse Anthropology'. Some of his important publications are: 'The Sacrifice of Human Being: British rule & the Konds of Orissa, (1995/2000), 'Forest Knowledge: Tribal people, their Environment and the Structure of Power' (1998), and with Samarendra Das, 'Cultural Genocide: the Real Impact of Development-Induced Displacement'2008 and 'Orissa's highland clearances: The reality gap in R & R, (2008).

H.V. Singh, M.Sc., Ph.D. (Anthropology), is an Assistant Professor, Arunachal Institute of Tribal Studies, Rajiv Gandhi University, Itanagar, Arunachal Pradesh. His present research interest lies in tribal health, HIV/AIDS and population genetics.

Jagabandhu Samal is a retired Professor in Economics. He has joined the Council of Analytical Tribal Studies, Koraput, Orissa, and is actively involved in action researches for tribal development. Ph.+91 9437233382, E-mail: coatskrp@rediff mail.com

Jagannath Dash, M.A., Ph.D.(Anthropology), is a Professor in Social Anthropology, Department of Anthro-pology, Utkal University, Vanivihar, Bhubaneswar-751004. He is an awardee of Commonwealth Fellowship (2000-01). He has extensively written on various issues, both theoretical and empirical, in social anthropology. His important work on *Human Ecology of Foragers* (1999) has earned him wide acclamation in the country and abroad. He is a member of various professional and advisory bodies including the one in Bhumiputra Foundation of India. Ph. No. 09437919198; E-mail: jdash1955 @gmail.com.

Jumyir Basar, M.A.(Anthropology), UGC-JRF and ICSSR Doctoral Fellow, is an Assistant Professor, Arunachal Institute of Tribal Studies, Rajiv Gandhi University, Itanagar, Arunachal Pradesh. She is actively involved in NGO and women movements of the State. Her research interest includes IKS, development and women issues. Presently she is working on *Indigenous Knowledge System in Developmental Policies and Programmes* for her Ph.D degree. Contact: +91 9436055264, E-mail: jumyir@yahoo.com

Kabiraj Behera is a Research Scholar, Department of Anthropology, Utkal University, Vanivihar, Bhubaneswar-751004. His research interest lies in shamanistic studies in the context of globalisation.

Kartikeswar Behera, M.A (History, English), Orissa Education Service(II), is a Senior Teacher Educator, DIET, Jeypore, P.O. Jeypore, Dist-Koraput, Orissa. His present research interest lies in folklore studies and popularizing English education among the tribal students through folklores. Cell: 09937452016. E-mail: kartike_swar@yahoo.com.

L. Jitendro Singh is a Research Scholar, G.B. Pant Institute of Himalayan Environment and Development (AI, MoEF, GOI), North East Unit, Vivek Vihar, Itanagar-791 113, Arunachal Pradesh, Telephone: 03602211773, 2216423

M.C. Behera, M.A., Ph.D (Economics), Associate Professor, Arunachal Institute of Tribal Studies, Rajiv Gandhi University, Itanagar, Arunachal Pradesh. Some of his recent works include *Globalisation and Development Dilemma-Reflections from North East India(2004), Globalisation and Rural Development-Understanding New Development Paradigm (2005), Globalising Rural Development: Competing Paradigms and Emerging Realities (2006), Making Gandhi Relevant, Rural Development in the Context of Globalisation (2009)* and *Foraging Mode of Thought and Forager Sulung's Social Self* (in press). His research interest lies in tribal studies, development in cultural perspectives and cultural syncretism. Ph.+91 9436252229, E-mail: mcbehera1959 @gmail. com.

Malsawmdawngliana, M.A., M.Phil (History), is a Faculty in the Department of History, St. Francis College For Women, Begumpet, Hyderabad -500 046, and a Ph.D Research Scholar in the Department of History, University of Hyderabad. His present research interest is Medieval Indian History. He is a member of Indian Historical Congress. Some of his recent publications include 'Thangchhuah Feast and their implications in Mizo Society' (2009), 'Re-thinking sacred geography of the Chin-Lushai in the historical Context' (2009), Critical Areas of Ensuring Energy Security (2009) and 'Sources of writing Mizo history and their limitations: Past and Future' (2009). Cell: +91 9949143027; E-mail: sawmpuia@gmail.com

Mihin Dollo is a Research Scholar, G.B. Pant Institute of Himalayan Environment and Development (AI,MoEF, GOI), North East Unit, Vivek Vihar, Itanagar-791 113, Arunachal Pradesh, Ph.03602211773, 2216423

Mritunjay Kumar, M.A (Ancient History), LL.B., a UGC-SRF, is a Ph.D Research Scholar at P.G. Department of History, Ranchi University, Ranchi. His present research interest lies in Socio-Economic History in general and of tribal communities in particular. Ph. 09334709042, E-mail- mritunjay 26june@yahoo.co.in.

Mrs. Himani is Academic Councillor, IGNOU, Department of Public Administration, Government College of Chamba, Himachal Pradesh

Nabam Nakha Hina, M.A (Political Science), L.LB, is an Assistant Professor in the Department of Political Science, Rajiv Gandhi University. He is an indigenous scholar belonging to Nyishi tribe of Arunachal Pradesh. His research interest lies in codification of customary laws of the tribes. email-nabamnakha@yahoo.co.in, Ph.+91 9436895325.

O.P. Monga, M.A. Ph.D. (Sociology), is a Professor of Sociology, Department of Sociology, Himachal Pradesh University, Summer Hill, Shimla-171005. His present research interest includes Sociology of Family, Gerontology, Child Development, Health Behaviour, Tribal Development, etc. he is a member of many international and national bodies like The International Union of Anthropological and Ethnological Sciences, Indian Association of Population Education, Association of Gerontology, Community Psychology Association of India, etc. Contact: Ph.09418126760, E-mail: opmonga2001@yahoo.com

Otem Moyong, M.Com, Ph.D (Commerce), is an Assistant Professor in the Department of Commerce, Rajiv Gandhi University, Itanagar. His research interest lies in the study of entrepreneurial activities in tribal communities in the context of globalisation. Ph.+91 9856329021, E-mail:otm_02@rediff mail.com

P.C. Mohapatro is a retired Professor of Economics and presently working as Director, Council of Analytical Tribal Studies, Koraput-764020, Orissa. He has extensively worked on shifting cultivation. His important work on the topic is *Economic Development of Tribal India (1987)*. Presently he is involved in district planning and tirelessly working for the up-liftment of the tribal communities in undivided Koraput district. Ph. (06852) 251708/09437094323, E-mail: pcmpatro@ yahoo.com.

Philip Mody, M.Com, is an Assistant Professor in the Department of Commerce, Rajiv Gandhi University, Itanagar. His research interest lies in the study of potentials of agro-based industries in tribal areas in the context of globalisation.

Pradeep Kumar Mishra, M.A. (Oriya, English, Education), M.Sc. (Environmental Sciences), M.Phil (Education), is a Chief Investigator, Swami Vivekananda Vidya Mandir (Govt. School), At/ Po-Umerkote, Dist: Nabarangpur–764073, Orissa. His present research interest lies in popularising English and science education among the tribal students. Cell: +91 94375 25105, E-mail: pradeepkumarmishra71@yahoo.com,

Prasanna K. Samal MA, Ph.D., Scientist In charge , G.B. Pant Institute of Himalayan Environment and Development (AI,MoEF, GOI), North East Unit, Vivek Vihar, Itanagar-791 113, Arunachal Pradesh. He is a Life Member in more than 10 scientific bodies/associations and Member in Editorial Boards of more than 5 Journals/Newsletters. He has worked on 17 National/International R&D Projects from organizations like SICI-CIDA (Canada); DST (Govt. of India, New Delhi), ICSSR (New Delhi), ICIMOD (Kathmandu), UNESCO and UNDP. His present research interest lies in Socio-economic development, Tribal Development, Culture studies, Technology Backstopping, Watershed Management, Indigenous Knowledge System, Gender, Resource Management, Impact Studies, and Participatory Development. Contact: Phone: 03602211773, 2216423 E-mail- prasannasamal @rediffmail.com

Preeti Misra, M.A (Economics), LL.M, LL.D, is an Assistant Professor of Human Rights, School for Legal Studies, Babasaheb Bhimrao Ambedkar University, Lucknow-226025. Her present research interest lies in the field of women and gender issues, ethnic minority, human rights of rural and urban poor, family violence, aging, education and development. Some of her important publications include Domestic Violence Against women-Legal Control & Judicial Response 2006, 'Growing Menace of HIV/AIDS-A Socio-Legal Study' 2007, 'Growing Menace of Incestuous Behaviour in

India- Calls for Legislation' (1999), 'Gender Justice–A Dream to be Fulfilled' 1998), 'Female Foeticide –A Violation of Human Rights', 'Policing the Police in Modern Context–A Critical Analysis' and 'Protection of Women From Domestic Violence Act, 2005-A Critical Evaluation' (2009) E-mail: misra9us@ gmail.com.

Priyanka Priyadarshini, M.A, Ph. D (Economics) is an Assistant Professor, Department of Economics, J.N. College, Pasighat, Arunachal Pradesh. Her research interest lies in the study of agricultural economics and institutional economics with focus on property rights in tribal areas. Ph.+9194360 53153

Rabindranath Sarma, M.A. Ph.D. (Folkloristics) is a Research Associate, UPE Project on Rice Myths of North-East India, NEHU, Shillong. Contact: +919863315243, rsfolk@ gmail.com

Rajiv Mili is a Research Scholar, G.B. Pant Institute of Himalayan Environment and Development (AI, MoEF, GOI), North East Unit, Vivek Vihar, Itanagar-791 113, Arunachal Pradesh, Telephone: 03602211773, 2216423.

Ramesh C Malik, M.A (Oriya), M.Phil (Translation Studies), is a Ph.D Research Scholar and Senior Research Fellow (UGC) in Centre for Applied Linguistics and Translation Studies, University of Hyderabad, Hyderabad-500046. His current research interest lies in General Linguistics, Translation Studies, Literary Criticism and Ethnography Studies. He has written extensively both in Oriya and English. His main works include '*Socio-Political Structure of Kandara Caste in Puri District*' (2004), '*Socio-Cultural Analysis of the Desia Kondh Kinship Terms*' (2006), '*The Multidimensional Facets of Ethnography: An Agenda for Research*' (2009); and which are jointly written, *Language, Culture and* (2008), *Ethnographic Discourses of the Others: Conceptual and Methodological Issues* (2008) and *Theory and Practice of Ethnography: Reading from Periphery* (2009). Contact No :=91 9989130450, E-mail: rameshmalik@gmail.com

Samarendra Das, MCA, is a prolific writer in both Oriya and English, an NGO activist and a producer of documentary films. *Wira Pdika* (Earth Worm: Company Man), 2005, Co-directed with Amarendra Das, a feature-length campaign documentary on the resistance of the tribal people in Orissa to the multinational mining companies trying to take their sacred mountains is widely screened in Italy, Germany, Spain, USA, UK, Iceland, Peru, France, Australia, Norway, Sweden, Finland, The Netherlands, Turkey, Brazil, Argentina in various festivals, seminar, and lecture tours. His another documentary with Amarendra Das , April, 2006, is on Tawa Matsya Sangh called *Ladat Jaare* – (a fishery co-operative run by the Korkus and Gonds, who were forcefully displaced in 1974 by dam construction, currently under combined threat from a tiger conservation project, a military test fire range, and a national park). Contact: 7F Belsize Park Gardens, London NW3 4LB, UK., E-mail-sadasorisa@rediffmail.com

S.K. Kataria, M.A., M. Phil and Ph.D (Public Administra-tion) M.A. (Sociology) Bachelor of Journalism and Mass Communication, is a social activist and presently working as an Associate Professor in Government M.S. College, Bikaner. He is a recipient of many national awards like Kautilaya Award by Planning Commission and G.B. Pant Award by Ministry of Home Affairs. He is a prolific writer in both Hindi and English. Some of his important publications include: *Economic Planning and Poverty Alleviation in India, Panchayati Raj Institutions: Past, Present and Future, Administration and Public Policy, Rural Development in India: Strategies and Challenges, Social Policy In India and Right to Information: Lessons and Implications*. Contact: Ph: +91141-2783871, Cell:+919929155 426, E-mail: skkataria64@redffmail.com.

Shyamal Kr. Jana, M.A., Ph.D (Anthropology), is a District Coordinator, District Programme Management Unit for Strengthening Rural Decentralisation, Office of the District Magistrate, P.O. & Dist. Jalpaiguri, Pin-735 101, West Bengal, Cell: +91 94344 38771,E-mail: shyamaljana@hotmail.com.

Srinibash Panda, M.A., Ph.D (History), is an Associate Professor in History, Jawaharlal Nehru College, Pasighat, East Siang District, Arunachal Pradesh. His research interest lies in imperialism in north-east India.

Tabang Mibang, M.A.(Political Science), M.Phil (Tribal Studies), is an Assistant Professor, Department of Political Science, Rajiv Gandhi University, Itanagar, Arunachal Pradesh. His present research interest lies in social capital, tribal culture and political theory.

Vinay Kumar Srivastava, M.Sc. (Anthropology), M.A. (Sociology), M.Phil. (Chinese Studies), Ph.D. (Social Anthropology), is working as Professor of Social Anthropology, Department of Anthropology, University of Delhi. He is a recipient of many awards including Commonwealth Scholarship National Scholarship to Study Abroad, Rashtriya Shiromani Award, 2006, by Delhi Telegu Society and Post-Graduate Research Award, University Grants Commission, 2006. He is/was associated with many academic and research institutions in different capacities including Fellow, Cambridge Philosophical Society; Fellow and Associate Editor, Journal of Human Ecology; Managing Editor, Journal of Social Science (2000-2). Editor, The Eastern Anthropologist, Lucknow (from 2001), etc. He has published widely in both national and international journals. His important books are: *Essays in social anthropology* (1990) *L'Inde des Tribus Oubliees* (with Declan Quigley) (1993), *Religious renunciation of a pastoral people,* (1997), 'On ethnography and the sacred cow controversy' (1982), 'Malinowski on freedom and civilization' (1985), 'The future of anthropology' (1999), 'Some responses of communities to social tensions in India' (2003), 'Tribes in Crises: Some Reflections'(2007), and 'On Renunciation, Alternative Society, and Sociology: An Essay Commemorating the Work of Professor Narendra K. Singhi' (2009) His research interest lies in the study of comparative religion, caste system, family dynamics, medical systems, and anthropological theory and methods. Ph. + 91 11-27666614/ 26276104, Cell: +91 9810 45 46, E-mail- vinaykumar srivas tava. vks@gmail.com

1

INTRODUCTION

M.C. Behera, Jumyir Basar

Pursuits on tribal development in India have been an interminable process since its Independence in 1947. Before Independence, due to the British policy of isolation, the tribal areas in India were loosely administered or virtually remained un-administered. (Sinha, 1981). However, there were cases where tribal communities encountered British administration when the later intruded into the resource base of the former. (see Damodaran, 2005; Singh, 1983). Further, in north-east India the tribes encountered the British in course of the latter's drive for territorial extension, security concern or trade expansion. (Mackanzie, 1884/1994; Gait, 1905/1963 and Behera, 1994:23-25; and also see Panda & Priyadarshini in this volume). Otherwise there were no any direct interventions by the British administration for socio- economic development of the tribes except the efforts of conversion. (Malsawm-dawngliana and Lalrozami in this volume).

It is only after Independence that the representative government of people of India intervened directly with planning instruments, constitutional provisions, etc. for the general welfare of tribal people.

NATURE AND SCOPE OF INTERVENTIONS

It is to be mentioned that there is no comprehensive tribal policy except the Draft of National Tribal Policy (A Policy for the Scheduled Tribes of India) 2006, was framed only recently and is awaiting the legal status. Similarly, The Forest (Recognition of Tribal and Other Forest Dwellers) Rights Act, 2006 is the first organised step in defining the rights of the tribals in an objective manner. However, the state policy of tribal development is in the line with Nehru's ideals of tribal development, the tribal *panchashil*[1] to be precise. (Pakem, 1992:82-100).

Before Independence, however, the issue of tribal development had found a place only in the election manifesto of the Congress towards the end of 1945. (Mantaw, 2003:10). Practically a concrete step in this regard was initiated when the issue was included in the Cabinet Mission Plan in 1946. In accordance with the provisions laid down in the Plan, the Constituent Assembly set up an Advisory Committee on Fundamental Rights, Minorities and Tribal and Excluded Areas. The Advisory Committee set up four sub-committees including one on North East Tribal and Excluded Areas of Assam and the other on Excluded areas other than those in Assam. In India, there are predominantly tribal states like Arunachal Pradesh, Mizoram, Nagaland, Lakshadweep, where general plan programmes are implemented for tribal development. (GOI, 1986-87). But in states like Orissa, Madhya Pradesh, Himachal Pradesh, Gujarat, Rajasthan, Assam, tribes are a part of general population and so there are special programmes and schemes such as Multi-Purpose tribal development Projects, Special Multi-Purpose Tribal Blocks (1956-1961), Crash Special Nutrition Programmes and Crash Employment Programmes (1969-1974) and Tribal Sub-Plan (1974-1979), to address the specific development needs of the tribal communities. The Tribal Development Blocks, Large Agricultural Multi-Purpose Societies (LAMPS), Tribal Development Corporation, Tribal Cooperative Marketing Development Federation of India Limited (TRIFED) have been created to provide institutional support (see Rao,1998) in the process of tribal development.

The Constitution of India provides for safeguarding the interest of all citizens in general, weaker sections and tribes in particular through the fundamental rights. (Sharma, 2001:209-255 and Mantaw, op cit. 13-21). Emphasis is laid on protective as well as development aspects concerning the tribal development. The protective aspects relate to the protection of the rights of the tribals in land and forests along with the safeguards against usurious or exploitive forces. The protection is also discriminatory in that there are special provisions, basically preferential in nature, like reservations to tribals. The development aspects relate to implementation of welfare measures, both development and protective discrimination aspects having the objective of raising their socio-economic standard at par national level. The provisions are contained in Articles 46, 244, 330, 332, 334, 335, 338, 339, 342 and Schedules V and VI to the Constitution of India. The concern for tribal development is evident, for example, in Art.46 which reads:

"The state shall promote with special care the educational and economic interests of the weaker sections of the people, and in particular, of the Scheduled Castes and the Scheduled Tribes, and shall protect them from social injustice and all forms of exploitation". Art.46.

Since the beginning of First Five Year Plan the national government has formulated a series of development policies pertaining to the welfare of Scheduled Tribes. The First Five Year Plan document outlines the national concern for tribal development, which evinces both the goal and perspectives of the government, as under:

"The conditions are now generally such that there has to be a positive policy of assisting the tribal people to develop their natural resources and to evolve a productive economic life wherein they will enjoy the fruits of their labour and will not be exploited by more organised economic forces from outside".(GOI,1951: 836).

After the implementation of Tenth Five Year Plan, tribal development policies and programmes could be viewed in the range from infrastructure building to empowerment, from collective welfare to individual/family welfare, from area development to integrated area development and from growth oriented development to sustainable and inclusive development.

As has been said, tribal development practically began with the beginning of First Five Year Plan. However, the policies and strategies get modified from time to time (see Singh, 1994) after evaluation of the welfare programmes by different governmental committees and individual scholars. There are various committees and commissions (Rath, 2006:32; Srivastava, 2006; Singh 1981:115-116; Mantaw, op cit. 23-24) like Committee on Special Multi-Purpose Tribal Development Blocks (Elwin Committee), 1959; Scheduled Areas and Scheduled Tribes Commission (Dhebar Commission),1961; Shilu Ao Committee, 1969 (The Study Team on Tribal Development Programmes on Plan Projects was set up under the Chairmanship of Shri P.Shilu Ao, 26-10-1966); Commission for Scheduled Castes and Scheduled Tribes and Parliamentary Committee on Welfare of Scheduled Castes and Scheduled Tribes. The recommendations of these committees guided subsequent policies and strategies on tribal development. For example, Shilu Ao Committee was set up firstly to study the problems and needs of the tribal communities in each state and secondly to appraise the working of tribal development programmes, especially of the Third Five Year Plan, and to make recommendations to be carried out during Fourth Five Year Plan. The 'Area Approach' and 'adopting to the felt needs of the areas' were two main recommendations of this Committee. The National Committee on the Development of Backward Areas (Sivaraman Committee) of Government of India, 1981 suggested for Integrated Tribal Development Project. (Rath, op cit.).

Formulation of policies, strategies and implementation of programmes were not the only objectives of tribal development programmes. There have been systematic monitoring and evaluation of tribal development programmes with a view to get feed back and to make recommendations for planning. The first important step in this regard was taken when a working group on tribal development was set up in the Ministry of Home Affaires in 1978. Evaluation work was entrusted to Directorate of Statistics/ Evaluation of the State Governments; Tribal Research Institute of State Governments; Programme Evaluation Organisation of Planning Commission; Regional Offices of the SC/ST Commission; and National Level Organisations like Administrative Staff College, Hyderabad; National Institute of Rural Development, Hyderabad; National Institute of Educational Planning and Administration, New Delhi; National Council for Applied Economic Research, New Delhi, Indian Institute of Public Administration, New Delhi; etc. Further, a number of professional and autonomous research organisations working in the field, including Department of Social Work, Economics, Anthropology, and other related disciplines of Universities were also entrusted the evaluation work. The monitoring of schemes, on the other hand, were entrusted to Monitoring Cells of the State Governments; Tribal Research Institute of State Governments; Tribal Cell of Central Ministries; and Directorate of Research, Monitoring and Evaluation of the Ministry of Home Affairs.(cf. Basu,1994:11-46).

In addition to the recommendations of the Commissions and Committees, and feed back report of various organisations there is also a Central Ministry namely Ministry of Tribal Affairs working as the nodal Ministry for overall policy, planning and coordination of programmes of development for the Scheduled Tribes. Its main focus is on tribal welfare-planning, policy formulation, research and training; scholarships to STs; promotion of voluntary efforts in development of STs; and administration with respect to matters concerning Scheduled Areas. The Ministry was setup in 1999 after the bifurcation of *Ministry of Social Justice and Empowerment (India)* to have a more focused approach on the integrated socio-economic development of the *Scheduled Tribes* (STs), the most underprivileged of the Indian Society. Before formation of the ministry the tribal affairs was being handled by different ministries as under:

- As Tribal Division under the Ministry of Home Affairs since after independence up to September 1985;
- Ministry of Welfare: From September 1985 to May 1998; and
- Ministry of Social Justice & Empowerment from May 1998 to September 1999.

For the tribal dominated northeast, the Ministry of Development of North Eastern Region (DONER) has been established in 2001 to act as the nodal Department of the Central Government to deal with matters pertaining to socio-economic development of the eight States of North East i.e. Arunachal Pradesh, Assam, Manipur, Meghalaya, Mizoram, Nagaland, Tripura and Sikkim. In states where tribal population forms a part of total population there are tribal research institutes to provide intellectual input to be translated into development actions. There are individual social workers and NGOs working for the development of tribal communities. The famous NGOs working for tribal development are *Akhil Bharatiya Adivasi Vikash Parishad* and *Akhil Bharatiya Vanavasi Kalyan Ashram*.

COMPREHENDING SOCIAL PROCESS THROUGH INTERVENTIONS

It is obvious from the foregoing discussions that tribal development is a state-induced[2] process. In other words, state interventions[3] have been instrumental in launching programmes and schemes of tribal welfare in Independent India. So, a preliminary attempt is made to forward an interventionist frame of analysis to study social transformation in general and development process in particular. Though the development process is the result of state intervention in the present context of analysis, intervention is considered to be more comprehensive including any type of external influence, intended or otherwise, affecting the community and its people in any aspect of the life.

There are many analytical concepts to understand the social process. Mention may be made of Marx's mode of production as an analytical category of the social process in an evolutionary perspective. It presents the social process through various stages of evolution like slave mode of production, feudal mode of production, capitalist mode of production and so on. Correspondingly, we are given to understand the process of social transformation through slave society, feudalistic society[4], capitalistic society[5] and socialistic society. The transformation of one stage to another stage is determined by a mismatch between forces of production and relations of production over a period of time. This mismatch may arise either due to external dynamics or through the operational complexity involved in the internal dynamics of the society. The resultant change say the capitalist society does not display all the characteristics of the feudalistic society out of which it evolved. To put it in different way new characteristics, mostly in the forms of antithesis to feudalistic ones, combined with feudalistic features evolved into capitalistic society. So, capitalist society is a feudalistic base of capitalistic mode of production. It is to be mentioned that mode of production has economic content in it in analysing the process of change. This is obviously a specialised way of understanding. But it is argued that interventions understood as simply as in our example also could provide an analytical frame of understanding of social process in a holistic perspective.

Now-a-days, the disciplinary rigidity is melting on the interdisciplinary cauldron of knowledge system. Consequently, emerging analytical frame to study interdisciplinary issues extends beyond disciplinary boundary. An analysis in order to be more revealing needs an interdisciplinary perspective. Here intervention is proposed as a frame of analysis to study the social process in a wider and more inclusive sense.

Nevertheless, there are a number of analytical concepts of specialised studies. It is in this context that mode of resource use which claims to be a better conceptual frame in presenting the social process needs mention. (Gadgil & Guha, 1992:11-

14). Again, mode of resource use is a specialised conceptual category (ibid.11-68) because a society cannot be understood in terms of resource use. Sometimes, binary concepts like, foraging mode of thought (Barnard, 2002; Behera, 2009a) also provides an insight into the social process of forager communities.

A cursory look at the past reveals that the distinct phases of history or stages of economic development in particular or the process of social transformation are evidently marked by one or other types of interventions individually or combined. At individual level the influence of Marx's Communist Manifesto (1848) or Sen's concept of entitlement (1982, 1986) or Darwin's survival of the fittest/natural selection (1859) or Einstein's $E = mc^2$ (1905; see Rigden, 2005 and Schwartz & McGuinness, 1979) in the transformation of human thought and social process is not a matter of debate. More often, individual ideas influence the social process through institutional support. The concept of Whitemen's burden[6] and racial superiority is very much associated with the process of colonisation and religious conversions. Colonisation is a coercive form of intervention whereas, religious conversion displays persuasion and manipulation. In all the cases the intervention is external to the community intervened. In other words, intervention needs to be understood from the perspective of the intervened. To cite an example, the European colonising efforts associated with conversion drive was an intended one. But from the point of view of the colonised the process was not intended, it is something induced. However, the situation does not negate the possibility of an intervention intended by a community itself. To cite an example further, the government of U.S.A during the great depression of 1930s intentionally put J.M. Keynes prescriptions into practice[7]. In 1971 war, Bangladesh intended military intervention of India to fight with the then West Pakistan. Though apparently an outside intervention, it was otherwise intended by the then East Pakistan.

Sometimes, a process of natural interaction between individuals and communities influence one another in different ways. Usually, technologically less developed communities adopt unconsciously some features of the technologically developed communities. The adoptions could also be a conscious act of the community which is nothing but the intended intervention. But unconscious influence results in replication which apparently is imitation. Such unconscious influences are a type of intervention because the adopted features are from outside and exist where it did not exist earlier. Needless to say, intervention, whether induced or intended or imitated, bring about changes in the intervened society. It is therefore argued that interventions can be conceptualised to develop analytical frames to study social transformation or social change.

Contrary to the concept of the police state, welfare of the citizen has been the primary concern of nation states. As a matter of fact, welfare of the people is the primary concern of democratic governments. To promote the welfare, the government introduces various policies and enacts various laws because welfare is a multidimensional concept and includes not only material welfare but also social, cultural and mental welfare. The rules and regulations, and programmes and schemes are interventions from above. That is why the planning process of India is a core-periphery syndrome (Behera, 2006:20-22), a top-down approach and centralised in nature in early years of planning and even today. It is the Planning Commission that formulates policies for the all round development of the people of India.

India is a vast country of many ethnic groups. Among them, tribal groups, as has been mentioned earlier, were almost put in isolation, away from the national stream, during the colonial period under excluded and partially excluded categories. After independence the government of India brought all these communities at par with other communities within the frame of its welfare drive. Needless to say, the process of development and transformation on tribal communities in India after independence has been the process of intervention by the government and later by both government organisations and non-government organisations. The government of India has been adopting plans and programmes following the shifting development paradigms which do not have a national boundary. (See Singh, 1994:51-62). It is the manifestation of international development discourse. In this context it is to be mentioned that the issue of empowerment was the focus of Ninth Five Year Plan and inclusive development of Tenth Five Year Plan. The essence of empowerment comes from the World Summit for Social Development held at Copenhagen in March, 1995. Similarly, inclusive development as a strategy of development comes from the Millennium Development Goals (MDGs) defined in the Millennium Summit in 2000 when participating nations recognised the need for working together in order to benefit the principles of inclusion and equality of opportunities, in the path of the fight against poverty and of a social, economic and human development. In other words, the national government in one way or the other is intervened and subsequently it intervenes with a view to bring about the welfare of the people of India in general and tribal communities in particular.

Tribal communities initially resisted to any outside intervention in various states. In many states except a few enlightened individuals, the general mass was either averse or nonchalant to the intervention. While the government tried to introduce formal education in the then NEFA and the education officer persuaded the people for the education, there were both reactions and indifference. The first education officer Mrs. Indira Miri writes in this regard, *'Hoi Akramon Nohai Polayan.'* (Miri, 2003, quoted in Begi, 2007:vii-viii). Needless to say, under such a situation the interventions could not produce the desired outcome.

THEMATIC ORGANISATION OF THE DYNAMICS OF DEVELOPMENT INTERVENTIONS

In spite of preferential treatment to tribals they are still technically and economically backward and impoverished. Many development projects in tribal areas without developing tribes (see Das and Banerjee,1962) had been found marginalising or excluding them from participation in the process of development. A casual observation even reveals that tribal areas like Rourkela, Durgapur, Ranchi, Bhilai, Jamsedpur have been developed but tribals have become more precarious in these areas. On September 6, 2001 a PTI report (*http://cricket.rediff.com/news/2001/oct/16oris.htm*) states that dried mango kernels were hurled at the motorcade of Orissa Chief Minister Naveen Patnaik during his visit to Kashipur village in Rayagada district to assess the situation following the starvation deaths of 19 tribals after consuming mango kernel gruel. Imran Khan reports (*http://cricket.rediff.com/news/2001/oct/16oris.htm*) the death of over 50 tribal children either due to malnutrition or hunger while some fell victim to diseases like diarrhoea in two and half months in Kalahandi district of Orissa on October 16, 2001. Needless to say, inspite of all the cares and concerns the tribal development seems to be a myth. They suffer from discrimination, indebtedness, land alienation, educational backwardness and lead a life of misery and destitution. The National Sample Survey Organisation (NSSO) in its 55th round, 2000 records highest tribal illiteracy in Andhra Pradesh, Orissa, Madhya Pradesh followed by Karnataka, West Bengal and Rajasthan. In rural Rajasthan the survey records of highest concentration of female illiteracy. In terms of workforce participation the lowest percentage is recorded in Haryana followed by Arunachal Pradesh and Tripura.

Evidently, tribal communities are still on the last rung of the national development ladder. But this does not ignore the fact that a small section of tribes has been benefited from the development interventions. There has been class formation[8] in classless communities in spite of general backwardness. (See Behera, Mohapatro and Hina in this volume).The trend in tribal development, as highlighted, is also the focus of discussion in various papers included in this volume. Each and every paper deals with a distinct issue relating to tribal development but the essence of discussion remains same: marginalisation, exclusion, etc. of the tribals in the process of development through interventions.

The volume includes twenty seven papers organised under seven thematic sections on the basis of issues undertaken for discussion. The changing context is evident in all the papers included in the volume. In fact, each and every paper deals with a number of issues in the context of transitional nature of tribal economy. But one or two predominant issues have been considered to classify the paper in one or the other thematic section; the classification merely being suggestive, rather than exclusive.

The first section namely *Contradictions in Interventions* includes four papers which primarily focus on various dimensions of emerging contradictions associated with development interventions in tribal areas. The development-induced displacement, marginalisation and exclusion, and constraints and initiatives relating to management of shifting cultivation and finally, jhumia community's nature of involvement in resource conservation for tourism development have been the essence of discussion in this section.

The second section focuses on a constrained space of development, a process that does not show a level of 'natural' growth concomitant to the potentials of development forces. In this section there are four papers out of which two papers highlight the prevailing economic conditions of two individual tribes. The other two papers deal with specific problems relating to shifting cultivation practices and commercialisation of ginger cultivation in response to development programmes of the government. That the level of achievement is less than the desired level is the common thread in all the five papers for which the section is entitled *Stunted Transformation*. The phrase stunted transformation does not negate development through interventions. But what it emphasises is a type of underdevelopment in the process; the speed and magnitude of development is not a 'normal' one in relation to the potentials of development forces.

The third section includes four papers under the theme *Specious Dynamics*. As it is clear from the title, development dynamics are quite apparent in tribal communities but with a grim reality underneath. The dynamics present the development scenario either superficially or negatively. It is to be made clear that the phrase *Specious Dynamics* addresses issues relating to the visible side effects or contradictions even with the slow speed of development. Further, the dynamics of transformation in general are viewed in cultural context contrary to the focus on 'below the normal level' of development.

The fourth section is entitled *Innovation as Intervention* under which the included three papers focus on the innovative interventions in promoting language skills of tribal students. Sincerity, seriousness and commitment to the purpose make innovative interventions more effective, while innovation as a routine work and linked with ills of the social system lacks in lustre and fails in objective realisation.

The fifth section includes three papers under the heading *Intervention Perspectives.* The perspectives evince intellectual foundation of empirical findings. One of the papers included in this section has a policy implication; it argues theoretically about the need of IKS based policies with reference to utilisation of bamboo for development of the community. The argument in the paper combines both theoretical foundation and a prescription for practical action. Another paper is critical about the intention of intervention in dealing with *Mautam* famine in Mizoram. The last paper prescribes, drawing on historical experiences, an intervention perspective with regard to look east policy in the context of globalisation.

The sixth section includes four papers under the sub-theme *Untended Context: Challenges in tradition.* The concept of development is no more an economic issue[9]. Over the years of experience with economic development it has been realised that development only in economic sense is a narrow perspective and does not ensure all round development. In recent years the concept of development has become more inclusive and broad in scope; it includes both economic and non economic aspects of development. In practice economic forces have been still predominant in the development exercises of nation states. A society is neither an economic entity nor a political expression. In reality, it is economics, polity, culture, etc., all are interwoven together to define a social reality. Infact on a point of time these various aspects of the society attain a manageable equilibrium. It is logical to think that when one aspect is given more predominance the manageable equilibrium is disturbed and other aspects are affected in different ways. Right from the beginning economic development not only ignored cultural factors but also considered them detrimental in the path to progress. But this idea is no more held. Cultural factors are also recognised as contributing factors to all round development[10].

As has been said, economic primacy is still there in development interventions which are inversely related to the cultural factors. The interrelationship between economic and cultural forces creates a tension zone in development process. Cultural forces interact with intervening forces, sometimes accepting and more often resisting them. These two value domains provide a context (Gudeman, 2008:4) that does not figure in interventionist development strategies. The four papers included in this section examine such untended issues in different contexts.

In thematic divisions two themes namely contradictions in interventions and the untended context challenging traditions seem to be similar in content. Hence this needs an explanation. In 'contradictions in interventions' the emerging opposite forces associated with development process have been the focus of discussion. For example development intervention aims at development of all, but development-induced displacement contradicts this aim. On the other hand in *Untended Context: Challenges in Tradition* the issue is about the conflicting zone between the culture and economic interventions that is not addressed in the development planning.

The final section, section-VII, is entitled *Rethinking the Context* and includes five papers which outline various perspectives of tribal development having contextual significance.

Contradictions in Interventions

All over India, especially in the tribal belt of eastern and central India, tribal and non-tribal farmers alike are asking basic questions pertaining to the model of development when thousands of people have been displaced and thousands are threatened in the name of development. This basic issue forms the subject matter of discussion in the joint paper of Felix Padel and Samarendra Das entitled *Resettlement Realities: the Gulf between Policy and Practice*. The authors highlight the protests of tribal people against development projects of corporate companies in tribal areas of Orissa. The protesters oppose the projects in view of the consequent displacement that would befall on them. Drawing on historical experience of the link between development projects and displacement and subsequent vulnerability of the displaced persons the protesters have exposed the inner contradictions in development ideology and practices that bring maximum good to a small section of people[11] (cf. Behera, 2006: 20-26), and also institutional attitude of subsequent neglect towards these displaced people. Padel and Das have compared the development activities of 18th-19th century Scotland and 20th-21st century Orissa and find an irreversible trend of miseries befalling on the displaced persons. This field reality provides the logic to their sympathy to protesters' apprehension and protest against present corporate activities.

In the era of globalisation development discourse emphasises on human development, which is sustainable, participatory and culture friendly. But who are the human whom development is meant for when a large number of human beings are excluded from their resource base and cultural setting, and above all are exposed to the conditions of vulnerability from a secured life? Is it a selected few? Why do not the Resettlement and Rehabilitation schemes succeed in ensuring pre-displacement promises? How does material aspect of development handle the mental wellbeing of weaker sections like the tribes for whom the latter is more meaningful in the realm of their faiths, beliefs and practices?

These are the issues the authors have taken up to understand present protests in Orissa, because generalised development interventions lead to particular cases of exclusion, both materially and culturally. In the words of the authors, development–induced displacement 'amounts not only to pauperisation, but also to Cultural Genocide, since every aspect of the social structure is fundamentally altered and undermined, including people's economy, political system, material culture and relationship with the environment, religion and system of values'. The contradiction in development intervention glares in between the mind set of capitalist interventionists accompanied by bureaucratic instruments[12] and tribals intervened; this is quite evident in discussions in the paper. Drawing on empirical data the authors have discussed the attitude of a senior bureaucrats in the state, the lacuna in R & R policies formulated by them and the concerns of to-be displaced people. The contradiction glares when deprivation is predominant in areas of industrial activities. Nalco-dominated Koraput is the poorest of all, with 78 per cent of the population below poverty line. There is also contradiction in development ideologies. As the authors write, 'development' defined in purely material and economic terms, loses all connection with the original aim of improving people's actual well-being'.

In the similar vein, M.C.Behera and Jumyir Basar in their joint paper entitled *Interventions and Exclusion: A Critique of Tribal Exclusion in Formal System of Education* have made a study of contradictions in development interventions by focusing on the nature of exclusion as inherent in development policies and practices drawing on the process of formal education introduced in tribal dominated state of Arunachal Pradesh after 1947. The authors have studied the nature of exclusion in development process by applying two measurers of exclusion: absolute and relative. The extent of any intra-category inequality is a measure of relative exclusion pertaining to any development programme. On the other hand, the deviation from hundred per cent achievements measures absolute exclusion. They have taken the process of formal education to understand this inequality. There is literacy gap across the gender among the districts and between rural and urban areas. Papum Pare district is recorded having highest literacy rate at 69.3 per cent while East Kameng the lowest at 40.6 per cent. Similarly, the highest male literacy is recorded 77.3 per cent in Papum Pare district in contrast to the lowest 52.4 per cent in East Kameng district. The same trend is noticed in female literacy rate.

The gender gap in overall literacy rate is recorded 20.3 percentage points for the state. This gap is 10.9 percentage points between the highest male and female literacy rate and the gap between lowest male and female literacy rate is 24.8 percentage points. Similarly, the gap between highest and lowest female literacy in the districts is 31.8 per cent. The overall gap between the urban and rural literacy rate is 30.5 percentage points. This gap in literacy rate, according to the authors, is a relative measure of exclusion. Clearly, females are more excluded than the males, some districts are more excluded than others, and rural people are more excluded than urban people in the field of education. In the opinion of authors this exclusion has policy implication which they find from the gradual coverage of the territory with various levels of educational institutions. Further they attribute the inequality and thus exclusion to urban bias of educational institutions privileging a selected few in better schools. The authors identify that initial practices of *unequal treatment to equals* and in later years, *equal treatment to unequals* have started the process of circulation of the elites and conversely, to the continuation of the excluded. Needless to say the development interventions by themselves have released contradicting forces which have created inequality and thus exclusion in undifferentiated tribal communities.

No component of agriculture, other than shifting (jhum) cultivation practice, has visible contradictions[13] even while appreciating this mode at ideological level. At one hand this practice is being criticised for its being uneconomical and ecologically destructive. On the other hand, it is glorified for its risk coping mechanism, inherent IKS with respect to conservation and sustainable aspect- maintenance of rich germplasm. Strangely, the government has been supporting the former views and as a result formulating policies to ban or replace the practice. In North East India right from independence the government has been trying to wean away the jhumias. Contrary to governmental interventions and discouragement, jhum cultivation still continues. In the efforts to check jhum cultivation better alternatives have been introduced. Line departments of the government have been implementing departmental schemes of the central and state governments for all round development of the tribal communities who are practising jhum cultivation. Ironically, jhum cultivation did not stop. Along with it other forms of land utilisation like terrace cultivation, horticulture have emerged. Of course, there are other development activities like road construction, commercialisation of timber and non-timber products and many others. Consequent upon these emerging land use pattern and development activities, jhum has become unscientific due to reduced fallow period from 15 to 20 years in 1950s to 3-7 years in 1990s. The other problems are soil erosion, biodiversity loss and declining fertility. Though, the changing nature of jhum cultivation is responsible to some extent for environmental problems, the contribution of developmental activities and new land utilisation pattern are completely ignored from the development parlance. The irony is that the debate still continues and shifting cultivation still exists with a change in tone in some quarters to make shifting cultivation more scientific with an adaptation of appropriate technology. Rajiv Mili, Mihin Dollo, Prasanna K. Samal and L. Jitendro Singh in their joint paper entitled *Shifting Cultivation in North East India: Transition and Contemporary Issues* focus on the debate on jhum cultivation and suggest an alternative, without discarding jhum, but through scientific management of the practice.

Intervention in the existing social structure is full of contradictions; it is a contradiction because it does not achieve what it is supposed to do. In other words, it accentuates the inequality inherent in social structure and thus adds to marginalisation of the marginalised. (see Mullaly, 2007:252-286). This is clearly evident in the paper of Debojyoti Das which is entitled *Communities, Conservation and the Challenge of Participation: An Ethnographic Detour of Conservation Programme and the Fate of Jhummias in Naga Villages.* With ethnographic data from two villages Das presents how conservation drive linked to the source of livelihood creates a change in the communities dependent on shifting cultivation and hunting. But underlying the changes are various contradictions. In the studied villages, SACON, State Government and the Baptist Church, more often with funding from abroad, acted as intervening institutions through organising training, workshops, seminars and conferences. As a result the members in the community participate in conservation of their natural resources and link it to tourism. In Khonoma village a sanctuary developed, while in Leangkangru, villagers developed bird watching project to attract tourists. The alternatives available for livelihood diverted the community from shifting cultivation and hunting. Apparently, the achievement is significant but beneath these achievements there is a conflict between elites who were actively involved and others who are not in sharing project money. As Das writes "The village elites and people holding positions of power and authority appropriate their personal interest through the images of conservation. Often these conservation efforts also lead to disenchantment among community leaders and create multiple factions within a village leading to clash of interest and fragmentation of the conservation effort".

The conservation drive did not create any conservation ethics as many villagers stopped hunting in the village itself but did not hesitate to hunt outside. Even the KNCTS members who did not hunt in the village did not find it wrong outside their village. The worst part of it is that animals were hunted during the visit of the political leaders in anticipation of grant of funds for conservation project. Before the projects, the government through Village Development Councils tried to introduce conservation measures but as Das reports, the money was used for different purposes like supplementing immediate needs of the beneficiaries and advancing loan to villagers at exorbitantly high rates of interest. The resource belonged to the community. In community's involvement in conservation drive naturally all members of the community are to benefit equally. But in practice the community shares the benefit unequally. The employees who worked outside the villages especially in urban areas returned to the village after retirement and gained from the tourism by providing logistics support, hospitality to the visitors. As Das writes the village farming community was completely at dark about the economies of bird watching which these town people have monopolised over the years. To earn income there was competition among the individuals contrary to the community participation. Community got fragmented and individuals contested over each others rights and claims. To quote Das, "The fragmentation of collective action in a post project phase speaks of the individual discourses of appropriation that are based on tropes of community/village and clan interest that stems from actors, conservators individual interest in such projects (Das, 2007)".

The community exercise of control led to exclusion of a section of the people. In Leangkangru village, community patrons appropriated resources and demarcated private land of others in the community who had no political power or clan representation in the village council or Village Development Board as part of conservation effort without sacrificing their individual plots. The intervention also attempted at modernising shifting cultivation by introducing commercial crops but the success in this regard ended up with non-marketing of the produce in the absence of market and market mechanism.

Stunted Transformation

There is no denying to the fact that the state and central governments are trying to modernise agriculture right from the First Plan Period. (Kapila, 2004-05:28). On of the strategies of this modernising efforts is to control shifting cultivation in tribal areas. The steps to control shifting cultivation has also been supplemented with various approaches like Special Multipurpose Tribal Development Blocks, Tribal Sub-Plan, Modified Area Development Approach, Cluster Approach, Dispersed tribal Development Plan and so on in Vth Scheduled areas. (Mohapatro, 2009:19-38). P.C.Mohapatro in his paper entitled *A Study of Shifting Cultivation Practices in Koraput Region*, however, has not touched upon these programmes of tribal development, though the essence of his paper draws on tribal development perspective at the backdrop. The author has presented the nature and extent of shifting cultivation in Orissa with reference to data of different periods and a comparison between the recent (1996) and earlier conditions (Mooney, 1951). Surprisingly, he finds almost similar conditions in that shifting cultivation is still the secured source of livelihood of the tribal communities in Orissa. (Behura, 2009:1-18). Though individual rights on land have been established contrary to characteristic practice of communal ownership under shifting cultivation, there is no legal record of ownership (see Mahapatra and Mohanty, 2009:59-80) available; as a result land can not be used as collateral to access to bank finances. Interestingly, Mohapatro finds a continuity of crops and cropping pattern in shifting cultivation practices followed in the recent years. Of course, there are some changes as he has noticed among some rich tribals who practise both wet rice and shifting cultivation. But for others the practice of shifting cultivation is the only source of livelihood in the absence of suitable alternatives. So writes Mohapatro, "The food security measures adopted by the Government till the end of the 10th Plan did not ensure them a sustainable means of livelihood".

Obviously, tribal development has not followed the right direction as it is evident from the paper. Attitude of some people to shifting cultivation, those who are closer to 'mainstream life' has changed, but they still practise it in the absence of alternatives. The provision of alternatives available to rich tribals even has not been effective in controlling shifting cultivation as they also practise it along with other sources of livelihood.

The exposure to 'mainstream' economy and life does not have any significant impact on Bhoxa economy. It is to be mentioned that Bhoxas have been exposed to external forces right from colonial period. Obviously, they have a long association with various interventions. The present socio-economic status of Bhoxa is the outcome of negotiation- both resilience and acceptance-with external forces. This understanding forms the subject matter of discussion in the paper *"We have Little hope to Survive in Future": Dilemma of Bhoxa – A Primitive Himalayan Tribe in Globalising India* written by Bina Shaklani. Because of refugee settlements in their areas during post-Independence period the Bhoxas experienced a declining relationship with natuıal resources. In subsequent years a large section of the population became landless and started working as labourers in their own ancestral land which was duped by the refugees from them. But after independence the development interventions rather came to their disadvantage. It accentuated their low socio-economic status and created intra-tribe inequality. As Shaklani records about 50 per cent of population in Bhoxa community comes under the category of very poor. Similarly, the traditional body politics has declined without a strong panchayat raj institutions. Because of their low literacy level and sharing the political niche with other comparatively advanced tribal groups, the community does not have any elected representative in local bodies like gram panchayats, forest panchayats, etc. So is the case with their educational status when 50 per cent of the population within age group of 18-50 and 92 per cent beyond the 60 are illiterate. Needless to say, the low level of skill formation even after a long association with development interventions excludes them from gainful employments. There are free studentship and free ration for the students, but still the dropout rate is high and more alarming among the girls because of their status role in patriarchy. In the health front the situation is also gloomy. But on the other hand the level of conspicuous consumption is found to be in the rise. Contrary to it, land alienation and indebtedness have become part and parcel of Bhoxa's life. The rule denying land ownership rights to non-tribals in Bhoxa area is perceived as a negative incentive for the Bhoxa youth who are duped by their people during land transaction. As the land cannot be sold to outsiders the Bhoxa's are deprived of competitive market price for their land. No doubt, the Bhoxa case is a development paradox that has emerged in course of their interaction with post independence development forces.

Development in terms of optimisation principle[14] is a mathematical presentation of economic efficiency (Dorfman, Samuelson, and Solow, 1958; Beale, 1968; Intrilligator, 1971 and Whittle, 1971) based on some given constraints and rational assumptions. The solution is based on some given variables and therefore lacks in other variables which influence the development but are outside the model. Development may be economically efficient, but it may not cover all sections of population in the society equally and in terms of both material and non-material wellbeing. Such an achievement is stunted, for development does not take a normal course covering both material and non-material domains of life and all variables that matter in holistic development.

The development does not take place in isolation. It necessitates many preconditions. Without preconditions and with the existing constraints the development may be economically efficient in maximisation model but it cannot be a desirable full growth. In other words, absence of preconditions is in itself an indicator of a development below the desired level. This is very much evident in the joint paper of Otem Moyong and Philip Mody. The paper entitled *Ginger Cultivation of Adi Community in Lower Dibang Valley District of Arunachal Pradesh in the era of Globalization: Constraints and Opportunities* makes a study of the ginger cultivation among the Adis of Lower Dibang Valley district of Arunachal Pradesh. The authors point out the shortcomings, if could be avoided would make the venture profitable. The success of ginger cultivation is constrained by high labour cost, imperfect market conditions, poor physical infrastructure, etc. There is no ingestible area to plough back whatever profit is earned. As a result the commercialisation of ginger cultivation does not have any spill over effect. As ginger is subject to the fluctuation of market price and the vagaries of monsoon there is no provision of insurance to cover resultant price or product risk. What is more important is the reproduction of the economy in response to economic transformation. Unless there is reproduction of the economy the development is not sustainable and lacks in a precondition, i.e. the availability of labour.

In this context it is to be mentioned that the genesis of development (Schultz: 1968:57) in a region is its population; and it is sustained growth of population that acts as an agent of development especially in the region inhabited by primitive communities. Moreover, in case of obtruded development - where external forces aggravate the internal contradictions leading to unexpected transformations (Pathy: 1982:30) – the population factor bears greater significance.

External thrusts of change aiming at planned development bring about economic transformation through a change in the 'mode of production' (Mathew, 1980: 8-9) of primitive communities. The existence of the new mode of production "requires that economic re-production should take place". (ibid:9). Economic reproduction requires production of the means of material existence and production of labour-force. In this context Engles observes that "the determining factor in history is ... the production and reproduction of immediate life. But this itself is of two fold character. On the one hand, the production in the means of subsistence,... on the other, the production of human beings themselves. (Engles, 1977:6). In a directed economy, the economic transformation is an exercise of plan directives. But conditions for reproduction of labour force within the economy do not exist in the short run to meet demand for labour in the process of economic transformation. So, the reproduction of the economy through obtruded development is crucially linked to the problem of reproduction of labour force. Consequently, the inflow of outside labour force to the economy is encouraged for initiating development measures and for providing social goods to those engaged in the process. Needless to say, economic reproduction is limited by shortage of labour force. To put it in right perspective, economic transformation does not take its normal course where production of material means of existence matches with the production of labour force within the economy itself. Of course, the reproduction of labour force to meet the requirements of diverse and large scale production of material means of existence may not be possible in a small community based economy. Then the question arises whether the small community economy, say, economy of a tribal community be looked differently in the process of national development in the image of preservation and protection of cultural heritage of the people.

Another example of stunted growth is the case of Lodhas of Pachim Medinapur district. S.K. Jana in his paper *Economic Life of the Lodhas of West Bengal: Past, Present and Future* has outlined the process of transformation concomitant to Lodhas' changing status from denotified tribe to PTG/Vulnerable Tribal Groups(VTG). Jana has not enumerated various programmes; but being a part of the national programme the objectives of plan programme are obvious. What is evident from his paper is the present status which is the outcome of past development interventions. Presently, Lodhas live in an abject state of poverty, because they are primarily still foragers, though a small section of population has adopted cultivation and a large section has been engaged in wage labour. Jana records 58.64 per cent of main workers under agricultural labour category and another 24.08 per cent under non-agriculture labour category. Only 13.61 per cent of the main workers are recorded as cultivators. Further he records 75 per cent of the population engaged in collection of minor forest products. Clearly, the livelihood is drawn from various sources of subsistence activities. Another interesting finding is intergenerational occupational mobility. Out of 75 respondents 12 respondents under cultivation category had their respective fathers in the same category; 46 respondents followed the occupation of agriculture labour of the father. Another 12 also inherited father's occupation of non-agricultural labour. However, in the 3rd generation there is a change in occupation. For example, out of 46 agricultural labourers in 1st and 2nd

generations, two have become non-agricultural labour, one has started a shop and 15 have taken up cultivation. So, the limited mobility in 3 generations points to the limited achievements through plan programmes. They have been further exposed to the forces of globalisation in recent years which has provided more scope for the continuity of their occupation of wage labour in nearby towns.

Specious Dynamics

Globalisation has removed the barriers of free trade, caused closer integration of national economies and thereby has made political boundaries porous. As a result, movement of people and goods has been tremendously increased with the accompaniment of communicable diseases like HIV-AIDS "which respect no boundaries". (Stiglitz, 2002:223). This means there are visible changes because of the intervention of global forces and these changes have apparent glamour and contradictions. This is the essence of discussion in H.V. Singh's paper entitled *Globalisation and Problems of HIV-AIDS and Child Trafficking in Manipur*. He has selected Moreh town, situated in the Indo- Myanmar border and known as "the golden triangle", as a case study. The place is notorious for being the major hub of drug trafficking which started in 1980s and since then it has affected almost all the North Eastern states and especially Manipur. Breakdown of local indigenous small scale industries due to influx of cheaper and better quality of smuggled products in the market had its adverse effects, worst being abject poverty.

Development discourse in the process of globalisation has identified cross border trade as an effective agent of economic development of participating countries/people. Manipur has the cross border trade relations with Myanmar. Moreh in Manipur and Lamphalong in Myanmar are two border markets for the cross border trade. It is found that from early 1980s till date Heroin No. 4 and other narcotic drugs enter into Manipur from Myanmar via Moreh. Many tourists, business-persons, police personnel, drivers and others who are mobile through the places are the in High Risk Groups (HRGs) of HIV infection. Drug-addicted youths who share needle syringes are also responsible for rising up of the statistics of HIV infection. Moreover, there are flesh trade centres in these areas. The frequency of widowhood due to Naga-Kuki clash and the tendency for illegal earning pushes many women to flesh trade. Without proper awareness/knowledge of HIV/AIDS and other Sexually Transmitted Diseases (STDs), they become easy prey to the disease. Besides, many young boys and girls who are easily accessing to pornographic channels such as magazine, video, computer, internet, mobile phones, etc. are easily motivated to indulge in premarital and extramarital sex. This increases the risk of HIV infection and other STDs. Women empowerment linking education with job market is an important feature of globalisation. In Manipur the consciousness for better education is high. But many parents fail to afford for higher education of their children. Besides, there are educated youths who do not get jobs easily. They involve in illegal practices for quick money. These practices range from drugs trafficking to terrorist activities. There is also attraction of promises of job and good education from unscrupulous persons pushing many girls into flesh trade and young boys into the hands of organ transplantation rackets.

Various studies on the impact of globalisation reveal that development process has been a threat to the economy and identity of weaker sections of the society, specifically to the women in general and tribal women in particular. In North East India tribal population constitutes 26.77 per cent of the total population of the region. Around half of it is women. The threat of globalisation is presumed to be more acute here as the region has already been labelled as technologically and economically backward. While the supporters of globalisation and liberalisation see it as a positive sign for the overall development of the tribes, the critics are vocal about the impoverishment and degradation in economy created by globalisation[15]. Daisy Nath's paper entitled *The Impact of Globalisation on Tribal Women in North East India with special reference to Angami Women* has examined the changing status of Angami women in response to development intervention in general and globalisation in particular. In the field of education tribal women have achieved a lot. But there is a conflicting situation between the emerging status role and traditional role of women in the patriarchal Angami community. The women have new challenges from the tradition in contrast to what they expect in the changing situation. The new challenges have deprived a woman from her rights of accessing to resources which she had in community land. She cannot depend on forest products of individually owned forest which is a feature in the present context. Obviously, such women have been marginalised while others with education do participate in the process of development. The newly defined household duties like educating the children and looking after the domestic chores in the line of the traditional roles has added to their plight. What seems to be a positive change at a macro level proves to be a painful experience to the tribal women. Such a paradox is the essence of which is the theme of discussion in Nath's paper. Undoubtedly, weaker partner becomes weaker in interventionist model of development.

Tribal communities in Arunachal Pradesh were isolated by the inner line regulation of 1873 from the process of colonial administration till independence[16]. These communities got exposed to developmental interventions through plan programmes after independence. The nature and extent of development dynamics depended on two factors: first, the political evolution of the state from North Eastern Frontier Tracts to NEFA and then to Union Territory in 1972 and subsequently to the full fledged state in 1987. Concomitant to this phase the administration has shifted from Ministry of External Affairs to Ministry of Home Affairs and then to direct administration during Union Territory phase and eventually to state government[17]. (Pandey,1997). For all practical purposes the forces of development introduced in the state follow central government's commitment to changing development perspective from time to time. Coupled with it is Nehru's tribal *panchsil* that provides a guideline to development approaches. Nevertheless, the tribal communities in general and the Nyishi community in particular that is covered in the paper of N.N. Hina have been exposed to development forces right from the beginning of planning era. Hina in his paper entitled *The Nyishi in the Process of Development: a note* has compared the present development scenario in the community with that of pre-independence situation from his own observation as he himself belongs to the tribe and with reference to the information collected from elders by conducting interview.

The axes of comparison include agriculture, forest activities, the institution of land tenure, organisation of labour, nature of production and manufacturing activities. Hina mentions of mobility of labour force from agriculture to government jobs. There are changes in the community in every aspect of life; some of the changes Hina cited are: breakdown of the joint family system, division of the society into classes, widening gap between the rich and poor, diminishing use of the traditional artefacts, etc. But the point he emphasises is that the change is not uniform in the community. A section of the Nyishi benefits from commercialisation of activity while a large chunk of population is still tradition bound. No doubt the community has been stratified along economic line which did not exist in traditional community. On the other hand in the institution of labour and technology or land tenure system, Hina has found changes and continuity. Mutual reciprocation for example of social appropriation of labour coexists with wage labour. The ethics of sharing, though has declined, coexist with accumulation. The change and continuity points to a level of change but the dynamics in it needs to be examined with regard to the requirements of benefiting from present commitment to globalisation. The question is: has Nyishi economy evolved to a position to compete for the benefit of efficiency from market driven development process?

Tribal development and subsequent transformation in tribal communities of Himachal Pradesh have taken place within the frame of single line administration, tribal sub-plan and constitutional provisions of protective discrimination. Later National Human Rights Commission and National Women Commission also safeguarded the tribal interest.

Consequent upon the above there are perceptible changes in literacy level, work participation rate and sex ratio. But these macro level achievements give a different picture across the gender. This is the focus of discussion of Ajay Kumar and Himani in their join paper entitled *Tribal Situation in Himachal Pradesh: An Overview*. The authors have recorded the gender gap in literacy rate as 24.4 per cent point as per 2001 census. Further there is regional variation in literacy level. The literacy rate in districts varies between 46.7 per cent in Una and 87.0 per cent in Shimla as per 2001 census. Further, the literacy rate among the schedule tribe, as the authors find, is quite low as compared to literacy rate of schedule caste. Surprisingly, there is a decline in the sex ratio in urban districts like Solan, Shimla and Shirmau. The declining sex ratio and rate of population is attributed to migration from rural areas. Evidently, the development interventions had urban bias neglecting rural development in the state.

Innovation as Intervention

Educational technology, whether in its simple form of chalk and blackboard or more sophisticated ICT, is an intervention in teaching learning process that makes, in general, the communication between teacher and learner easy, effective and meaningful. In particular, its use influences the cognitive, affective and psychomotor domains of the learners and ensures better learning outcome. In his paper, entitled *Folklore and Audio-Cassette in Teaching Language Effectively to Tribal Students at Primary Level -An Experimental Study*, Kartikeswar Behera on the basis of an experimental study, though conducted in a small scale, prescribes for folklore teaching with audio-visual aids in language teaching. He argues, drawing on the result of his experiment, that the innovative intervention in language teaching through folklore and audio-cassette expands the horizon of comprehension and application and develops language skill of the learner. That is why the group (Experimental Group-1) with folklore-cassette intervention has a higher mean difference between pre- and post- test scorings than the one treated with traditional method. This difference marks the measure of effectiveness of folklore-cassette intervention. The innovative intervention, on which Behera has developed his experimentation includes supplementary lessons relating to a prescribed topic in the syllabus; selection of lessons from the cultural setting of the learner; and use of ICT in general.

A similar intervention is evident in the paper of Pradeep Kumar Mishra which is entitled *Role of Tribal Folklores in Developing the Communicative Skill of Tribal Children in English at Elementary Level under S.S.A.* Children in general and tribal children in particular are fond of songs, riddles and any teaching-learning process incorporating them in the delivery system, no doubt, would be effective means in realising the teaching-learning objectives of improving learners' communicative skill in English. It is because songs, riddles and stories would provide a familiar situation which they are accustomed to in the process of informal learning in the culture. However, the formal system does not provide such a process and tribal students ultimately lag behind in learning communicative skills. A teacher, by applying stories, rhymes in the teaching learning process in the class room, makes an innovative intervention to create an enabling environment for the development of the communicative skill of the learners of English language. Such an intervention has four major philosophical dimensions along motivation, activity based approach ensuring participation of the learners in listening and speaking, child centred learning and situation specificity in terms of focus on specific needs of society by drawing on local inputs. This philosophy of effective teaching learning process is translated into practice by Pradeep Kumar Mishra when he experiments it with Class-IV students of Swami Vivekananda Vidyamandir under Umerkote Block in the district of Nawaraangpur of Orissa state. He uses songs, rhymes, etc. on experimental basis to teach the students with a view to develop their communicative skill. He has assessed the impact by conducting tests before and after the intervention. He finds10.18 as mean difference between the pre- and post-test scorings which is a crude measure of gauging effectiveness of the situation specific interventions drawing on local and familiar resources to develop the communicative skill of tribal students, a socially disadvantaged section of population in the country, in English.

'Level play ground' is a catch word associated with the process of globalisation when the issue of equality becomes the focus of discussion. Globalisation is characterised by competition,but competition between unequals is not a natural justice. The job market is linked to skill endowments. The skill development on the other hand depends on better education and training which usually marginalised groups like tribal people cannot afford. They not only lack in better education, they also lack in communicative skill especially in English which is a prerequisite to enter into the competitive job markets. There are various measures to develop the language skill of tribal children. These measures include education through mother tongue and development of language skills especially in English. In developing countries like India the efforts of education through mother tongue are the routine work of government departments. It is a known fact that corruption, insincerity and bureaucratic high handedness are part and parcel of the government efforts. Moreover, these attributes are detrimental to objective realisation. This is clearly presented both implicitly and explicitly in the paper of Ramesh C. Malik which is entitled *Bilingual Primers in Tribal Languages in Orissa: Inconsistency in Efforts to Develop Tribal Languages.* Analysing critically the lapses in the primers he hints at inconsistency to the purpose of intervening efforts. The way indigenous linguistic practices have been translated into dominant linguistic power of the state within the bureaucratic structure is the central issue of discussion in his paper.

Intervention Perspectives

It may be mentioned that development perspective is neither an exercise of intellectual speculation nor an action without contemplation. It is a broad based comprehensive translation of ideology into practice. However, behind every action there is mental.[18] (Godelier, 1986). This mental reality could be speculation of a specialised thought as is natural in reductionist thinking or interdisciplinary and comprehensive being consistent with system/holistic approach. More often intellectual foundation precedes action but now-a-days the intellectual foundations behind any strategy formulation and subsequent action are more comprehensive. No doubt, David Ellerman (2005) criticises World Bank's approach to development assistance drawing intellectual inputs from educational theory, management theory, community organisation, psychology and philosophy. The purpose is to lay intellectual foundation for an alternative approach to World Bank's policies. Needless to say, intellectual speculation provides for a launching pad to development action.

Behind a material there is a mental. In other words, whether it is a material object or an action, there is a thought process, the ideology at the backdrop. Policy interventions, to be precise, are not bereft of any ideological base. As ideology changes, policies are also required to be changed. The problem arises when a choice has to be made from among the ideological alternatives available or when the policies once formulated does not respond to changing ideologies. A. Wati Walling in his paper entitled *Rethinking Tribe and Scientific Knowledge Based Policies: A Sociological Analysis on Bamboo Development in Nagaland* deals with such a problem relating to IKS and general policy frame with reference to Government's policy on bamboo development.

There are two important issues which Walling has examined in the paper. First, he has contested 'tribe' as the term of discourse in Indian context and repudiated the practice of considering 'tribe' as a homogenous category in policy frame of tribal development. He argues for tribe specific policy intervention in order to link IKS, which also is culture specific, with development policies. He finds its absence in the policy of bamboo development with Ao tribe of Nagaland as case study. Significantly, bamboo has an undisputable place in the material and non-material culture of the Ao community. By ignoring Ao's IKS in bamboo development policy, he finds, there is privileging to certain knowledge in the policy frame which may not be relevant to address the problems of different takers. Obviously, the issue of privileging certain knowledge is the problematic relating to the choice from among alternatives.

The other dimension of the problem has a theoretical basis. The knowledge that forms an ideology shifts and with it there arises anomalies challenging the premises of existing knowledge. Walling's argument draws on the perspectives of Thomas Kuhn and Paul Feyerabend on normal scientific knowledge. He takes a clue from the paradigmatic shifts in scientific knowledge to argue that different communities, particularly, tribal communities, have different paradigms of knowledge system. As the shift to new paradigm challenges the existing one, so also the development paradigm of one community differs from that of the others. Uniform treatment to divergent paradigms by privileging one knowledge system is therefore not logical. That is why Walling criticizes privileging certain knowledge system in policy frame while planning for the community with a different system of knowledge, for the knowledge of the community does not get a space in development process.

Privileging of certain knowledge is also evident in the perspectives of the individuals and institutions while addressing to bamboo famine in Mizoram during both colonial and post-colonial periods. The joint paper of Malsawmdawngliana and C. Lalrozami, which is entitled *Mautam Famine in Mizoram: The Politics behind the Catastrophe,* deals with such privileging in perspectives. British government's intention to create governable subjects influenced their relief measures during famine. Similarly, Missionaries took the vulnerability of people during famine to the advantage of their conversion drive. Needless to say, intervention perspective during colonial period through 'humanitarian' considerations was for conversion and administrative control of the Mizos while they were victims of recurring bamboo famine. Post-colonial interventions in addressing the issue of famine have different perspectives for different individuals and institutions. The government of India had integration perspective, i.e. to integrate the Mizos and their territory with Inida. The new elites from among the tribes took famine as an issue to criticize traditional elite for their inability to deal with the situation and formed into different forums like Mizo Union, Mizo Cultural Society, Mizo National Front, etc. These organizations articulated the people's demand which had at the core the concern for mitigating the horror of famine. Even the separatist movement was started and spearheaded under the leadership of Laldenga.

After Mizoram became a full fledgcd state, representatives of the Mizo people formed the government. But the government formed by MNF party was not successful in implementing long term plans like ginger cultivation meant for addressing famine effectively. The opposition took advantage of it by ousting the government in the election to the State Assembly in December, 2008.

All the interventions have one or the other perspective. The policy intervention of Government of India within the frame of Look East Policy has both present and past perspectives. The past perspective is nothing but the historical perspective as this policy marks the beginning of an era of establishment of economic relation with eastern neighbours of India, with whom there was a long tradition, but neglected historically after independence. The context is to look at the Look East Policy through the leaves of the history to which Panda and Priyanka's paper *Look East Policy through the Singpho Corridor:A Study in Historical Perspective* provides a comprehensive perspective with reference to British Singpho relation in this regard. The Look East Policy has two common questions: who shall look towards east? And what should be the role of the local people in this matter? The answer lies in the multilinear approach to a visible issue of security needs of the British India and of lesser visible trade relations. British approached the issue through diplomatic relation with Java administration, study of the local tribes for their involvement in the trade and becoming a cushion against any invasion, exploratory tours to different areas and other administrative measures like experimenting trade relations with Burma. This multilinear approach provided an alternative by establishing Tomo-Morey road in Manipur. Had there been a linear effort perhaps it could have ended up without any success but multilinear approach provided an alternative to their advantage. The important part of the exercise was that the problems of the locals were translated to the advantage of the British by involving them in the greater agenda of the British interest. The Signphos were troubled by the Burmese so, they became the entry point to realise the British objective. Though implicit, the argument in the paper hints at the multilinearity about the intervention and involvement of the local people for the success of intervention of Look East Policy.

Untended Context: Challenges in Tradition

Though globalisation is seen primarily as an economic phenomenon through increasing interaction of national economic systems for the growth in international trade, investment and capital flows, one can also see it through cross-border social, cultural and technological exchanges. But one cannot obviously ignore its impact on the indigenous socio-cultural systems of the traditional societies. All the societies may be benefited economically but globalisation may also bring in a change in their socio- cultural system especially in the field of indigenous knowledge. The basic tribal development policies experimented in India after Independence are also no way different from the goals and consequences of globalisation. One cannot deny such a drastic change as fatal for an indigenous society like that of the tribals. For the time being they may feel better with an economic betterment but ultimately the death of a tradition can be realised.

In the above line of thinking, Jagannath Dash and Kabiraj Behera in their joint paper entitled *The State of Shamanistic Knowledge System in the Face of Globalisation: Need for a Policy Dialogue* examine the issue of globalisation and declining shamanistic knowledge system with reference to 'Paraja' tribe in South Orissa. There is no denying to the fact that economic development is a necessity for the Parajas but economic development, as the authors find, is directly related to the declining role of the Shaman. In Paraja society, shaman is the cultural hub that defines Paraja identity. One finds how their age-old Shamanistic knowledge system has protected and maintained the indigenous knowledge system of the tribe due to the least impact of the modernisation in general. The Constitution of India is also committed to safeguarding the culture of all the people. Further, globalisation also emphasises on the importance of IKS. The situation that exists in the Paraja society consequent upon development interventions is obviously dichotomous. The culture and IKS are threatened because of economic development. At the same time economic development can not be sacrificed for the sake of preservation of culture. The authors therefore strongly argue for a policy dialogue so that economic development takes place without destroying the institution of the shaman, the symbolic representative of the culture.

The apprehension of Jagannath Dash and Kabiraj Behera is also evident in clear terms in Tabang Mibang's paper entitled *Contextualising Traditional Social Capital in the Age of Globalisation: Local Organisations and Sustainability among the Tribes of Arunachal Pradesh.* In response to development interventions in Arunachal Pradesh after 1947, the traditional institutions have either declined or disappeared. Social ties, fellow feelings, mutual trust, connectedness and sharing are gradually slipping away and individual preoccupation is making inroad into the social domain of the state. But it is realised that social capital in terms of mutual trust, mutual reciprocation and fellow feelings is an important prerequisite for effective development. This fact is well recognised by modern thinkers like Anthony Giddens, R.D. Putnam, A. Portes, B. Bourdeiu, J.S. Coalman and many others which Mibang has discussed in his paper. Obviously the context is a contradiction: social capital is an important condition for economic development, but empirical evidences from Arunachal Pradesh find that social capital has declined due to economic development. This dichotomous situation needs to be thoroughly addressed which is conspicuously absent in tribal development policies in India. Though new social capital is emerging, there is a mismatch among new social capital, traditional social capital and the modern forces of development which creates a situation of confusion to a large section of tribal people.

A similar problem is outlined with reference to the traditional institutions of family and marriage in O.P. Monga's paper entitled *Social Transformation of Kinnaura tribe: Change and Continuity in Family and Marriage*. Monga has listed five year plan, particularly the tribal development programmes coupled with planed schemes, urbanization and effective network of communication, establishment of educational and health institutions as external dynamics of development which have influenced socio-cultural life of tribal community. Market oriented dynamics of tribal development require an institutional setup quite different form the one that exist in traditional tribal communities. The traditional tribal institutions are compatible to the subsistence nature of economy with small scale economic activities and therefore are unsuitable to propel the market driven surplus economy with economic activities of different magnitudes. Monga's study shows that the development forces have not molded the traditional institutions to the changing requirements; rather there is a continuity and change of the tradition in the emerging new institution. Needless to say, such institutional support lies half way between traditional and modern forces of development and therefore are not compatible to the requirements of the changing needs. The context of the situation does not figure in the policy frame for tribal development. Associated with such changes the traditional social capital is declining whereas the modern social capital has not taken definite shape.

Rice has a spread in the culture of the rice producing communities having been interwoven in folklores-songs, dances, performances, festivals, religion, etc. The concept of goddess of wealth, domestication of animals and value to draft animas, and social appropriation of labour are examples to be cited to show all pervasive nature of rice in cultural life of people. The customs and rituals are inextricably tied to the tradition of rice which people grow. The technique of growing rice has shaped the indigenous technical knowledge of the community to a large extent. The myth of rice has assumed new meanings and interpretations in relation to globalisation. The cultural practices around rice are documented. The products from the rice find a market in non-rice producing areas. But the question is whether the dynamics of rice myth is powerful enough to benefit from globalisation, like such other dynamics as IT intervention and multinational companies' intervention, in the process and control of production. This is the thematic focus in Rabindranath Sarma's paper entitled *Globalisation and Rice myths of North-east India.* Globalisation has undoubtedly introduced dynamics into rice myths of North East India through mass media which documents and disseminates the tradition. The rice myth is not an individual knowledge system. It belongs to various communities and thus becomes a community property. How far the community is benefited from documentation and dissemination of the knowledge and who are the people to benefit from such documentation and dissemination. Though implicit, these are the areas where globalisation has yet to give a definite answer.

Rethinking the Context

Stereotypes about the tribes, that they live in isolation, their economy is subsistence in nature and non-monetised, they engage in primary sector activities, their method of shifting cultivation is harmful to environment and that they are illiterate, have been the bases of delineating a development frame for them in the development planning in India. But these stereotypes are no more the context to be considered for tribal development. Today tribes have been integrated to national economy in different degrees through national planning. (Gupta, 1993:323-336). Tribal elites and various Acts concerning their specific problems have brought in the forces of modernization in these communities. They participate in electoral politics (Bath, 2009) of the nation. In fact tribes in India did not exist in isolation as colonial anthropologists have made us to believe. That is why, 'tribe', the term of discourse, is being contested and thus the inclusion in the list of STs of Indian Constitution.

The economy of a tribe is no more a self-sufficient community based pursuits in a substantive sense. The economy has been diversified with the growth of and integration to secondary and tertiary sector activities in the community and occupational diversification of members of the community. (Mishra, 2007; Gyatso, 2004-05). Tribal people are found working in government and private agencies and engaged in business activities[19]. Nevertheless there is a hangover of substantivist approach to understand tribal economy today in many quarters. There is no doubt that the economy is in transition and hence it is difficult to understand the process in either of the approaches- substantivist or formalist.

The four papers included in this section maintain the changing context of tribal economy both from theoretical and empirical perspectives. The discussion, however, contains an implicitly strong urge for rethinking this changing context beyond stereotypes while planning tribal development effectively and meaning fully in the process of globalisation.

In his paper entitled *On Tribal Economy and Society*, Vinay Kumar Srivastava has emphasized on this changing context when he puts that tribal economies 'are no more unmonetized; no more are their markets of ceremonial importance; no more are they part of the domestic economy'. In the process of development, tribal communities have been decimated consequent upon building of nuclear plants, experimental rocket ranges, large industries and mining operations along with exploitation of their natural resources to meet the demand in national and international markets. Surprisingly, the wrong done to the tribes has a support base in state institutions (Padel and Das in this volume) which otherwise would have actually protected them to safeguard tribal interests according to Constitutional and legal provisions. Ironically, tribal elites or an advanced tribe whose members are influential in state machinery (for example Meena tribe of Rajasthan, see Kataria in this volume) act to their own benefits.

What is significant in Srivastava's paper is that the tribes themselves want development which they voice from different platforms, may be a seminar, or through 'their own movements', or founding their 'own organisations'. Two important points which emerge from Srivastava's paper give a clue to understand the changing perspectives in tribal development. This perspective no doubt has an emic appeal contrary to earlier parental approach to planning for tribal development. In other words, the essence of top-down approach to planning, which otherwise is macro in nature and sectoral in coverage and which has been, and still is (see Behera, 1994) the dominating process of development, is challenged in tribals' changing perspective on development. That the process has not delivered and still tribes are techno-economically backward, an excluded section and want to change is enough to substantiate to inadequacy in top-down approach.

Though plan experiments have not delivered to the extent what it should have, still there are development dynamics to be noticed in tribal communities in different degrees. Education, occupational diversification, monetisation, etc. are some dynamics in earlier tradition bound subsistence economy of the tribes. What is important in this context are the efforts of facilitating their empowerment which has made them to voice their concerns for their development. Needless to say, emerging development dynamics in tribal communities consequent upon the introduction of plan programmes has been instrumental in their changing development perspectives in the first place.

Secondly, what Shrivastava wants to share with us has a theoretical grounding. The tribal person is not exclusively a 'social man' as conceptualised from earlier writings, opposite to the 'economic man' of industrial and modern societies. In fact these seemingly two opposite concepts are two approaches to explain the economic phenomenon; in one, economy is passive while in other it is an active process. Precisely, in the former, the objective is 'social gains' from economic pursuits while in the latter the objective of 'economic gains' goes together with economic pursuits. In tribal communities, there is 'social context of economic behaviour'. In the same line of reasoning we may add predominance of 'economic context in economic behaviour' to the concept of 'economic man'. In both 'social' and 'economic' men, there is economic context with a primary objective. In 'social man' category, the 'economic context' was to add to a tribe's 'social gains'. Nevertheless, as Srivastava puts, "the 'primitive man', like the modern, was equally interested in his well-being, increasing his life chances of survival, gaining a high status". He cites the example of Kula, to which Malinowski described as "efforts and strategies (of wooing) that Trobriand men made to acquire the best gift, *in terms of exchange value* (emphasis is ours), from their partners, since it would raise their prestige among their community people. Srivastava has strongly put this economic context of 'social man' referring to the writings of Evans-Pritchard, 1940 and Oscar Lewis, 1966. Undoubtedly, the 'social man' was also an 'economic man' (cf. Sen,1977), but with a difference, which was neglected because of the importance given to understanding of tribal economy in a substantive sense initially till formalist views gained ground. Currently, also in many quarters, tribal economy is projected in their stereotypes emphasizing on the substantive sense of understanding.

But what a tribal economy reflects today is neither the substantive nor the formalist characteristics (Gudeman, 2008); it is rather a transitional economy (see Desai, 1982: 505-518; Thakur, 1986; Nair, 1987; Behera, 1994 and Das, 1995) combining the features of both in different proportions. At this juncture, globalisation has brought the importance of social capital- community cooperation, mutual trust, environmental protection, IKS and other cultural factors to the fore in the process of people centred development. Needless to say, these strategic parameters have been the strength of traditional tribal communities which did not figure positively in the earlier discourse on development. But in today's changing context, tribal culture assumed significance in development parlance.

At the same time, the institutional set up and the status of social capital in the present tribal communities are in transition. Despite the changes these are not strong enough to meet the requirements of forces of globalisation. There is continuity in change and it is not possible to change cultural outlook of tribal people over night by replacing everything or creating an enabling environment compatible to globalisation. So, what wisdom demands is to plan for tribal development by integrating the strengths in the culture with market forces.

The above argument is also at the core of discussion in the paper *Rethinking Sustainable Tribal Development in a Cultural Perspective* by Jagabandhu Samal. The contention of the author is that most of the tribal development programmes failed because the felt needs, skills and over and above cultural values of the tribes were ignored both at planning and implementation levels. He identifies the dignity of labour in general and tribal women's work ethics in particular, artistic value of tribal arts and crafts, tribal way of curing diseases, mutual reciprocity, IKS in maintaining and preserving environment as potential factors of their development in the era of globalisation.

In this era of globalisation corporate sectors play a significant role in the process of economic development. Interestingly, tribal communities have a rich tradition of corporate life. (see Pertin, 2009). Their traditional body politics is an example of participatory democracy which has been identified as a pre-requisite to decentralised grassroots development. Introduction of Panchayat Raj institutions has the same logic. No doubt, tribal communities have all the pre-requisites which have been recognised in recent development discourse. But what tribes do not have is a sense of competition and market orientation for which, as Samal writes, their traditional arts and crafts have declined. Arguably, infusing a sense of competition and preparing tribals for it in the competitive market bear significance in tribal development perspective. That is why Samal strongly argues for sustainable tribal development in a cultural perspective.

As tribal culture of sharing is anti-thesis to competition, so is also reservation policy to safeguard against competition.

Surprisingly, there is an agitation for reservation under ST status which S.K.Kataria reports in his paper entitled *Gurjar Agitation in Rajasthan: Issues and Impacts.* Gurjar agitation has many dimensions in the context of globalisation. As has been mentioned, it is obviously an anti-thesis to competition, the basic underlying principle in market efficiency. It is interesting to note that the agitation for reservation was opposed by Meena tribe, known as the advanced tribe in India, when the community filed two civil writ petitions (SB civil writ petition no. 4695/07 Shri Lakhan Singh v/s state of Rajasthan and SB civil writ petition no. 5526/07 Shri Narayan Kemala v/s state of Rajasthan) in Jaipur bench of Rajasthan High Court to avoid any hasty decision by the state government under undue pressure. It is interesting to note that the agitation by Gurjars to minimise competition in sharing state resources did not go without a tough competition from a privileged tribespersons who enjoyed the benefit in a reservation regime. The motive to check any further increase in the number of competitors is implicit behind the sophisticate way of opposing to Gurjar agitation by the Meenas.

More importantly, Gurjar agitation substantiates to the point that it is now tribals, for that matter economically backward communities, who want their own development in their own perceived way. Evidently, the agitation has also brought to the fore the irrelevance of the criteria determined by Lokur Committee on the basis of which a community is enlisted as Scheduled Tribe (ST)[20]. Not surprisingly, the Assam government also made claims in 2005 to include the tea garden tribes in ST list. The agitation, over all, has decelerating effect in both social and economic spheres. To Kataria this includes "Gurjar-Meena split, civil disobedience, polarization of politics, set back to tourism industry of Rajasthan as well as Agra (Taj Mahal), emergence of pressure politics, low morale of police force and destruction of public property including highways and Delhi- Mumbai railway track. The Gurjar agitators had built their huts on the railway track".

World Bank (2002) while recognizing economic development in terms of social development maintains that lack of social development increases the sphere of social movements. Needless to say, World Bank's concern is quite valid in the context of Gurjar agitation. Further, the agitation has ethnic dimension as across the globe ethnicity and thereby inclination towards own caste, race, religion, creed and language is increasing[21]. (see Stavenhagen,1990; Sharma,1993; cf. Miri, 1993; Dasgupta, 1993; Basu, 2006; *Linkenbach, 2005* and Sarkar, 2006). Necessarily, Gurjar agitation touches upon diverse issues and perspectives and further draws attention to the understanding of the context of tribal development from a broad perspective.

There is another context to look at tribal development- through the frame of human rights. This is evident in the joint paper of Alok Chantia & Preeti Misra, which is entitled *Impact of Globalisation on Tribal Groups in India (An Anthropological Study on Dhankut of Bahraich District, U.P.)*. Strangely, the members of Dhankut (the name of the community and also the people) with a population of 2687 and a social set up resembling those of tribal communities have not been enlisted under ST category. Though they are categorised as general caste, their caste/ caste position is not Constitutionally recognised so far and so they do not have any specific caste status. Their demand for tribal status in 1973 is yet to be fulfilled. Obviously, a doubt is cast on the relevance of Lokur Committee's criteria in determining a community to be enlisted under ST category. Dhankut people are conscious of the benefit of good housing, quality education, better economic life, etc., but they do not have means to afford for them. Development interventions over the years have ruined their main traditional source of livelihood, i.e. trading grains, by exposing them to competition. Instead of it the Dhankut people have got no suitable alternatives, as a result of which they have remained poor. Various agencies talk about their possible development from globalisation and human rights perspectives, but the irony is that, as the authors have recorded, 91.30 per cent of people have not heard of what these globalisation and human rights are all about. The situation is a precarious one; the people want development but they are not aware of globalisation and human rights which provide operational frame of development. Moreover, the Dhankut people do not have the minimum pre-requisites like high literacy rate, good education, housing facilities, health facilities and job opportunities on which development dynamics can better work. On the other hand, these people have organised into *Dhankut Sangharsh Samiti* to fight for their identity, status and development. Needless to say, Dhankuts also want development, but to achieve it they are in a situation of change and continuity which is not favourable to development dynamics in the context of globalisation.

Mritunjay Kumar in his paper entitled *Situating Asurs of Jharkhand in Socio-Economic Perspective* highlights a contradicting perspective among the Asurs of Jharkhand state of India who were once famous for iron smelting. As Kumar writes, their traditional occupation was neither polluting nor environment-damaging unlike the modern steel mills. Development of area due to the introduction of modern technology and steel mills did not develop the tribal people; it rather displaced them from their traditional source of livelihood. Asurs are still tribes but without their tribal economy. On the other hand they are situated somewhere in the periphery of non-tribal (modern) economy.

Development interventions have brought about new opportunities in the field of credit institutions, education, and information and communication technology in the area inhabited by Asurs. These facilities promise benefits to this group. But are the Asurs prepared for that when, as Kumar writes, "they are cut off from the mainstream economic activities"?

At various stages of intervention – colonial rule, adhoc development plans, land alienation, finance capital, to mention a few - Asurs have been loosing traditions without proper hold on new economic opportunities. Globalisation seems to be a bye-passing experience for them because they are not skilled enough to benefit from competitive market forces and financial sector services.

Asurs have lost their traditional sources of livelihood. Accessing to available sources seems to be far from reality. But still they want development in the modern line. The question is how?

It follows that the issue of tribal development in the present context is different and therefore needs an understanding beyond stereotypes. The fact is that tribals are no more stereotypes in their economic pursuits, health problems or the like. It is evident when Srivastava (in this volume) writes that minor Chenchu and Lambada girls work as cheap agriculture labour in chilli and tobacco farms, where they are exposed to harmful chemical pesticides. Children are most prone to sexual exploitation; there are cases of Lambada girls sold for trafficking. Local NGOs have found incidences of HIV/AIDS among the Yanadi girls living around the temple and tourist town of Srisailam. Juvenile crime, which was non-existent among tribes, is now an issue of concern. As a consequence of these factors, the children fall prey to ill health, alcoholism and other vices".

Tribes now-a-days have their own response to money and money markets. There are also impacts of technological interventions on their economies. In this context the development approach needs to be different in which "the tribes (and other down-trodden communities) have the freedom to choose the line and the programme of development they want, the way in which they would manage their natural resources; have the freedom to choose the leaders who would govern them in a participatory way; and have the freedom to protest against unjust systems and uninformed decisions". (Srivastava in this volume).

CONCLUSION

From the foregoing discussions the following issues emerge explicitly though some are implicitly striking:

- There are intended interventions in India since Independence to develop the tribals.
- There are inter and intra level variations among the tribal communities on the scale of development.

- The overall development of the tribals is far behind the national average by any standard
- The development project more often has created ambience of exclusion for the tribal persons in the process by marginalising and displacing them from their root.

Associated with the above issues of tribal development is the issue of situating tribal communities in the process of globalisation. Are they prepared to manage their development in the context of globalisation?

It is to be mentioned here that in spite of all the forces operating in favour of globalisation at national level, the tribals are still local. They are local because they need special attention for their development even after more than 60 years of Independence. They need reservation in jobs, in educational institutions and in Lok Sabha seats. The protectionist approach to their development is enough to consider them as weak partner in the process of national development and hence local. The issue is serious when we think of situating tribals in the scale of globalisation.

ENDNOTES

1. Nehru, 1958, in Elwin, 1959:xiii. See Samal (in this volume). He has enumerated five principles known as Tribal Panhashil.
2. The development is planned and implemented through state agency. see Basu,1994:11-46 for tribal development administration.
3. Also see 10 papers included under the section entitled Planned Interventions & Development, Samal,1996:363-486.
4. See McNeill, William H. (1963 [1991]).
   The author has explored human history in terms of the effect of different world civilizations on one another. Western feudalism, evolving in turbulent eighth-century France, offered aristocratic landowners potential security in the absence of law and order. By concession or usurpation, major landowners assumed substantial legal and governmental power from the central government and proceeded through private arrangements with lesser landowners to create local militias for defensive purposes.
5. See Strasser, Hermann, 1981 The contributions in clouded in the volume deal with various theories of social change including the change from feudalistic to capitalist society.

6. The White Man's Burden is a poem by the English poet Rudyard Kipling. It was originally published in the popular magazine McClure's in 1899, with the subtitle The United States and the Philippine Islands. It is a Eurocentric view of the world, in which non-European cultures are seen as undeveloped. This view proposes that white people consequently have an obligation to rule over, and encourage the cultural development of people from other ethnic and cultural backgrounds until they can take their place in the world by fully adopting Western ways.
7. In the 1930s, Keynes spearheaded a revolution in economic thinking, overturning the older ideas of neoclassical economics that held that free markets would automatically provide full employment as long as workers were flexible in their wage demands. Following the outbreak of World War II Keynes's ideas concerning economic policy were adopted by leading Western economies. During the 1950s and 1960s, the success of Keynesian economics was so resounding that almost all capitalist governments adopted its policy recommendations.
8. This is evident from the emergence of tribal political elites. (See Dubey, 1975; Bandyopadyay,1985; Panigrahi, 1998 and Karlo,2005).
9. To understand the present standing that the concept of development is no more viewed in terms of economics only see Behera (2006:13-14).
10. For relation between culture and development and recognition to the importance of cultural factors in development see Vidyarthi, 1981; Yatsushro, 1953; Bisht, 1996; Brinkman, 1991 and Chatterjee & Ghosh, 1996.
11. Robin Hahnel (quoted in Reich,2002:38) attacks 'corporate sponsored globalisation...which widens the gap between rich and poor, and hastens environmental destruction...'.Also see Behera, 2009, 8:15 for the discussion on ' the other side of development', i.e imperial nature of globalisation.
12. For a detailed discussion on bureaucrats' understanding of people's development see Barnard, 1998, quoted in Behera,2006;21; Chambers, 1983 and 1993:69-110.
13. For the debate and other details on shifting cultivation see NEICSSR, 1976; NEC, 1982; Sharma, 2003 and Sachidananda, 1989.
14. The principle of maximization is criticized in actual life situation. Sen conceptualizes human development through his moral philosophical position (Sen,1984) and emphasizes on the role of factors such as 'commitment' and 'sympathy'. (Sen, 1977). Contrary to maximization behaviour of an economic man, a committed man may choose an act that he believes will yield a lower level of personal welfare to him than the alternate that is also available to him (ibid , 327). Also see Sen, 2002. Sen scrutinizes and departs from the standard criteria of rationality, and shows how it can be seen in terms of subjecting one's values as well as choices to the demands of reason and critical scrutiny.

    From Behera, 2006:18; also see foot note-3, ibid. Behera (2009:23-35) has critically discussed the limitations of maximisation principle on the basis of rationality and has advocated Gandhian economy which is more inclusive and does not suffer from specialised treatment to socio-economic problems.

15. See Bello,1999; Sachs and Vajpai,1998; Sinha ,1995 and Sobhan ,1995 for empirical support to the emergence of inequality in the process of globalisation. Also see Chandrasekhar and Ghosh.2006.
The authors, on the basis of empirical data hold that market strategy of globalisation has not just failed to deliver sustained growth, but has had damaging consequences from the point of view of employment, poverty alleviation and equity.
16. After Independence, the national government also continued the Regulation, but the territory (now the state of Arunachal Pradesh) is not isolated, it is integrated to the nation politically, economically, etc.
17. See The Arunachal Pradesh Code, various volumes. Itanagar: Law and Judicial Department, Government of Arunachal Pradesh.
18. Material means (trap) and intellectual means (skill, knowledge, etc.) roughly make up productive forces (Godelier: 1986:131) and reflect two realities; material (physical) and mental, in man's production activity.
19. A few village studies (Mamung, 2009; Phukan, 1999-2000; Priyadarshini, 2008, etc.) present the picture of economic diversification and workforce distribution in different sectoral activities. The workforce has shifted from traditional primary sector activities to secondary and tertiary sector activities which did not exit in the community/village earlier.
20. The debate on the relevance of the concept 'tribe' as a discourse also has been presented in details in Misra, 2008, Atal, 2008; Behera, 2008; Chana, 2008; and Prasad, 2008).
21. See 10 papers included in section-2 entitled Tribal Unrest, Political System and Identity Crisis, in Chaudhuri, 1982:99-232.

REFERENCES

Atal, Yogesh (2008), "A Note on the Concept of Tribe", in *The Eastern Anthropologist*, Vol.61 (4), New Delhi: Serial Publications, pp.441-450.

Bandyopadhyay, P.K. (1985), *Leadership among the Mizos*, New Delhi: B.R.Publishing Corporation.

Barnard, A. (1998), "Hunter-gatherers and Bureaucrats' Reconciling Opposing World Views", quoted in Behera, 2006.

——(2002), "The Foraging Mode of Thought", in Henry Stewart, Alan Barnard & Keiichi Omura (eds.). 2002. *Self-and- Other Images of Hunter-Gatherers*, Senri Ethnological Studies-60. Osaka: National Museum of Ethnology.

Basu, Ashok Ranjan (1994), "Tribal Development Administration in India", in Ashok Ranjan Basu, Satish Nijhawan (eds).1994. *Tribal*

Development Administration in India. New Delhi: Mittal. pp.11-46.

Basu, Sajal (2006), "Ethno-regionalism and tribal development : Problems and Challenges in Jharkhand", in Govinda Chandra Rath (ed). 2006. *Tribal Development in India: The Contemporary Debate*. New Delhi/Thousand Oaks/London: Sage Publications. pp.133-152.

Bath, Nani. (2009), *Electoral Politics in Arunachal Pradesh*. Varanasi: Pilgrims Publishing.

Beale, E.M.L.(1968), *Mathematical Programming in Practice*. New York: Pitman.

Begi, Joram (2007), *Education in Arunachal Pradesh since 1947 (Constraints, Opportunities, Initiatives and Needs)*, New Delhi:Mittal Publications.

Behera, M.C. (1994), *Planning and Socio-Economic Development of the Tribals*, New Delhi: Commonwealth.

——*(2006), "Introduction", in M.C.Behera (ed).2006. Globalising Rural Development: Competing Paradigms and Emerging Realities. New Delhi: Sage.*

——(2008), "Definitional Limitations in the Use of the Term Tribe: An Overview with Reference to the Padam of Arunachal Pradesh", *The Oriental Anthropologist, A Bi-Annual International Journal of the Science of Man* 8 (1-2, January-December. pp. 143-157.

——(2009), "Introduction", in M.C.Behera (ed.). 2009. *Making Gandhi Relevant-Rural development in the Context of Globalisation*. New Delhi: Commonwealth.

—— (2009a), *Foraging Mode of Thought and Forager Sulung's Social Self*. Dudweiler Landstr, Germany: VDM Verlag Dr. Müller Aktiengesellschaft & Co.

Behura, N.K. (2009), "Primitive tribal Groups: Their Problems and development", in Mohapatra, P.M. et al (eds). 2009. *Sustainable Development in Bonda Hills*.Koraput, Orissa: Council of Analytical Tribal Studies.

Bello, Walden (1999), "Asia Heads Back into Underdevelopment"?. *The North-East Daily*, 2 January.

Bisht, B.S. (1996), "Cultural dimensions of economic development", in Prasanna K.Samal (ed).1996. *Tribal Development: Options*. Nainital: Gyanodaya Prakashan, pp.222-230.

Brinkman, Richard L. (1991), *Cultural Economics*. New Delhi: Heritage Publishers.

Chambers, R. (1983), *Rural Development: Putting the Last First*. New York: Longman & Scientific Technical.

—— (1993), *Challenging the Professions: Frontiers for Rural Development*, London: Intermediate Technology Publication.

Chandrasekhar, C.P & Jayati Ghosh (2006), *The Market That Failed: Neo liberal Economic Reforms in India*. New Delhi: Leftword Books.

Channa, S.M (2008), "Tribe: The Concept and its Relevance in Post-Modern World", in *The Eastern Anthropologist*, Vol.61 (4), New Delhi: Serial Publications, pp.461-471.

Chatterjee, A.K. & B.N. Ghosh (1996), "The impact of culture on development: a critical response", in Prasanna K.Samal (ed).1996. *Tribal Development: Options*. Nainital: Gyanodaya Prakashan, pp.155-161.

Chaudhuri, Budhadeb (ed). (1982), *Tribal Development in India, Problems and Prospects*. New Delhi: Inter India Publications.

Dalton, G. (1961), "Economic Theory and Primitive Society", *American Anthropologist*, Vol 63(1), pp. 1-25.

Damodaran, Vinita (2005), "Indigenous Forests: Rights, Discourses and Resistance in Chotanagpur, 1860-2002", in Gunnel *Cederlöf and K. Shivaramakrishnan (eds.). 2005. Ecological Nationalisms: Nature, Livelihoods and Identities in South Asia. New Delhi: Permanent Black.pp.115-150.*

Darwin Charlse (1859), *On the Origin of Species*. London: John Murray.

Das, A.K. and S.K. Banerjee (1962), *Impact of Industrialisation on the life of Tribals of West Bengal*. Calcutta: Cultural Research Institute.

Das, Gurudas (1995), *Tribes of Arunachal Pradesh in Transition*. New Delhi: Vikas Publishing House.

Dasgupta, P.K. (1993), "Quest for Ethnic identity by the Tribes in India", in Mrinal Miri (ed).1993. Continuity and Change in Tribal Society, Shimla: Indian Institute of Advanced Study. pp 158-164.

Desai,A.R. (1982), "Tribes in Transition", in Budhadeb Chaudhuri (ed).1982. *Tribal Development in India, Problems and Prospects*. New Delhi: Inter India Publications.

Dorfman, Robert; Paul A. Samuelson, and Robert M. Solow (1958), *Linear Programming and Economic Analysis*, New York: McGraw Hill Book Company.

Dubey, S.M. (1975), *Modernisation and Elites in Arunachal Pradesh.* Shillong: Directorate of Census, Government of Arunachal Pradesh.

Ellerman, David (2005), *Helping People Help Themselves: From the World Bank to an Alternative Philosophy of Development Assistance.* Ann Arbor: University of Michigan Press.

Engles, Fredric (1977), *The Origin of Family, Private Property and the State.* Moscow: Progress Publishers.

Gadgil, M. & R. Guha (1992), *This Fissured land, An Ecological History of India,* Delhi: Oxford University Press.

Gait, E.A. (1905/1963), *A History of Assam.* Calcullta:Thacker Spink & Co.

Godelier, Maurice (1986), *The Mental and the Material,* London: Verso.

GOI (1951), *First Five Year Plan.* New Delhi: Planning Commission, Government of India.

GOI (1986-87), *Report of the Commissioner for Scheduled Castes and Scheduled Tribes,* 28th Report, New Delhi: Government of India.

Gudeman, Stephen (2008), *Economy's Tension, The Dialectics of Community and Market.* New York/Oxford: Berghahn Books.

Gupta, Malabika Das (1993), "Tribal Developemnt Programmes and their Impact: Continuity and Change", in Mrinal Miri (ed).1993. Continuity and Change in Tribal Society, Shimla: Indian Institute of Advanced Study. pp 323-336.

Gyatso, Wangda (2004-2005), "A Study of Employment and Income Situation in Small-scale industries (SSIs) in Tawang District of Arunachal Pradesh". *Unpublished M. Phil Dissertation,* Submitted to Arunachal University (presently Rajiv Gandhi University), Itanagar.

Herskovits, Melville J. (1952), *Economic Anthropology,* New York: Alfred A.Knopf.

Intrilligator, M.D. (1971), *Mathematical Optimization and Economic Theory,* New Jersey: Prentice Hall, Inc.

Kapila, Uma (2004-05), "Indian Economy at Independence", in Uma Kapila (ed).2004-05. *Indian Economy since Independence,* New Delhi: Academic Foundation.

Karlo, Rejir (2005), *Emerging Pattern of Tribal Leadership in Arunachal Pradesh.* New Delhi: Commonwealth.

Linkenbach,Antje (2005), *"Nature and Politics: The Case of Uttarakhand, North India"*, in Gunnel *Cederlöf and K. Shivaramakrishnan (eds.). 2005. Ecological Nationalisms: Nature, Livelihoods and Identities in South Asia. New Delhi: Permanent Black.pp.151-169.*

Mackenzie, A. (1884/1994), *The North-East Frontier of India.* New Delhi:Mittal.

Mahapatra,L.K. and R.P.Mohanty (2009), "Land Rights, Land Use, and some Aspects of Developemnt in situ in Bonda Hills", in Mohapatra, P.M. et al (eds). 2009. *Sustainable Development in Bonda Hills.* Koraput,Orissa: Council of Analytical Tribal Studies.

Mamung, Millo (2008-09), "Transformation of Tribal Economy and Workforce Participation in Arunachal Pradesh (A Case Study of the Apatanis)". *Unpublished M.Phil Dissertation,* Submitted to Rajiv Gandhi University, Itanagar.

Mantaw, N. Helina (2003), *Tribal Gevelopment.* New Delhi: Classical Publishing Company.

Marx, K. & F.Engels nd. *Manifesto of the Communist Party.* New Delhi: People Publishing House. (This is the Indian reprint of the text of Italian edition, 1893, translated by Samuel Moore in 1888 from the original German text of 1848).

Mathew, T. (ed). (1980), *Tribal Economy of North Eastern Region.* Guwahati: Spectrum Publications.

McNeill, William H. (1963) 1991, *The Rise of the West: A History of the Human Community* [With a Retrospective Essay]. Chicago: University of Chicago Press.

Miri, Indira (2003), *Moi aru NEFA,* Guwahati: Spectrum Publications. (Trans. *Me and NEFA*)

Miri, M. (1993), "Identity and Tribesmen", in Mrinal Miri (ed).1993. Continuity and Change in Tribal Society, Shimla: Indian Institute of Advanced Study. pp 165-174.

Mishra, Deepak K. (2007), *Rural Non-Farm Employment in Arunachal Pradesh- Growth, Composition and Determinants, NLI Research Studies Series, No.075/2007,* Noida: V.V.Giri National Labour Institute.

Misra, K.K. (2008), "On "Tribe" and "Tribalism"", in *The Eastern Anthropologist,* Vol.61 (4), New Delhi: Serial Publications, pp.430-440.

Mohapatro, P.C. (2009), "Problems of Tribal Developemnt in Orissa", in Mohapatra, P.M. et al (eds). 2009. *Sustainable Development in Bonda Hills.*Koraput, Orissa: Council of Analytical Tribal Studies.

Mullaly, B. (2007), "Oppression: The Focus of Structural Social Work", in B. Mullaly (ed), *The New Structural Social Work,* Don Mills: Oxford University Press.

Nair, M.K. Sukumaran (1987), Tribal Economy in Transition. New Delhi: Inter India Publications.

Nehru, J. (1958), "Forward to the Second Edition". In Verrier Elwin, 1959 (1988 reprint). *A Philosophy for NEFA.* Itanagar: Directorate of Research.

North East India Council for Social Science Research (1976), *Shifting Cultivation in North East India,* Seminar Proceedings, Shillong: NEICSSR.

North Eastern Council (1982), "Shifting Cultivation in North-Eastern Region". *NEC Publication, No. 17,* Shillong: Directorate of Information and Public Relations, North Eastern Council.

Pakem, B. (1992), "Jawaharlal Nehru's Panchashila and Hill People of North-East Inida", in B.Datta Ray and C.D.Tripathi (eds.). 1992. *Jawaharlal Nehru and the Disadvantaged.* Sillong: NEICSSR.

Pandey, B. B. (1997), *Arunachal Pradesh-Village State to Statehood.* Delhi/ Itanagar: Himalayan Publishers.

Panigrahi, P.K. (1998), *Political Elite in Tribal Society,* New Delhi: Commonwealth.

Pathy, J. (1982), "An Outline of Modes of Production in Tribal India", in B. Chaudhuri (ed).1982. *Tribal Development in India, Problems and Prospects.* New Delhi: Inter India Publications.

Pertin, Otem (2009), *Rethinking Tribal Institutions,* New Delhi: Commonwealth Publishers.

Phukan, Purneswar (1999-2000), "A Study of Employment Structure and Income in an Arunachal Village (A case study of Rayang village under Ruksin circle of East Siang District of Arunachal Pradesh". *Unpublished M.Phil Dissertation,* Submitted to Arunachal University (presently Rajiv Gandhi University), Itanagar.

Prasad, R.S (2008), "Is Tribe a fiction?", in *The Eastern Anthropologist,* Vol.61 (4), New Delhi: Serial Publications, pp.451-460.

Priyadarshini, Priyanka (2008), "Tribe and Tribal Economy: A Study of Two Tribal Villages of Arunachal Pradesh", in Journal *of Social Anthropology*, Vol.5 (1&2), New Delhi:Serial Publications, pp1-16.

Rao, P.V. (1988), *Institutional Framework for Tribal Development*. New Delhi: Inter-India Publications

Rath, Govinda Chandra (ed). (2006), *Tribal Development in India: The Contemporary Debate*. New Delhi/Thousand Oaks/London: Sage Publications.

Reich, Jonathan D. (2002), "Ashes to Ashes and Dust to Dust: The Relevance and Future of the Anti-Globalization Movement", *The Journal of Politics and Society*, Vol.XIII ColumbiaUniversity,pp.36-53, *http://www.helvidius.org/files/2002/2002_Reich.pdf*

Rigden, John S. (2005), *Einstein 1905: The Standard of Greatness*. Cambridge and London: *Harvard University Press.*

Sachchidananda (1989), *Shifting Cultivation in India*, New Delhi: Concept Publishing.

Sachs, J.D. and I .N.Vajpai (1998), "Money Order", *The Telegraph*, 21 December.

Sarkar, I. (2006), "The Kamtapur Movement: Towards a Separate State in West Bengal", in Govinda Chandra Rath (ed). 2006. *Tribal Development in India: The Contemporary Debate*. New Delhi/ Thousand Oaks/London: Sage Publications. Pp.153-165.

Schultz, T.M. (1968), *Economic Growth and Agriculture*. Bombay-New Delhi: Tata Mc Graw Hills Publishing Company Ltd.

Schwartz, J.and M. McGuinness (1979), *Einstein for Beginners*, New York : Pantheon Books.

Sen, Amartya (1977), *"Rational Fools: A Critique of behavioural Foundations of Economic Theory", in Philosophy & Public Affairs, 6 (4), Summer, pp.317-344.*

——(1982), *Poverty and Famines: An Essay on Entitlements and Deprivation*, Oxford: Clarendon Press,

——(1986), *Food Economics and Entitlements*, Wider Working Paper 1. Helsinki.

——(2002), Rationality and Freedom. *Cambridge MA: Harvard University Press.*

——(2002), *Rationality and Freedom*, Harvard: Harvard Belknap Press.

——(1984), "Goods and People", in Amartya Sen 1984. *Resources, Values and Development*, Oxford: Basil Blackwell, pp. 509–532.

Sharma, B.D. (2001), *Tribal Affairs in India: The Circular Transition*. New Delhi: Sahyog Pustak Kuteer (Trust).

——(2003), *Shifting Cultivators & Their Development*, New Delhi: Sahyog Pustak Kutir (Trust).

Sharma, K .L. (1993), "The Question of Identity and Sub- Nationality: A Case of Jharkhand Movement in Bihar", in Mrinal Miri (ed).1993. Continuity and Change in Tribal Society, Shimla: Indian Institute of Advanced Study.pp.463-473.

Singh, Bhupinder (1981), "Tribal Development: Strategy and Approach" in L.P.Vidyarthi (ed). 1981. *Tribal Development and its Administration*, New Delhi: Concept Publishing Company.pp.111-131.

——(1994), "Challenges of Development: The Shifting Scenario of Tribal Development", in Ashok Ranjan Basu, Satish Nijhawan (eds), 1994, *Tribal Development Administration in India*. New Delhi: Mittal. pp.51-62.

Singh, K.S. (ed). (1983), *Tribal Movements in India, Vol-II*, New Delhi: Manohar.

Sinha, S.P. (1981), "Tribal Development Administration- A Historical Review, in L.P.Vidyarthi (ed). 1981. *Tribal Development and its Administration*, New Delhi: Concept Publishing Company.pp.65-81.

Sinha, S.L.N. (1995), "Mexican Financial Crisis: Implications and Lessons", *Southern Economists*,33(20).

Sobhan, Rehman (1995), "Down and Out in Outer Mongolia- lessons from Economic Reform from 1995". *Economic and Political Weekly*, 30(10): 495-501.

Srivastava V.K. (2006), "Commissions and Committees on Development of Indian Tribes", in Prakash Chandra Mehta (ed), 2006, *Development of Indian Tribes*, New Delhi: *Discovery Publishing House*.pp.77-126.

Stavenhagen, R. (1990), *The Ethnic Question: Conflicts, Development and Human Rights*. Tokyo: United Nations University Press.

Strasser, Hermann (ed). (1981), *An Introduction to Theories of Social Change*.London, Boston and Henley: Routledge & Kegan Paul.

Thakur, D. (1986), *Socio-Economic Development of Tribes in India*. New Delhi: Deep & Deep Publications.

Vidyarthi, L. P. (1981), "The Cultural Factors in Development Process: Case Studies from Bihar", in L.P.Vidyarthi (ed). 1981. *Tribal Development and its Administration*, New Delhi: Concept Publishing Company.pp.3-18.

Whittle, P. (1971), *Optimisation Under Constraints: Theory and Applications of Non-linear Programming*. New York:Wiley Interscience.

World Bank (2002), *Globalisation, Growth and Poverty-Building an Inclusive World*. Washington DC: World Bank Publications.

Yatsushiro, Toshio (1953), "Economic Development and Cultural Dynamics", *The Eastern Anthropologist*, 2(1), pp.5-18.

SECTION–I

Contradictions in Interventions

2

RESETTLEMENT REALITIES: THE GULF BETWEEN POLICY AND PRACTICE[1]

Felix Padel, Samarendra Das

Several glaring discrepancies exist between the policies and promises as against what actually happens. To start with, the literature on displacement rarely brings out people's voices, yet what they say is a social fact more basic than any statistics.

Among the main reasons for the gulf between policy and practice is a lack of acknowledgement or analysis of the corruption, intimidation and exploitation that happens at every stage of a "development project", or of the environmental degradation involved. To understand the strength of resistance to displacement-projects it is vital to analyse the clash of ideologies between a belief in development as something based on material constructs and mining-based industrialisation, as against village people's belief in their own culture and way of life. When farming communities are displaced, especially tribal villages, what is involved amounts to not only to pauperisation, but also to Cultural Genocide, since every aspect of the social structure is fundamentally altered and undermined, including people's economy, political system, material culture and relationship with the environment, religion and system of values. From being self-reliant, rooted to the land, remarkably egalitarian and growing most of their own food, displaced people are forced to the bottom of a ladder, to become dependent on obscure and cruel corporate hierarchies, losing their former freedom and control over their labour and environment. This lowers the position of women and children in particular. The vast drop in displaced people's quality of life is acknowledged in most serious literature, yet remains little analysed, in particular its discrepancy with CSR (Corporate Social responsibility) models of "Sustainable Development".

THE PHENOMENON OF DISPLACEMENT

Bhagaban Majhi, one of the leaders of the Kashipur movement against the Utkal alumina project, questions mainstream ideas about development in the light of the grim reality of displacement.

"We have sought an explanation from the Government about people who have already been displaced in the name of development. How many have been properly rehabilitated? You have not provided them with jobs; you have not rehabilitated them at all. How can you again displace more people? Where will you relocate them and what jobs will you give them? You tell us first. The Government has failed to answer our questions. Our fundamental question is: how can we survive if our lands are taken away from us? We are tribal farmers. We are earthworms [matiro poko]. Like fishes that die when taken out of water, a cultivator dies when his land is taken away from him. So we won't leave our land. We want permanent development." (Das & Das, 2005).

How do mobile phones, wide roads, cars and skyscrapers represent development if they only benefit the rich? (Majhi, 2005) All over Orissa, people are resisting displacement, where before they gave into the terror and acquiesced. Today's generations have witnessed the wretched conditions of people displaced by numerous projects, in Bhagaban's case in southwest Orissa, by the upper Kolab and Indravati reservoirs and Nalco's refinery in particular.

Our aim in this paper is to draw attention to a number of very grave aspects of what is termed "development-induced displacement"–aspects neglected by much of the literature, because they are not subject to measurement. There is a tendency in social science to give importance only to *chrematist* (monetary) values, at the expense of a broader sense of well-being. For various reasons, many aspects of displacement are hard to measure and define. With some aspects this is because of an institutionalised attitude of neglect towards displaced people – for example, no reliable statistics have been kept either of the number of people displaced by most projects or of what happens to them in following years. (Fernandes, 2008 : 90). Effects of displacement are often especially dire when communities are dislodged from regions of exceptionally rich biodiversity, which they have adapted to and helped maintain over generations, as is the case in many areas of Orissa. Maps of India's mineral deposits, rivers and forests highlight the very areas richest in traditional cultures. (Sunil in Das & Das, 2006). Hence the resource curse: natural resource abundance becomes a curse for inhabitants displaced by mining and dams. (Ross, 1999).

Other vital aspects of the displacement process can only be understood if people are prepared to open their hearts and minds to other ways of being. Measurement has little place here. The *social construction of reality* in tribal culture is worlds away from mainstream culture, and it is a real challenge for the bureaucratic, technology-focused mindset which guides development projects to comprehend the enormity of what is involved when tribal people are uprooted from their land and villages to a resettlement colony.

It is precisely because of this reality gap that resistance to projects is so intense, so the people who manage projects and resettlement would benefit greatly from trying to understand it. What follows is drawn from the insights of social anthropology, and based in an intimate knowledge of the realities on the ground in project areas – among people already displaced, and among people resisting displacement now, as well as in areas where traditional social structures still exist and displacement is still only a distant threat.

In this first section we make a holistic appraisal of the phenomenon of displacement taking place in Orissa – its historical roots, and an over-view of what actually happens. In the next section we examine an alarming disjunction between policy and practice that lies at the heart of the displacement trauma, and explains why Resettlement & Rehabilitation (R & R) schemes almost always fail to raise the living standards of displaced people. In the third section, we look at what is happening in terms of Cultural Genocide - the extinction of people's communities and social structure - which largely explains why they fight so strenuously to resist displacement. In the next three sections we examine the clash of belief systems and attitudes to Law underlying displacement- the gap between different actors' realities of life and outlook, taking stock of the impoverishment experienced by Project Affected Persons (PAPs), before drawing our conclusions in a final section.

Future historians of Orissa are likely to look at the last 60 years, 1948-2008, as a period of mass dispossession of communities who lived and worked on the land since time immemorial - an extinction of vibrant cultures by industrialists and planners focused on accelerating growth through industrialisation, without a proper appreciation of what they are destroying.

Displacement arises out of a clash of ideologies. On one side, there are value systems of traditional cultures, where relationships with land and community are more important than money. On the other, an ideology of industrialisation-as-development, in which market forces and swift financial profit override other values.

The particular phase we are in now is marked by traumatic events that symbolise a struggle by communities to put a stop to this trend and avoid being displaced, while on the other side, deals for new projects accelerate even further the pressure to acquire more farmland for industrial projects. The police firings that killed tribal people at Maikanch village in

December 2000, and Kalinganagar industrial area in January 2006, are key symbols of this struggle in Orissa. Cultivators look on industrial projects that lower their standard of living and destroy their communities as the opposite of real development. While "anti-development" is what those promoting industrialisation and their foreign investors call farmers who take a stand against displacing projects.

Dispossessing vast numbers of people from their land in the name of development is a phenomenon that has accelerated rapidly since India's Independence. Displacement during colonial times has a hidden, unrecorded history. Numerous communities were displaced by tea plantations in Assam, Kerala and present Bangladesh. In Orissa, British demands for increased revenue from the land caused the eviction of thousands of tribal people from their territories. (Currie, 2000 and Padel, 2000). It is significant that the legal apparatus for displacement was put in place during colonial times, with the Permanent Settlement (1793) and the Land Acquisition Act (1894). W.W.Hunter expressed succintly the set of values which many British rulers saw as their main legacy to India:

"It is by what we have implanted in the living people, rather than what we have built upon the dead earth, that our name will survive. The permanent aspect of British Rule in India is the growth of Private Rights."

"By a wise limitation of our state ownership we have raised up a permanent Proprietary Body, composed of mutually hostile classes; but each of which, from the grand seigneurs down to the Resident Husbandsmen, holds its lands under documents issued by British officials." (Hunter 1872 pp.201, 277, quoted in Padel, 2001 p.80).

This *divide and rule legacy* of British colonialism is bearing fruit now, in internal colonialism carried out through large-scale privatisation of resources, and takeovers of huge tracts of cultivated land, by mining and construction companies, in Orissa and neighbouring states. The ideology of industrialisation sweeping Orissa now stems from the same essential belief system that motivated the industrial revolution in Britain, the USA, the USSR, China and other countries. It is well to bear this history in mind. A collective forgetting of what was done and said in preceding centuries leads to a compounding of past mistakes and mistaken belief systems.

In fact, the modern pattern of displacing people from their land to make the land more profitable was set far away from India. European colonists exterminated indigenous tribes all over America and Australia, and forced survivors to cede their land and move to reservations, where a policy of detribalisation was imposed. This pattern is also embedded in the history of the colonising countries themselves. In Britain, the Enclosure Acts between 1760 and 1840 started a process of privatising land that evicted small-scale farmers in vast numbers all over the British Isles – a precedent for the land-grabs by the already-rich going on in Orissa right now, that are reducing the already-poor to a poverty worse than anything they knew before. Orissa today witnesses the same kinds of injustice, and very similar justifications, to those evident in 18th and 19th century Britain. Understanding these deeply embedded patterns gives a clearer view on the whole issue of R & R.

Britain's remote northern areas suffered a particular trauma known as the Highland Clearances. The Scottish clans lived a highly traditional life based on small-scale crofting in the highlands and islands, characterised by a distinctive culture and an independent spirit. During the 19th century, English rulers persuaded the Scottish lairds (zamindars) to make their land more profitable by expelling these crofters in huge numbers – just as they persuaded Rajas in Orissa around the same time. Intellectuals of the "Edinburgh Enlightenment" painted a picture of these crofters as sunk in poverty and warfare, their stone houses as dirty hovels, and their lifestyle as backward and uneconomic. Using this justification, hundreds of communities were permanently erased, and thousands of people died from starvation and disease. (Prebble, 1969). Of those that survived, many had to become factory workers. Thousands emigrated to Britain's colonies, in America, Australia and South Africa, where they displaced the natives just as they had been displaced themselves. Many served in the army in various outreaches of the British empire, including India. The Kond areas of west Orissa that are now the scene of invasion by aluminium companies were forced under British rule by a series of Scottish highland officers, named Macpherson, Campbell, MacViccar, and McNeill. (Padel, 2000).

The Highland Clearances in Scotland cleared people from the land and erased communities, but also cleared forests and farmland to make way for sheep and plantations of foreign trees for timber and paper. Another phase of clearances started in the early 20th century when some of the world's first dams were built to generate hydro-power for aluminium smelters. These reservoirs fill valleys emptied of their people. The water level is low and a sterile gap of at least 30 feet separates the water from land vegetation. Even back in 1910, when about a third of the world's aluminium was being produced in Scotland, a union leader contrasted the British aluminium company's picture of its main smelter enclave as a "Garden of Eden", with the "misery and degradation" which workers endured. (Perchard, 2008/2009). Then as now, this included a high incidence of industrial diseases among smelter workers, whose true extent has never been revealed.

In Orissa, hundreds of communities have ceased to exist, and hundreds more are threatened with extinction. Local tribal and non-tribal politicians and landlords in Kashipur and Lanjigarh have sold out their communities just as the Scottish Lairds did. (Saroj, 2008). There is no "empire" for Orissa's displaced people to emigrate to. Factory and construction work is every bit as dangerous and degrading as it was in 19th century Britain, but in the present age of mechanisation, permanent jobs are much fewer.

Also, environmental degradation works alongside the decline in living standards, even more than in industrialising Britain. Around the Upper Indravati reservoir, displaced people cut down the remaining forest, because they have lost their land along with their traditional forest-based livelihood system. Selling the timber as firewood is all that saves them from starvation.

The aluminium companies are entering the Kond region of western Orissa after the bauxite deposits, which are sited on the summits of the biggest mountains, so although the planned mines, unlike dams and factories, may not displace people directly, they erode the water-bearing capacity of the mountains, and thereby threaten the local Konds' cultivation of millet, maize, turmeric, ginger, orange, pineapple and dozens of other food crops which they depend on for sustenance and income. Mining bauxite from these mountain tops is also an assault on their religion. For Kond religion recognises mountains as prime sacred entities and sources of life–a connection which geologists recognised when they named the base rock of these bauxite-capped mountains as Khondalite. (Fox, 1932:136 and Padel and Das, 2007).

DISJUNCTION BETWEEN POLICY AND PRACTICE

The official version of Orissa's modern history tends to reflect the developers' self-image, and focuses on the growth rate, and the development of roads, railways, airports, sea ports, mobile phone networks and the exploitation at last of the state's minerals. What is left out of this version is the realities on the ground. If displaced people suffer–so did people in "developed" countries. The suffering is often seen as a necessary sacrifice for overall development–the cost of progress. Overall, or eventually, it is believed that most people's standard of living goes up - even though "trickle down economics" has been shown to be false, and most people can see clearly that poverty is getting worse. Company officials often say "there was nothing here before we came" – only "mud huts".

According to R & R policies formulated by the World Bank, DFID and UNDP, as well as the Governments of Orissa and India, people's standard of living is supposed to go up, not down. It is generally acknowledged that this hardly ever happens in practice. (Mathur, 2008:179).

This exemplifies the reality gap at the centre of Resettlement & Rehabilitation. Between what is supposed to happen and what actually happens is a gulf–often no correlation at all. Since most projects have no Social Impact Assessment, since displaced people are not made part of the decision-making process, and there is no proper check on the success of R & R, or even proper ways to assess this, let alone any disciplinary action against officials responsible for failure, this reality gap remains almost completely outside the approved discourse on R & R.

To bring it in, we need to address several issues of fundamental importance on the ground that finds little or no mention in most of the literature on displacement. One set of issues involves Cultural Genocide and the sacrificing of people's quality of life, along with all the non-measurable factors that make up their culture and community.

Another basic problem is that in most, if not all the project areas, various forms of intimidation and coercion appear to be standard procedure towards people unwilling to be displaced, by police and administrative authorities, as well as by a mafia network of *goondas*. This intimidation also operates around people who have been displaced from traditional communities to a resettlement colony. In a traditional tribal village, differences of status are relatively small: everyone is of approximately equal status and value. Once displaced from their village and land, they find themselves at the bottom of a hierarchy that is often extremely cruel and corrupt.

This corruption is conspicuous by its absence from most models of R & R, and at the heart of the fundamental discrepancies between theory and practice. In the awarding of contracts, for constructing a colony, and at every stage of a displacing project, corruption is rampant (Dash, 2008). This starts with the deals mining companies make, but percolates down to the lowest level. Workers often attest that even labouring jobs, that should be theirs by right, can only be had by paying bribes. Villagers living below Nalco's bauxite mine have informed us that they gave bribes of several thousand rupees just to get preferential selection for labouring jobs up the mountain paid at just 68/- rupees per day. Often, it seems that large bribes are more or less mandatory even to get standard land title documents, which small-scale farmers need as a basic security, since without *patta*, they are not entitled to compensation for their land - and often, even after bribes, no documents materialise. Corruption only exists among lower officials because it is tolerated at higher levels. In November 2003 the Minister of Environment & Forests was captured on camera receiving a large bribe from an Australian mining company for leases in Orissa and Chhattisgarh, with words that reveal much about modern attitudes to money: "*Paise khuda to nahi, par khuda ki kasam, khuda se kam bhi nahi.*" ("Money isn't God, but by God, it's no less than God", *Sunday Express* 16.11.03).

This materialism did not start from India, and the reality gap appears to be a feature of most development projects. A study by social anthropologist David Mosse finds almost no correlation between policy and practice in a major agricultural project funded by the DFID (Dept for International Development of the UK Govt.) in Madhya Pradesh, for which he was a consultant. (Mosse D., 2005).

Most of Orissa's first wave of industrial projects has been notorious for their lack of adequate R & R, such as the Rourkela steel plant, the Hirakud, Upper Kolab and Indravati dam projects, and also Nalco in Koraput, sometimes cited as a model of good practice, but actually, as we shall see, they are anything but good.

So the present situation in Orissa involves several high profile struggles of people opposing displacement in Orissa. Three companies in particular face protracted opposition, in a series of projects some of which have already caused displacement or are currently causing agitation, while others (e.g. iron-ore mines) have yet to be finalised: Tata at Kalingnagar and Gopalpur (steel plants), Naraj (thermal power plant near Cuttack), Dhamra (port), and north Orissa (iron-ore mines), Posco at Jagatsingpur (steel plant & port) and north Orissa (iron-ore mines), and Vedanta at Lanjigarh (alumina refinery), Niyamgiri (planned bauxite mine), Jharsaguda district (smelter & giant power plant), near Puri (university-cum-business-centre), and Gandhamardan (another bauxite deposit). Several other projects, which have recently displaced people, or where people have taken a strong stand resisting displacement, include the Utkal alumina refinery, numerous steel plants and sponge iron factories by Bhushan, Jindal and other companies, and the Lower Suktel dam.

The resistances to all these projects by people opposing displacement are of immense significance. From the viewpoint of the companies, and members of the Government of Orissa and Government of India supporting them, the protestors are holding up foreign investment worth many crores of rupees. From the viewpoint of protestors threatened with displacement, they are being treated with a fundamental injustice. The authorities appear not to understand or care that these people's whole lives are being torn apart. What else is Government for if not to listen to and serve these people? This is the essence of the reality gap: a gulf of understanding between those imposing and suffering displacement.

Displacement tends to be seen as a peripheral aspect of a development project, and the officials in charge of overseeing R & R are neither well-trained nor well-motivated to help in what we now understand is a highly traumatic process for nearly everyone undergoing displacement. (Mathur, 2006 :48, 69-70). Most of the people faced with displacement do not see the projects as development at all, since far from raising their standard of living, they lower it. As Bhagaban says of a meeting with the Superintendent of Police:

"I put a question to the SP. I asked him, 'Sir, what do you mean by development? (Agya, unnoti boile kono?) Can you call displacing people development? The people, for whom development is meant, should reap its benefits. After them, the succeeding generations should enjoy its benefits. That is development. It should not be merely to cater to the greed of a few officials.' " (Das & Das, 2005).

Since 1995, the Kashipur movement has been at the forefront of questioning what is meant by "development" (Lingaraj, 1995 and Pradhan, 1995). Defined in purely material and economic terms, "development" loses all connection with the original aim of improving people's actual well-being.

Education, health, levels of nutrition and employment are among the important indices often used to study people's well-being, and where reliable statistics on these aspects have been collected, they do indeed confirm that industrialised tribal areas are among the most impoverished in India. Nalco-dominated Koraput is the poorest of all, with 78% of the population below the poverty line. (CSE, 2008 :254, 322). But it is not enough to collect statistics. Not just because we all know how easily statistics can be massaged. People's own perception of their well-being is also vital, and most studies of people who have been or are due to be displaced fail to even include these people's voices! This is disturbing. For often, the perceptiveness and wit Adivasis express when they speak freely beat anything in written discourse. The trouble is, they know most outsiders have no wish to hear what they say or to learn from them.

CULTURAL GENOCIDE

Cultural Genocide is the least recognised but perhaps most painful aspect of the drastic drop in the quality of life of people who are displaced (Padel & Das 2008). This is why so many farmers say "we'll die rather than give up our land", recognising that all their values are at stake, since these are rooted in their land and physical community. When Bhagaban says a cultivator dies when his land is taken away, he is not referring just to a physical death, from hunger or other causes. He means: people die inside-a soul death. The deaths at Maikanch and Kalinganagar are taken as symbolic of a collective death. This is something hard to communicate in words to people who have no experience of the kind of rootedness at the heart of Adivasi society. It echoes the decision to die rather than leave their land of many indigenous peoples in America, where physical genocide–meaning the extermination of all members of a tribe–often went alongside cultural genocide: the killing off of cultures. (Brown, 1975; Padel & Das, 2008).

Briefly, social anthropology analyses the social structure of a tribal (or non-tribal) village in terms of several spheres of life, each of which is radically altered and dismantled by displacement:-

- The economy is completely changed when people who have been essentially cultivators are removed from the land and turned into an industrial labour force. Food security vanishes, and money assumes far greater importance in defining relationships between people.
- People's identity is also radically altered. From being largely self-sufficient for their basic food wants and material needs (e.g. making their own houses, and channelling the water to their fields), they become dependent on a hierarchy outside their control for jobs, and every aspect of life. Their fields and houses were often made by their parents or remote forefathers, so losing their land and ancestral village creates a traumatic break with previous generations.
- The political system and power structure in traditional tribal villages is remarkably egalitarian. Differences in status and wealth do exist, but are counteracted by a strong tendency towards sharing and equality. These differences were accentuated by colonial rule, and displacement makes them much greater. From being in control of most aspects of their daily life and the area around their village, people find themselves at the bottom of a corporate hierarchy, dependent on a wide range of more powerful people, many of them outsiders to the area. In other words, displacement disempowers villagers and lowers their status.
- Women's position is often particularly badly affected, even where education, health centres and self-help groups (SHGs) are provided for oustees. The reason for this is that in a tribal village, women often retain a large degree of control over their own labour, working essentially for themselves and their own families, at times of their own choice. Even when they do coolie labour, this tends to supplement work on their own land as they see fit. Losing their land, they become

more dependent on their husbands, and often bear the brunt of men's frustration, in a situation where work ceases to be on their own terms. Tribal women who retain their land go to market to sell their own produce. The dignity from this self-sufficiency is destroyed by displacement. SHGs have an ideology of raising women's status that is often contradicted by ground realities, especially once pressure to repay loans kicks in (Das, 2000; Muhammad, 2006 and Saroj, 2008). There are frequent testimonies of displaced women being forced into prostitution, even in the colonies built for them.

— A village's material culture is altered out of all recognition by displacement. From making most of their own food, tools and houses, villagers become dependent on factory-made goods. An influx of cars and trucks into their area make life more dangerous and pollute the atmosphere, as do the factories that become the centre of the local power structure.

— Religious life is also transformed. Seeing the incomers around them tearing nature apart, and participating in blasting rock formations and cutting down trees to earn money, undermines people's sense of sacredness in nature which lies at the heart of traditional tribal religion. For example, a woman who had just been removed from Kinari village to make way for Vedanta's refinery said to us "*Amoro deveta bi nasht kole*" – "they even destroyed our deities" – referring to the *darni vali* (earth goddess stones) that form the centre of a Kond village, which had been bulldozed into rubble along with the houses as soon as villagers were evicted. Similar testimony is given by people displaced by the Indravati reservoir, who say "Our deities were drowned".

— In this context, the dances, songs, stories, and customary ways of behaving that are commonly understood as "culture" also lose their meaning and vitality. Many displaced by the Indravati dam attest

> that when times were hard before, the better-off would help those in need. Now everyone is struggling to survive.

An easy way to understand Cultural Genocide is through the original meaning of "culture", deriving from Latin *cultus*, which links the meaning of culture, cult, and cultivation. In other words, cultures which still retain their own system of cultivation, linked with a cult of nature-based deities, are bound to be undermined by removal from their land. For those of us who lost any sense of being part of a community rooted to the soil hundreds of years ago, it is very hard to understand the Cultural Genocide implicit in this kind of displacement.

Cultural Genocide applies most clearly to tribal cultures, which differ markedly from mainstream orientation in their lifestyle's groundedness in nature. When the Balimela dam was being constructed in the 1960s a team from the Anthropological Survey of India were commissioned to study the small, distinctive Didayi tribe, a large part of which was about to be displaced. (Guha, 1970). But it also applies to non-tribal farmers, such as the betel-vine cultivators resisting Posco, and the farmers who resisted Tata's Gopalpur steel plant plans in the 1990s (Shiva, 1998), as well as thousands of farmers in West Bengal resisting takeovers of their land at Singur and Nandigram. The village culture these people are defending is the same "village *swaraj*" which lay at the heart of Gandhi's conception of Indian culture.

So the various peoples in Orissa and other states who are striving to protect their land from corporate takeover are actually campaigning for much more – to preserve India's cultural integrity and independence against the forces of global finance. And even more than this: to preserve India's natural environment that forms the basis of life itself.

There is a widespread recognition now that biocultural diversity co-exists with biodiversity in nature – that indigenous cultures preserve many of the world's most important areas of nature, because the values of these cultures differ fundamentally from those of the industrial society that grew up in the West, "built on the misconceived and ultimately ruinous belief in humans' separateness from Nature and dominion over it." (Maffi, 2008: 10 and Kothari & Pathak, 2008). The World Conservation Congress promotes the concept of Indigenous Community Conserved Areas (ICCAs). In Orissa one of the outstanding such areas is the forested mountain summit in Niyamgiri where Vedanta plans to mine bauxite. This is an example of a project that may not cause direct displacement, but strikes at the heart of a cultural heritage that is also the heart of one of Orissa's best preserved forest areas. The reason is the Dongria Konds and their religion, which centres on Niyam Raja, Lord of the Law, whose abode is the mountain summit. The tribe maintain a taboo on cutting trees up there in Niyam Raja's name, out of a recognition that the natural vegetation conserves the fertility of their land through an abundance of streams. So, mining of bauxite from Niyamgiri and other Khondalite mountains in south Orissa is bound to cause an erosion of Kond spiritual values as well as an erosion of Orissa's natural environment and fertility. (Dash, 2008).

DIVERGENT VALUES AND BELIEFS

As we write, several other calamities are affecting Orissa, which have an extremely close, though hidden, connection with the subject of displacement: terrible floods, violent attacks between Hindus and Christians, and a number of violent attacks by Maoists and consequent repression. It will be helpful to examine these connections, as a way of leading in to an appraisal of the influence in causing displacement, and compounding its trauma, of differences in what social scientists call the *social construction of reality.* (Berger, 1966).

The floods sweeping Orissa in September 2008 have displaced about 180,000 people, and marooned about 1,500,000. It seems that mismanagement of Hirakud and other dams is a significant factor (*Hindu,* 21.9.08; *Tehelka,* vol.5 issue 39, 4.10.08). Although flood control was given along with irrigation and hydro-power as a main reason for building these dams, recent events have shown that supplying water and power to new factories is the dams' main purpose. Far from controlling floods, evidence suggests that the dams have actually compounded them by releasing water inappropriately, and through the ever-present threat of bursting - the main cause of the disastrous 2008 Bihar floods, after a dam was breached on the Kosi river in Nepal, and officials in Bihar failed to act in time (times online 28.8.08, bihartimes.com 12.9.08). On 7th November 2007, protest by 30,000 farmers in the Hirakud area highlighted the fact of industry taking water at the expense of irrigation for farmers. The farmers drew a "*chashi rekha*" (farmers' line) against factories' further intake of water. (POKSSS, 2008).

Dams thus cause widespread displacement in two other dimensions in addition to their large-scale direct displacement: first, through catastrophic floods in times of excessive rain, and second, by reducing canal or river flow that thousands of farmers depend upon. When Nehru laid the foundation stone for Hirakud, he saw dams as the "temples of modern India" – a view he later regretted–and his words are a poignant illustration of the reality gap: "The Hirakud project is a work which will not cause more misery to the people, but which will bring about the end of their miseries" (*Tehelka*, above). Chief Minister Nabakrushna Choudhury also promised the dam would bring an end to poverty in Orissa. After at least 150,000 people had been displaced, and two Tehsildars had been murdered by furious villagers, causing severe police repression, Hirakud was a main factor in Choudhury's resignation in 1956 (Dhalo, 2007). Sudden release of water by the Hirakud dam caused widespread displacement and loss of life and property in 1980 and 1999 as well as 2008.

The Hindu-Christian issue was sparked in December 2007 by the application of certain Panos (the main Scheduled Caste) in Kandhamal district to change their status from Scheduled Caste to Scheduled Tribe on the basis that they speak the Kond tribal language Kui–an application that angered Konds, and fanned the flames of a double split in society that broke out in violent attacks: SC (Pano)–ST (Kond), and Hindu–Christian. The latter split broke out with renewed ferocity in August 2008 following the murder by Maoists of the VHP leader Laxmanananda Saraswati, whom they held responsible for instigating communal violence in December. August-October 2008 has seen the burning of countless villages and churches, and the displacement of tens of thousands of Christians.

What we are dealing with here is the spread of a *polarising tendency* in society. The primary issue we address in this paper is a polarisation between those who believe in or promote industrial development-cum-displacement, and those resisting it. The Kandhamal violence demonstrates the power of several related polarisations-Hindu-Christian, and SC-ST-and highlights the position of the Maoists in this process.

Increasingly, people who resist displacement are being branded as Maoists, especially in the Kalinganagar and Posco areas (as also at Singur & Nandigram). To what extent Maoist influence is penetrating these areas is often difficult to gauge. What is clear is that these movements against forced displacement are primarily motivated by farmers' wish to retain their land and communities, and if Maoist influence enters, the main reason for this is people's exasperation at the injustice they face, and the Maoists' readiness to capitalise on this, since supporting fights against injustice is at the core of their ideology. It is also apparent that labelling protestors as Maoists makes it easier to justify repressive measures against them.

Before examining the ideology of the protestors, or of the Maoists, we need to look more deeply at the mainstream ideology of development that is the prime cause of displacement. By ideology, we mean the patterns of values and beliefs that motivate people and form their perception of what is real and right–the *social construction of reality*.

As we showed in the first section, the phenomenon of displacement taking place in Orissa now comes out of a history of industrial revolution in a succession of countries, motivated by a nationalistic faith in "progress" that shows relatively little variation from 18th-19th Britain and America, to communist Russia and China, to Orissa/India today. The heart of this belief system is *materialism*: the belief that a high growth rate and increased material production and construction lead to a rise in the general standard of living. In each of the countries mentioned, millions of people were displaced from their land and faced starvation conditions as a result of rapidly imposed industrialisation. In the case of Russia, Stalin's first five year plan caused the death of around 7 million people through starvation in Ukraine in 1932-33, and Mao's Great Leap Forward in 1958-61 caused the death of an estimated 30 million people due to an enforced shift from agriculture to steel production. (Chang, 1991, 2005 and Short, 1999:480-505). In other words, no-one seems to have tried to impose industrialisation more swiftly and cruelly than Mao. This fact alone would make Maoism a very strange ally of people who are resisting industrialisation.

Coming back to the main ideology, it seems that capitalists and Marxists alike believe in industrialisation as a necessary stage of development. They also share a belief in violence, as a means to impose their will. No-one analysed the inequities of capitalism better than Marx, but he was limited by the belief systems of his own time, when hardly anyone could see the environmental consequences of large-scale industrialisation in catastrophic climate change etc, now plainly visible, and when everyone was excited by a new "scientific" vision of progress through set stages of development.

This view of human societies as developing through certain fixed or necessary stages of development is known as *social evolutionism*. Originally it was seen as an application to society of Darwin's theory of evolution of natural species, causing Marx to offer to dedicate a volume of *Das Kapital* to Darwin. Unfortunately, the application of the theory of evolution to society by Herbert Spencer and others was misplaced, since thousands of natural species each develops on its own unique path in relation to changes in other species, while social evolutionists posit the same path of development for every society, forcing diverse cultures into a single paradigm of unsolicited cultural uniformity. (Padel, 2000, chapter 7).

So one aspect of social evolutionism, and therefore of the mainstream values promoting industrial development in India and Orissa today, involves a set of negative stereotypes about tribal people, and other small-scale farmers: as "primitive", "backward", "uneconomic", "unsustainable" etc. This has actually been the dominant view of tribal cultures since European moderns first encountered them (Meek, 1976), and causes an immense undervaluation of tribal culture, which helps justify destroying it, through the idea that resettlement will aid tribal people's development in the long run, even if it causes pain now.

A core aspect of the ideology of industrialisation relates to a faith in certain economic theories. In particular, the idea that a high growth rate in the overall economy is bound to trickle down to the poor, has continued to find currency, even though it has been repeatedly discredited, and flies in the face of the evidence all around us. Neoliberal economics gives prime importance to a belief in "market forces", on the view that if everyone follows their own interests, market forces will produce the proper adjustments in society. This belief, promoted by Adam Smith and others in 18th century Britain, still forms a core belief in the ideology of developers, even though it is clear that it has led to the rich getting richer and the poor getting poorer. It is forgotten that Adam Smith also attacked the power of corporations, the East India Company in particular, warning of their tendency to make a "conspiracy against the public." (Robbins, 2006:61).

From the perspective of tribal cultures, the idea that everyone should follow their self-interest promotes selfishness on a dangerous scale. Even the idea of private property, which Hunter outlined as the core colonial legacy to India (above), is seen by indigenous people as a cause of environmental devastation. As a leading native American leader, Oren Lyons, sees it, "Private property is a concept that flies in the face...of the reality of life...a human conception, which amounts to greed."(Lopez, 2008:28).

The privatisation of resources such as land, minerals and water going on now is seen by environmentalists as a danger to the fabric of life, and contrasts with the advice in the famous Constitution of the Six Nations of the Iroquois confederacy, that any important decision should be assessed on the basis of its likely effects on the seventh generation to come. (ibid. p.29).

This kind of long-term planning is also the reason that Adam Smith distrusted corporations: their thinking is confined to extremely short-term calculations of profits and costs. As we would express this now: wider environmental costs, costs to people being displaced by their projects, and costs likely to fall on future generations are *externalised*, so that they are not borne by the companies who incur them.

In other words, the displacement process involves double standards. A proper Cost Benefit Analysis of any project would offset financial and employment benefits against environmental and social costs, and consequent costs to future generations. The way these are externalised so that companies have to pay nothing, or at most, guarantee a token 5 per cent of profits to compensate for these costs, shows that development projects are defined by the companies and their beneficiaries.

RULE OF LAW

A blatant double set of values is apparent in the application of Law. While protestors against the Utkal, Posco and Tata projects are harassed by countless "false cases" that tie them into a drawn out and highly exploitative process at the local law courts, the big corporations are seen to wriggle out of legal injunctions with ease, e.g. in the notorious bribes paid by mining companies to ministers, and in the way that Utkal and Vedanta proceeded to build their factories without having first acquired proper environmental clearance for the mines they were depending on. (IPTEHR, 2006 headed by Justice Bhargava, Samantara, 2007 and Goodland, 2007). Vedanta/ Sterlite's clearance for mining Niyamgiri came after the Norwegian Government Council on Ethics released a report that detailed a long list of transgressions of Law by the Sterlite-Vedanta group, and abuse of the environment and human rights in India and other countries (2007).

The use of *goondas* (hired thugs) by mining companies is a particularly blatant example of double legal standards. As "Outrage against displacement spreads", (*Statesman*, Bhubaneswar, 23.5.06), it is clear to observers in Orissa that the orchestration of *goondas* in support of mining companies is a nexus that involves certain politicians and senior administrators, as well as the mining companies they promote (Dash 2008). The murder of gangster Biranchi Das in Bhubaneswar on 13th April 08 pointed to senior administrators' involvement in campaigns to terrorise displacement protestors. Raja Acharya, who was arrested for this murder had a close connection with a senior IAS officer, (*name omitted*) whom Raja stated offered him a contract working for Posco. (*Kalinga Times* 5.5.08).

In the Kalinanagar area, leading activists of the *Bisthapit Birodhi Jan Manch* (People's Platform Against Displacement) have been attacked, and one murdered, while another activist was killed in the Posco area. Amin 'Shyam' Banara was gunned down on 1st May 2008 by goons who accosted him near the Tata factory site – a crime for which gangster Arbind Sing was later arrested. A month before, another activist, Jogendra Jamuda, was shot in the back while driving his mother and wife on a motorbike past the Kalinganagar police station. As Chakradhara Haiburu, 60-year old spokesman for the BBJM said, "If Maoists were involved then it would be Arbind Sing lying dead, not Amin Banara." (see Samadrusti TV: "Tata steel bullets" on youtube.com). The main Kalinganagar activists have all received death threats for their opposition to Tata.

The anti-Posco activist Dula Mandal was killed by pro-Posco goons in his village of Govindpur on 21.6.08, after a day's work alongside hundreds of others, dredging the Jetadhari river mouth. Villagers had alerted the authorities to the importance of this task to avert floods, but after huge delays, and offers of a 20 crore contract for the job, the villagers had decided to do it themselves, which angered businessmen who had hoped to get this contract. After completing the dredging on 30th June, they held a memorial for Dula attended by 3,000 villagers and supporters. A few days later, villagers captured several goons who had used violence, along with six boxes of home made bombs and other weapons, from the school in Govindpur. (*Statesman*, 26.6.08). When serious violence erupted before this, on 29th November 2007, and bombs had been thrown by goons at a crowd consisting largely of women, 'the said senior IAS officer' had made a statement on TV that "those people have been taught a lesson".

Similar intimidation, by goons as well as police, took place at a Public Hearing for a Tata thermal power plant at Naraj, near Cuttack on 10.3.08, that would displace several villagers (Samadrusti TV: "Tata Muscle power" on youtube.com). In this instance, villagers entirely new to this kind of intimidation were beaten up and began the process of making a stand against displacement.

Another area where intimidation by goons has escalated is around Maliparbat, a mountain in south Orissa threatened with bauxite mining by Hindalco, where most villagers have come together to oppose the project (Patnaik, 2008), where goons attacked the village of Maliguda on 20th July. Ten villagers were seriously injured and taken to Koraput hospital. Women and girls were molested.

Villagers who maintain a stance against displacement need the utmost strength and courage, not just because the power nexus confronting them links gangsters and mining companies with people in the Government who do secret deals with the companies, but also because of a *manufacturing of consent* by the media. Posco's invitation of journalists to Korea, and Vedanta's invitation of journalists to Lanjigarh, and the money on offer to journalists who promote positive news for these companies, is well known. The number of journalists and editors prepared to take a stand for truth and report what is really happening on the ground, or give a voice to the anti-displacement protestors, is relatively few. So in *the social construction of reality* around the issue of displacement, *The Manufacturing of Consent* by corporate interests making use of the media plays a significant part. (Chomsky & Herman, 1988).

Tata and Posco followed Vedanta's example of trying to construct their factories before getting mining clearance, in order to exert leverage in their bids. The primary object of their desire is the iron-ore in the few as-yet untouched mountains in north Orissa, in a race with Rio, Tinto and Mittal. Yet the pollution and devastation of large areas of north and central

Orissa by existing iron-ore, chromite and coal mines, and about 90 sponge iron factories, has already made life hell for countless Adivasis (Dash, 2008). Sukinda, adjacent to Kalinganagar, has been named one of the ten most polluted spots on earth (Dutta, 2007 nd CSE, 2008 :247). Posco at first did not even want to build a steel plant in Orissa, but was persuaded that this was a condition of gaining access to north Orissa's rich iron deposits. Meanwhile, all the bauxite-mountains in south Orissa are exposed to imminent threat of mining clearance. BHP Billiton, Alcoa and Dubai Aluminium are among the companies known to be manoeuvring for bauxite deals.

Among the most important aspects of development is access to equal justice for all – rich and poor alike. A lot of evidence from the ground indicates that far from getting better, the corruption and intimidation are getting worse. Mining companies, in fact, are notorious for spreading not just material pollution, but also a corruption of values and the dividing of communities.

The pattern for this behaviour was set in the age of the "robber barons" in 19th century USA, when the biggest capitalists often showed contempt for the process of Law. Corrupting elected politicians and Supreme Court Judges was a basic part of this system. Cornelius Vanderbilt, one of the first "railway kings" once remarked when challenged, *"What do I care about the law? Hain't I got the power?"* In 1866-8, during the ferocious "railway wars", rival companies bribed SC Judges, and one party was exposed as paying over 1$million in bribes, describing it in his expenses as *"extra and legal services"*. There was an established system for purchasing elected politicians and judges. As Collis P. Huntingdon, another of the railway kings, put this in a letter of 1877:

"If you have to pay money to have the right thing done, it is only just and fair to do it ....If a man has the power to do great evil and won't do right unless he is bribed to do it, I think the time spent will be gained when it is a man's duty to go up and bribe the judge." (Josephson, 1962: 15, 352, 354).

The prevalence of this corruption explains why Abraham Lincoln, shortly before he was assassinated in 1865, drew attention to the dangers of company power for America:

"Corporations have been enthroned...An era of corruption in high places will follow and the money power will endeavour to prolong its reign by working on the prejudices of the people...until wealth is aggregated in a few hands...and the Republic is destroyed". (Korten, 1995 :58).

"Breaking rules at opportune moments" was one of the secrets of Carnegie's success (Josephson, op.cit. p. 43), and for the other Robber Barons too, laying down a pattern of "dancing with the Law", in which politicians and the judiciary were in effect making and implementing the Law at the Robber Barons' bidding - a pattern painfully visible in corporate takeovers today, in Orissa and worldwide.

The difference in values and beliefs between corporate attitudes to Law and those of Adivasis could not be starker. The Kond concept of Niyam Raja as upholder of Law unites a universal with human conceptions of Law, like the ancient Indian concept of *dharma*. In fact, hearing that a judge in India's Supreme Court was effectively selling Niyamgiri to Vedanta, by asking the company to set aside fixed sums for tribal development and compensatory afforestation, a Kond elder, in our hearing, said something that demonstrates this connection: *"Taro Karma, Amoro Dharma"* (his the sin, ours the *dharma)*.

Another example we witnessed took place during a session of the Inquiry by Justice P.K. Mishra into the Maikanch firing on 29.5.02, when Utkal's Chief Executive Officer was in the witness box, and stated that he could not get the balance sheet to explain where an unaccounted-for 70 crore rupees had gone - listed under "miscellaneous" in Utkal's accounts, and allegedly set aside for bribes. Unable to account for these missing funds, he passed on responsibility to Ola Lie, the head of Norsk Hydro (resident in London), indicating that Mr. Lie was in effect his superior in Utkal, which was then a Hindalco-Norsk-Alcan joint venture. The Judge made a joke about the appropriateness of Mr. Lie's name given Utkal's reputation for tampering with the truth. After the Utkal executive, two women were called, an Adivasi and a Dalit, who had witnessed the shooting in Maikanch, and whose relatives were shot. The whole time each stood in the witness box she kept her palms joined in *Johar/Namaste,* in a symbolic plea for justice and truth in that alien environment of the courtroom, where the Judge kept an impartial aloofness, while the company lawyers pretended friendliness, but tried to trip them up with complicated lines of questioning about who had paid for them to come to Rayagada that day, and where they were during the shooting, implying that they couldn't have seen it, or to cow them with scorn. For example, in answer to the question *"Occupation?"* when one of the women answered *"Chaso"* (cultivation) the lawyers led a round of titters, as if to dismiss her as an illiterate peasant. Before the end of the session, when the witnesses had left, the Judge made the whole courtroom stand while he said that lawyers can be more violent than guns, and that treating villagers with such little respect will erode their faith in our courts.

Indeed, if it is true that Maoists' appeal is on the rise, village people's despair of getting justice at the courts should be counted as a significant factor. The call to armed struggle appears as radical and progressive empowerment for oppressed people who lack legal redress for their grievances. To many observers it seems that, at the grassroots level, money usually decides who wins a case, making a mockery of the idea that the Law is impartial between rich and poor. There is little question that police lodge court cases for unreal offences against activists to de-activate them. Over 500 arrests were made against anti-mining villagers in Kashipur up to 1999 alone (Mahapatra, 1999), and villagers attending the court every few weeks for these cases say they have to pay fees or bribes to a large range of lawyers and court officials.

A summary of Mishra's report was finally released to the media on 10th October 2003, when *Dharitri* published an account under the title "Maikanch firing was justified". Basically, according to the extracts released, the report reaches the contradictory conclusions that grossly excessive force was used, but that the firing was justified. It singles out the OIC (Officer in Command) of Kashipur Police Station "for continuing with firing beyond requirement", after the

Magistrate had given the order to fire, and also admonishes this Magistrate, for giving an open-ended order to fire. The excerpts released mention the 19 rounds fired as excessive, and question the prior intent of the police visit to "investigate" and "maintain law and order", but they do not highlight the height at which bullets were fired (i.e. with intention to kill), nor the live ammunition in the guns, which implies a prior intention to cause harm. The report accepted the villagers' account that the incident was provoked when police laid their hands on two of the women. But critics of Utkal had hoped Mishra's inquiry would reveal the collusion between politicians and ministers, police, and company officials. The fact that the report did not apparently touch on the question of who called out the armed police, or how this decision was reached, implies to critics that the whole exercise was basically a whitewash. Most controversially, the report went beyond its brief to justify the alumina project, stating that "the state cannot afford to remain backward for the sake of so-called environmental protection"– an ideological statement.

One of the best-known books about mining in 19th Wales is called *The Rape of the Fair Country* (Cordell, 1959), and opponents of the proliferation of mining projects talk about a rape of Orissa - its resources as well as its people. Indeed, with the sidelining of legislation that protects India's forests, coasts and land rights by the SEZ and other recent Acts, conservationists as well as rights activists are worried that India's resources are being looted on a scale that even the East India Company could not dream of, and in the violence and manipulation of law and finance the ongoing corporate takeover of farming and forest land represent a kind of reincarnation of the EIC - an undermining of India's Independence in which members of the ruling class are colluding with foreign-based financial institutions for short term gain. In effect it is the very people and communities living most sustainably that are being sacrificed.

The American legal expert Cormac Cullinan's book *Wild Law: A Manifesto for Earth Justice* (2002) raises the question of whether systems of Law now shouldn't make protecting the basic fabric of life a fundamental concern. As he says,

"Most lawyers and legislators do not know enough about natural regulatory systems, and in any case, do not believe they are relevant to humans.....

We need to

"recognise that at the moment the governance systems of most countries and of the international 'community' actually facilitate and legitimise the exploitation and destruction of Earth by humans. (2002, p.30).

Much of what is being called "development" is essentially destructive: the removal of unrenewable resources (in the case of Orissa's minerals), and dangerous overuse of water, as well as destruction of communities living basically in harmony with nature. And much of this "development" promotes an *over-consumption*:

"while economists look with pride on the fact that the world economy expanded sevenfold between 1950 and 2000, and world trade is expanding more rapidly, ecologists see that these are based on a profligate use of Earth's 'natural capital'. (ibid. p.38).

Cullinan calls for a swift change in countries' legal systems with a view to protecting the fabric of life in a world which most ecologists see as entering a period of severe environmental crisis caused by economic growth out of control. The irony of displacement in Orissa is that the very tribal people being displaced in Orissa have been at the forefront of protecting the environment, living sustainably in the true sense of the word.

The threat of accelerating climate change is a case in point. Orissa is a frontline region in climate change causes as well as effects. As it builds new metal factories, deforests its mountains and valleys for mines, depletes its water and food sources, and accepts a virtually uncontrolled increase in pollution in order to serve foreign investors, it is heating up its own climate as well as making a major contribution towards pushing the whole planet towards the tipping point of inevitable runaway global heating. What we need is a fundamental shift of consciousness. We should be learning from Orissa's indigenous people, not dispossessing them of the land they have safeguarded over centuries.

IMPOVERISHMENT: A DRASTIC FALL IN PEOPLE'S QUALITY OF LIFE

Most studies of R & R agree that oustees very rarely regain their previous standard of living, let alone raise it. Orissa's 3 million oustees, and people faced by further displacement now are bound to be cynical about the new R & R policies, when even many areas often mentioned as positive examples of resettlement, such as Nalco's Damanjodi area, prove anything but positive. Will the new policies really remedy the situation, or simply entrench an already ingrained pattern of un-met promises?

When the ILO, and the recent UN declaration on the rights of indigenous peoples, insist that the provision of land of similar quality for land being taken away is the minimum requirement to safeguard indigenous people's quality of life, and this provision is not in the recent R & R policies; and the UN Declaration, like the Extractive Industries Review, insists that people faced with displacement have the right to Free Prior Informed Consent, and this too is not in the R & R policies, it cannot be said that these R & R policies are generous.

One symbol of the reality gap is a cheque for just six rupees we have photocopied, dated 29.9.07 and presented as compensation to Umesh Chhatria of Koindapali village in the Lower Suktel area, for his house by the Special Land Acquisition officer, Balangir. What can be bought for six rupees?

When Company people say of a tribal area where they have erected a factory "there was nothing here before – only mud huts", this shows how the dominant mindset equates development with modern, material constructs, such as roads and buildings. Most R & R schemes assess traditional tribal houses as without any economic value. For example, an official account of Nalco's R & R at Damanjodi states that:

"The Government of Orissa as well as the NALCO have taken the view that the homesteads lost by the tribal families were practically of no value as they were small mud huts. As no compensation could be paid for loss of such homesteads, durable houses (partly pucca) could be constructed for them at the cost of NALCO. Secondly, the concept of rehabilitation was based on the fact that it was necessary for NALCO alumina project to create certain amount of community relationship with those who have lost all their assets in the larger interest of the nation..." (Muthayya, 1984: 2, *emphasis ours).*

The contrast between houses before and after displacement demonstrates a far-reaching difference in values and culture. Traditional tribal villages, without too much outside interference, have a high quality of life in that each man and woman is self-employed on their own land. They have clean water and a daily bath in a flowing stream – better than the most expensive bathroom! They make their own houses out of earth and wood, and though these houses are officially classified as mere "mud huts" - and on this basis people receive minimal compensation for them when they are destroyed to make way for a project - they are far superior in many ways to pukka concrete houses. They remain cool in summer and warm in winter, unlike concrete buildings in resettlement colonies. They are beautifully painted with clays and well-mixed natural glazes; and have many secret spaces for cooking, storing things, and worship of gods and ancestors. Traditional houses are an expression of cultural pride, while the pukka houses that are "gifted" to oustees as if far superior are soulless, inconvenient, and alien in culture. Since the people rarely have any design input, the houses lack the spatial arrangement that binds people into a living community.

The following are some of the areas of life where displaced people generally see a marked decline in their living standards:-

- Food security lost along with people's land,
- Self-employment replaced by humiliating dependency on a supply labouring jobs,
- Egalitarian social structure replaced by a low place in an extreme hierarchy,

- Splits in the community between people for and against a project/company,
- Access to fresh stream water ends, replaced by pump water, often polluted & unreliable (residents in many rehab colonies testify to a dire water shortage),
- Deterioration in community values, corruption, and oppression by *goondas*.

Offsetting the deterioration in standards, are various schemes of "sustainable development" and CSR (Corporate Social Responsibility). Vedanta's 2007 Report devoted 60 pages to SD and CSR. The main evidence of good works is statistics of money spent on schools, health centres and SHGs, accredited by a London-based accountancy firm. Investigation on the ground in the Lanjigarh area reveals that schools and hospitals are functioning barely if at all, while SHGs are open to the problem that once loans are disbursed, repayment pressure is intense and affords a means of control over the indebted population – problems reported by several researchers from Bangladesh, where the SHG model first took off. (Muhammad, 2006). It is true that Vedanta gave training to a number of local youths, but the participation by these youths in repeated demonstrations at Lanjigarh demanding jobs gives the lie to claims that the company offers major opportunities for local people. Local people insist that most well-paid jobs go to outsiders. (Dash, 2008).

The basic problem with privatised models of development is that they bypass democratic social controls that developed through intense campaigns since Independence. Officials have been heard to say, e.g. in the Kashipur region, that once the Utkal project is underway, proper development in terms of schools and hospitals will be given by the company. But the companies involved in Utkal have changed: from Indal, Tata and Norsk, to Alcan and Hindalco, to just Hindalco. So when officials say "*company debo*" (the company will give), the actual company involved shifts its form, and this statement is an echo to words that might have been said 200 years ago about the EIC and its promises. How to ensure that companies keep their promises? What punishments should be meted out to company executives who deceive people with false promises?

In this context, the specific problems with the new R & R policies are that:

— They say it is best to avoid displacement, but there is no serious or publicly transparent process of pursuing alternatives,

— The promise of one job per family has often been made (e.g. at Rourkela and Damanjodi) but has rarely if ever been kept in practice,

— Land is often bought for absurdly low prices, a major factor of discontent at Kalinganagar, where land was resold by IDCO to Tata for ten times the price paid,

— People without *patta* are classed as "encroachers on government land", even though they have often farmed this land over generations,

— The value of houses is grossly underestimated by classing them as "mud huts",

— Cash compensation is the norm, and accepted uncritically in the R & R policies, even though it has been shown repeatedly that business sharks invariably pursue those in receipt of cash and new bank accounts, with offers of vehicles or schemes that enmesh oustees immediately into debt. (Das, 2000),

— Even recent suggestions that mining companies should give 5 per cent of their profits for local area development, or make displaced people shareholders are unenforceable and likely to compound the exploitation.

What adds insult to injury is the dehumanised discourse that is customary concerning people who have been or may be displaced. A study commissioned by Tata soon after the Kalingnagar firing is a case in point (Harsha, 2006), giving statistics of DPs (displaced persons) and PAPs (project-affected persons). Meeting with opposition from villagers whose friends and relations had been killed, the team *"repeatedly emphasised to them that this survey has been initiated only to strengthen the cause of the affected people. Sometimes it worked, paving way for future deliberations."* (ibid. p.10) Which contrasts strongly with the tendentious assumption that *"The very fact that the displaced persons have spelt-out their options and preferences for their relocation, resettlement and rehabilitation indicates that they are willing to accept the project. It also indicates that they are mentally preparing themselves to get displaced to give way for the project."* (ibid. p.iv) Posco, like Tata, has spent a lot of money studying the people resisting displacement, and a visit to the Posco office in Bhubaneswar revealed a site map where resisting households were marked with red dots, pro-Posco households with green, and fence-sitters with blue. In other words, the companies keep lists of "agitators" to be "targeted".

The takeover of Adivasi lands in Orissa's tribal areas follows the same pattern as Scotland's Highland Clearances. Any visitor to Scotland will see clan maps, which show the territories of the Highland Clans, before their villages were burnt and their land was cleared of people to make it more profitable.

In tribal villages that still remain far from industry, there is a silence. The peace at night vibrates with the song of *jhintika* (crickets). When a factory is nearby, this peace is shattered by many sounds of heavy machinery and vehicles, together with the shattering of the community's social structure, and the pollution by dust and smog.

In the Scottish highlands today, the glens (valleys) are full of a different kind of silence–a silence which thousands of tourists come to enjoy–a silence of a land emptied of its people: post-industrial silence, post-people emptiness... (Prebble, 1969). Basically the 'Scottish Enlightenment', in 18th century Edinburgh, promoted market economics, while simultaneously, English armies were slaughtering the Jacobite rebels, who fought for Scottish independence. Scottish as well as English intellectuals wrote about the wretched poverty of the highland crofters and their hovels, and when famine and cholera swept the land, this was taken as a sign, not of the outrageous exploitation, but of the crofters' lack of economic sense. It was Scottish Lairds (*zamindars*) who got their factors and bailiffs to drive the people out of their hamlets and set the crofts on fire, which fitted like hand into glove the English military policy to break the power of the clans. These crofts were made of stones and their ruins are still visible, far and wide.

From 18th-19th century Scotland to 20th-21st century Orissa, essentially the same discourse: a view of clansmen and Adivasis as unruly, uncouth, uneducated, backward, and above all uneconomic and standing in the way of progress. Yet the reality was, and in Orissa still is, that these people grow a large variety of foods on their land, and if the process is labour-intensive, it also involves a huge variety of experience and communication-bathing in the stream, complex songs, dances, myths related to the local landscape, visits between communities, clan feasts–and careful preservation of the natural environment.

Scotland too had its mines, dams and factories. When Kinlochleven aluminium smelter was built in the 1900s and Lochaber smelter in the 1920s, they were the world's largest, and the hydro-schemes to supply them with water and electricity were among the world's first big dams, the Blackwater dam supplying Kinlochleven, and 3 dams built for Lochaber, with a series of pipes 50 miles long bringing water to fall down an incline through the shoulder of Britain's highest mountain, Ben Nevis - a model for the Indravati hydro-scheme.

Thousands of people laboured to build these dams, and smelters, and their associated roads and railways. Conditions were close to slave labour. One of thousands of Irish navvies employed to build Kinlochleven in the 1900s wrote a famous book about the experience: *Children of the Dead End* (McGee, 1914), and during the first world war, hundreds of German Prisoners of War were brought in to build a road to Kinlochleven on the north side of Loch Leven, while hundreds of British conscientious objectors (pacifists, jailed for refusing to fight in this war) were forced to build a road on the south side.

From the silence of tribal villages at night, to the silence of the vanished crofts cleared or drowned from glens and lochs, to another kind of silence: our own silence, when we don't speak about what is really happening.

CONCLUSIONS

A recent review of the state of human rights in India by the UN Committee on Economic, Social and Cultural Rights (UNESCR) expresses deep concern about the displacement and forced evictions of millions of families, and their inadequate R & R, especially the adverse impacts on Adivasis and Dalits, and the harrassment of human rights campaigners attempting to help people assert their rights. The Committee recommends the enforcing of laws that prohibit forced evictions and guarantee proper compensation (2008, paragraphs 31 & 71).

1. As Bhagaban Majhi says, no more displacement ought to happen in Orissa until already-displaced people have first been properly resettled and their standard of living has improved. At the very least, a much more stringent attempt should be made by the authorities to avoid displacement. The principle of Free, Prior Informed Consent should be applied, as set out in the UN Declaration on the Rights of Indigenous Peoples (September 2007), which says they "have the right to require that States obtain their free and informed consent prior to the approval of any project affecting their lands, territories and other resources."
2. The process of consulting with people slated for displacement should be a real and equal procedure, far removed from the present scenario of Public Hearings, where coercion has become the norm, and people's voices have no impact on the outcome. The provisions of the 5th Schedule of the Constitution, the PESA, and the Samata Judgement should be applied to protect tribal people's land rights in Scheduled Areas, at the very least. People's voices should be heard and quoted in official discourse to counteract the proliferation of stereotypes.

3. Social Impact Assessments should be required. R & R should be carried out by properly trained and well motivated officials in charge of resettlement, with an attitude of serving the people. In present circumstances, this is almost unimaginable, so it needs to start from a correction of existing stereotypes about tribals, and an awareness of the reality gap, along with a collective determination to bridge it. If people are opposing major projects, it needs to be clearly understood that this is because they are trying to save the land that forms the core of their culture and community. If these people are sometimes angry at the injustice and intimidation they meet with, it needs to be widely accepted that their anger is justified, and that their movements against displacement are seen by many people as an attempt to safeguard saving the fabric of life itself.

**We are grateful to researchers Subrat Sahu and Mamata Dash for their inputs into this paper*

ENDNOTE

1. This article is a re-writing (based partly on comments by Romy Kraemer) of an article entitled "Orissa's Highland Clearances: the reality gap in R & R", published in the Dec 2008 issue of Social Change. (S.Das is co-author of this & other articles, & our book Out of This Earth: East India Adivasis & the Aluminium Cartelis due to be published this year).

REFERENCES

Berger, Peter L. (1966), *The Social Construction of Reality: a treatise in the Sociology of Knowledge*. London: Thomas Luckmann.

Brown, Dee (1975), [1970]. *Bury my heart at Wounded Knee*. London: Pan.

Centre for Science & the Environment (2008), *Rich Lands, Poor People: Is Sustainable Mining Possible? State of India's Environment. Citizens' Report no.6*. Delhi: CSE.

Chang, Jung (1991), *Wild Swans: Three Daughters of China*. New York: Simon & Schuster.

——(2005), *Mao, the Unknown Story*. London: Cape.

Chomsky, Noam and Edward Herman (1988), *Manufacturing Consent*. New York: Pantheon.

Cordell, Alexander (1959), *The Rape of the Fair Country*. Blorenge Books, Church Lane, Llanfoist, Abergavenny, Monmouthshire NP7 9NG, UK.

Council on Ethics, Norwegian Govt Pension Fund May 2007. *Report on Vedanta Resources plc*. Oslo: Ministry of Finance.

Cullinan, Cormac (2002), *Wild Law: A Manifesto for Earth Justice*. Totnes: Green Books, with the Gaia Foundation, www.thegaiafoundation.org

Currie, Bob (2000), *The Politics of Hunger: A Study of Democracy, Governance And Kalahandi's Poverty*. London: Macmillan.

Das, A.&S. Das (2005), *Matiro Poko, Company Loko* (Earth Worm, Company Man).

Documentary film about mining in Orissa (sdasorisa@rediffmail.com).

______ (2006), *Ladaat Jare* (The Struggle) (sdasorisa@rediffmail.com)

Das, Samarendra 7 Nov. (2000), *"Dalalanko kobjare Kondhomaloro gramoporibohono byobostha"* (Into the clutches of the brokers: Kondhomal's village transport system). Berhampur: *Dainik Asha*.

Dash, Suryashankar (2008), *Niyamgiri, the Mountain of Law*. Documentary film.

Bhubaneswar: Samadrusti TV.

Dutta, Madhumita Dec. (2007), *Sukinda: Top of the Dirty Thirty heap*, in Infosys

Environment at *http://infochangeindia.org/200712016704/Environment/*

Features/Sukinda-Top-of-the-Dirty-Thirty-heap.html

Dhalo, B. Krishna (2007), *"Sarkar Javaab diantu!"* ("Government, explain!") in *Dharitri* newspaper, Bhubaneswar, 23.10.07.

Fernandes, Walter (2008), "Sixty Years of Development-induced Displacemnet in India: Scale, Impacts, and the Search for Alternatives", in Mathur (ed) 2008 (pp.89-102).

Fox, CS. (1932), *Bauxite and Aluminous Laterite: a Treatise Discussing in Detail*...London: Technical Press. (1st edition, *Bauxite*, 1927).

Goodland, Robert March (2007), *Utkal Bauxite and Alumina Project: Human Rights and Environmental Impacts*. Washington: Rbt Goodland@aol.com

Guha, Uma *et al.* (1970), *The Didayi.* Calcutta: Anthropological Survey of India.

Harsha Trust (2006), Xavier Institute of Managament & District Action Group (Jajpur), Nov. *Empirical Study on People Affected and Displaced due to Tata Steel in Kalinganagar, Orissa.* Bhubaneswar: Harsha.

Hunter, WW. (1872), *The Annals of Rural Bengal,* vol.II. London: Smith, Elder & co.

S.N. Bhargava Oct. (2006), *Kashipur: An Enquiry into Mining and Human Rights Violations in Kashipur, Orissa.* Mumbai: IPTEHR.

Kothari, Ashish & Neema Pathak (2008), "Defenders of Diversity", in *Resurgence* Issue no.250, Sept-Oct. 2008, *Indigenous Intelligence: Diverse Solutions for the 21st Century* (pp..36-7). Ford House, Hartland, Bideford, Devon EX39 6EE, UK.

Korten, David C. (1995), *When Corporations Rule the World.* London: Earthscan.

Lingaraj March (1995), *Kashipur re Andolanara swaro: bikashara chaka nabinasharo bulldozer*? (The wheels of development or the destruction of the bulldozer?) *Pragativadi,* Bhubaneswar.

Lopez, Barry (2008), "Faithkeeper: Interview with Oren Lyons", in *Resurgence,* issue no.250 (pp.26-30).

McGee, Patrick (1982/1914), *Children of the Dead End.* Pittsburgh: Caliban books.

Maffi, Luisa (2008), "Cultural Vitality", in *Resurgence,* issue no.250 (pp.10-11).

Mahapatra, Richard (1999), "Confrontation", in *Down to Earth,* Delhi, 15 April.

Majhi, Bhagaban 4 Jan. (2005), *"Bikash banama jana andolan"*, in *Samaj,* Bhubaneswar.

Mathur, H.M. (ed) (2006), *Social Change, Special Resettlement Issue.* Delhi: Council for Social Development.

——April (2006), "Resettling People Displaced by Development Projects: Some Critical Management Issues", in *Social Change* vol.36 no.1 (pp.36-86).

——Dec. (2006), "Development Projects and Displacement of Tribal Peoples", in *Adivasi,* vol.46, no.2. Bhubaneswar.

——(ed) (2008), *India Social Development Report 2008 (Development and Displacement)*. New Delhi: Oxford University Press/Council for Social Development.

——(2008), "Managing the Consequences of Development-induced Displacement", in Mathur (ed) 2008 (pp.179-195).

Meek, R.L. (1976), *Social Science and the Ignoble Savage*. Cambridge: Cambridge University Press.

Mosse, David (2005), *Cultivating Development: An Ethnography of Aid Policy and Practice*. London: Pluto.

Muhammad, Anu (2006), *Monga, Micro-credit and the Nobel Prize, www.countercurrents.org/gl.muhammad04126.htm,* retrieved on 4 Dec.

Muthayya, B.C. *et al.* (1984), *Rehabilitation of Displaced Villages: A Study in Nalco Complex, Damanjodi, Koraput District, Orissa*. Hyderabad: National Institute of Rural Development.

Padel, Felix. (2000), *The Sacrifice of Human Being: British Rule and the Konds ofOrissa*. Delhi: Oxford University Press.

——and Samarendra Das (2007), "*Agya*, what do you mean by development?" in Rakesh Kalshian ed., *Caterpillar and the Mahua Flower: Tremors in India's Mining Fields*. Delhi: Panos. (pp.26-46)

——(2008), "Cultural Genocide: The Real Impact of Development-induced Displacement" in Mathur (ed) (2008) (pp.103-115).

Patnaik, K.Sudhakar (2008), "Project at Mali Parbat: How Environmentally Friendly",At *http://www.merinews.com/catFull.jsp?articleID=132320,* retrieved on 12 April, 2008.

Paschim Orissa Krushak Sangathan Samanyay Samiti Feb. (2008), *Chashi Rekha*. Sambalpur: POKSSS.

Perchard, Andrew (2008), "Sculpting the 'Garden of Eden': Patronage, community & the British Aluminium Company in the Scottish Highlands, 1895-1982." Paper presented to a seminar on Bauxite in Paris in 2008, part of a book to be published in 2009, *Aluminiumville: Metal, the British Government & the Scottish Highlands*. Lancaster: Carnegie Publishing.

Pradhan, Jagdish (1995), "*Aluminium prakalpo birodhare janaa andolaan*", in *Sarvodaya*, vol 51, no 6, 15 March 1995.

Prebble, John 1969 [1963]. *The Highland Clearances*. London: Penguin.

Robbins, Nick (2006), *The Corporation that Changed the World: How the East India Company Shaped the Modern Multinational.* Hyderabad: Orient Longman.

Ross, Michael (1999), "The Politicasl Economy of the Resource Curse", in *World Politics* No.51. January, 1999.

Samantara, Prafulla (2006), *Niyamgiri: Waiting for Justice.* Berhampur: Lokshakti Abhiyan (Orissa unit).

Sarangi, Deboranjan (2004), "*Odisharo khanija sampada o baurashtriya Company*" (Orissa's mineral resources and the transnational corporation), in *Samaj,* p.3, 6 June 2004, Bhubaneswar.

Saroj Jan. (2008), "*Kashipur Andoland*", in *Bikolpo Bichar* for July-Dec. 2007. Boroghoro.

Shiva, Vandana and Afasar H.Jafri (1998), *Stronger than Steel: People's Movement against Globalisation and the Gopalpur Steel Plant.* Delhi: Research Foundation for Science, Technology and Ecology.

Short, Philip 1999. *Mao: A Life.* London: Hoddon & Stoughton.UN Committee on Economic, Social and Cultural Rights (UNESCR), 40th session 28 April – 16 May 2008. *Concluding Observations, India.*

http://www.pwescr.org/docs/Concluding%20Observations.pdf

UN Forum for Indigenous Rights 13 September 2007. *UN Declaration on the Rights of Indigenous Peoples, www.un.org/esa/socdev/unpfii/en/declaration.html*

3

INTERVENTIONS AND EXCLUSION: A CRITIQUE OF TRIBAL EXCLUSION IN FORMAL SYSTEM OF EDUCATION

M.C. Behera, Jumyir Basar

INTRODUCTION

Tribal communities in India had an informal system of education before their encounter with the formal system of education. The encounter happened through interventions both before and after Independence. Before Independence the tribal communities which came under the direct administration of the British government encountered the formal system of education through state interventions. Besides, missionary activities also introduced formal system both in British administered territories and out side. Formal system of education in tribal areas of Meghalaya, Nagaland, Mizoram, and Rajasthan, and in South and Central India was introduced as a part of conversion activities of the missionaries. But after Independence the national government at New Delhi introduced plan programmes for the general welfare of the all sections of people including the tribals. Introduction of formal system of education is an important component of such plan interventions.

Education caters to the societal needs of members of a society/nation, *interalia,* of securing livelihoods. Informal system of education was compatible to the subsistence needs of the tribal communities. The knowledge system, both as ideological perception and skill endowment, was the total worldview which got manifested in their faiths, beliefs, social relations, social norms, customs and ways of securing material means of existence by way of their interaction with nature. The knowledge was transmitted from generation to generation by words of mouth and participation in various performances and activities such as dance, child rearing, making of utilitarian objects and production for livelihoods. In particular, the skill of cultivation, hunting, fishing, weaving and making of handicrafts were learnt from observation, imitation and participation. (Basar and Tok, 2004; Begi, 2007:24-27; Perme, 2008:25-33 and also see Pertin, 2009).

But as has been said these communities encountered formal system of education as interventions. In Meghalaya and Nagaland missionaries introduced formal system of education before Independence. Although there was Missionary efforts in the present Arunachal Pradesh to introduce formal education as a part of their conversion activities it did not become a success. (Begi, op cit.:73; Perme, op cit.:21-27). Infact, formal education began after independence through plan programmes under Community/Social Services sector (Agarwal, 1985:305 and Behera, 1994:135) with an objective to: "train and build up a team of their own people to do the work of administration and development". (Nehru, 1958 in Elwin, 1959: xii).

It is to be mentioned that in the informal system of education inclusiveness was expressed in terms of learning the required skill for meeting out the subsistence needs of the self and family. Every able bodied person participated in the production system according to age, sex and cultural prescriptions. It was difficult to find a normal person excluded from production system because of lacking in skill. Efficiency differed but participation was ensured. Persons physically unable to participate in the production system were insured through the social norms and network of sharing. Sharing as risk coping mechanism was a social obligation.

But in the formal system of education a person has to go through some stages of education before s/he utilises it for the purpose of gainful employment i.e. participation in nation's production system in contrast to the community production system. Precisely, the stages refer to elementary and secondary stages of education as there are minimum eligible qualifications for entering the job markets. There are also eligible criteria for skilled workers which require technical and professional education.

Naturally, those who do not attain the minimum level of education under formal system of education are excluded from the market driven production system of the nation. Jha (1985:173-175) has noted that the problem of unemployment was related to high rates of drop outs and thus non availability of candidates with minimum level of qualification. Attainment of a particular level of education is a condition for inclusive development; but the essential condition is the availability of job opportunities for them which more often is limited by, first, due to less supply of opportunities than demand and second, by competition. So, all the eligible persons do not have guarantee for employment. The extent of unemployment of eligible persons is a measure of exclusion. Further, there is another dimension to it. All the equally eligible persons do not get equal jobs in terms of income, status, power, etc. Limited in opportunities and associated competition to posts exclude many eligible persons. Though all graduates are eligible for Indian Civil Services only a negligible percentage of them enter into it due to limited posts and competition. This situation is also an aspect of exclusion.

Denial of conditions of equal opportunity breeds the ground for exclusion of this type. It is not difficult to find schools of different standards and inability of many to avail of the opportunity of better schooling. Obviously, schools of different standards promote different standards of human resources at the same level of schooling. As a result, competition takes place among unequals and the better one wins. This practice is another dimension of exclusion.

The present study makes an attempt to describe the nature and extent of exclusion in tribal state of Arunachal Pradesh with respect to opportunities available at various levels of education in the state. It also focuses on the nature and extent of opportunities provided through government and/or non-government interventions in the field of formal education.

Arunachal Pradesh is selected because educational interventions started from 1947 after Independence through plan programmes and subsequently institutions in formal system of education covered various regions of the state in a phased manner. It is to be mentioned that the strategy to impart education was discriminatory from the beginning. This is evident in Elwin's writings. As Elwin writes, the aim of education in the beginning was "to discover and develop boys and girls of exceptional promise and train them upto the highest standard possible so that they can in time take their place as leaders and administrators of their own people" and "for the great mass of tribes men" to supply a "combination of ordinary and Basic education, suitably adjusted to tribal needs". (Elwin, 1959:191).

DYNAMICS OF INTERVENTIONS

As the study is designed to understand exclusion in the process of development of education it is but natural to present briefly development dynamics operating in the state of Arunachal Pradesh after Independence. It is to be mentioned that Arunachal Pradesh is a predominantly tribal state with 64.22 (Census, 2001) per cent of tribal population, unlike in states where ST are placed under the Vth Schedule of the Constitution.

The tribal society of Arunachal Pradesh was very much tradition bound before independence. (see Haimendorf, 1946, 1962; Elwin, op cit.; Jha, op cit. ; Behera, op cit.). Precisely, the economy was operating at subsistence level in between the stages of food gathering and food production. An idea of the state of underdevelopment is evident from the fact that there were only two lower primary schools with less than 100 enrolments, 13 health units, mostly to cater to the needs of Assam Rifles, and 168 jeepable roads in plains at the time of Independence. Women folk had to walk 3-5 kilometres to fetch water in the bamboo containers which they carried on their backs. (NCAER: 1967). But after independence, the representative government at Delhi took interest in the all round development of tribal people and therefore, introduced general plán programmes. (GOI:1986-87:36)

Therefore, from the very beginning, the policy for the tribal development has been based on (i) protection and promotion of their interests through legal and administrative support and (ii) implementation of development schemes to raise their level of living (ibid.). Accordingly, tribal development and planning in Arunachal Pradesh are essentially political and administrative approaches to development since independence.

At the outset, plan measures were exclusively aimed at penetrating into Arunachal Pradesh with administrative network. The first concern of the government of Independent India had been to cover the entire territory administratively. That is why circle headquarters have been set up in remotest places of the territory. During 1948-49, a total expenditure of a little less than Rs.7,00000/- (seven lakhs rupees) was incurred for the whole area. It was about Rs.10, 00000/- (ten lakhs rupees) in 1949-50 and about Rs.12,00000/- (twelve lakhs rupees) in 1950-51. There was further rise in expenditure and it came to a total of Rs.30,00000/- (thirty lakhs rupees) during 1951-52. All these years the government spending accounted primarily and almost exclusively for the speed administration across the inner-line. (Chowdhury: 1982:246).But the first accent on development was spelt out with the inception of First Five Year Plan 'when a full scale development programme for the area was put into operation from 1953 with definite allotments for different heads of expenditure' (ibid.).

During First Five Year Plan, four sectoral activities namely, agriculture and allied services, industry and mineral, transport and community/social services were introduced. Two additional activities were undertaken under rural development and economic services sector during the Second Plan. During Fourth Five Year Plan, three more activities were added to the previous sectors. The expenditure incurred during the First Five Year Plan was about 30000000/- (three crores) of rupees which was stepped up to 50000000/- (five crores) in the second Five Year Plan and further to 70000000/- (seven crores) in the Third Five Year Plan and to 18,0000000/- (eighteen crores) in the Fourth Five Year plan (Behera 1994 Ch 3 and 4; 1997). During 5th, 6th, 7th, 8th, 9th and 10th plan periods, the expenditure has been recorded at Rs. 63 corers, Rs. 223 crores, Rs. 552 crores, Rs. 1729 crores, Rs. 3570 crores and Rs. 3888 crores (agreed outlay) respectively. (Govt. of Arunachal Pradesh: 2000, 2007). It was a top down plan approach to development with government departments as implementing agencies. (Behera, op cit.). During independence, tribal communities in Arunachal Pradesh were economically non-hierarchical.

Education was one among the sectoral activities with which the development intervention began in Arunachal Pradesh. Of the four sectors, community/social services sector was second in sharing the total budget allocation which amounted to Rs.106.81 lakhs (32.37%) in the total budget allocation of Rs. 300 lakhs. The allocation in transport sector was highest with an amount of Rs. 135 lakhs which comes to 35.06 percentage. (Behera, op cit: 104,109). The same trend continued during the first four plans. The allocation in this sector during four plan periods was 25.9 % of the total plan allocation as against 41.67% under transport sector. (ibid. :118).

What is important is that education was given priority right from the beginning of the plan period. This is evident from the tribal *panchseel* of Nehru as mentioned earlier and in the general policy frame for tribal development in Second Five Year Plan in the then NEFA. The development interventions revolved round the objective of developing human capital to undertake the work contemplated in National objectives and presumably, undertaken by people outside the state. (ibid.:102). No doubt, education in Arunachal Pradesh in the beginning had a wider connotation encompassing all the line departments. (Elwin, 1959: 190-191). But here the concept of education is used to mean its general sense of formal education.

ESTABLISHMENT OF EDUCATIONAL INSTITUTIONS

In the present Arunachal Pradesh the formal system of education started with the opening of schools and appointment of Education Officer at Sadiya in 1947. Though Begi (op cit.) has enumerated more than 10 schools before Independence the Techno-Economic Survey of North-East Frontier Agency reports (NCAER, *op.cit*) that education first came to NEFA in 1947 when two lower primary schools were started.

Growth of educational institutions in the state after Independence: a general profile

During the period from 1947-48 to 1950-51 only one middle school and 63 Junior Basic schools were established raising the total number of educational institutions to 68 (67 Junior Basic Schools including earlier 3 schools and one middle school). GoAP, 1997:2). Needless to say, there was no middle school prior to it and no secondary or higher secondary schools by that time in the territory. However, during the First Five Year Plan, the period between 1951-52 and 1955-56, secondary schools, three in number, were established. During First Five Year Plan also 14 middle schools and 28 Junior Basic/Primary schools were established. (ibid.:4).

During the Second Five Year Plan, the period between 1956-57 and 1960-61, 2 Sec/Hr.Sec. schools were added by upgrading 2 middle schools. But there was a total reduction of 23 Junior Basic schools due to upgradation to middle schools and for some other reasons. That is why Junior Basic schools recorded at 152 earlier were reduced to 129 in 1961. (GoAP, nd[1].5). But subsequently the institutions increased to 567 during the decade covered by the 1971 Census. In 1972, there were 572 educational institutions in total in the state. Further,during 1980-81, there were 49 pre-primary, 845 primary, 117 middle and 44 secondary/higher secondary schools in the state. The census report 1991 records 284 pre-primary, 1,144 primary, 73 secondary and 48 higher secondary schools.

Census 2001 records 3863 rural habitations and 20 urban centres in the state. In 3863 rural habitations there are 1263 primary, 309 upper primary, 109 secondary and 47 higher secondary schools. On the other hand, in 20 urban centres there are 74 primary, 51 upper primary, 23 secondary and 25 higher secondary schools. During the year 2007-08, there are 1561 primary, 664 upper primary, 163 secondary and 97 higher secondary schools, both aided and unaided, recorded in the state. Out of them there are 126 primary, 51 secondary and 12 higher secondary schools under private sector. This leaves 1435 primary, 565 upper primary, 112 secondary and 85 higher secondary schools in government sector which includes one Kendriya Vidyalaya(KV) and three Jawahar Navodaya Vidyalayas(JNV) at upper primary level, four Kendriya Vidyalayas and seven Jawahar Navodaya Vidyalayas at secondary level, and seven Kendriya Vidyalayas and six Jawahar Navodaya Vidyalayas at higher secondary level.[1]

At the level of higher education, the first degree college started in 1964 followed by the second one in 1979, after 15 years interval. Colleges in private sector and professional institutions are late entrants in the state. There are three institutions, which provide B.Ed course. Except NERIST, technical education at diploma level started in 2002. Till date there are two such institutions in the state.

ESTABLISHMENT AND DISTRIBUTION OF SCHOOLS

A few schools were reported to have existed in the present state of Arunachal Pradesh before Independence. These schools were established through both private and government initiatives. All these schools, however, did not exist during Independence except two government schools. Real beginning was made in the field of formal education after Independence through government initiatives which were later followed by private ventures.

Government Initiatives

Formal system of education began in the state of Arunachal Pradesh only after 1947. It is noteworthy that the efforts in this regard begun as government initiatives through plan programmes.

Government of Arunachal Pradesh[2]: In 59 years from 1947 to 2005 the distribution of establishment of schools is very uneven and erratic (Begi,2007:213-217)[3]. Out of 16 districts there were only 9 schools established in 5 districts during 1947. Similarly, in 1948 also there were 10 schools opened in 6 districts out of which 7 schools in earlier 4 districts. In the present Kurung Kumey district the account of the educational institution opened only in 1958. There are some districts like Changlang, Tirap, West Siang and East Siang which received more attention than districts like Dibang Valley, Anjaw, and Lower Dibang Valley. Though in Papum Pare there were only 10 schools upto 1970 the number increased thereafter consequent upon the selection and establishement of state capital in present Naharlagun which is in the present Papum Pare district. Establishment of schools in all the years except in 2005 became regular feature after 1971. (ibid).

The schools are not evenly distributed over time and space. All the districts do not have a school established in each year. Moreover, the number of schools varies from district to district ranging between 16 and 257. In West Siang, East Siang and Changlang districts, except a few years, which stand at 6,7, and 8 respectively, schools were established in all other years. Districts like West Kameng, Papum Pare, Kurung Kumey, Lower Subansiri, Lohit and Anjaw did not have any school for 13,19,17,17,10 and 13 years respectively. Similarly, Tawang, East Kameng, Upper Subansiri, Upper Siang districts did not have schools for 22, 21,22 and 21 years respectively. Present Dibang Valley and Lower Dibang Valley districts surprisingly did not have any school for 46 and 30 years respectively. In some districts schools opened very late but in others even though schools were opened in early years, the efforts did not continue in later years. Though number of schools in a district depends on the number of villages to justify the differences in the number, what is important is that all the districts have not got same attention while opening the schools. (ibid).

There is another way to look at inequality in the distribution of schools. The Census of 1961 records 148 educational institutions and 2451 villages. A simple calculation shows that each Junior Basic/Primary school roughly covers 17 villages on an average. Even to this day all the villages do not have a primary school (GoAP, 2002, 2007-08)[4]. All the villages have not been covered by a school. Of course, there is an improvement of the situation in 2007-08 over 2001. Still all the villages do not have schools at elementary level. Besides in 2001 there was one school in about 50 sq.kms. This difference is glare at inter-district levels. While in Dibang Valley and Lower Dibang Valley districts (former undivided Dibang Valley), there is one school on an average in 228 sq.kms, it is 16 sq. kms in Tirap. Further, the villages covered by one school are lowest in East Siang and highest in former Lower Subansiri district (presently Lower Subansiri and Kurung Kumey). The growth over 6 years is not uniform. It is recorded highest, 93.83 per cent, in Papum Pare district and lowest, 7.66 per cent, in West Siang district followed by Changlang, Tirap and Lohit (present Lohit and Anjaw) districts. The growth rate is recorded below two digit figures.(ibid).

As per available data 2535 villages are unserved by schools at primary stage while 52 villages do not have primary schooling facility at all. (GoAP, 2005: 51-52). Though all the habitations do not have primary schools, about 51.62 per cent (2168) of habitations have primary schools within a radius of one kms and 1309 have upper primary schools within the radius of three kms. (ibid).

Central Government Schemes: Under the management of Central government there are two schools in the state; one is Kendriya Vidyalaya and the other Jawahar Navodaya Vidyalaya. In Arunachal Pradesh the first Kendriya Vidyalaya was established at Tenga Valley under West Kameng District in 1975-76 (GoAP,1981:12). At present there are 14 Kendriya Vidyalayas (Begi, op cit.:39-40) in Naharlagun, Itanagar, Pasighat, Nirjuli, Aalo, Kimin, Rupa, Tawang, Tezu, Tenga Valley, Khonsa, Miao and Roing to meet the needs of the children of the employees of central government and central government undertakings. Keeping in the line of the objectives National Policy of Education 1986 Jawahar Navodaya Vidyalayas have been established in all the districts except Kurung Kumey. (ibid.:40). Establishment of a Sainik school in West Kameng District is in the progress[5]. It is to be mentioned that except Vivekananda Kendra Vidyalayas other private schools are located in administrative headquarters including the capital complex and thus have urban bias. Vivekananda Kendra Vidyalayas are located in some rural settings like Amliang, Sunpura (about 9 kms from Sunpura circle head quarters) Sher, etc.

Private Initiatives

As has been said the spread of formal education in Arunachal Pradesh is a state induce-exercise at the beginning. Later, private initiatives followed with the establishment of Rama Krishna Mission Schools in 1960s. During 1990s schools in private sector became a profit earning enterprise (Behera & Mantaw, 1998:221) and it is so even now. During the first part of this century, private interest was noted in the fields of higher and technical education. Though data before 1994 are not available, it is still evident from table-1 that establishment of educational institutions under private initiatives practically started form 1990s excluding R K Mission schools, Sharada Mission Schools, Vivekananda Kendra Vidyalayas, Donyi-Polo Vidya Bhawan and Boum Kakir Mission schools which strated in 1960s, 1970s and in 1980s. It is Donyi-Polo Mission which has started Donyi-Polo Vidya Bhawan and another school for hearing impaired children. The growth of schools shows erratic trend at various levels. For example the number of primary schools during the period 1994 to 1996 has dropped to 20 in 1998. This is due to the reason of upgradation of primary sections to middle level. Of course, with upgradation there is new establishment of schools. From field observation, it can be stated that private schools have been established in administrative headquarters with more concentration at district headquarters and state capital.

Table 1
Growth of Schools through Private Initiatives

Year/ Schools	*Hr. Sec*	*Sec/ High / Post-Basic*	*Middle*	*Primary*	*Pre-Primary*	*Physically Handicapped*
1994-1996	5	3	9	26	-	1
1998	6	10	21	20	16	1
1999	6	12	27	54	20	1
2001	13	25	36	74	28	1
2002	14	28	51	75	-	1
2003	14	36	49	82	-	1
2006	19	49	65	117	-	1
2007	24	52	87	127	-	1

Source: Computed from Statistical Abstracts of 1994, 1995, 1996, 1998, 1999, 2001, 2002, 2003, 2006 and 2007. Directorate of Economics and Statistics, Government of Arunachal Pradesh, Itanagar.

ESTABLISHMENT AND GROWTH OF INSTITUTIONS OF HIGHER AND TECHNICAL EDUCATION

In early years, the government of Arunachal Pradesh used to nominate/select students for higher and technical education outside the state. The same practice also prevails now for courses which are not available in the state. Moreover, students who go on their own for higher education in courses available in the state or for which the government does not have provision also get financial assistance. A small but significant beginning was made in the field of higher education with the establishment of a degree college in 1964-65 in the state.

Government Initiatives

For all practical purposes, the beginning in higher education was made with the establishment a degree college at Pasighat through government initiatives. The first technical institution in the state is NERIST, an institute of Central Government. However, in the field of higher and technical education noticeable achievements have been made from 1980s.

Government of Arunachal Pradesh: As has been said, a beginning in the field of higher education was made through government initiatives with the establishment of a general degree college, namely Jawaharlal Nehru College at Pasighat in 1964-65. So far there are eight government degree colleges

Table 2
Institutions of Higher and Technical Education under Government Management

Programmes	*No. of Institutions*	*No. of Institutions in* *Capital Complex*	*District Hqs*	*SDO/ Circle HQs*	*Year of Establishment*	*Remarks*
General UG	08	01	04	03	1964, 1979, 1986, 1988, 1996, 1996, 1997, 2007	
General PG	01	01	-	-	1984	Converted to Central University on 8/4/2007
Technical Diploma	01	01	-	-	2002	
Technical PG	01	01	-	-	1984	
Professional UG	01	-	01	-	2001	College of Horticulture and Forestry under Central Agriculture University, Imphal.

Source: Basic Information on Institutions of Higher and Technical Education, Arunachal Pradesh, 2008-09, Directorate of Higher Education, Govt. of A.P, Itanagar.

located in administrative headquarters including the capital complex as can be viewed from Table-2. The University which was established in 1984 has been converted to a Central University in 2007. Surprisingly, government initiatives in opening up institutions for technical and professional courses have been very late. However, in 1984 the first institute, namely North-eastern Regional Institute of Science and Technology (NERIST), was established to cater to the needs of all the states in the region. There is only one technical institution, namely Rajiv Gandhi Polytechnic, which was established in 2002 with the initiatives of the state government. The College of Horticulture and Forestry at Pasighat, which was established in 2001 is a campus of Central Agriculture University, Imphal. Needless to say, the initiative of the state government in establishing professional and technical institutions in diverse courses is not at all encouraging.

Central Government: Under central government sector there are two universities at present, one is NERIST, a Deemed University and the other is present Rajiv Gandhi University, a Central University from 8th April, 2007. The College of Horticulture and Forestry, which is a campus of Central Agriculture University, Imphal, was established at Pasighat, East Siang district in 2001.

Private Initiatives: Initiatives from private sector to establish institutions of higher and technical education in the state are also not encouraging. It transpires from Table-3 that there are only 4 degree colleges of general education; the first one, namely Don Bosco College, only began only in 2002 in capital complex. All the degree colleges are run by missionaries and trust. There is only one technical institution providing diploma course which was established in 2006 in Basar of West Siang district. The professional institutions include only medical, law and B.Ed courses. The medical institution, established in 2002 in Itanagar, provides degree in homoeopathy. The B.Ed course also started late and still late is the course in law. However, Department of Education, Rajiv Gandhi University is providing B.Ed degree from 1988.

Table 3

Institutions of Higher and Technical Education under Private Management

Programmes	*No. of Institutions*	*No. of Institutions in* Capital Complex	District Hqs	SDO/ Circle HQs	*Year of Establishment*	*Remarks*
General UG	04	01	03	-	2002, 2003, 2004, 2007	3 colleges by missionaries, 1 by trust.
Technical Diploma	01	-	-	01	2006	Polytechnic at Basar
Professional UG	03	-	03	-	2002-medical 2006- B.Ed 2007- Law	1- Medical 1- Law 1- B.Ed
Total	20	05	11	04	-	-

Source: Basic Information on Institutions of Higher and Technical Education, Arunachal Pradesh, 2008-09, Directorate of Higher education, Govt. of A.P, Itanagar.

EFFORTS TO WOO CHILDREN TO SCHOOLS

The introduction of formal system considered the effectiveness of a familiar setting in order that the beginners do not feel a sense of total alienation.(See Elwin, 1959:190-201 and Perme, 2008: Chapters IV and V). So, the structure of schools resembled the tribal house structure and agriculture, dance, picnic, etc. were included in the school curriculum. The teachers, government officers and officials and a few traditional elites tried to motivate the parents to send their children to schools. In fact the administration made it a point that at least one of the children of the same parents be sent to school. Often the brother to whom others considered 'good for nothing' in their traditional standard was sent to school to avert the displeasure of the government. Only in one case the traditional institution was linked to the school education. The Buddhist monasteries in Khampti area became the hostels for school children. While staying in monasteries Khampti boys learnt religious texts and other traditional knowledge as they used to do earlier and at the same time joined school education.

SELECTION OF STUDENTS TO SCHOOLS OUTSIDE THE STATE

With a view to create human resources from among the tribal people themselves and enable them to shoulder the responsibility of their own development, the government used to nominate students to different institutes for study. There was no entrance examination up to 1970s for selection of students to medical or engineering courses. Those who passed in science subject and mathematics at secondary level were nominated to diploma courses. Further science students after higher secondary were nominated to medical and engineering courses.

In recent years, Directorate of Higher & Technical Education, Government of Arunachal Pradesh conducts Joint Entrance Examination for medical, engineering and other technical courses and nominates candidates to institutes outside the state. These students are also provided with stipend, book grants, etc.

The government on the basis of entrance examination also nominates students to Vanastahli at Rajasthan[6], Sainik School at Imphal, Bhubaneswar and Goalpara, Jawahar Navodaya Vidyalay, Kendriya Vidyalaya in Gaziabad, Vishesh Kendriya Vidyalaya in Delhi, etc.

FINANCIAL INITIATIVES

The children in tribal communities used to be a part of workforce, right from looking after siblings to helping parents in their works, depending on age. Education seemed to the people a means of loosing working hands in the family. Moreover, education required money which the non-monetised tribal people did not have. That is why as per the provisions of the Constitution and various Acts, the government provided stipends, free admission, books grant, free accommodation and many other incentives (Behera, 1994:265) so that schooling did not put a burden on the parents.

ANALYSIS OF FINDINGS

Educational interventions in the tribal state of Arunachal Pradesh have different implications. First and foremost outcome of such intervention is that people have been included in the formal system of education and through it acquire knowledge and develop skills compatible to the requirements of market economy. But what is evident from such achievement is a variation in literacy rate and thus a process of exclusion in the development process. Of course, literacy is not the true measure of skill development, or it does not give a picture of access to higher education, but it is the foundation stone in this regard. Needless to say, variation in literacy rate across the gender, districts and rural-urban divide for the total population as shown in Table-4 marks the extent of exclusion from formal system of education. Literacy rate less than 100 per cent marks the extent by which the population is excluded from the system. Similarly, inter-group variation also gives the picture of a comparative exclusion; the group with low rate of literacy is more excluded than the higher ones.

Table 4

Rural-Urban and Sex Wise Distribution of Literacy Percentage in the Districts of Arunachal Pradesh

Name of District	District Literacy			Rural Literacy			Urban Literacy		
	Male	Female	Total	Male	Female	Total	Male	Female	Total
Tawang	60.3	30.0	47.3	44.9	25.0	35.1	93.1	66.6	87.2
West Kameng	70.3	47.5	60.8	69.0	44.8	58.9	84.2	71.3	78.3
East Kameng	52.4	28.6	40.6	41.8	20.8	31.3	79.9	52.7	67.4
Papum Pare	77.3	60.4	69.3	68.3	49.0	59.0	85.4	71.3	78.9
Lower Subansiri & Kurung Kumey	53.4	36.0	44.8	48.7	31.3	40.1	83.6	69.8	77.1
Upper Subansiri	59.5	40.7	50.3	50.5	32.5	41.5	80.5	63.0	72.5
Weat Siang	66.6	51.6	59.5	60.7	46.7	53.9	86.7	73.0	80.9
East Siang	68.4	52.4	60.7	63.5	47.5	55.7	81.9	67.2	75.1
Upper Siang	58.7	38.8	49.8	58.7	38.8	49.8	-	-	-
Changlang	62.1	39.2	51.3	58.7	35.4	47.6	89.0	75.4	83.2
Lohit &Anjaw	65.7	44.5	56.1	61.3	38.8	51.0	83.4	69.3	72.2
12L/Dibang Valley & Dibang Valley	67.2	48.7	58.9	62.0	42.5	53.1	89.3	78.1	84.5
Tirap	53.4	28.8	41.7	46.2	21.2	34.2	87.9	73.1	81.4
Arunachal Pradesh	63.8	43.5	54.3	57.7	36.9	47.8	85.2	69.5	78.3

Source: Directorate of School Education, Government of Arunachal Pradesh, Itanagar

There was no formal system of education and so no literacy gap when educational interventions were initiated in the state. Rural-urban and gender gap in literacy rates among the Arunachalee (Table-5) indicates the existence exclusion between the groups and within the group in general in terms of achievements less than 100 per cent of literacy. (table-4). Besides, the gradual increase in literacy rate in all categories in succeeding censuses could be attributed, among other things, to gradual provision of opportunities available by opening of schools in a phased manner in the state. So the paper argues that the inequality and thus exclusion emerged from the process of educational interventions. Further, the paper attributes this inequality to 'unequal treatment to equals' and 'equal treatment to unequals'. The former refers to gradual establishment of schools which created inequality of the opportunity in accessing to school education. This is also true for higher and technical education as transpires from Tables -2 &3.

Table 5
Literacy Rates of Arunachalee Population

	Male			*Female*		
Category	*1981*	*1991*	*2001*	*1981*	*1991*	*2001*
Total	12.43	44.0	64.07	5.16	24.94	44.24
Rural	12.25	41.50	NA	4.95	22.89	NA
Urban	19.34	81.97	NA	15.61	60.17	NA

Source: Census reports of 1981, 1991&2001
• *Literacy rates for population of all category were recorded 7.13, 11.29, 20.79 and 41. 59 percents in 1961, 1971, 1981 and 1991 respectively. The rate was estimated for population of 4+ age groups in 1961 and 1971, and for 6+ age groups in 1981 and 1991.*

The attribute of 'equal treatment to unequals' refers to the provisions of equal facilities and opportunities to socially and economically differentiated groups. Due to unequal treatment to equals, inequality emerged among the equals. But there is no preferential treatment to unequals and the weaker section does not get any boost to come to the level of the stronger section. As a result inequality perpetuates and the process of exclusion continues unabated.

UNEQUAL TREATMENT TO EQUALS

Overall achievements in literacy front display gender bias in terms of variations of achievements between sexes as can be seen with reference to literacy rates (Table-5) and enrolments (Table-6). In 2004-05 about 10.74 per cent of total male students in the state were from rural schools while 26.85 from urban schools at secondary level of education. In case of female students the figures were recorded 8.93 and 22.70 for rural and urban categories. (Begi, 2007: 107). Evidently, external forces of change have benefited male population more than the female population. As changes have been introduced directly through plan expenditures, it would not be out of place to state precisely that these forces of change are essentially economic in nature. Alternatively, economic forces of change have affected changes in socio-economic life of the tradition bound people and communities of Arunachal Pradesh with a greater leverage to male population.

Table-6 shows that there is a gradual decline of enrolments at successive higher levels of education. Due to non-availability of comparable time series data for analysis, average student per class is calculated for each level. At primary level the average enrolment per class is 29456 which has reduced to 5872 at higher secondary level. The difference in enrolments in successive higher level of education marks the extent of exclusion which might have also occurred due to stagnation or dropouts[7] or retention. But the fact that number of schools at higher secondary level is less as compared to primary level is indicative of inadequate opportunities available at higher level of education. This is also true when there is only one Law College or a homoeopathy college in the state. For technical education at PG and UG levels there are only 159 ST students enrolled (Table-7) which constitutes 15.35 percent of total enrolment in NERIST. This figure refers to total ST students of NE states and so the ST students of Arunachal Pradesh pursuing technical education at NERIST are still less. The reservation quota restricts opportunities to a greater extent. Fewer opportunities in general and expensive opportunities in private sector in particular deprive many from accessing to technical education. Obviously, lack of opportunities is an important causative factor of exclusion.

The nature and extent of exclusion in terms of differences between the percentage distribution of population and primary schools in the districts and in rural areas can be viewed from the Table- 7. The difference in percentage points between the percentage of primary schools in the district and that of in rural areas in the district is negative in all the districts except Upper Subansiri where it is zero. Evidently, the comparative higher percentage for the district total as compared to rural figures shows relative measure of rural exclusion but urban concentration of schools.

A comparison of differences between percentage points of population and ST population respectively in the districts shows an erratic trend. Further, there is also variation between the percentage point differences of ST population and schools in rural areas. For example, the percentage point difference between per cent of population and per cent of rural ST population in Papum Pare district is - 4.22 and in Changlang +1.57. Corresponding per cent point differences in the said districts and rural areas are - 0.61 and - 0.07 respectively. A negative percentage point difference shows more concentration of urban people while a positive one shows less as compared to rural concentration of ST population. A positive percentage point difference of rural ST population and negative percentage point difference of primary schools show a wider gap between urban-rural concentration of schools than when differences in both the cases are positive. To put it in simple terms, the degrees of inter- and intra -district variations as transpires from the table of reference marks the nature and extent of inequality in accessing to the opportunities of schooling and thus exclusion of people from formal system of education.

It is noteworthy that from among the Arunachalee students very few were available who passed out higher secondary standard with science and mathematics successfully. Up to 1994, passing in mathematics was not compulsory in Class-X standard in CBSE examination. So there were very few

Arunachalee students enrolled in science stream at higher secondary level. That is why till date science stream has been opened only in two colleges, namely J.N. College Pasighat and D.N. Government College Itanagar[8].

Not only enrolment in science stream was low in higher secondary level, there were very few higher secondary schools having science stream. Science streams were introduced in the beginning in the higher secondary schools at Paighat, Ziro, Along (now Aalo) and Tezu. So the early batches of doctors, engineers and other professionals belong to these places.

In Arunachal Pradesh a little above 4 per cent of eligible population within the age group of 18-24 years has excess to higher education. (Begi, op cit., and Behera, 2006). Obviously, around 95 per cent of eligible population is excluded from availing the benefit of higher education. From this 4 per cent a higher concentration could be with all probability in eight (8) districts out of 16 districts in the state which have general colleges. In total, there are 20 institutes of higher education. Of all the institutes of higher education, the state capital has one University; one deemed University, the IGNOU Regional

Table 6
Enrolment of Arunachalee Students, 2007-08

Educational Institutions		*Boys*	*Girls*	*Total*	*Average*
Primary schools		77782	69494	147276	29456
Upper Primary		27917	24219	52136	26068
Secondary schools		12238	10741	22979	114895
Hr. Secondary schools		6662	5082	11744	5872
Colleges (general)		4771	3908	8674	2891
University(PG)		393	408	801	400
Technical & Professional	NERIST	121(777)	38(259)	159(1036)	-
	Law	84	10	94	47
	B.Ed	26	31	57	57
	BHMS	16(30)	39(59)	55(89)	11
	Horti & Agriculture	13(64)	12 (44)	25 (108)	12
	Technical (Diploma)	382(111)	163(73)	545(181)	182

Source: Government of Arunachal Pradesh (2008-09

Note: Data relating to College/University pertain to the year 2008-09.

Centre, three general colleges, one law college, one polytechnic and one Homeopathy college, in all nine institutes. Except the two universities and one general college other colleges are in private sector where education is comparatively expensive, thereby depriving higher education to economically disadvantaged groups.

All the colleges have urban bias except three colleges situated at Kamki (1996), Changlang (1996), and Yachuli (2007). But these colleges are lacking in infrastructure with very low enrolment. For example, during the year 2005-06 the total enrolment in Rang-Frah Government College, Changlang was reported 191 (Begi, *op.cit*). While urban government colleges have more enrolment, the rural colleges have less. This implies that candidates of interior villages have less access to higher education. In Changlang the total enrolment in three years degree course during the session 2008-09 happens to be 230 while it is 1842 in J.N.C.Pasighat and 2001in D.N.G.C, Itanagar, the capital complex. The next highest enrolment stands at 831 in IGGC Tezu. In the same line of thinking and from empirical observations we find districts without colleges have less access to higher education. For example in East Kameng district there are only two (2) graduates among the Puroik community who earlier happened to be subordinate to major tribes in the district. (Deori, 1982). Likewise from among the Meyors there is only one lady graduate. Needless to say, Meyors who live in interior villages along the international border do not have access to higher education at Tezu where there is a college. Of course, the new district bifurcated from Lohit that is Anjaw does not have a college either. The Buguns, another tribe in West Kameng district with a college also do not have more graduates due to their earlier dependency relation with their neighbours. By 2008, there are three graduates, out of whom one is a post graduate and the other is a student in post graduate course. Two girls and three boys have been recorded enrolled in Under Graduate course at Bomdila College during the session 2007-08[9].

Though there is no quantitative data available, an observation in government offices reveals that most of the human resources have come from West Siang and East Siang districts followed by Lower Subansiri, Lohit, Upper Siang, Papum Pare, Tawang and West Kameng. In Changlang and Tirap the attention to education has been given form the very beginning and with a regular commitment as for less then 10 years there was no establishment of schools during the period of 59 years. Despite the comparable literacy rate with Siang districts there is backwardness in terms of evolution of human resource. During field study one of the authors found the social structure around the chieftaincy responsible for the situation. Even educated girls had to work in the royal family.

EQUAL TREATMENT TO UNEQUALS

In response to unequal treatment to equals in the process of establishing educational institutions in a phased manner and nomination of children to various educational institutions outside, a selected few got initial exposure to education. There emerged an elite class from among these selected few in course of time in undifferentiated tribal communities of Arunachal Pradesh. People of this section undoubtedly were the first group to participate in the development process of the state. This class reasonably understood the importance of education and had the means-in terms of awareness, information, nearness to power and money–to provide quality education to their children. Not only they sent their children to good private schools both inside and out side the state, they also managed to avail opportunities from the process of selection to government quota to good educational institutes. A casual researcher can find that almost all the Arunachalee children studying in good schools and later in technical institutes belong to the first generation of the elite class[10].

Mention may be made that Mrs. Boromoti Dai (Yirang) was the first graduate from among NEFA girls in 1966. During the same year Mrs.Disi Mihu passed PU(Arts) from the women college Varanasi. Nang Vina Namchum and Nang Narika Namchum, daughters of Chowkhamoon Gohain, the first M.P. nominated to Lok Sabha from NEFA, passed PU (Sc) from cotton College Gauhati. (NEFA Information, 1966 1(1), p.17).

There were no other girls from NEFA pursuing education after high school by that time. Mrs.Dai has retired as the Principal of a Higher Secondary school. One of her children is an Engineer. Mrs Mihu also retired as the Director in the Department of Social Welfare, Women & Child Development, Government of Arunachal Pradesh . Her daughter; Ms. Indira Malo, is the first lady IAS officer from Nyishi community. Nang Vina Namchum and Nang Narika Namchum were Chief Medical Ofiicers and have recently retired. One of Dr.Vina Namchum's daughters is working in London after her Masters in Social Work from Delhi University. Mr. Jamin Tayeng who was pursuing his Law degree during that year (NEFA Information,1966,1(2),p.17) became the first IAS officer. Two of his children are in State Administrative Services. Similarly, two children of Mr.Martin Dai, who retired as the Chief Secretary of the State got selected in Indian Civil Services. His daughter, Ms. Mamang Dai, an ICS of Foreign Service cadre and the first lady ICS from the state, resigned her post and now is a freelance journalist. Mr. Tago Basar was a student at R.K.Mission school, Narendrapur in 1967 (NEFA Information,1967,II (2),p.27). He is the present Director, Department of Agriculture. Mr.Kuru Hassang who was studying at Sainik School in 1967 at Bhubaneswar (ibid.) joined IAF and became the first pilot from the state. These persons are the elites in the state and have been able to provide better education to their children.

It is to be mentioned that the tribal education is subsidised. There are stipend and other facilities like books grants, free hostel accommodation, etc. available to tribal students, even from the elite class, at all levels of education. This provides a respite to those who want to send their children to private colleges but marginally fall short of the money requirement.

Unequal treatment to equals has another dimension. Traditional role expectations of girls deter their education. (cf. Behera:1991). Food habit and traditional life style in villages have not changed to any significant extent. Girls entertain the guests in the evening around fireplace, prepare food for them and help women folk of the house in house hold management.

Table 7

Percentage Distribution of Population and Primary Schools in the Districts of Arunachal Pradesh[1]

Districts	*% of Population in the District*	*% of Rural ST to total Population[2]*	*% of Primary Schools to total in the state*	*% of Primary Schools in rural areas to total in the state**
Tawang	03.55	3.51 (-0.04)	4.33	04.03 (-0.30)
West Kameng	06.79	7.80 (+1.01)	8.37	07.38(-0.99)
East Kameng	05.21	4.85 (-0.36)	8.37	08.21(-0.16)
Papum Pare	11.11	6.89 (-4.22)	5.55	04.94 (-0.61)
Lower Subansiri / Kurung Kumey	08.95	9.87 (+0.92)	8.97	08.21(-0.76)
Upper Subansiri	05.04	4.55 (-0.49)	7.30	07.30 (-0.00)
West Siang	9.46	9.52 (+0.06)	12.93	12.40 (-0.53)
East Siang	7.96	7.52 (-0.44)	8.14	07.45 (-0.69).
Upper Siang	3.04	3.83 (+0.79)	3.88	03.73 (-0.15)
Changlang	11.42	12.99 (+1.57)	10.34	10.27 (-0.07)
Lohit & Anjaw	13.07	13.42 (+0.35)	9.58	09.13 (-0.45)
Dibang & Lower Dibang Valley	05.26	5.47 (+0.21)	2.90	02.59 (-0.31)
Tirap	9.14	9.77 (+0.63)	9.28	08.67 (-0.61)

Source: GoAP 2002: *Statistical Abstract of Arunachal Pradesh.*

Notes:

1. Population figure corresponds to Census, 2001 and primary schools to 2001-02.
2. Figures in the parentheses show percentage point variations of ST population and rural primary schools over the district.

* Includes only Arunachal Pradesh Government Schools. There are no data available on the basis of rural-urban classification. Primary schools, numbering 75 under private sector, have been taken as urban schools. There are about 30 government primary schools in 20 urban centres, including the state capital. Similarly, there are also some Vivekananda Kendra Vidyalayas, recorded under private sector, in rural areas. Considering the above facts and non-availability of data on rural-urban basis, primary schools under government sector have been considered rural schools for the convenience of substantiating to the fact that there is inequality in the distribution of primary schools in the state which is an indicator of the nature of exclusion in the process of implementation of plan programmes for the growth of education.

During festivals, they spend a lot of time in preparing food not only in their respective houses but in the house of their clan members. For daily consumption, collection of edibles from the jungle falls usually on their lot. They help in collecting firewood, growing vegetables (mostly in Khampti area) in kitchen garden and during agricultural season, in various stages of agriculture. Girls learn to earning and to earn for the family. That is why there is a gender gap in literacy and also in enrolments.

During early periods of planning boys were more responsive to education than girls, presumably because of the fact that girl students were not sent to schools. The first education officer, Mrs Indira Miri, on her tour to Denning in the September of 1948, found only 13 Mishmi boys enrolled in the school[11]. Later also the enrolment in schools had male bias. The coefficient of variation of enrolment of boys at all levels of education during VIth plan period was 65.20 per cent as against 68.13 per cent for girls. Needless to say, the enrolment of girl students was comparatively more variable than boys. Further the enrolment of boys at each level of education was more than 60 per cent as compared to below 40 per cent for girls. (Behera, 1994:219).

Apparently it seems that social structure along gender line is responsible for the exclusion of the girls from the system of formal education. But in reality exclusion is inherent in the general nature of educational interventions in which specific needs of boys and girls were not addressed separately.

CONCLUSION

The process of tribal education in Arunachal Pradesh, which has created exclusion, is marked by two distinct factors, namely unequal treatment to equals and equal treatment to unequals. The exclusion manifests in rural-urban and gender gap in literacy rates consequent upon the nature of urban bias of educational institutions and their establishment in a phased manner. It is obvious that people of all the districts and all sections of people in the same districts did not get equal access to education from the beginning of the development interventions. Besides, the educational institutions offering few programmes have limited the choices and access to technical and professional courses. So people are excluded from undertaking education in these courses. This type of exclusion has a greater implication when compared with the availability of technical and professional personnel in the areas in which Arunachalees are deprived of due to lack of opportunities. The opportunity of available courses/programmes is further limited in every succeeding higher level of education.

With the beginning of planned development, the administration selected students, especially boys, for education in Sainik Schools, Vanasthali, Rama Krishna Mission Schools and Vivekananda Kendra Vidyalayas in spite of the fact that there were efforts by the government to introduce formal system of education in the state right from the day of Independence. The quality education envisioned in the JNVs and KVs for bright students who are selected through a merit test is the process of excluding a larger section of students from it. Similarly, the KVs cater to the educational needs of children of the employees of central government and central government undertakings.

As mentioned, before Independence the tribal people were homogenous and undifferentiated in terms of their accesses to community's informal system of education. By selecting a few from among the equals the administration did exclude a large section of people from the initial benefit of quality education. Not only administration but also voluntary organisation of various denominations followed the same practice by picking up a selected few for education. It is to be mentioned that in private and cooperative sector there are schools like Donyi-Polo Vidya Bhawan for the high elite class and Indira Academy, or Green Mount, or Kingkup public schools for children of middle class families. Obviously a few have access to quality education while many are excluded from it.

To conclude, from among the members of the same tribe two distinct classes namely elites and non-elites have been emerging and getting perpetuated. The non-elites fail to participate in development process because of the low level of capacity building (human resource development) as compared to the elite group whose earlier participation provides opportunity to sustain and maintain the *status-quo.*

ENDNOTES

1. Directorate of School Education, Government of Arunachal Pradesh, Itanagar.
2. Earlier Arunachal Pradesh was divided into frontier tracts, further designated as divisions and still further as districts. There were five districts namely, Tirap, Lohit, Siang, Subansiri and Kameng which have been reorganized into present 16 districts. The schools have been distributed in these districts considering the place name in which school was established and the district to which it belongs to presently.
3. Data have been taken from Begi, 2007, Appendix 4.1, pp.213-217.
4. Computed from Statistical Abstracts, 2002 and 2007-08 issues, Government of Arunachal Pradesh, Department of Economics and Statistics, Itanagar.
5. Field data. The site of the school id located in Sanchu village near Tenga Valley.
6. During 1966 seven girl students from Arunachal Pradesh were studying in Vanasthali Vidyalaya, Rajasthan. (NEFA Information, 1966,1(1),p.17; 1(5), p.22.).
7. At primary stage the dropout rate has been recorded 64.85 %-boys 45.86% and girls 48.01%- for the year 2004-05. This rate has increased to 62.63 %- boys 63.22 and girls 61.90 % at elementary level (Begi, 2007:171). For the years 2007 -08 and 2008-09 the Directorate of School Education has recorded Cohort dropout at 5.69 and 9.0 respectively within the age group of 6-11 and 7.06 and 5.6 for age group of 11-14 during the same period.
8. In J.N.College only Botany and Zoology subjects were introduced in 1980-81 and later in 1989-90 Physics, Chemistry and Mathematics were introduced. In D. N Government College three subjects, namely Botany, Zoology and Chemistry have been introduced in 2005-06 only.
9. Based on field data collected during January 2008.
10. One of the authors had conducted a preliminary survey in December, 2007 in connection with a project under distance mode of education. He found that during 2006-07 academic session 98 per cent of female learners and 87 per cent of male learners from among the Arunachelee students pursuing PG courses in Rajiv Gandhi University belonged to at least second generation of the elite families. The elite families belonged to the families in which at least one of the parents is in government job, or in contract/business or in direct politics.
11. Tour Diaries of Education Officer,NEFA, Memo No.Edn 3T-982,15th October,1948.

REFERENCES

Agarwal, A.K. (1985), *North-East India: An Economic Perspective*, Allahabad: Chugh Publications.

Basar, Jumyir and Boa Rina Tok (2004), "Traditional System of Informal Education in Tribal Communities in Arunachal Pradesh-an overview". Presented in the national seminar on *Indigenous Educating Process among various Tribes of Arunachal Pradesh*. October 29-30, 2004, Itanagar: Arunachal University (presently Rajiv Gandhi University).

Begi, Joram (2007), *Education in Arunachal Pradesh since 1947 (Constraints, Opportunities, Initiatives and Needs)*, New Delhi:Mittal Publications.

Behera, M.C. (1991), "Education in Cultural Perspective", *Arunachal Times*, July,7-8,1991.

——(1994), *Planning and Socio-Economic Development of the Tribals*, New Delhi: Commonwealth Publishers.

——(2006), 'Contextualising Human Resource Development in Arunachal Pradesh: Open and Distance Learning (ODL) at Perspective', Paper presented at 2nd Biennial Conference & National Seminar on *Challenges of Higher education in the present Perspective and Role of Distance Mode*, 3rd-4th November,2006, Tripura University, Agartala.

——and Helina Mantaw (1998), "Growth of Entrepreneurship in Arunachal Pradesh: Problems and Prospects–A Study with reference to the Khampti Tribe". In B.Datta Ray and Prabin Baishya (eds), 1998. *Sociological Constraints to Industrial Development in North East India*. New Delhi:Concept.

Chowdhury, J. N., (1982), *Arunachal though the Ages*, Shillong.

Deori, R.K. (1982), *The Sulungs*, Shillong: Research Department, Government of Arunachal Pradesh.

Elwin,V. (ed.). (1959), *India's North East Frontier in the Nineteenth Century*, London: Oxford University Press.

GOI (1986-87), *Report of the Commissioner for Scheduled Castes and Scheduled Tribes*, 28th Report, New Delhi.

——Censuses of 1961, 1971, 1981, 1991 and 2001.

Government of Arunachal Pradesh (1981), *Twenty Years' Development Activities of Arunachal Pradesh since 1960-61 to 1979-80*. Itanagar:

Directorate of Economics and Statistics, Government of Arunachal Pradesh.

Government of Arunachal Pradesh. (nd[1]). Basic Statistics of Arunachal Pradesh (1950-51 to 1986-87), Itanagar : Directorate of Economics and Statistics.

——1991, 1994,1995, 1996,1998,1999, 2001, 2002, 2003, 2002, 2006, 2007. *Statistical Abstract*. Itanagar: Directorate of Economics and Statistics, Government of Arunachal Pradesh.

——(1997), *50 Years Space of Development in Arunachal Pradesh (1947 to 1997)*, Itanagar: Directorate of Economics and Statistics, Government of Arunachal Pradesh.

——(2000), *Economic Review of Arunachal Pradesh*, Itanagar: Directorate of Economics and Statistics, Government of Arunachal Pradesh.

——(2005), *Report of Provisional Statistics, Arunachal Pradesh, Seventh All India School Education Survey*, Itanagar: Department of Education.

——(2008-09), Basic *Information on Institutions of Higher & Technical Education, Arunachal Pradesh*. Itanagar: Directorate Higher & Technical Education.

Haimendorf, C.Von.Furer (1946/1950), *Ethnographic Notes on the Tribes of the Subansiri Region*, Shillong: Assam Government Press.

——(1962), *The Apatanis and their Neighbours (A Primitive Civilization of the Eastern Himalayas)*. London: Routledge and Kegan Paul.

Jha, S.D. (1985), *The Wealth of Arunachal Pradesh*. New Delhi: Mittal Publications.

NCAER (1967), *Techno-Economic Survey of Arunachal Pradesh*. New Delhi:NCAER.

NEFA Information. 1966 1(1), 1(2),1(5); 1967 II(2). Itanagar: DIPR.

Nehru, J. (1958), "Forward to the Second Edition". In Verrier Elwin, 1959 (1988 reprint). *A Philosophy for NEFA*. Itanagar: Directorate of Research.

Perme, Onong (2008), "A Study on the Culture and Process of Education in Arunachal Pradesh with the Adis of East Siang as Case Study". *M.Phil Dissertation*. Itanagar: Arunachal Institute of Tribal Studies, Rajiv Gandhi University

Pertin, Otem (2009), *Rethinking Tribal Institutions*, New Delhi: Commonwealth Publishers.

4

SHIFTING CULTIVATION IN NORTH EAST INDIA: TRANSITION AND CONTEMPORARY ISSUES

—— Rajiv Mili, Mihin Dollo, Prasanna K. Samal, L. Jitendro Singh ——

INTRODUCTION

In the North-East Himalayas, shifting agriculture commonly known as jhum, which was once considered to be an efficient system of cultivation being sustainable, both ecologically and economically (Ramakrishnan, 1992), is gradually becoming untenable under pressure from a number of factors and besieged with conflicting views in regard to the degradation/ conservation of ecosystem and the way of life for the upland people. This situation has led to a number of dialogues; one section perceives the practice as ecologically destructive, uneconomical and, therefore undesirable, hence advocates to ban or replace the practice by other alternatives such as agroforestry based farming system. (Borthakur, et al. 1979; Ingty and Goswami, 1979; Borthakur, 1992; Mokopathy, 2000). Alternatives like horticultural, floriculture, coffee or rubber plantations, etc. are being introduced to prevent deterioration of environment, soil erosion and forest cover loss (GOI, 1983, Syiem, 2002), however with limited success.

The other section, considering the social and economic dependency of the ethnic communities on this practice, regarded it as a way of life that integrates both material and non-material culture. They discard the opinion of the former labelling it as a top down approach that neglects the very basic needs of the shifting cultivators and their inherent knowledge with respect to conservation. (Brown and Schreckenberg, 1998). They emphasize on the unique resource ownership and utilization pattern of the shifting cultivators, which according to them, makes the system ecologically and economically sustainable. (ICIMOD, 2006). They also opined that the efforts to wean farmers away from shifting agriculture and to replace shifting agriculture have not been successful (Das, 2006) and such projects encroached the cultivable land ultimately shortening the jhum cycles. (Darlong, 2004).

Paradoxically, efforts of the government to find solutions through settled agricultural practices have been responsible for marginalization of the practice and the, resultant vulnerability of the practitioners. (Choudhury and Sundriyal, 2003). Further, ecologists who made extensive studies on shifting cultivation in Northeast India opined that any development in the region should be jhum centered as the region is not having any viable alternative to shifting cultivation. (Ramakrishnan, 1988). It is also suggested that the beneficial spin-off of shifting agriculture in terms of societal gains, particularly equitable gains to the members of the village community and the maintenance of the societal norms of harmony and equity. (MoEF, 2006).

Nevertheless, in the present global context, documentation of country's traditional ecological knowledge (TEK) particularly those associated with natural resources management has assumed high priority. Over the centuries, the tribal and other traditional forest dweller communities have accumulated a rich and time tested traditional knowledge on the management of natural resources for their livelihood sustenance. The management practices adopted by these ethnic communities are ecologically and culturally suited to their habitat. The need of hour is to acknowledge and build on it for sustainable development on highly complex ecosystem.

The North-Eastern region of India is well recognised as one of the Mega Biodiversity Hot Spot' zones of the world. The region is not only known for biological diversity but also has tremendous significance in evolutionary history of biological resources. Besides, it has high cultural diversity, as reports suggest that approximately one third of the ethnic groups of the nation are found in it. The rich cultural heritages of the region are well entranced with diverse traditional ecological knowledge, which help to manage the resource sustainability.

Irrespective of the conflicting opinions, shifting agriculture, which is closely woven with the socio-cultural fabric of the region, continues to be the predominant land use system and primary livelihood option. This often is the only agricultural practice available to address the need for food security of the majority of the upland communities. It is imperative to synchronize the traditional resource management strategies and customary practices of the shifting cultivators with appropriate low cost technological interventions and government policies, respectively, to make it ecologically, economically and socially viable.

TRANSITION

Dynamics of Jhum Cycle

In the contemporary global milieu, maintenance of long jhum cycle is one of prerequisite parameters to sustain the traditional shifting cultivation practices throughout the globe. Over the centuries, keeping the cultivation plot as fallow for a long period resulted in good recycling of soil nutrient that maintained the balance of both ecosystem of the cultivation plot and its adjoining habitat. But in recent past, due to the assemblance of various factors, for example, rapidly increasing population pressure, fast growing of developmental activities, intrusion of inappropriate modern technologies etc. are severely affecting the maintenance of long jhum cycle which in turn disrupts the sustainability of shifting cultivation. During fifties the cycle was maintained at least upto 30 years by the tribes practising shifting cultivation whereas the cycle has declined upto 3-7 years in late nineties. The shortening of jhum cycle not only interrupts the ecological balance of the cultivation practices, but also affects adversely the entire system of the surrounding landscape. Thus, it stands as major challenge in the millennium for the policy makers, academicians, researchers and the farming communities of the globe.

In North Eastern region of India, shifting cultivation is considered as primary means of economic mainstay with exception to the plains of Assam, Tripura and valley areas of Manipur. (Darlong, 2003). Almost all the tribes living in the uneven topographic region (except the Apatanis of Lower Subansiri district, Khamptis of Lohit district and the Monpas of West Kameng district in Arunachal Pradesh) of northeast India are practicing shifting cultivation which in another sense is the only source of subsistence for the people. Several programmes and schemes of both central and state government departments have been implemented to replace the practice; however no appropriate alternative, which is suited to the socio-economic and eco-cultural setup is implemented.

Numbers of multi-disciplinary studies on shifting cultivation have been conducted in the region from time to time and the reports clearly highlighted gradual decline of jhum cycle in past few decades. (Ramakrishnan, 1993; Borang, 1997; Darlong, 2004). The cycle was maintained upto 5-15 years in Arunachal Pradesh and Meghalaya. It has been recorded as high as of 24 years in East Siang and West Siang districts of Arunachal Pradesh (table 1). However the maintenance of the cycle varies from location to location and also from tribe to tribe. The Tangkhuls of Ukhrul district in Manipur maintains at least 9 years but the Hmars for 6 years. Similar observation was found among the Khasis and Garos of Meghalaya where the former maintains a fallow cycle of 10-15 years in Khasi Hills while the later maintains a cycle of 5-6 years. Although there is little variation in maintenance of jhum cycle among

Table 1
Dynamics of Jhum cycle in North East India

State	Study Area	Community	Year of Study	Jhum Cycle (Years)	Fallow Period (Years)	References
Arunachal Pradesh	Balijan (East Kameng)	Nyishi	1990b	5	4	Maikhuri & Ramakrishnan, 1990b
	Kameng	Idu Mishmi	2003	4	3	Satapathy et. al, 2003
	West Siang	Adi	2008	15	14	Primary Survey (GBPIHED, 2008)
	East Siang	Adi	2008	24-36	23-35	Primary Survey (GBPIHED, 2008)
Assam	Karbi Anglong	Karbi	2003	6	5	Satapathy et. al, 2003
	N.C Hills	Kuki	2003	6-7	5-6	Satapathy et. al, 2003
Manipur	South West	Hmar	2003	6-7	5-6	Satapathy et. al, 2003
	Ukhrul	Tangkhul	2007	9-15	8-14	Primary Survey (GBPIHED, 2008)
Mehgalaya	Khasi Hills	Khasi	1981	10-15	9-14	Rao & Ramakrishnana, 1981
	Khasi Hills	Khasi	2003	4-7	3-6	Satapathy et. al,2003
	Garo Hills	Garo	2003	5-6	4-5	Satapathy et. al,2003
Mizoram	South	Pawi	2003	8-9	7-8	Satapathy et. al,2003
	South	Lakher	2003	8-9	7-8	Satapathy et. al,2003
	North	Lusai	2003	8-9	7-8	Satapathy et. al,2003
Nagaland	Wokha	Lotha	2003	8-13	7-12	Satapathy et. al,2003
	Mokokchung	Ao	2003	8-11	7-10	Satapathy et. al,2003
Tripura	South & North	Reang	2003	6	5	Satapathy et. al,2003

the tribe or community but the overall scenario represents the clear shortening of the cycle. So, the transition in maintaining fallow cycle in the region has now been reduced from favourable 15-20 or more years to as low as 3-7 years (Ramakrishna, 1990, Darlong, 2003) with an average of 6-7 years. (Satapathy *et.al*, 2003). Thus, the current practice of short cycle in the region has resulted in poor economic yield due to break down of ecological process, degradation of soil ecology and insecure livelihood of the communities. In order to make shifting cultivation sustainable, several workers suggested a jhum cycle of 10 or more years. (Ramakrishnan, 1990, Darlong, op.cit).

Table 2
Crop Germplasm Varieties in Shifting Cultivation Fields of North East India

Crops	*No.s of Germplasm*
Upland Rice	298
Brinjal	37
Ginger	60
Chillies	68
Maize	674
Turmeric	60
Grain Legume	200
Sweet Potato	5
Cucurbits	76
Taros	250
Yams	242

Source: NBPGR, Barapahi Shillong

Inspite of the drastic reduction of jhum cycle in the region, several communities are still maintaining the system effectively. For example the Adis of East and West Siang districts of Arunachal Pradesh, Tangkhuls of Ukrul district in Manipur etc. are managing this agro-ecosystem effectively with diverse traditional ecological knowledge. The Adis of Siang districts maintain well defined *patat* system where they maintain the fallow period of 14-35 years. The entire land of the village has been divided into number of blocks or patches locally called *Patat* with specific name to each *patat*, which is being cultivated according to the cycling period. The land use division for shifting cultivation helps the farmer in counting the exact year of cultivation for the current year and also for the next consecutive years. The entire process is governed fully by means of age old traditional norms with various customary practices of the community and is executed purely through local level institutions. According to the community perception, forests including shifting cultivation fields are owned by the community, and the village controls over the resource use pattern. They cultivate the land for livelihood but simultaneously observe customary norms for conservation of biological resources for future use. Even though, variations exist on the norms and functioning of such institutions, a common characteristic is that they are based on locally acceptable cultural values and are functional within each community, including in the management of natural resources. (Darlong, 2003; Kerkhoff & Sharma, 2006).

DIVERSITY OF CROPS AND CROPPING PATTERN

Shifting Agriculture is a unique type of cultivation practice that can be characterized by diverse crops and cropping patterns. The basic difference of this practice with the settled agriculture lies in the fact that varieties of species are cultivated at a time in the same plot in Shifting Agriculture. About 35-46 crop species have been documented at a single time which are cultivated in jhum cultivation system in the region. (Ramakrishnan, 1985). The high crop diversity not only helps to sustain the nutrient requirement but also food security as it has been well adopted with diverse ecological conditions and, environmental and pathological stresses. (Abalu, 1976; Singh, 1981, Summer *et.al*, 1981; Walker *et.al*, 1983; Mogina, 1999; Hore, 2005).

While, the region is well acknowledged for its rich traditional crops and biological diversity which support the sustenance of the entire region (Dollo & Sundriyal, 2003), the region has also been identified by the Indian Council of Agricultural Research as a centre for rice germplasm, while the Forest Survey of India reported it as a centre that harbours

Table 3
Major Crops and Cropping Patterns in Upland Agro-ecosystems

Land Use	*Cropping Type*	*Cropping Pattern*	*Sowing-harvesting Time*
Traditional	Mono#	Dry rice/fallow	May-Sept
		Finger millet/fallow	June-Dec
		Jobs Tear/fallow	June-Dec
		Ginger/fallow	Apr/May-Dec
	Mixed	Dry rice; maize; pulses; spices; vegetable	May-Sept/Oct; June-Dec; July/Aug-Dec; Apr/June-Dec/ Jan;Apr/May- throughout the year.
Emerging (Transformed)	Mono	Wet rice	June/July-Nov-Dec
		Orange	Apr/May-Sept/Dec
		Large Cardamom	Mar/May-Sept/Oct
		Jenkins Palm	Mar/Apr- Dec/Jan
	Mixed	Ginger; Mustard; Maize; Finger Millet; Vegetables	Apr/May-Dec; Feb/Mar- May/ June; June-Dec; Apr/May- throughout the year.

Note: # rarely practice, particularly in 2nd yr of cultivation wide range of species with greater endemism. Major share of crop diversity is contributed by Arunachal Pradesh, as 616 numbers of rice germplasm were recorded from the state in between 1987 and 2002. Hore (2005) reported a total of 128 rice land races while Singh et al., (2004) reported a total of 245 land races of cereals, pulses, oil seeds, fruits, vegetables, coarse cereals, spices and fibre crops from Changlang and Tirap districts of the state. Many indigenous varieties of cereals (mainly paddy and millet crops), pulses, oil seeds, vegetables and spices are being conserved under the shifting cultivation system. There are 74 indigenous varieties of crops in East Siang District, which are locally grown, conserved and used to fulfil the diversified needs. (Singh, 2007).

The mixed cropping is a common practice where rice and maize occupied the major share since they are the staple food crops of the region. Rice and maize are associated with other cereals and pseudo cereals, fruits and leafy vegetable, tubers, spices and condiments, rhizomatous crops etc. Among the principal food crops maize (674) has the highest diversity followed by rice (298), taros (250), yam (242), grain legume (200) (table 2) The sowing and harvesting periods of diverse crops in shifting agro-ecosystem vary as per the socio-ecological conditions of the region (table 3).

Community dimension

The North East India is known for high biocultural diversity having 130 major tribes and 300 sub-tribes out of the total 507 tribal communities inhabiting in India and is often referred to as "Biological Hotspot". (Myers et al. 2000). Besides, the region has huge potential of forest based natural resources that sustain the livelihood of the ethnic communities living in upland habitat. Unlike the main stream populace, the people of the region primarily depend on the forest based natural resources for food, medicine, fuel wood, housing materials, ritualistic items and other daily needs. The agricultural system is purely forest based. The practice has evolved from time immemorial and is still evolving. The practice is a mixture of various activities which are intricately linked with the traditional norms and customs. Starting from the plot selection to harvesting, communities observe numbers of socio-ritual practices, which are been strictly followed by the shifting cultivators. Initially, the plots are selected by the village head or tribal chief through focus group discussion with their deputies or open panel discussion with the villagers and the plots are allocated among the families according to the need i.e family size and traditional norms. After allocation of plot, villagers get together for community fencing to protect the crops from the grazers of both domestic and wild animals. The slashing and clearing is done with simple machinery tools such as axe and *Dao*. The slashed wood and branches are allowed to dry and are set fire on it. The debris that remains after burning is cleared. Unlike the plain land cultivation, in shifting cultivation seeds are sown with the help of stick by dibbling with pointed portion. Since the practice is a mixed cropping type hence sowing or broadcasting is done sequentially according to the timeframe of the crop.

Weed is a common problem, which starts growing more rapidly in jhum field. Weeding is done 2-4 times in a season based on the weed population. The first phase of weeding is done simultaneously with the seedlings. It may vary from location to location even differences may observe among the communities of the same locality. The second phase of weeding is done at the mature stage of the crops. In some places it is done just before harvesting of principal crop. Both male and female farmers of the family engage actively in the cultivation process. However, hard works such as felling of big trees, cutting of jungle, fencing construction, construction of temporary hut, etc., are exclusively done by the male farmers only whereas females are engaged in weeding, sowing, harvesting, winnowing etc. Carrying of agronomic product is done by both male and female.

In recent past, extensive land use interventions by the state and central government, have distorted the traditional land use practices and also have reduced the land availability for shifting cultivation. Further, the economic diversification has impacted the labour availability within the community, resulting dependence on external labour. Disruption of community labour by engaging external labour force affects the socio-ecological sustainability of the shifting agro-ecosystem, which not only eroded the traditional ecological knowledge but also risk the long term sustainability.

Land Tenure and Customary Practices

The land tenure systems of the North Eastern states are unique and quite different from the rest of the country except for the plains of Assam, Tripura and the valley areas of Manipur. The local customary laws govern the land tenure systems of the region. (Darlong, 2003). The traditional laws are enforced by the traditional institutions headed by the tribal head or village headman, which vary from location specific to tribe specific.

In the upland region of North East India, land either belongs to the individual, clan, village or community, however management and distribution of land are solely based on democratic decision making headed by the village head. It has been recorded that during the course of migration, the communities had settled down in the uneven and formidable forest areas of the region and started cultivation in the adjoining location, which was bit far from their settlement areas.

Depending upon the soil fertility land is being cultivated consecutively for not more than three years and these also left fallows, which allow recuperation of soil nutrition lost during cultivation. Once the land is left fallow, the community or village institution has resumed its right on the utilization or transferring the same to any family within the village. The demarcation of allotted land to the families or clan is made by putting pointed stone boulder along the boundary line or mark on the structures such as big trees, mountain ridge or stones, valley and ridge, which are easily recognised from distance. The allocation of land among the clan and families had been governed by traditional village or community institutions with oral norms and custom. For that traditional institutions have strong oral bindings, which have to be strictly obeyed by the villagers. If anybody found to be violating the traditional norms, the violator may be a penalty is imposed on him/her based on the gravity of the violation.

The forest resources such as bamboo, cane, timber, leaves etc. could be extracted sustainably for the house hold utilization like construction of houses, granaries, bridge and agricultural implements. Any disputes relating to the land, water and forest resources are solved through the village council chaired by the village head.

EMERGING ISSUES

The traditional cultivation practice, particularly shifting cultivation, has enormous importance for the farmers of North Eastern hill region since it is linked with the socio- cultural attributes of the tribal communities. However, in recent past a number of changes are taking place in the traditional practice of shifting cultivation, making itself as a critical issue for the policy makers, researchers and the academic institutions. Gradual decline in forest cover, expansion of agricultural land and declining of jhum cycle are linked with high rate of soil erosion and runoff, shrinkage of biological diversity, CO_2 emission and global warming, questioning the present sustainability of Shifting Agriculture.

Change in Forest and Vegetation Cover

Changes in forest cover adversely affected the ecosystems of both tropics and subtropical regions of the world. (Fearnside, 2000; Lele and Joshi, 2008). The forest not only helps in mitigating the excess CO_2 emission but also provides ecological services such as maintaining the hydrological cycle, soil erosion, release of oxygen level in the atmosphere, etc. Besides, it provides diverse resources to the traditional communities living along the margin of the forest. The recent reports on forest cover have highlighted regular declining of the geographical area under it, which resulted into global warming. (Fearnside, 2000; Boucher et. al., 2009). Among the various reasons blaming Shifting cultivation is also clubbed as a factor for deforestation in the tropical region. (Fearnside, 2000; Ickowitz, 2006; Ickowitz & Jacqueline, 2008).

Like other parts of mainstream India, the states of North East India have also been losing forests and vegetation cover in last decades. During the course, Assam has lost the highest forest cover (1472 km^2), followed by Meghalaya (833km^2), Mizoram (746km^2), Nagaland (230 km^2), Tripura (208 km^2) and Manipur with 91 km^2 (Table 4). In contrast, Arunachal Pradesh is maintaining its vegetation cover reporting an increase of 4715 km^2 in between 1987-1999, which is the highest in India. Regionally, it is interesting to note that North-Eastern states have recovered good forest vegetation increasing with 1135 km^2 in between 1987-99 years as compare to mainland India where nearly 3526 km^2 of forest cover has been lost.

On the other hand, shifting cultivation, as a major factor for declining forest cover is debated over the years. (Kerkhoff & Sharma, 2006). The forest survey report shows that the net change in forest cover of North East India during 1987-97 was 316 km^2 where shifting cultivation has affected 152 km^2 only (Table 5.). Among the North Eastern States, Assam has lost maximum forest cover with the loss of 237 km^2 where more than the half of the total cover loss was due to other reason (143 km^2) rather than shifting cultivation (State of Forest Report, 1997). Further, interestingly, Mizoram and Tripura have tremendously recovered forest cover from shifting cultivation areas with total gain of 199 and 8 km^2 respectively.

Soil Erosion

It is the carrying away of the land surface by physical forces (rainfall, flowing water, temperature change, gravity) or other natural or anthropogenic agents that abrade, detach and remove soil or geological material from one point on the Earth's surface to be deposited elsewhere. (Thompson,2007). Normally it is a noticeable intrinsic natural phenomena occurring over geological timescales but the rate has been significantly increased by anthropogenic activity such as poor land use practices which accelerate erosion and become a process of degradation and thus an identifiable threat to soil health. Land that is used for the production of agricultural crops generally experiences a significant greater rate of erosion than that of land under natural vegetation.

Table 4
Dynamics of Forest and Vegetation Cover in North East India (km²)

Year wise Assessment								*Change*
State	*1987*	*1989*	*1991*	*1993*	*1995*	*1997*	*1999*	*1987-99*
Arunachal Pradesh	64,132	69,002	68,757	68,661	68,621	68,602	68,847	+4715
Assam	25,160	24,832	24,751	24,508	24,061	23,824	23,688	-1,472
Manipur	17,475	17,685	17,685	17,621	17,558	17,418	17,384	-91
Meghalaya	16,466	15,645	15,875	15,769	15,714	15,657	15,633	-833
Mizoram	19,084	18,170	18,853	18,697	18,576	18,775	18,338	-746
Nagaland	14,394	14,399	14,321	14,348	14,291	14,221	14,164	-230
Tripura	5,953	5,535	5,535	5,538	5,538	5,546	5,745	-208
NE India	1,62,664	1,65,268	1,65,777	1,65,142	1,64,359	1,64,043	1,63,799	+1,135
All India	6,40,819	6,38,804	6,39,364	6,39,386	6,38,879	6,33,397	6,37,293	-3,526

Source: State of Forest Report 1999

Table 5
Loss/Gain in Forest Covers in Northeast India (km^2)

	Shifting Cultivation			*Other Reasons*			
State	*Loss*	*Gain (Nat.reg)*	*Change (A)*	*Loss*	*Gain*	*Change (B)*	*Net Change (A+B)*
Arunachal Pradesh	75	56	- 19	-	-	-	- 19
Assam	257	163	- 94	159	16	- 143	- 237
Manipur	603	463	- 140	-	-	-	- 140
Meghalaya	75	20	- 55	2	-	- 2	- 57
Mizoram	292	491	+ 199	-	-	-	+ 199
Nagaland	573	503	- 70	-	-	-	- 70
Tripura	-	4	+ 4	3	7	+ 4	+ 8
Total	1,875	1,700	- 152	164	23	- 141	-316

Nat. reg.: Natural regeneration in shifting cultivation
Source: State of Forest Report 1997

Table 6
Soil Erosion in Shifting Cultivation Areas of Meghalaya

Land Use	*Soil Loss (ton/ha/year)*
1st year of Jhum	146.6
2nd year of Jhum	170.2
Abandoned Jhum (1st year)	30.2
Bamboo forest	8.2

Source: Agriculture in NER–D.N.Borthakur

Soil erosion in various land uses including forest has been viewed as one of the serious global threats in meeting sustainable development throughout the tropics and subtropical region of the world. The available reports (Borthakur, 1992; Brady, 1996; Harwood, 1996; Devendra and Thomas, 2002; Borggaard et al., 2003; Gardner & Gerrard, 2003; Rasul et al., 2004) on the subject have accused Shifting cultivation as a major agent of causing soil erosion in agricultural land use of mountain ecosystem. The practice has been considered as one of the primitive means of cultivation that is detrimental to the physico-chemical and microbiology of soil through severe loss of soil particles. In Meghalaya, nearly 316.8 tonnesha^{-1} year^{-1} of soil loss was reported in two successive shifting cultivation years where the second year of cultivation phase in the same plot has found more severe (Table 6). The loss of organic rich soil particle from the surface area leads to physico-chemical imbalance in soil agroecosystem. The burning of plant debris and other organic biomass on the surface kills the microbes that play vital role in holding the soil particles in the ground level. (Mubyana-John et.al., 2007). On the other hand the land mass of the region is comparatively younger than those of other mountain range whose physiography is characterised by rugged and steep terrain with rather erosive soils. (Putjaroon & Pongboon, 1987). In addition to these factors another notable reason is that it is the most wetted region in the world with heavy rain fall throughout the year. The heavy rain water runoff directly washes away relatively loose and organic rich upper surface layer of the soil profile that directly affects the soil texture and finally making the surface area to barren land mass. Since, the region is considered as one of the erosion prone areas of the nation with heavy soil loss, there is every possibility of causing serious soil erosion which may adversely affect the yield and productivity of crops.

Decline in Fertility

Maintaining fertility in agricultural land use is one of the prerequisite parameter for sustainable development of agroecosystems, which support the livelihood sustenance for majority of the farming communities. Over the centuries, various techniques have been adopted to maintain soil vigour in agroecosystem throughout the world. But in recent past due to assemblance of various factors such as excess input of inorganic fertilizer, adoption of inappropriate technologies, mass scale harvesting of agricultural product for commercial purposes, etc., threatens the fertility maintenance and becomes major serious global concern for both policy makers as well as the farming communities.

Shifting cultivation is often being blamed for this serious decline of soil fertility. (Lal, 1974). The system involves with slash and burn practice that destroys the soil micro flora and fauna which are actively engaged in fertility maintenance. (Mubayana-John et. al., 2007). The burning of organic debris severely alters the physico-chemical properties of the soil. Further due to shifting cultivation, the porosity of the soil decreases tremendously directly affecting water holding capacity as well as pH of the soil. (Kanchanatanaset, et.al., 2000). Drying up of soil in the upper surface directs quick flow of soil runoff towards downwards levels that disrupts the proper percolation and also checks in meeting required water content in the breakdown of organic matter to successive level of the soil profile. The lowering of pH leads to acidification that tends to susceptible to souring and putrefactions, rather than undergoing the sweet decay processes associated with the decay of organic matter. When pH is too low the nutrients present in the soil become locked-up. The long term acidification decreases the concentration of potassium (K), magnesium (Mg) and calcium (Ca) in soil solution. Moreover, the north east region falls under the most precipitate location where excess leaching gradually depletes the basic soil cations (Ca, Mg, K). Besides the physical properties, the soil chemistry is also adversely affected by shifting cultivation in upland agroecosystem. The major nutrients, NPK have depleted in the system due to the inappropriate treatment of soil by the farming communities. During the cultivation phase, Phosphorus (P) act as one of the most limiting nutrients in tropical forests (Vitousek1984, Cleveland et al. 2002) that tied up to forests productivity. The loss of available inorganic P and total organic P is a principle cause of declining agricultural productivity in the tropics. (Tiessen et. al., 1983, Tiessen et. al., 1994). The restoration of these P pools during the fallow period is key to the recovery of soil fertility under shifting cultivation. (Diekmann, 2004). The other essential organic nutrients i.e Organic carbon (OC) and Nitrogen (N) also decrease upto three to four folds in shifting cultivation than that of the natural vegetation significantly affecting the nutrient pool (Rasul et.al., 2004; Emadi, et.al., 2008) of the soil ecosystem.

Biodiversity Loss

The north eastern India is highly acknowledged for its rich biological diversity which falls under the "Eastern Himalaya" often being called as one of the mega biodiversity hot spots of the world. The region shelters about 10000 plant species and 1927 animal species in both terrestrial and aquatic ecosystem of which 31.6 per cent falls under the endangered categories of plants and per cent of animals. (*http://www. biodiversity hotspots.org*). The formidable undulating topography and remoteness of the region helps in creation of suitable habitat for these plants and animals living with great harmony. Despite their apparent remoteness and inaccessibility, the North Eastern India has not been spared from human-induced biodiversity loss. In recent decades, greater access to the global market has increased the demand for natural resources in the area encouraged by immigration from outside. Also, the population growth is adversely affecting the biodiversity in the region, due to extensive clearing of forests and grasslands for cultivation, and widespread logging. Both legal and illegal loggings often occur on extremely steep slopes, resulting in severe erosion. Although cultivation has a general upper limit of about 2,100 meters on slopes exposed to monsoons, people grow crops such as barley, potato and buckwheat at high elevations in the inner valleys and trans-montane regions. The land is also often cleared in the summer months for livestocks. The use of fire to clear land poses an additional threat to forest land, as fires sometimes spread out of control. The conversion of forests and grasslands to agricultural land and settlements has led to large-scale deforestation and habitat fragmentation in the region while overgrazing by domestic livestock is widespread in the lowlands and alpine ecosystems. Fuelwood collection and non-timber forest product extraction, both for domestic consumption and export, has inflicted severe damage to some forest ecosystems.

One of the salient features of traditional farming systems throughout the developing world is their high degree of biodiversity. Shifting cultivation, traditional farming systems of the North East India has emerged over centuries of cultural and biological evolution and represents accumulated experiences of indigenous farmers interacting with the environment without access to external inputs, capital, or modern scientific knowledge. (Chang, 1977; Grigg, 1974). But this practice of cultivation clears the existing vegetation of the surrounding forest cover where numbers of biological species take shelter. The forest can be regenerated after keeping fallow while the animal species once left would not come back to the original habitat for which the cultivation practice have often being blamed for the biodiversity shrinkage in the region. (Wang & Young, 2003).

CONCLUSION

In the mindset of the traditional shifting cultivators of North East India both forest and jhum practices are interlinked and intertwined. (Darlong, 2003). It might indeed be paradoxical to imagine that the basic philosophy of shifting cultivation has been "to create forests and not to destroy forest" for without the forest the next jhum cannot be cultivated. The idea of "Forests" in this context was to convert the land occupied by the tall and large tropical or sub-tropical trees into cultivable land by clearing such areas by slashing, burning and allowing it to fallow with fresh re-growth of vegetation for sufficiently long enough period until the same area becomes suitable for cultivation and repeat the cycle. (*ibid*).

In the context of shifting cultivation a healthy growth of secondary forests with enough biomass had to be maintained without too many big trees as clearing of large size trees are time consuming and not conductive to the simple implements and tools available. The balanced and sustainable shifting cultivation has got disoriented due to varieties of reason such as population increase, the conversion of large forest areas into reserve forests or protected areas, changes in ownership of forest land, unsustainable logging and development of other land use systems including expansion of settled agriculture and cash crops plantation. (*ibid*).

The practice of shifting cultivation may be highly sustainable in terms of its impact (Fox, et al. 1998) on forest cover and associated biological and hydrological systems, and that government effort to stabilize or resettle shifting cultivators may be misguided. Low levels of net deforestation suggest that more attention should be paid to improve fallow management and its role in crop diversification and food security. The study also shows a strong correlation between rates of deforestation and forest fragmentation and changes in government policy. From a technical standpoint, the Pathfinder approach permits the rapid analysis of forest cover change over large areas, albeit using a very simplified classification scheme. As such, it may be suitable as the basis of an operational forest monitoring system.

In view of the transition and emerging issues in the current practice of shifting cultivation, we strongly advocate for consideration of the following issues:

— Reviewing of the state and central policies and laws in the forest and agriculture sectors dealing with shifting cultivation and ongoing schemes and programmes of state and central Governments for control and regulation of shifting cultivation;

— Indepth study of the land tenure and customary laws of selected ethnic communities relating to shifting cultivation;

— Documentation of TEK on soil conservation, water resources and forest resource management and validation of indigenous soil and water conservation practices;

— Analysis of impact of shifting agriculture on faunal diversity with special reference to avifauna and mammals; and

— Need based assessment and identification of potential interventions and their application.

It will be worth to mention here that G.B. Pant Institute of Himalayan Environment and Development, North East Unit in one of its projects is trying to address the above issues.

REFERENCES

Abalu, G. 1976. A Note on Crop Mixtures Under Indigenous Conditions in Northern Nigeria. *Journal of Development Studies*, Vol. 12.

Borggaard, O.K., Gafur, A. & Petersen, L., (2003). Sustainability appraisal of shifting cultivation in the Chittagong Hill Tracts of Bangladesh. *Ambio*, Vol. 32, pp 118-123.

Borthakur, D.N., Prasad, R.N., Ghosh, S.P., Singh, A., Awasthi, R.P., Rai, R.N., Verma, A., Data, H.H., Sachan, J.N., & Singh, M.D. 1979. Agro forestry based farming system as an alternative to Jhuming. Seminar Proceeding on Agro Forestry Seminar, Imphal, May 16-18, ICAR.

Borthakur, D.N. 1992. Agriculture of north eastern region. Guwahati: BeeCee Prakashan.

Borang, A. 1997. Shifting Cultivation among the Adi tribes of Arunachal Pradesh, In. Mahanta, K.C (ed.), *People of Himalayas: Ecology, Culture Development and Change* Delhi: Kamla-Raj Enterprises, pp 145-151.

Brady, N.C. 1996. Alternatives to slash-and-burn: a global imperative. *Agriculture Ecosystem & Environment*. Vol. 58, pp 3-11.

Brown, D.M. & Schreckenberg, K. 1998. Shifting Cultivation as an Agent of Deforestation: Assessing the Evidence Overseas Development Institute, Natural Resources Perspectives-29. (http://www.odi.org.uk/nrp/29.html).

Boucher, D., Movious, D., Fitzhugh, E., Roquemore, S. & Patricia Elias, P. 2009. Tropical Deforestation and Global Worming: A Solution, Tropical Forest and Climate Initiative, Union of concerned Scientists. Two Brattle Square, Cambridge (http://www.ucsusa.org)

Chang, J.H. 1977. Tropical agriculture: crop diversity and crop yields. *Econ. Geogr.* Vol. 53, pp 241-254.

Choudhry, D. & Sundriyal, R.C. 2003. Factors contributing to the marginalization of shifting cultivation in northeast India: micro scale issues. *Outlook on Agriculture*, Vol. 32, No. 1, pp 17-28.

Cleveland, C.C. Townsend, A.R. & Schmidt. S.K. 2002. Phosphorus limitation of microbial processes in moist tropical forests: evidence from short-term laboratory incubations and filed studies. *Ecosystems*, vol.5, pp 680-691.

Das, D. 2006. "Demystifying the myth of shifting cultivation agronomy in the north east". *Economic and Political Weekly* (XLI) 47: pp 4912-4917.

Darlong, V.T. 2003. "To Jhum or Not to Jhum Policy Perspective on Shifting Cultivaton. The Missing Link (TML)". Society for Environment and communication, India, pp 143.

Devendra, C. & Thomas, D. 2002. "Smallholder farming systems in Asia". *Agricultural system*. Vol.71, pp 17-25.

Diekmann, L.O. 2004. Soil Nutrient dynamics during shifting cultivation in Campeche, Mexico. *Unpublished Ph.D. thesis* submitted to University of Virginia, Mexico.

Dollo, M. & Sundriyal, R.C. 2003. "Agricultural status and future potential in the state of Aruanchal Pradesh". *Arunachal University Research Journal*. Vol.6, No.2, pp 21-33.

Dollo, M 2004. "Shifting cultivation and conservation laws of Arunachal Pradesh". *North Lakhimpur Law's College Magazine*, Vol. 1, pp 43-45.

Dollo, M. & Choudhury, D. 2006. Eco-cultural heritage of Arunachal Pradesh. In Proceedings of National Seminar on *Interpreting the Heritage of the North East*. INTACH, New Delhi, India, pp 42-59.

Emadi, M., Baghernehad, M. & Emadi, M. 2008. "Effect of shifting cultivation on distribution of nutrient elements and carbohydrates within water stable aggregates in Northern India Iran". *Pakistan Journal of Biological Sciences*, Vol. 11, pp 195-201.

Fearnside, P. 2000. "Global Warming and Tropical Land-Use Change: Green house Gas Emissions from Biomass Burning, Decomposition and Soils in Forest conversion, Shifting Cultivation and Secondary Vegetation". *Climate Change*, Vol. 64, No. 2, pp 115-158.

Fox, J., Truong, D.M., Rambo, T., Tueyn, N. P., Le Trong cuc & Leisz, S. 1998. *Shifting Cultivation with Deforestation: a Case Study in the Mountains of Northwestern Vietnam, mimeo.* Honolulu, HI: East-West Center.

Gardner, R.A.M. & Gerrard, A.J. 2003. Runoff and soil erosion on cultivated rainfed terraces in the Middle Hills of Nepal. *Applied Geography*, Vol. 23, pp 23-45.

GOI. 1983. *Task Force Report on shifting cultivation in India*. New Delhi: Government of India, Ministry of Agriculture.

Grigg, D.B. 1974. The Agricultural Systems of the World: An evolutionary approach. Cambridge: Cambridge University Press.

Hore, D.K. 2005. Rice diversity collection, conservation and management in northeastern India. *Genetic Resources and Crop Evolution*, Vol. 52, pp 1129-1140.

Harwood, R.R. 1996. Development pathways toward sustainable systems following slash-and-burn. *Agriculture, Ecosystem & Environment*, Vol. 58, pp75-86.

ICIMOD. 2006. Debating Shifting Cultivation in the Eastern Himalayas. *Farmers' Innovations as Lessons for Policy*. Kathmandu: International Centre for Integrated Mountain Development.

Ickowitz, A. 2006. Shifting Cultivation and Deforestation in Tropical Africa: Critical Reflections. *Development and Change*, Vol. 37, pp 599-626.

Ickowitz, A. & Hacqueline, G. 2000. Shifting Cultivation and Forest Transition in the Tropics: Research Advances and Remaining Challenges, *Land-Use Transitions in the Tropics*. (http://magrann-conference, rutgers.edu/2008/_abstracts/abstract)

Ingty, P.S. & Goswami, N. 1979. Shifting Cultivation in North Eastern Hills- A new approach to the problem. Proceedings on Agro forestry seminar, Imphal, May 16-18, ICAR.

Kanchanatanaset, K., Boonsaner, A. & Thitirojanawat, P. 2000. Soil Property Changing by Shifting Cultivation Effects. Forest Research Office. (http://www.forest. Go.th/Research/English/abstracts_water/wse2.html)

Kerkhoff, E. & Sharma, E. 2006. Debating Shifting Cultivation in the Eastern Himalayas: Farmers' Innovations as Lessons for Policy, Kathmandu, ICIMOD, pp 82.

Lal, R., 1974. "Soil erosion and shifting agriculture. In: FAO". (Eds.), *Shifting Cultivation and Soil Conservation in Africa*. FAO, Rome, pp 49-71.

Lele, N. & Joshi, P.K. 2008. Analyzing deforestation rates, spatial forest cover changes and identifying critical areas of forest cover changes in North-East India during 1972-1999. *Environ Monit Assess*. (http://www.springerlink.com/content/pk62716302422582/)

Maikhuri, R.K. & Ramakrishnan, P.S. 1990b. Comparative analysis of the village ecosystem function of different tribes living in the same area in Arunachal Pradesh in North East India. *Agric. Systems*. Vol.35

Ministry of Environment and Forests MoEF. 2006. Report of the National Forest Commission. Government of India, Ministry of Environment and Forests. (URL: http://www.envfor.nic.in/divisions/nfr.html)

Mogina, J. 1999. Maintenance of crop diversity and food security in rural Papua New Guinea: Case studies from Cape Vogel and Good enough Island, *Development. Bull.* No. 50 (http://devnet.anu.edu.au/DB50PDF/8mogina50.pdf)

Mokopathy, S. 2000. "Shifting Cultivation: From knowledge to Unsustainability; Can Agroforestry remediate it". In: *Agroforestry and Forest Products*. Proceeding International Workshop, Aizawl, Nov. 28-30.

Mubyana-John, T., Wutor, V.C., Yeboah, S.O. & Ringrose, S. 2007. Fire and its influence on microbial community structure and soil biochemical properties in the Okavango Delta, Botswana, *Scientific Research and Essay* Vol.2., No.2, pp 47-54. (http://www.academichournals.org/SRE)

Myers, N., Mittermeier, R.A., Mittermeier, C.G., da Fronseca, G.A.B & Kent, J. 2000. "Biodiversity hotspots for conservation priorities". *Nature,* Vol. 403, pp 853-858.

Pimentel, D., Harvey, D., Resosudarmo, P., Sinclair, K., Kurz, D., McNair, M., Crist, S.,Shpritz, L., Fitton, L., Saffouri, R. & Blair, R. 1995. "Environmental and economic costs of soil erosion and conservation benefits". *Science,* Vol. 267, pp 1117-1123.

Pimentel, D. (2006). "Soil erosion: a food and environmental threat". *Environ. Dev. Syst.* Vol.8, pp 119-137.

Putjaroon, W. & Pongboon, K. 1987. "Amount of runoff and soil losses from various land. Use sampling plots in Sakolnakorn Province, Thailand". In: *Forest Hydrology and Watershed Management* (Proceedings of the Vancouver Symposium) Vol.1, No. 167.

Rasul, G., Thapa, G.B. & Zoebisch, M.A. 2004. "Determinants of land-use changes in the Chittogong Hill Tracts of Bangladesh". *Applied Geography,* Vol. 24, pp 217-240.

Ramakrishnan, P.S.1984. "Problems and prospects of conservation of north-eastern hill region of India". In. Jain & Mehra (ed.) *Conservation of plant resources.* Botanical survey of India, Howrah. pp 172-180.

Ramakrishnan, P.S.1985. "Tribal man in the humid tropics of the north eastern India". *Man in India,* Vol. 65, pp 1-32.

Ramakrishnan, P.S.1990. "Shifting agriculture and rainforest ecosystem management". In Nair, K.K.N., Bhat, Sharma, J.K. & Swarupandan, K. (ed.) Tropical forest *ecosystem conservation and development in southeast in Southeast Asia.* Proc. MAB Training workshop. Kerala Forest Research Institute, pp 41-43.

Ramakrishnan, P.S.1992. "Shifting Agriculture and sustainable development. An interdisciplinary study from North-Eastern India". *Man and the biosphere series,* Vol. 10. UNISCO Paris and Oxford University Press, New Delhi.

Ranjan, R. & Upadhyay, V.P.1999. Ecological problems due to shifting cultivation. *Current Science,* Vol. 77, pp 1246-1250. (http://www/ias,ac.in/currsc/nov25/articles12.html)

Sample, I. 2007. Global food crisis looms as climate change and population growth strip fertile land. 'Ignorance, need and greed' depleting soil, *The Guardian,* Friday31August(http://www.guardian.co.uk/environment/2007/aug/31/ climate change. food)

Satapathy, K.K., Sarma, B.K., Goswami, S.N. & Verma, D.N. 2003. Developing Lands Affected by Shifting Cultivation. Department of Land Resources. New Delhi: Ministry of Rural Development, Government of India.

Singh, R. P. 1981. Crop failure and intercropping in the semi arid tropics of India. Economic Programme Progress Report. Patancheru, India: 21 ICRISAT.

Singh, J.K., Sarma, B.K. & Pattnayak, A.K. 2004. "Collecting crop diversity from Changlang and Tirap districts of Arunachal Pradesh". *Indian J. of Hill Farm.* Vol. 17 No. 1 & 2, pp 150-152.

Singh, R.K. 2007. Agrobiodiversity and Food Security in risk prone agro-ecosystems: An appraisal of tribal's wisdom. Personal communication at College of Horticulture, Pasighat.

State of Forest Report 1999. *Forest Survey of India.* Dehradun: Ministry of Environment and Forest, India.

Sumner, D. R., doupnik, B. and boosalis, M. G. 1981. "Effects of tillage and multicropping on plant diseases". *Annual Review of Phytopathology*, Vol.19.

Syiem, B. 2002. "Agricultural transition in the hill areas of the North Eastern Region. Proceedings of fourth conference". *The North Eastern Economic Association*, Shillong.

Tiessen, H.J., Stewart, W. B. & Moir, J. O. 1983. "Changes in organic and inorganic phosphorous composition of two grassland soils and their particle size fractions during 60-90 years of cultivation". *Journal of Soil Science*, Vol. 34, pp 815-825.

Tiessen, H., Cuevas, E. & Chacon, P. 1994. "The role of soil organic matter in sustaining soil fertility". *Nature*, Vol. 371, pp 783-785.

Tiessen, H. 1998. "Resilience of phosphorus transformations in tropical forest and derived ecosystems". In. Schulte, A. & Ruhiyal, D. (eds). *Soils of tropical forest ecosystems.* New York: Springer-Verlag, pp 92-98.

Thompson, D. 2007. "Soil Erosion". A workshop in support of the Thematic Strategy for Soil Protection Common Criteria for Risk Area Identification in the Soil Framework Directive BGR, Hannover, 25 April.

Vitousek, P.M. 1984. "Litterfall, nutrient cycling, and nutrient limitation in tropical forests". *Ecology*, Vol. 65, pp 285-298.

Walker, T. S., Singh, R. P. and Jodha, N. S. 1983. "Dimensions of farm level diversification in the semi arid tropics of rural south India. Economic Program Progress Report, Patancheru, India.: 51 ICRISAT.

Wang, Z.J. & Young, S.S. 2003. "Difference in bird diversity between two swidden agricultural sites in mountainous terrain, Xishuangbanna, Yunnan, China". *Biological Conservation*, Vol. 110, pp 231-243.

5

COMMUNITIES, CONSERVATION AND THE CHALLENGE OF PARTICIPATION: AN ETHNOGRAPHIC DETOUR OF CONSERVATION PROGRAMME AND THE FATE OF *JHUMMIAS* IN NAGA VILLAGES

Debojyoti Das

INTRODUCTION

Herbert Simon in his Nobel lecture 1973, deliberated on the idea of bounded rationality and cognitive behaviour in economies that challenged mainstream economic assumption of all human relations being 'bounded rational'[1]. Here I use Simon's cognitive behaviour thesis to understand how swidden farmers are imagined as bounded irrational in state and trans-national funded projects on conservation and improvement in native life world. Planners, scientific experts and community facilitators today engage with the idea of forest degradation caused by swidden farming through promotion of participatory conservation and address conservation issues under a community driven development project to bring about improvement in native life. Through the working of the project communities share doubts about the future of conservation and how it will work in the post project phase. The uncertainties are maintained. The project facilitators who organise in mapping village resources with the help of village elders, village council and village development board[2] members systematically involve in documenting valuable resources and generic species that server broader goals of the project to identify potential villages for biodiversity conservation.

The aims of the conservation facilitation are based on the project goals of biodiversity maintenance through various participatory mechanisms like community resource mapping that do not impose the will of the planners on the community but work through consensus building with the community. Through participation planners claim to evolve consensus and work through communities social capital. The representations in this ethnography are based on participant observation; taped interviews and long term stay in two villages of Nagaland where conservation efforts proceeded before the NEPED (Nagaland Environment Protection and Economic Development through Peoples Action) team embarked on this project of biodiversity conservation with technical support and financial assistance from SACON (Salim Ali Centre for Ornithology). A focus on two village, spread over two development spaces was useful to develop ethnographic details that would help in narrating how conservation policy are reworked and reshaped on the ground and why markets, experts, and planners triumph to create community conservation by restricting hunting, game and collection of forest products- practices that are alien to communities that subsist on them for their daily dietary needs.

I met Asoba, a key informant in the whole narrative while travelling from Tuensang to Kohima. He was travelling to Kohima in the same bus for a training workshop. Asoba worked as a grass root member of the NEPED team as Facilitator of Community Conservation (FCC), hereafter FCC, in Samatur. My understanding of the NEPED programme before I met him was quite conventional, that the NEPED project was aimed at bringing improvement in swidden farmer's life through the promotion of alternative farming practice and initiation of micro-credit. However as I interacted with the FCC facilitator I realised that there were broad scheme of intervention that the NEPED project now engages with today along with ideas of conservation that takes place through diffusing ideas and values of conservation. The FCC facilitator comes from a Yumchanger Naga village and has 16 villages under his supervision. While interacting with him I realised that he was constrained by his own education in humanities, - social sciences. In the workshops people from the Salim Ali Centre for Ornithology (SEKON), Coimbatore come and train FCCs how to use G.P.S and make them aware of taxonomies of plant species that were valuable and demands identification, documentation and thereafter conservation. Questioners are filled and GPS are feeded with geo-coded data that are later extrapolated to map village landscape and resources for policy makers in different funding and donor agencies and NEPED planners working in the state capital, Kohima.

The FCC member had successfully mapped the village boundary and learned the use of G.P.S but was finding it difficult to remember botanical nomenclatures of species. They took the help of local villagers to identify the species, but were unable to define the botanical nomenclature. A similar problem was faced by the SEKON research assistants who were inducted to develop a data bank. This research group composed of scientific experts who were specialised in various botanical fields but their task did not match their expertise. One of the respondent replied that it was very difficult for him to identify plant species as he was a specialist in toxicology and mammals.[3] These researchers were further unaware of the local customs, traditions and nomenclatures of botanical names used by the native Nagas. They were themselves alien to the researched community. Their main task was to produce a glossary of plant species, their local names, botanical nomenclature and its economic use. This would lead to the publication of a plant and animals species found in the area like the Red Data Book. This activity they argued would lead up to conservation initiative in the area. They even referred to two community conservation sites that have been recently started in the Saramati mountains in Tuensanag district already declared as biological hot-spot. Their approach was technical and scientific based on taxonomical classification and identification of species. Community involvement was seeker to know the local names of species and their traditional uses. For example certain plant species as used for making dies, have medicinal values or are used as herbs for curing ailments. The economic importance of bio-diversity and why these species should be conserved were underpinned by a discourse on global warming, deforestation, biodiversity loss and resultant desiccation crisis.

The 'crisis narrative' produced in their discussion was real. Nagaland was a perfect site for conservation. However, they had very little understanding of a community beyond their 'epistemic community' of experts. Here we will show in the following paragraphs how project practice simplifies the image of the community as 'irrigational institutions' needing scientific and technical support to produce sustainable future and effective conservation strategy.

Asoba the NEPED fcc member who was closely working with the SEKON team observes that he is disturbed with the manipulation of grants in the village by VDB (Village Development Board, hereafter VDB) members that were selected as part of the conservation practice.[4] He cited the lack of awareness among the villagers about development grants that create avenues for siphoning of funds by the VDB in connivance with district officials. He too was sceptical about the project as there was no financial assistance on plan that would create alternative livelihood for farmers. He even exclaims that before his selection in the project he was unemployed. The project has engaged him productivity in the village. But there was nothing for the villagers to fall back upon for their subsistence. Hunting and game were natural and inevitable as it supplemented their daily dietary needs. His interaction with villagers, farmers made him aware of village life. His location in a small town made him distanced from rural life. His participation in the village as FCC worker among the Yumchunger Nagas brings out an ethnographic details of his pedagogy in school, collages and later in a development agency that constructs his idea of villagers, his clan members and all that was good with conservation. It explains his subjectivity, agency that is 'bounded rational'; premise on maximization of economic befits and cash income through commercialisation and promotion of exotic and economically valued species.

Developmental intervention in a Naga village in Tuensang district as is the case for rest of Naga Hills is mediated these days through Village Development Board (VDB),[5] the village council (VC) and the village council members (VCM) and the various political, factional and bureaucratic intermediaries (community patron) who act as gatekeepers, brokers and translators, facilitating developmental and community work in villages. The village patrons (V.C and V.C.M members) are nominated as state agents to facilitate development planning of the village, who sanitize information act as envoys between the district-sub division administration and the council and act as community- clan leaders. They are the nominated members of *khels*, clan and the village community who work in the best interest of their clan and village. The FCC members by training and long detachment from rural life image their village folk as destroyers of forest; people who are inclined to make quick profit. However, in their common perception *jhumming* is still considered sustainable with a ten years cycle. The *jhum* land is revered by the villagers as pricest as it can produce every crop of their dietary need. A study of the dietary habits of Yamchunger Nagas will also speak of the changes that have occurred in their daily life.

The image of the community as destroyers of forest and hunters of wildlife comes from the scientific imagination of place, space and habitat. The people from the Salim Ali centre had visited the FCCs village several times in the past year to document wildlife. Observing and identifying birds, their habitat and their procreation activity is an integral part in documenting species and record information that are vital for conservation strategy. The third phase of the NEPED programme has picked up biodiversity conservation, watershed management as the new *mantra* for rural livelihood improvement in the backward districts of Nagaland. The biodiversity conservation project is in operation in four backward districts of Naga Hills Tuensang, Khipri, Longling and Mon. As my FCC informant observed these regions have been declared by the forest and wildlife department in Naga Hills as biological hotspots. Similarly people in these backward districts of Nagaland completely depend on *jhumming* for their livelihood.

The state has historically had limited control over these blank space[6], as these were the territories of independent Nagas. Right after India's independence they became part of NEFA and later NHTA till 1963. These were the least interfered districts from the instruments of developmental planning. The native life was preserved, excluded and marginalized from outside interference with the exception of Baptist Missionaries and the military administration that territorialized the native life world as frontier areas and as buffers to the nation state. The decades of Naga nationalistic struggles kept these tribes in pristine isolation. In the post 1970's period the development intervention of the Indian state diffused to these backward tracts once 'excluded areas of the British Empire-trans frontier tract', through the promotion of new agricultural technologies-Terrace Rice Cultivation (TRC) that was introduced as an attempt to contain *jhum* cultivation through diversification of farming and the utilization of lowlands that were kept as waste by the *jhummias*. The promotion of TRC was done with the appointment of WL officer by the agriculture department locally known as the *Kelu Babu* (water man). The *Kelu Babu* came from Angami areas on deputation and stayed in Yumchunger Villages and also in my study village Leangkongru to teach local farmers about the techniques of wet rice farming and how to maintain the fields. This change brought about by state interventions were complimented by the Baptist church. The church was looked upon as an institution of improvement and an icon on modernity, civility and hygiene. The socialization of church were based on spread of puritan and protestant ethics,- abstinence from bad habits- drinking of alcohol, committing feuds, head hunting and revenge killings. The Church organised the village youths as work force based on 'age-set' or 'age-groups' to conduct important work of public importance. The age-group worked on wage payment on public works, building roads, canals and culverts. The wages were collected and contributed towards payment of church expenses. The practices of 'feast of merit'[7]or community feast after a rich harvest were declared irrational, uneconomical and acts of insanity and waste.

The diffusion of paddy farming has had a remarkable change in the study area (Leankongru village). The food habits, dietary needs have changed with the changes in cropping and the permanent settlement of fields. The landscape is dotted with moon crescent *jhum* plots, but the practice on making new *jhum* plots every year is on a slow but tangible decline. There are more permanent plots in the *jhum* fields these days. The adoption of plantation farming along with the cultivation of *kholar* long beans that are grown in combination with maize have made *jhum* plots permanent. The relay cropping keeps the soil fertile for multiple seasons thus stabilizing the soil. Farmers grow rice in freshly cleared forest in the first year followed by a crop combination of maize and *kholar* that maintain soil stability and nutrient content unlike millets and job tears that were grown during the NEFA days.

Kholar or long beans have become prominent in the farmers crop cycle in recent years, as the market value of this crop has grown. There is a myth in Leangkongru that their soil is the best in Tuensang and even in the whole of Nagaland. NEPED a Canadian funded development programme aimed at improving local livelihood through the promotion of IK (indigenous knowledge) of the farmers and alternative livelihood strategy sanctified the myth and adopted the village as one of its model village for improvement. Conservation was top of their agenda. After six years of project intervention and an investment of Rs seven lakh as revolving fund the villagers continued with *kholar*, rice and maize cultivation. The promotion of cardamom cultivation, ginger plantation and micro-credit failed to improve farmer's livelihood as farmers experienced crops failed and market glut with ginger produce. The NEPED loan dissolved as most of the funds were distributed among the village Council and Village Development Board members. The church also got a large share of the NAPED loan. My ethnography showed that most of the loan money was used to supplement the immediate need of the beneficiaries. Some people further advanced the loan to other villagers who had no access to institutional lending at exorbitantly higher rates of interest. Building house, paying children's admission fees, medical treatment and further landing at a higher rate of interest were the main purpose for which the NEPED loan was uses. Very little of the revolving fund was put to cultivate new crops and improve livelihood. In fact the meaning of revolving fund as resources to generate more cash and disposable income for the farmers through agri-business and plantations of commercial crops that would permanently settle *jhum* plots was understood differently by the beneficiaries. Most of the beneficiaries sow the grant as an opportunity to improve their housing, financing child education and as reinvestment in loans at higher rates of interest to clan and community members who had no access to credit. The exorbitant rate of interest 10% per month turned most of the lenders as defaulters and the people who repaid their loan were worse off at the end of the term as they had to sacrifice their cattle and mortgage their household valuables to repay their loan amount.

The question of bounded rationality becomes evident here. The beneficiaries from this account, economist would claim were bounded irrational as they speculated and invested the loans in non-remunerative areas. The minority of the beneficiaries who used the fund for agrarian improvement failed to repay their loans in light of bad harvest and the vagaries of market that spoiled good produce of ginger. The farmers continue with Long beans *(khullar)*, *jhum* rice (*mutsu*), maize (*manzi)*, millets *(tanji)*, soya been *(akuni)*, Naga dal and sweet potato cultivation in their *jhum* plots and wet rice (*kelu*) in their terrace fields. The NEPED project has had limited impact on the overall agrarian improvement in Yumchunger Naga life. The intensive crop management practiced by the Leangkongru villagers enticed NEPED officials to select it as one of their beneficiary village. However the project officials misrepresented the social context of Leangkongrus success in indigenous fallow management that were based on changes in their farming practice brought about by the impact of Christianity, protestant ethics, the diffusion of new agricultural technology and the constraints imposed by topography and the limited availability of cultivable land. The efficient farming practice based on extending cropping seasons and limited rotation was picked up as an outcome of communities collective solidarity and the social cohesiveness. However, when development funds entered to aid this process of progress made till them through an investment on plantation farming, farmers showed little interest as these new crops posed tremendous challenge towards their management. And once produced they had no ready market for sale. Thus it worked adversely towards people's interest. On the other hand development grants were seen as resources for appropriation and the powerful village interest got self interested by selecting beneficiaries from their own clan affiliations and often themselves appropriated the resources. The collective solidarity as represented in the funder's discourse got quickly fragmented and community stewards became co-optors and appropriators of the project denying poor landless farmers in the village their designed share.

Nonetheless, these notified backward districts have evolved from their semi-nomadic mode of production. *Jhum* is no longer so intensive as it used to be in the past. Fresh fields for cultivation are reducing with increasing fragmentation of land, changing cropping pattern and the growth of plantation for timber and horticulture. The *jhum* cycle in Leangkongru village is maintained by continuous cultivation in one single plot for more than three years. Fresh plots are only cleared for *jhum* rice cultivation as it yields best in the first year. The dependence on market rice is growing day by day as farmers cannot produce enough from their fields. The myth of excellent soil is undermined by the change in cropping pattern that restores soil fertility and permits settled farming. Decades of agrarian intervention by the Land Resource department, Soil Conservation, Agricultural and Wasteland Department have introduced new ideas of conservation and management of land resources. With the establishment of different department and a separate department for underdeveloped areas known as the Department of Underdeveloped Areas (DODA), in 2003, with special central assistance for improving native life, the ethnic life world of the Yumchunger Nagas of frontier Naga villages are fast changing as dynamic spaces of accumulation, privatisation and individual ownership of land are catching up in the community. Today there are more than thirty government departments in Nagaland. These underdeveloped districts are completely dependent on Swidden farming for their subsistence.

Conservation is a key word that is fast catching up in Naga Hills. While conservation policies of the government, forest and wildlife department have been constrained by innumerable violation, encroachment and defaulters who hunt indiscriminately. The civil society and communities aided by conservation societies, NGOs global and national funding agencies have done well in organising communities to conserve resources and to impose ban on their resources bringing about moral codes of obedience and a ban on hunting. Several villages in Kohima, Phek and Mokokchung have set up community forest and eco parks. The KNCTS, Khonoma Nature Conservation and Tragopan Sanctuary have been the most important civil society organization that started operating in 1998. Today KNCTS is cited nationally as a success story. Members of KNCTS frequently visit national seminars and international workshops on conservation and present how the Khonoman's have achieved an impossible task a few years back. Khonoma attracted a lot of tourist after the establishment of the Tragopan sanctuary. Bird watchers from all over the world come and book seasons. Bird Watching as part of eco-tourism has gained and supersedes all other forms of tourism in the village as it brings considerable income to the village patrons who often do not reside in the village for such business throughout the year. Similarly cultural tourism and as the local people narrate historical tourism had picked up as Khonoma is declared as the heritage village.

These community conservation initiatives have spread far and wide. In Tuensang conservation seems to be a far cry. The NEPED- FCC members face a variety of constraints in promoting the idea of conservation. The latest effort has been to map the Traditional Ecological Knowledge (TEK) of the farmers. The people behind the project are SEKON and the Tata Dorajbi Trust as funding and technical support team, and operationalised in the field by NEPED team leaders, FCC grass root workers and research assistants who are engaged in compiling project reports. These institutions have initiated their funding and training programmes to materialise the idea of conservation. The following narrative will show how ideas of conservation get translated into opportunities and avenues for attracting development fund and how it gets translated in actual practice on the field by gatekeepers- the village patrons who appropriate their own self interest and constrain communities as well as project interest. The narrative will further unfold the context and complexities through which conservation works and how global ideas of risk are appropriated in local discourses of loos and destruction of nature. Power, patronage and agency of participants in conservation efforts play significant role in articulating the meaning, nature, text and the context of conservation. Successful conservation as I will show takes place through coercion and imposition of decisions on the public by influential man who collectively pass social writs- resolution that act at torts and as whips against violation.

To study conservation efforts among the Nagas I have selected two sites one lies in the developed areas among the Angamis in Khonoma village and the other among the Yumchungru of Samatur. The NEPED intervention has selected Tuensang as a site for biodiversity conservation. While in Khonoma I look at the evolution of KNCTS that has been produced in conservation literature as a success story.[8] The need to produce success stories is undermined by subjectivities and aspiration for improvement on the part of the people who initiate such projects. KNCTS was formed in 1998 by T. Sakhrie when he was the vice chairman of Khonoma Village Development Board.[99] As T. Sakhrie writes in the draft to one of his public lecture, that the 'Khonoma Nature Conservation and Tragopan Sanctuary' was declared open on the 11th of December 1998, with the theme "Care For Nature" by the then Commissioner and Secretary to the Government of Nagaland, Department of Forest, Ecology, Wildlife and Environment, Shri Thepfulhouvi Angami , IFS. The idea for forming a nature conservation society like KNCTS emerged in the late 1980s. However as Sakhrie recollects the villagers lack of conservation consciousness failed to develop any interest.[10] It was only during his tenure as VDB vice chairman that he engaged the Khonoma villagers, the students bodies, church groups, *khel* members and representatives of various denominations and pedigrees in each *khel* to adopt resolution that would impose a ban on hunting. As Sakhrie recollects it took several rounds of meetings more than nine with the representation from different fractions that led to the conservation effort. With the end of his tenure as VDB vice chairman, things have changed in the village. In 2003-4 the Khonoma Tourism Development Board was formed by the Village Council as an overarching platform to look at the Green Village project.

The project as Sakhrie claimed started because of their initiative. But the KNCTS members were sidelined in the whole scheme. The fresh nominated Village Council and VDB members underplayed the concerns of KNCTS president. A Sum of Rs 2 crores was sanctioned by the ministry of Environment and Forest to produce Khonoma's ecological success. Eco-friendly solar panels were put to light the streets with extensive networks of metalled pathways and memorable roads that were constructed at the expense of clearing secondary forest and bushes. All the village roofs were painted green and dustbins were set up in every nook and corner of the village road. Concrete pits were built as inseminators for garbage dump from households. Water tanks were constructed in every ward to facilitate clean and safe drinking water at community's doorsteps. The project brought cheer to some while it disappointed others. The villagers like Sakhrie and a former student union president whom I interviewed recollect that the Village Council and Village Development Board members benefited the most from project grant as they siphoned on large sum of the project money as the account were manipulated and never placed before the common public. A select group of village elders who were part of the council made fortunes with the project money with no tangible environment benefits. With the completion of the project phase khonoma remains in Naga peoples memory a symbolic icon of conservation that attracts huge number of tourist every year and especially bird watchers.

Conservation activities carried out by community organizations are today premiered as more efficient, less corrupt and free of political manoeuvres and bureaucratic cajoling. However these claims come from the broad Non Governmental civil society groups who do not critically engage with community and the micro politics of village elites and interest groups who act as important actors, gatekeepers, brokers and translators of conservation. It is these people who imagine the communities as backward, unscientific, irrational and short sighted to the whole conservation effort in Naga Hills. The KNCTS was organised to protect Tragopan the state bird of Nagaland. Today khonoma resonates as a conservation site and has become an important birding site in North Eastern part on India. The success story of Khonoma has got wide publicity in conservation literature in India (Kothari 2007). Nearly 300 kilometres away among the Backward Nagas of Samatur Sub division similar associations of eight villages led to the establishment of the Alotshu Wild life Control Committee in 2006. The main purpose of this organization was to control stag, an important animal attached to the socio cultural life of the Yumchungru Nagas of Samatur range. Nagas as many of my respondents claimed are passionate about hunting and to give it up is a big challenge. Many people in Khonoma depended on hunting for their livelihood before it was banned. The discourse of conservation gains popularity and scientific support from the crisis narratives produced in the name of "climate change". That climate change matters is today unequivocally prompted by the Baptist Church, the popular media and the enlightened citizens. Daily news papers present the crisis narratives through pictures, presentations and statistic (graphs and equations), remote sensing imageries that image the real danger posed by deforestation and destruction of animals to the local environment. These narratives are then picked by local activist, global NGOs to present and educate people from stopping the mayhem. The consciousness for conservation has even found its place in gods home. When I visited the Clark Theological College in Mokokchung, I found a poster fenced in the college's notice board that read Climate Change and the Gospel. The gospel had verse that talk of the great disaster brought by extremes of climate. This brings me to pose several questions:

What is the trope of conservation? Why some people have started taking conservation collectively beyond the state support and what makes conservation work? How do the global discourse on climate change, desiccation and bio-diversity loss captivate native mend? And why particular species become so important as symbols and icons on conservation in rural Nagaland?

These are broad questions that I have set to resolve in this essay through my engagement with the ethnographic I undertook during my fieldwork in Khonoma and Samatur. I will also argue that the conservation efforts popularised by these civil society and community initiative recreate success overlooking the social context and the contest for resources that takes place once the success is produced and donor agencies start fund such initiatives. I will also like to show how the success is diffused to attract global and national funding that gets co-opted and represented in the 'scientific' and 'technical' discourses surrounding conservation effort. Conservation even takes different meanings and creates different notions of improvement for village folk as they see such efforts attracting development grants for area development, creating new avenues for employment and offer new prospects for eco-tourism. These trails of events are underpinned by the micro–politics of community participation and the appropriation by elites who initiates these programmes.

KHONOMA POST CONSERVATION

Khonoma is an Angami Village located 20 kilometres away from Kohima in the southern Angami territory. It has a picturesque landscape dotted with broad valleys and green hills. The landscape presents a perfect conservation site. Villagers in Khonoma recollect that their forefathers were wise enough to have developed terrace rice fields that are well knitted by a network of irrigated channels that are regulated by norms of reciprocity and collective action. On the hill slope virgin forest are not disturber by annual *jhum* cycle as the villagers have adopted alder based fellow management that allow fixed rotation of fields with limited destruction of the standing vegetation.[1] The *Alder* trees are annually pollard and not cut from their stump to cultivate a new field. The *alder* leaves mulch the soil and make it nutritive for multiple cropping seasons. The Khonomans further take pride in their resistance movement against the British and the legacy left by Phizo during the post independence era. The idea of conservation came to the village in the late 1980 when the Chief Conservator of Forest introduced to Mr T, Sakhrie a former contractor and the son of the first graduate in the village to form a committee for conservation. Sakhrie readily accepted this idea as he himself had never practiced hunting in his youth and was averse to such practice. But his social position as a common citizen in the village did make little impact on the villagers. But his efforts were relentless. In 1996 he was elected vice chairman to the village council and this gave him solid grounding to cherish his dream. The KNCTS came up in 1998 after nine rounds of deliberation with various communities in the village.

The KNCTS came up in 1998 after nine rounds of deliberation with various communities in the village. The

KNCTS has given rise to many other activities in the village that needs broad discussion. For it successful functioning the organization mapped out a virgin forest in the surrounding mountain that was reserved for conservation. In the words of Sakhrie the protected Tragopan sanctuary covered 'twenty square kilometres as the crow flies, is estimated to be about seventy square kilometres if the contours of the vales and hills are taken into account.'[12] This geographical description of the landscape was supported by a proper survey, and instrumentation work. Six village guars were selected from the village representing the three *Khels*. Destruction of wildlife was banned with the imposition of fine. Any defaulters were penalised by the council on behalf of the KNCTS. The failure to pay fines meant not only social exclusion but even collect economic expulsion of the individual alone but also his clan/ khel and pedigree from the developmental grants that were annual guaranteed by the government and distributed by the village council and VDB. Thus community coercion was exercised by the village council to make defaulters pay for the violation of rule. This social norm proved to be the hallmark of Khonomas success. The Village Council decided on these coercive rules of obedience and thus the position of Mr Sakhrie as a low implementing body in the village became important.

In 2008-09, the village sow a dramatic change in the nature of conservation. For one month during the month January the KNCTS relaxed the ban on hunting in Khonoma. The common answer was people need to hunt, as that is part of their culture.[13] The answer seemed less convincing. However, this explanation quickly made me realise the local politics. One of the agricultural graduates whom I intervened recently informed me that the real cause for relaxation was the result of negotiation between the village elders and the student's body who felt cheated in the 'Green Village project'. The inability of the council to produce a balance sheet on expenditure incurred in the Green Village project led to the relaxation. It satisfied the students union as they hunted hundreds of birds during the period. T. Sakhrie exclaimed that most of the day's people came empty handed, as there were no birds left. His narrative seemed to co-opt outsiders concerns. The failure to catch birds did not imply conservation was forged. Rather it was reinforcing that the relaxation did not impact the overall population of birds in the wildlife sanctuary. On further intervention it became apparent that most of the conservation conscious people who also acted as members of KNCTS in various capacities did not find it wrong to hunt wildlife outside the village where they worked as teachers, government servants and as contractors. One of the KNCTS office bearers, a school teacher from Khifri, whom I mat on my journey to the village was carrying a game cat and an exotic bird in his bag. He even invited me to taste the meat. It was not wrong for the KNCTS members to hunt outside their village while they pleaded for conservation in their own village.

The school teacher was a board member of the conservation society and he revealed that the NGO has done well in the initial years to attract governmental and non-governmental funding. The WWF and IUCN had earlier funded KNCTS, which were never revealed in public. T. Sakhrie handed over to me a speech he recently delivered at a conference held in Indian Institute of Sciences (IIS), Bangalore where he writes that the KNCTS had received small grants from many charity and philanthropic organization, and paltry amounts that have barely sustained the organizations. The Gerald Durrel Memorial Fund, Pennsylvania, USA, had contributed $5000 to KNCTS on persuasion of the then Commissioner and Secretary, Government of Nagaland.

With the decline in funding the village guards have also vanished. The creation of Khonoma Tourism Development Board in 2003, the KNCTS got marginalized by the council members from major decision-making process during the 'Green Village project'. As Mr T. Sakhrie observed in his interview that his name was included in Khonoma Tourism Development Board (KTDB) core committee but he was never invited in its meetings and sessions where the decision on how to use the grant were decided and planned. Although his efforts led to the emergence of the project in the village the exclusion of Sakhrie was marked by new political groupings in the village who took control of the conservation grant. Dunning his tenure as Village Development Board member he developed good links in the government, NGO sector that attracted funds and technical support as well as privileged him to attend various environmental forums to present khonomas ecological success story.[14] But all these were now fading off.

The other fallout of the KNCTS effort has been the increase in tourist visit and the emergence of tour operators in the village, the rise of a mini tourism industry in the village managed and organised by villagers who claim to be guides for bird watchers.

I was guided by one such individual who facilitated my stay in the village during the fieldwork. His personal narrative, anxieties and subjectivities explains how conservation dream had personalised natural resources that are collectively owned by the village and how the village council exercised control over the community and decided upon conservation. The person was the former Khonoma student union president and is also an active member of the village church and the present chairman of the village conservation board initiated by the village council. He also aspires to start his own nature club that he claimed to be more robust, based on scientific study of birds available in the sanctuary and a correct assessment on forest resources and mapping of birds habitat. He was once an expert hunter, but he claimed that Mt Sakhrie and his organization transformed him and his outlook on conservation. He was worried and anxious upon the fact that his own villagers betrayed him. The village Council Chairman had allowed in the recent past a research to conduct his fieldwork in the village on Tragopan. This decision was taken by the council without his consent. He claimed that these people act as bio-pirates in the village and argued for stringent action to be taken against such perpetrators who work with the community in disguise for their selfish projects. However, his concerns were also underpinned by the sense of loss that he experienced in spite of being the president of the conservation committee. His concern being bypassed by the village council made him anxious and suspicious of the council and the head GB (village headman). He aspired to take control over the total bird watching business by placing community interest at the centre stage. And tourist should take his consent before venturing into the forest. He acted as guides for bird watchers in the village but occasionally other teams came for bird watching through other connections and tour operators that challenged his monopoly and knowledge over the region.

His subjective position for leadership in the village in matters relating to wildlife control was disguised in his inability to successfully employ the gate keeping business. His social position as conservation secretary gave him powers to act as gatekeeper in matters relating to conservation efforts in the village. But he saw his power overlooked by the head GB (Village Headman) who was also the village council chairman. Bird watching has become an interesting avenue of income generation for city dwellers; villagers who had roots in Khonoma but were migrants from towns and cities as ex-public servants, school teachers who find providing logistical support-hospitality to birding teams as highly remunerative. The village farming community was completely at dark about the economies of bird watching that these town people had monopolised over the years.

Bird watchers who come to the village presented a more interesting story. I met the leader of the bird watching team who visited annually to Khonoma. His name is Peter Lobo a Goanese who comes from Sikkim. Bird watchers as he exclaimed were attracted to khonoman purely for all kinds of wildlife and not specifically a particular species of bird that khonomans and the KNCTS presented- Tragopan that were protected and visible in Khonoma village alone. Tragopan had emerged in the local discourse of village gatekeepers as the most threatened species that found solace in Khonomas protected regime chaimed by villagers like T. Sakhrie who have made conservation their day today business.

Peter Lobo explained that his annual visit in the village was a means to sustain the village tourism economy by helping villagers. This is how he claimed conservation works. He identified the village hosts, the urban elites who were engaged in catering and lodging business as poor. Birding teams come to India's most sought after wildlife reserve to see exotic bird species of the tropics. Birding middleman and tour operators like Lobo contact such teams in their official engagements in London every year. These selected birding cites are sold to their customers as seasons reserved for one nation or multiple nations. This story was narrated to me by my host Baby who was engages in this business in Khonoma for several years. The practice as I understood draws similarity to virtual water trade. By virtual trading of birds in the international market the local is produced through the global trans-nationalism. Money is made and contracts signed without any visible trade in commodities or goods. The aesthetic value of bird watching and the privileged to access these sites are traded. Bird watchers take photographic memories from the field. Bird watching thus provided great avenue of income generation for people who were integrated to this network of trade that have very sophisticated mechanisms of business. Khonoma as a birding site evolved with KNCTS nature conservation efforts that are alien to the village folk who are primarily dependent on wet rice and alder based swidden cycle. A small group of village elites who had well build houses in the village, and those who had developed links with the tour operators, can speak good English and had exposure to the outside world benefited from this trade through rent remuneration and hospitality business.

Lobo felt that state intervention towards conservation had failed because of its rigidities and red tapeism. Conservation efforts carried out by community effort as in Khonoma was the ideal example of participation where communities benefited from such associations and collective ban. The tourist come and enjoy bird watching in an environment where there are no administrative constrains and official protocols to follow. Bird watchers seemed to have bought licence to enter the reserve wherever they wished as they paid money.

Lobo's presence was already contested by the conservation committee chairmen who sow his bird watching business constrained by free access of lobo to the village. He shared that lobos visit was perhaps the last. From now onward people need to register, give details of their work plan and get permission from the council before any birding or research exercise in the village takes place. Reckless entry of outsiders was seen as a threat to their identity and invited prospects of bio-piracy. Inherent in his concerns were his personal subjectivities and difference that had developed with other tour operators who narrower his prospects of income through conservation tourism.

He even proposed to establish his own nature club and had already proliferated his ideas by creating business friends in other districts of Nagaland. He even claimed to have the best knowledge of Khonoma and the location of Tragopan in its landscape. It is through the word of mouth he believed that the message of conservation will spread to the outside world and would attract people to visit the area. Beyond Khonomas mountain peak lays another exotic landscape, which the Khonomans call the Zuku Valley. They valley has large tracts of pastures dotted with exotic flowers that are endemic to the region and have in recent years become hot spots for conservation and tourism. The Khonoma village provides one train to the valley while the Visama village provides the other trail. People prefer the later route. Here again the village conservators want a control over the route that gives access to Zuku valley.

The exercise of control over resources in the name of conservation has become an important aspect of community efforts. This was also true for Leangkongru village where community patrons appropriated resources, demarcated private land as part of the conservation effort without sacrificing their individual plots but others in the community who had no political or clan representation in the village council or VDB. Often consensus that is seen as basis for community effort is encrypted in the social and economic sanctions that council/clan representatives impose on their members for their self interest. For Example, KNCTS imposed a fine of Rs 5000 on every defaulter. Even after imposition defaulters emerged and ambivalence prevailed on the identification of suspects as community members quickly denied their involvement on the pretext of lack of evidence. To prevent such scenarios that would allow free ridership, denial of charges and the failure of conservation efforts the community leaders made the individual Khel/clan/pedigree collectively responsible to compel community members from payment of fines and obedience to law passed by the council. In the event of failure on the part of individual defaulters to pay fines the Village Council sanitized the development grants and denied the particular members their relatives from participating in government programmes and blacklisted them from being beneficiaries of village development schemes. Through such collective coercion exerted by the Council and the VDB community citizens were compelled to abide.

At one level it presented a success story that is today cited nationally. (Kothari 2007). While on the other, success is produced through collective coercion exercised by a handful of community patrons who enjoy seats of privilege as decision makers in the village. I have tried to show how peoples self interest constitute much of community constituted conservation practice. Donor agencies, advocacy groups and NGOs on the other hand work through these institutional categories, explore communities social capital that are not homogenous neither linear and bank upon communities collective action. (Kothari, 2007, 2000, Kothari, 2004, Kothari et al 1998; Madhusudhan and Raman, 2003). A vast foray of literate that has been produced over this year's site such success as instruments of a discourse that make communities as champion conservators and state as predators. But I have shown till now how communities are fragments and contested over each other's rights and claims. The fragmentation of collective action in a post project phase speaks of the individual discourses of appropriation that are based on tropes of community/village and clan interest that stems from actors, conservators individual interest in such projects. (Das, 2007).

PRE PROJECT PHASE IN LEANGKANGRU VILLAGE

The next section looks at a pre project phase in Samatur and engages with the initiators of Alitiso Wildlife Conservation Committee. My engagement in Samatur was designed to understand how community leaders engaged with the idea of conservation that were floated by NEPED FCC members through workshops, personal meetings, participatory resource and IEK mapping and filling of questioners and their engagement with the idea of climate change and forest destruction. However, my ethnography was enriched and informed by individual responses and agency that was embedded in personal narratives and aspirations of village commoners who participated as active respondents in my ethnographic sojourn. Prior to the arrival at my field site I had interacted with Asoba who sow the NEPED project as inherently good but showed exception scepticism on the function -ability of the project to attract villagers.

When I asked how the NEPED project will work. He answers:

'People see no tangible economic benefits from conservation. If economic incentives are provided I hope it will work.'

What about the village intermediaries and middleman?

He replied, 'there lays the big danger. I am sceptical about community leaders they are only after project money. It's difficult to say if conservation at all will be successful with this mentality".[15]

The villagers according to Asobas narrative were short sighted and incapable to understand the impact of global warming.[16] A local newspaper recently reported on Samaturs growing crisis posed by swidden farming and the rapid clearing of agricultural fields. The newspaper reported that due to increasing temperature Samatur has seen an exceptional change in cropping patter and farmers reported unexpected rise in certain kinds of fish that were never to be seen in their rivers.[17] The extensive cultivation of *Kolhar* (long beans) and the presence of an unexpected fish species in Tizu river that are otherwise abundant downstream in the Chindwin river of Burma are used as examples to present the crisis narrative and to grow consciousness among the people that global warming is becoming real. However, these changes were very hurriedly captioned in the newspaper, based on a quick visit to the filed site misses the larger picture in which changes in farming practices have taken shape in Tuensang district of Nagaland. Long beans have become a characteristic feature of local farming in recent years with the diffusion of WTRC (Wet Terrace Rice Cultivation) in the early 1970 and the change in cropping pattern in the region from a predominantly millet and job tears dependent food economy to rice in the 1990s. Similarly this has triggered changes in cropping pattern particularly of maize and *kolhar* that are now grown more extensively then ever before. The market demand of *kolhar* and villagers need for cash have triggered increased production of *kolhar* in the recent past. Scientific determinism is quickly used to justify the spread of particular crops and to fethesize *jhum* cultivation and the destruction of forest as irrational, uneconomical and ecologically disastrous.

These narratives produce powerful discourse that mould young minds like Asoba towards scientific practice of conservation. But they underplay the cultural politics and moral economy of conservation. Asobas anxiety to instil ideas of conservation among his villagers spells the failure to produce economic benefits as the project did not promise any livelihood or economic substitute to hunting that keep communities disinterested to participate. Some sow conservation as a practice that would employ villagers as forest guards while others had more practical sense for conserving wild species in their forest. As many villagers exclaimed that they conserver wildlife to prey animals when big politicians and bureaucrats visit their village. The social purpose of conservation was thus inscribed in their response. For uncle Sojhiba, the president of Alteso Wildlife Conservation Committee, conservation of stag was a symbol and pride of the Yumchungers and a site for prosecution and authority. The defaulters had to pay Rs 15000. In the past years since the Alteso Wildlife Conservation Committee came up fifteen people have been penalised. The collected fees were used in conducting various meetings on conservation. The creation of this wildlife sanctuary was also underpinned by the desire to attract the governments attention. Uncle Sojhiba responded that the government should take interest in their reserve and fund it. My narration of Khonoma and the grants they received from central government as part of the conservation package excited Sojhiba and he requested me to write a letter in english addressing the concerned department that could bring their conservation effort to the notice of higher authorities. The intension was to get public fund for their community initiative. Inherent in this claim was also the idea of appropriating and co-opting public funds for person use in the name of conservation. Conservation is reproduced as a measure of development that was seen as attracting donor grant and project money.

My interaction with Asoba exposed this fact. His survey for the project by then was barely over. He expresses, "people are after after project money they are least interested in conservation. They don't understand Climate Change. They are in fact short sighted". This expression speaks of communities recklessness. However, in an economy that was once dependent on communiterian ethics, fast changes were evident with growing private ownership of land, paid labour and the growth of plantation agriculture, horticulture and agri-silviculture. Cash is fact becoming the most important exchange value that has replaced reciprocal exchanges within villagers. But reciprocity still exists and works as acts of patronage. For example, my interview with the hunters revealed, conservation is good as it helps villagers to protect wild animals like stag and offer these as exotic meat to government officers and politicicians with the expectation that officials declare projects and offer assistance in return.

Such reciprocal exchanges presents a more articulate sense of give and take relationship not necessarily based on cash bribes but by offering game animals as gifts, or shall we call modern day tributes. The intervention of market, the will for improvement imparted through education, the values of protestant ethics instilled by the church and the rise of cash payment and individualism in predominantly barter economy has made communities as economic subjects. Communities will not conserve unless they see tangible economic benefits coming from the state. Our interviews with people saw an overwhelming support that the idea of hunting is bad with few respondents claiming that such practices will affect the livelihood of poor farmer. Inevitable every affluent household in the village owned a gun to hunt wild animals and birds. Conservation is also vehemently claimed by these households who enjoy power, prestige and authority over the village. The Aletso Wildlife Conservation committee president also enjoyed such position in the village. He is the vice president of Nagaland Pradesh Congress Committee, Samatur areas and was one of the crusaders of conservatation effort. However, his nine-bore rifle had hunted much wildlife in the last decade since he purchased it from a native villager in 1988. He was interested in stag that attracted a premium state concern towards its conservation. It was declared as a threatened species. He explains that the animal is big, rare to observe and is a part of their culture hence they have resolved to conserve it. For other animals it was impossible to put a ban as hunting formed as part of their culture. Every hunter exercises a magic trick before going for hunting. The particular alignment of beads as they get arranged on the ground after a toss of ones finger indicates the favourability for hunting. Hunters claimed that unfavourable symbols inevitable leads to a spoiled game. They attach great value to this magic trails as they act as foretellers of failure or success that averts them of misadventure. Every male in the village presented a sharp shooter and was an inborn hunting. The practice of hunting wild animals and birds with catapult, air gun and rifles was an inborn practice in which generations of young man were trained. With the eclipse of head taking and the advent of Baptist missionaries in these frontier tracts, the hunting of wild animal has remained the only means of expatiating masculinity among these frontier tribes.

However, that time in memorial practices are today loosing value. People have become more rational and are integrated into the market. The birds killed are sold in the local bazaar and highways at amazing low and at through away prices Rs.15-20 per bird. Exotic species are hunted for a paltry cash income that is used in buying daily rations and cloths by the hunter's family. Hunting thus provides additional income and substitutes their dietary needs. The scarcity of cow, goats and other domesticated animals in the Naga villages had historically enticed people to the taste of dry meat that are smoked and preserved for a long time. Smoked meat meets people's daily requirement of protein. The idea of conservation in such hunting and game dependent communities seems trivial. None the less conservation has set in through various discouces promoted by the church, the civil society and educated youths who see conservation as essential to maintain bio-diversity and nature.

In the rural environment however conservation initiatives have caught a new high with communities organising and participating in nature conservation without state support. These campaigns have become fashionable with the NGOs and civil societies engagement with ideas of social capital and communities collective bond that are exploited to create successful conservation. Through this brief narrative I have explored how community driven conservation effort tend to misrepresent participation. Rather the social text of participation is underlined by elite construction and coercion imposed through fines and the exclusion of defaulters and their associate clan and family members from the process of development. The social whip is exercised to demonstrate that native communities present as repositories of 'social capital' and 'collective action'. The village elites and people holding positions of power and authority appropriate their personal interest through the images of conservation. Often these conservation efforts also lead to disenchantment among community leaders and create multiple factions within a village leading to clash on interest and fragmentation of the conservation effort.

The KNCTS and AWCC that I studied presented perfect case-studies in which through participation resource dependent communities were made part in the decision-making, power structure and accountability process of community based conservation programmes. However, this was achieved by the engagement of the village elites who enjoyed political affiliations, were well informed and were self-interested in these programmes and sow these grants as another avenue to attract funding from the government. The post project phase sow the disquiet between various groups that emerged to appropriate the funding assistance sanctioned by the government to improve the village environment. In Leangkangru village the village interest group is pushing hard for such reciprocal incentives and packages for village development from the government that will bring conservation in these backward villages to limelight and attract funding for improvement in peoples lives. People like I. Sakhrie have been popularising Khonoma as a success story in various national and regional forum through conferences, workshops and presentation in conventions. The success of Khonoma has been reproduced time and again. My interview with the former Khonoma student union president and present tour operator revealed that KNCTS had not undertaken any survey in the village nor they were aware what was the exact population of birds that they were conserving. Their moral authority in the community as elders and as initiators of conservation practice was strongly felt in the village. Community conservation in this respect presents more complex norms of power, patronage and self-interested village publics organised in the disguised of collective action in Naga villages.

ENDNOTES

1. See, Herbert A. Simon, 'Rational Decision Making in Business Ornization', Nobel Memorial Lecture, 8th December 1978. nobelprize.org/nobel_prizes/economics/laureates/1978/simon-lecture.pdf.

2. The Village Development Board was organised in the 1980 by the Nagaland Government by passing the Nagaland Village Development Act 1980, which provides for financial devolution and decentralization of resources to the villages themselves for their economic development.
3. My interface with Parmanandam on 28.5.09 at Tuensang revealed this point. His co-workers in SEKON who were part of the project faced similar problems.
4 The Village Development Board was formed in 1980 by a notification passed on 21st of November 1989 by the Government of Nagaland, Department of Rural Development. The main objective behind creation on VDB was economic decentralization through which villagers were made responsible for their own development through the dispersal of grants directly to the VDB and making them in charge in the selection of beneficiaries and implementation of programmes.
5. The Village Council were formally enshrined in the administrative structure of Nagaland with the passing of the Nagaland Village Council Act, 1978, that empowered villagers the GB (gau buras) who form the council members to resolve disputes and to look after the village through administering justice based on customary codes, torts and mores of Naga tradition. In the preceding period there were other village council acts but they are amended and replaced by this act. In the past three decades several amendments have been made to improve administration and to simplify local governance. See for detailed clause of these acts, Z. Angami,2008, Nagaland Village Empowerment Laws, A Compilation,Novelty printing press, Kohima.
6. The term 'blank space' has been used by Edmund Leach to explain territories that lay beyond colonial administrative control in the Bengal Eastern Indian Frontier including the eastern Naga territories of Burma. See, Leach, E. R. 1960. "The Frontiers of Burma." Comparative Studies in Society and History 3 (1): 49-68.
7. Stoner, C. R., 1950. 'The Feasts of Merit among the northern Sangtam Tribe of Assam', Anthropos, Vol. 45.
8. As Ashish Kothari writes in Khonoma Tragopan Sanctuary in Nagaland the NGO education is helping the local communities to work out a sustainable tourism plan from which locals will benefit. The tourism incentives for Khonom were also revealed in my intercourse with one tour operator who regularly visited the village every season with bird watchers. See, Ashish Kothari, 2007, Birds in out Lives,University Press, Bangalore.
10. My interface with T.Sakhrie in Khonoma. Dated 27-02-2009 revealed this point.
11. For an elaborate description of alder based fallow management one can refer to the NEPED resource handbook published in 2000, titled 'Building Upon Traditional Agriculture in Ngaland', p. 24-30.
12. My taped interview with T. Sakhrie, President, KNCTS on 12 January 2009.

13. My interaction with T. Sekhrie and other villagers like baby, Anungle revealed this point. Interview dated 25th of February, 2009.
14. T. Sakhrie narrated in his interview that the conservation initiation brought him in contact with many influential and nature lovers from all over the country. He hosted Asish Kothari a renowned conservator and NGO activist in Khonoma village. As a reciprocal gesture Kothari had promised to bring a mega funding for the village which was ultimately dropped because of non participation of the Village Council and the Village Development Board members. He also befriended Dr. Abdshesh Gangwar of the Centre for Environmental Education (North East India) and Shri James Hindon of the Darwin initiative, UK. All these networks and contacts helped Khonoma draw attention of environmental funders and donors to protect the village.
15. Interface with Asoba in Samatur town 7th March , 2009.
16. This has been a standard explanation by all NEPED (FCC) and SEKON project workers. Climate change is presented as the new crisis and it can only be challenged by adopting sustainable farming and bio-diversity conservation.
17. See the Newspaper Report 'Climate Change: More real than felt, in Nagaland', Morung Express, dated March 30, 2009, Monday. Also my interface with B.S Chauhan the former Vice–Chancellor of Nagaland University, a soil scientist revealed the scientific explanation of soil fertility and how Global Warming contributes to sustained soil fertility. He explained that due to rising temperatures the mineralization of soil takes place sustaining its fertility status. Thus he concluded that the decline in new Jhum plots and extended cropping in existing Jhum plots in Leangkangru village may be related to mineralization and the impact of Global Warming.

REFERENCES

Das, Priya (2007), 'The Politics of Participatory Conservation: A Case Study of Kailadevi Wildlife Sanctuary'. In Ghazala Shahabuddin and Mahesh Rangarajan (eds). *Making Conservation Work*. New Delhi: Permanent Black.

Kothari, Ashish, Neema Pathak, R.V. Anuradha and Bansuri Taneja, (eds) (1998), *Communities and Conservation, Natural Resource Management in South and Central Asia*. Delhi: Sage Publishers and UNESCO.

.Kothari, A. (2000), "Conserving Nature with Communities: Lessons from Real Life Experiences in South Asia". Paper presented at the second World Conservation Congress of IUCN, Amman, 3-11 October 2000 (Web Publication).

Kothari, A. (2004), 'Participatory Conservation: Paradigm Shift in International Policy. A Compilation of Output from Global Events

Relating to Participatory Conservation'. IUCN World Commission on Protected Areas; IUCN Commission on Environment, Economic and Social Policy; Themes on Equity and Protected Areas (TILCEPA) and Kalpavriksh, India.

Kothari, A. (2007), *Birds in our Lives.* Bangalore: University Press.

Madhusudhan and T.R.S Raman (2003), 'Conservation as if Biodiversity Matters: Preservation versus Sustainable Use in India'. *Conservation and Society*,1. Pp. 49-60.

SECTION–II

Stunted Transformation

6

A STUDY OF SHIFTING CULTIVATION PRACTICES IN KORAPUT REGION

P.C. Mohapatro

The variety of soils, climate and vegetation is responsible for many types of agriculture in the world. A close observation of global cultivation practices reveals that development of agriculture has passed through two distinct lines: plains cultivation and hills cultivation. Shifting Cultivation falls in the latter category. This system of cultivation has been considered to be the most ancient, dating back to the Neolithic period between the years 13000 to 3000 B.C. (FAO Staff, 1957:9) and considered to be a stage in the evolution of human culture. (Tripathy, 1952:10). Shifting Cultivation is a system which consists of cutting of trees on tops and slopes of hills, burning the fallen trees and bushes and dibbling or broadcasting seeds in the ash covered soil and rotation of fields with long fallow periods. (Conklin, 1961 quoted in Sachidananda, 1989:3; Hodder, 1973: 44-45 and Plezer,1958). The rest is left to nature's care. Good crops are harvested for the first two or three years at a diminishing rate and then the land is abandoned until it regains its fertility through renewed vegetation. This process continues until the fertility of land is completely exhausted due to soil erosion and loss of moisture content in land when no more forest growth is possible. The land is then abandoned finally leaving only 'bald hills' devoid of any economic or ecological importance. Then a new clearing is opened for fresh cultivation. The cultivation is thus shifted from one patch of land to another ultimately abandoning one after another bringing large scale devastation in its trail. (Mohapatro, 1987: 128).

SHIFTING CULTIVATION OVER THE GLOBE

Shifting cultivation is practised with some variations throughout the tropical and sub-tropical regions of the world. It has been tentatively estimated by FAO that 200 million people scattered over 36 million sq. kms. of the world are depending on this system. They constitute a little over 10 per cent of the world's population and are spread over 30 per cent of its exploitable soils. (Shah, 1970 quoted from P.H. Nye and D.J. Greenland, 1960). The indigenous communities of 63 countries in Africa, Asia, South America and Central America follow this practice of agriculture.

Shifting cultivation is practised by a number of tribes in the world. The Yoruba of Congo basin, the Bemba of Northern Rhodesia, the Yao of Southern Nyasaland, the Melanesian of Solomon Islands, the Boro of Western Amazon Forest, the Bakairi Indians of Upper Xingu Region in South America, Hill Tribes of North Borneo and Veddah of Ceylone are few instances of tribes who are still practising the primitive cultivation. (Nag, 1958: 410-418).

Shifting cultivation is known by various names in different countries. The primitive cultivators of West Africa call it 'Farming' and it is known as 'sortage' in French and Belgian Ardennes. It goes by the name of 'Kholo' among the natives of South-east Solomon Islands. The Veddah of Ceylone call it 'Chenna' and the Burmese hill tribe as 'Taungya'. (ibid.)

SHIFTING CULTIVATION IN INDIA

Like other parts of the world shifting cultivation occupies a distinct place in the tribal economy of India. It is found largely in the States of Andhra Pradesh, the hill districts of Assam,

Arunachal Pradesh, Meghalaya, Mizoram, Manipur, Nagaland, Orissa and Tripura. The system also exists in some parts of Bihar (now Jharkhand), former undivided Madhya Pradesh, Gujarat, Maharastra, Karnataka and Kerela. The percentage of S.T. population of different states depending on shifting cultivation is presented in Table-1 below:

Table 1
Percentage of ST Population of Different States Dependent on Shifting Cultivation in India

State	*Percentage of Total S.T. Population Dependent*
Assam	47.0
Manipur	73.5
Tripura	60.0
Orissa	66.6
Bihar	06.0
Madhya Pradesh	01.0
Maharastra	01.6
Karnataka	32.0
Andhra Pradesh	51.0
Kerela	39.0
Tamilnadu	02.6

Source: B.N. Pal in Vidyarthi and Sahay (ed), 1980 : 117.

The above data reveal that the States most affected by Shifting Cultivation are Manipur, Tripura, Orissa, Assam and Andhra Pradesh.

The Tenth Report of the Commissioner for Scheduled Castes and Scheduled Tribes, 1960-61 has enumerated the names of different tribes practising shifting cultivation in various states and union territories, their population, kinds of crops grown, names of districts where it is carried on and approximate area of land in which it is practised. The report mentions that 26 lakhs of tribal population belonging to 109 different tribal communities, living in interior hill districts of various states and union territories carry on shifting cultivation. It is practised on a large scale in the states and union territories of Andhra Pradesh, Assam, Bihar, Madhya Pradesh, Orissa, Manipur and Tripura and to a smaller extent in States of Gujrat, Kerala, Maharastra, Madras, Mysore, Uttar Pradesh and West Bengal.

In various regions of India, shifting (swidden) cultivation is known by different terms. In Assam, Meghalaya, Nagaland, Mizoram, Manipur and Arunachal Pradesh, Swidden cultivation is widely known as 'Jhum'. In some parts of Nagaland it is known as 'Teknaglue'. The Adis of Arunachal Pradesh call it 'Adi-arik', whereas among the Rang of Tripura, it is known as 'Hooknismong'. In Madhya Pradesh among the Baiga, it is known as 'Bewar' where as among the Ahujmaria Gonds of Bastar it is known as Penda and among the Korku of Melghat forest it is known as Dahya. In Tamilnadu, South Kanara of Karnatak, it is called 'Kumari' among the Sologa of Karnatak and in Andhra Pradesh it is known as Podu. In Orissa, the Kandoh, the Koya and other Dravidian speaking tribes refer to it as Podu; Gudia or Dangar Chasa, the Soura call it 'Buguda'. It is known as 'Angwal' among the Lanjia Soura. Some divisions of the Kandha of Orissa call it 'Rama' and the Kutia Kandha of Phulbani name it 'Berenga'. In northern Orissa, among the hill Bhuyans, it is known as Komanchas. It is known as Dahi (Firing), Kaman (saving) and Taila (upland) among the Juang of Keonjhar hills as Biringa or Kaman among the Paudi Bhuyan of Bonai sub-division and Bhuyan Pirh of Keonjhar district.

SHIFTING CULTIVATION IN ORISSA

Orissa is one of the major states of India, where shifting cultivation is widely practised among the Scheduled Tribes. The cultivation is extensively practised in the undivided Koraput, Phulbani, Ganjam, Kalahandi, Sambalpur, Sundargarh and Keonjhar districts. Like in other parts of the country, the greatest limitation of a proper study of shifting cultivation is regarding the availability of reliable data.

The credit of earliest survey made in Orissa on the subject goes to H.F. Mooney who wrote a report on shifting cultivation in Orissa (1951). Mooney who had worked as a Forest Adviser to ex-states in Orissa and subsequently as Conservator of Forests, Orissa had made a survey of shifting cultivation in Orissa in 1951. He estimated that about 12770 square miles or about one fifth of the total land surface in the State is affected by shifting cultivation and 9,35,700 tribal people were dependent on this method of cultivation for their livelihood. Area affected by Shifting Cultivation in different districts of the State is given below in Table–2 :

Table 2
Shifting Cultivation in Orissa

Name of the District	*Area affected in Square miles*	*Name of the Tribe*	*Population*
	NORTH ORISSA		
Keonjhar	460	Bhuyans	20,000
		Juangs	8,000
Sundargarh	300	Bhuyans	10,000
		Erenga Kolas	1,000
Dhenkanal	100	Bhuyans	2,000
Sambalpur	410	Bhuyans	7,000
		Kandha	8,000
Sub-Total (North Orissa)	1270		56,000
	SOUTH ORISSA		
Kalahandi	2000	Kandha	1,11,000
		Kutia	1,300
		Kamaras	1,600
		Bhunjias	5,400
Ganjam	4500	Kandh	2,06,800
		Saoras	95,600
		Jatapu	600
		Koraput	5000
		Kandh	1,76,500
		Saora	52,500
		Jatapu	15,200
		Paraja	1,45,700
		Gadba	34,300
		Koya	28,000
		Others	3,800
TOTAL	12,770		9,34,300

Source: Shifting Cultivation in Orissa, 1961, Department of Agriculture, Govt. of Orissa, Soil Conservation Organisation: P.2.

Mooney's estimate suffers from the limitation of 'eye estimation' and has been opened to doubt.

The Indian Council of Agricultural Research estimated in 1956 that around 10 lakhs people were dependent in shifting cultivation and 4 lakh acres of forest land affected by this primitive method of cultivation in Orissa. (I.C.A.R. 1958). The commissioner for Scheduled Castes and Scheduled Tribes in its Tenth Report for the year (1960-61) has estimated that 9,35,700 tribal people of Orissa were dependent upon this practice of cultivation and the total forest land affected was about 4 lakh acres. The D.F.O Forest Resource Survey, Orissa estimated in the year 1971-72 that 10,000,00 tribal people were dependent upon shifting cultivation for their livelihood and the total forest land affected was 34,59,400 acres.

The Tribal and Harijan Research Cum Training Institute (THRTI) of the Government of Orissa conducted a Bench Mark Survey in Tribal Development Agency areas of Gunpur–Rayagada of undivided Koraput district. Calculated on the basis of this survey the total land affected by the shifting cultivation was estimated at 46,500 acres and the total population engaged in Shifting Cultivation in Orissa was about 2,40,000 people. (Mahapatra and Devi, 1973: 13).

Table 3

District Wise Distribution of Land under Shifting Cultivation in the Sub-Plan Area of the State

Name of the District	*Area in Sq. Km.*	*Percentage to the Total Geographical Area of the District*
Koraput	10973.17	49.36%
Phulbani	5668.94	25.51%
Kalahandi	1076.82	4.84%
Ganjam	2354.00	10.59%
Sambalpur	12.89	0.06%
Keonjhar	1296.31	5.83%
Sundargarh	844.86	3.81%
TOTAL	22226.99	36.94%

Source: N. Patnaik, Tribes of Koraput (Their Pre-agricultural economic life), Adibasi, Vol.XXVIII No.1, March, 1988, P.6, T.H.R.T.I., Govt. of Orissa, Bhubaneswar.

Another estimate made by T.H.R.T.I. Orissa in 1975 shows the areas affected by shifting cultivation in various districts of Orissa and the tribal population which depends on this method of cultivation for their livelihood. According to this estimate the total area affected by this method of cultivation was 30977.91 Sq. Km. and the approximate size of the population of Orissa dependent was 6,92,000. (Patnaik, 1977: 18-20).

On the basis of Pondichery Institute data on shifting cultivation under different ITDAS has been made by the T.H.R.T.I., Bhubaneswar. The following table indicate district wise distribution of land under the shifting cultivation in the sub-plan areas of Orissa State.

Thus, it is found that there is a wide variation of the estimates made on the extent of the area affected under shifting cultivation and the number of people dependent on it. Instead of only academic exercise, if the estimates would have been made by Government of Orissa through the Tahasildars the estimate could be more reliable. The Revenue Inspectors and Amins could have given an accurate estimate in their respective area of operation. However, such an attempt is yet to be taken up.

SHIFTING CULTIVATION IN UNDIVIDED KORAPUT DISTRICT

In the undivided Koraput district Shifting Cultivation is widely practised by mainly eight tribes i.e. Bondo, Didayi, Koya, Gadba, Paraja, Kutia Kandhaa, Dongaria Kandha and Lanjia Saora. The Kandha, the Koyas and other Dravidian speaking tribes refer to it as *Podu, Gudia* or *Dongar Chas,* the Saora call it *Bagoda,* the Bondos name it *Livang* or *Kunda Chas* and the Koyas call it *Lankapadsenad.* It is called as *Saura Chasa* by the Kutia Kandhaas and *Haru* by Dongoria Kandhas. H.G. Turner, the then Special Assistant Agent, brought to notice the existence of *Podu* or *Dongar* cultivation in Koraput region as early as 1872. (Bell, 1945).

PODU CYCLE OR JHUM CYCLE

It has already been mentioned that a plot of Podu land after being cultivated for two or three years is left fallow for a number of years to regain its fertility. In the intervals a cultivator cultivates other such plots or hill slopes which he possesses. Afterwards the Podu cultivator returns to the original plot of land. The period during which the land is left fallow is known as 'Jhum Cycle'. "The fallowing period is mainly dependent upon the density of population of a particular area, availability of suitable hill slopes, composition of the soil and capacity of the same to recoup its fertility through natural processes". (Sachidananda and Pathak, 1983: 43). As population increases, the Jhum cycle become shorter and soil fertility is not fully restored, yields decline and further areas are brought under Jhumming, so that Jhum cycle is further shortened. (Gupta, and Sambrani, 1978: 2).

With the increase in the pressure of population, in recent years, the fallow period which was 8 to 12 years at Koraput region has reduced to 4 to 6 years in 1973 and 2 to 5 years in 1978 has further decreased to 2 to 3 years at present. (Sample Survey, 1996). The fallow period which was 22 years among the Juangs of Keonjhar has reduced to 10 to 12 years. (Banerjee, 1972: 113). In the sample blocks of Koraput region, it was found that the cultivation period and fallow period has become more or less equal, i.e. 2 to 3 years of cultivation period is followed by 2 to 3 years of fallow period. However, in case of Bondas inhabited in Bonda hills of Khairaput Block it was found that in some cases the fallow period may extend to 4 to 6 years, if the owner has a number of Hill slopes.

In 1996 the author conducted an investigation entitled, "A Study of Shifting Cultivation Practices in Koraput Region". With the help of the Research Assistant of the Council of Analytical Tribal Studies (COATS), Koraput. The main objectives of the study were:

(i) to analyse the causes of the shifting cultivation practices in Koraput region;

(ii) to assess the extent of the area and the number of people engaged in this practice;

(iii) to find out and analyse the effects of shifting cultivation practices;

(iv) to examine the various measures to eliminate/ control/regulate this method of cultivation; and

(v) to bring out a few suggestions to do way/regulate/ improve this method of cultivation.

METHODOLOGY ADOPTED IN THE STUDY

Out of the four districts in Koraput region shifting cultivation was practiced in three districts i.e. Koraput, Rayagada and Malkangiri. Two blocks from each of these districts were selected on the basis of simple random sampling method. Three villages from each of the blocks so selected were selected on the basis of simple random sampling method. To make the study more useful two additional villages were selected in the same process from Bissam Cuttack block of Rayagada district. Thus, 20 villages of seven blocks of the study area constituted the sample study. An effort was made to cover at least twenty households from each village so selected on the basis of systematic random sampling method. However, in some villages the respondents were not available. A total of 393 households were covered during the Survey.

CHARACTERISTICS OF SHIFTING CULTIVATION

There are certain essential features of shifting cultivation regarding the ownership right of land, selection of sites, performance of rites, crops grown, cropping pattern, etc. These are discussed below to understand the systems followed in different regions of Orissa.

Ownership of Land

In most of the hill areas of northern Orissa, land is owned by the community as a whole. According to customary rights of the Juangs and Paung Bhuiyans of Keonjar district the land under shifting cultivation of a village in the communal property owned by all the villagers in common. The land is allotted by the headman and the priest to each individual family of the village according to necessity by mutual consent. The ownership of land after allotment is transferred to the head of the household for a period of two to three years till he cultivates it actively. But as soon as it is left to rest it becomes the property of the community.

In contrast to this usual practice the communal ownership of land under shifting cultivation is completely absent in Southern Orissa. The Bondas, Saoras, Kandhas, Koyas and other tribes recognise private ownership of their respective hill clearings. Each household owns a number of sites on the hill sides which may be situated even outside the village boundary. The Bondas even sell their clearings to one another and mortgage them when they are in need. (Elwin, 1950). However, there is no legal title to such lands in any part of Orissa. The ownership of land is accepted only by the common usage and practice.

As right to land is safeguarded only by public opinion and there is no individual record of right, farmers do not take any interest for any improvement of their shifting land. Besides, due to lack of individual record of right over the cultivable land, tribals are unable to get the facilities of individual credit for investment in agriculture against land as security.

Selection of Sites and Primitive Method of Cultivation

Selection of sites for shifting cultivation is made on a number of considerations i.e. fallow period, growth of wild plants to be slashed, nearness to village, nature of slope, supernatural deviations, etc.

The selection of sites and methods of cultivation influences the extent of soil erosion and productivity. "The tribes of Southern Orissa cut the trees high above the ground leaving the stools of about 2 feet in height where as those of northern Orissa cut the trees flush with the ground." (Patnaik, 1977: 2).

In northern Orissa shifting cultivation is carried out both on hill slopes and on hill tops in contrast to Southern Orissa where it is practised mostly on hill slopes. The soil erosion is more in Southern Orissa in spite of the stumps left on the ground as this cultivation is mostly followed on the hill slopes.

Most of the tribal communities work with the soil in the swiddens by means of hoe. The tribes of northern Orissa sow the seeds during the monsoon. But in Southern Orissa the tribes sow the seeds before the monsoon. The Dongoria Kandha sow the seeds of Ragi, Suan, Arka, Ganthia mixed together during April and May all over the dongars. Pulses, oil seeds and bean are sown by Koyas in their Podu lands locally known as 'Elka'. The Bondas sow millets in their Swidden during the month of May.

The women are forbidden to take part in the Jungle clearing among the Juangs and the Bhujans where as there is no such taboo associated with this work among Saora, Dongaria Kandha and other tribal communities of Southern Orissa. The women toil hard from dawn to dusk. They cut the shrubs with the males, lit fire, level the ash and till the plots with the hoe, broadcast the seeds, weed the grasses and finally harvest the crops. Winnowing, threshing and storing are also done by both men and women. (Aprajita, 1994: 126).

Crops Grown in Swidden Cultivation

Shifting Cultivation has very little scope for specialisation as diverse crops are sown in a single plot of land. Mixed crops of hilly Paddy, Minor Millets, Pulses, Oil Seeds are grown in this type of cultivation and they are harvested in succession. Unlike the Saoras and Dongia Kandha who have their threshing floors and harvests each crop once, the Bondas reap a small quantity every day, just enough for the days' food threshing it with their feet on Verandah, husking, cleaning, cooking and eating immediately. (Elwin, 1950). Reaping in small quantity of crop every day and absence of threshing floors indicate that the primitive tribes like Bonda do not have the power to sustain stocks of the produce. This indicates a very primitive level of economic performance and very low standard of living.

Cropping Pattern

It has been already stated earlier that shifting cultivation is resorted to on a particular land for a period of two to three years. In the 2nd and 3rd year felling of threes is not required to be carried out. Hence, pressure of work is much less in the subsequent years. Generally, crops grown in the 2nd and 3rd year are of a different variety from those of the previous years.

The cropping pattern changes due to the declining fertility in the successive years.

Among the Bondas the first year of Swidden Cultivation is called Susang Biri and in this cultivation millet is mainly produced with side crops of pulse varieties like Widar, Jhudunga and Musri. Apart from this, oil seeds like niger is also grown as another main crop.

The second year of cultivation is called Susang Nurulu Biri. During this period niger is mainly produced with other pulse varieties crops called 'Kankadakhi', black gram and the like. The third year of cultivation is called Budi Biri means old Biri. During this year the land becomes infertile and hence the Bondas do not like to cultivate the most important cereals produced in the 1st year of shifting cultivation.

Among the 'Koyas' the 1st year of Swidden cultivation is called *Puna Elka*. In this land Ragi, Millet, Bean, etc. are mainly produced. After the harvest is reaped, the *Puna Elka* or the new patch of Jungle becomes *Pantia Elka* or old one.

Watching the Crop

Crop raising in shifting cultivation is a hard task. Besides the occasional pests and diseases, there is a fear of birds, rats and wild animals destroying the crop both during the day and night. Parrots, wild cocks, rats, wild bears, peacocks, rabbits, wild cats, monkeys, etc. are the enemies of crops. In order to save the crop from these enemies, the Swidden Cultivators in many areas, construct watch houses either on the ground or on high platforms. These temporary watch huts are mostly constructed out of the natural resources available in the near by forests and take generally two to three days of labour of a family.

The Koyas construct their watch hut known as 'Ketul' and blow 'Ahkum' (Horn made bugles) as well as beat drums to drive away the animals from the crop fields. The Dongaria Kandha, Kandhas and Kutia Kandhas of Chandrapur, Bissam Cuttack, Kalyansingpur and Narayanpatna blocks construct watch huts in their shifting land both on the ground as well as on high platforms and watch the crops for a period of two to three months.

Performance of Rites

Performance of rites at the time of selecting the shifting land, before clearing, before sowing and during harvesting is a universal phenomenon among the tribals. The village priest of Bondos ceremonially initiates the task of cutting by performing "Sume Gelirack" in March. During the 'giag-gige" ceremonies in April, there is a little rite or the collection and reburning of half consumed stumps of trees and branches. (Elwin, 1950). However, now-a-days this is not a heavy work as it is difficult to see on old forest in Bondo Hills.

Among the Dongaria Kandha sowing of seeds commences after performing the Bihan Puja. An auspicious date is fixed and all the villagers participate in this ritual which is communal in nature. The priest, Jani, the Shamans and Bejuni mix together all the seeds to be sown and consecrate these before earth Goddess Dharani Penu. The ritual incantations continue all through the night. Early next morning the Jani distributes the seeds to all the villagers.

Similar elaborate rites are performed by all the tribes with little variations.

Weeding

Weeding is one of the most strenuous and labour consuming method of shifting cultivation. It is essential in shifting cultivation as without it the farmers cannot harvest a good crop. Weeding is done solely by human labour. Among the Bondas weeding begins in the months of June and takes a great deal of women labour through out the rains. Among the Kandhas weeding takes place in the month of June and July and the work is done both by men and women. However, weeding is never done by the Koyas.

Harvesting

Before harvesting small families move to their respective shifting cultivation sites where they camp till their harvesting is over. This sort of proximate living helps them to collect all the produces of their cultivation and toil to the fullest extent.

Different crops are harvested at different times and this operation continues from October to April.

EXTENT OF SHIFTING CULTIVATION AND TRIBES ENGAGED IN THIS PRACTICE

The various estimates made on the acreage covered and people engaged in shifting cultivation in respect of Koraput region is presented below in Table-4.

It has already been pointed out earlier that Mooney's findings are the starting point of the estimation and is pioneering effort on the issue. His estimation is an eye estimation and therefore suffers from limitation. His estimate that 32 lakh acres or 5000 sq. miles are affected under shifting cultivation is highly exaggerated in view of the fact that the total forest area in Koraput district was only 4100 sq. miles as per 1951 Census.

The estimate made by DFO, Forest Resource Surveys is not supported by Surveys and hence cannot be accepted as correct. However, the estimate made by the THRTI has taken into account only those blocks where the practice of shifting cultivation is intensively followed and is based upon a number of studies conducted by the institute at different points of time. However, it has been admitted by the institute that as the estimated area also includes other types of cultivation akin to shifting cultivation, the area of shifting cultivation would be much less. The estimate of THRTI in 1988 was a rough estimate made on the basis of vegetation maps of India prepared by the Institute of Francis, Pondichery. The coverage of shifting cultivation given here includes not only the Swidden Plots but also immediate adjacent areas which are seriously affected by the shifting cultivation.

The estimate made by the author in 1966 is based on a sample survey of 20 villages of seven blocks (i.e. Khairaput, Podia, Chandrapur, Bissam Cuttack, Kalyansingpur, Narayanpatna and Kundra) and on the basis of the studies made by others in the region.

Table 4

Estimates Made on the Acreage Covered and People Engaged in Shifting Cultivation in Koraput Region

Year of Estimate	*Source of Estimation*	*No. of Tribal Communities practising Shifting Cultivation*	*No. of the Tribals Depending and their Percentage to the Total Tribal Population*	*Total Area Affected in Acres and their Percentage to the Total Forest Area*
1951	FH Mooney	08	4,56000 (87.21%)	3200000 (100%)
1971-72	DFO Forest Resource Surveys, Orissa		500000 (43.43%)	1482600 (36.89%)
1977	THRTI, Orissa	08	330000 (28.66%)	2848701 (77.89%)
1988	THRTI, Orissa		924923 (67.44%)	2711654 (33.35%)
1996	P.C. Mohapatro, COATS, Koraput	09	492360 (30.09)	1122580 (60.85)

Sources: 1. Govt. of Orissa, Agriculture Department (Soil Conservation Organisation) : Shifting Cultivation in Orissa, OGP, 1961. 2. N.C.A.E.R. : Perspective Plan of Economic Development of Orissa (1973-74 to 1983-84), OGP, 1977, P.155. 3.N. Patnaik : Shifting Cultivation in Orissa, Adibasi, Vol.XVI, No.4, January, 1977, OGP, 1978, P.18-19. 4. N. Patnaik: Tribes of Koraput District (Their Pre agricultural economic life), Adibasi, Vol.XXVIII- No.1, March, 1988. 5. P.C. Mohapatro : A Study of Shifting Cultivation Practices in Koraput Region, 1999 (Memiographed).

CAUSES OF SHIFTING CULTIVATION

In spite of the primitive character of shifting cultivation, the system has continued till today and is not going to die down in the near future. Hence, it is necessary to find out the causes which sustain it for such a long period.

Historical Background

Shifting cultivation wherever it exists has a historical background. History stands as a witness that in many parts of the world the aboriginals were pushed to inaccessible forest and mountainous areas by immigrants who were superior in arms and strategy. As all good lands were grabbed by the plains, they are at last practically banished to the rugged and the mountainous regions where the hill slopes are the only space left for them to grow their crops for their livelihood. The tribals felt more secure in the uplands as the exploiters cannot intrude such inconvenient pieces of land on the hill slopes.

Socio Cultural Stage

Dr. Verrier Elwin is of the opinion that, shifting cultivation is a socio cultural stage in the progress of human behaviour and he cites the instance of Gonds of Madhya Pradesh who are now keen settled cultivators though sometimes back they were also resorting to shifting cultivation.

Isolation

The primitive tribes generally inhabiting on the hill slopes find the available land on the slopes in close proximity to them for exploitation. Pushed to inaccessible secluded and isolated areas devoid of new ideas, new schemes and general awakening for ages to come, they suffer from the alternative means of gainful employment that may be available to them. Their life style of primitive isolation is in consonance with the primitive style of cultivation like shifting cultivation.

Socio-Cultural Imperatives[1]

Among certain tribes shifting cultivation has a deep religious significance. Their economic and religious life is interwoven to such an extent with this practice that it is difficult to isolate the economic factors for separate treatment. It has been rightly pointed out that "shifting cultivation has a special significance in the ethos of concerned tribal society and the social relationship, cultural values and mythical beliefs are directly linked with it. Tribal values orientation is one of the basic causes underlying the continuance of shifting cultivation among most of the tribes of hill regions". (Sachidanand, 1989: 63).

"For the Koyas Podu cultivation is not a mere set of agricultural practices, it contains a whole nexus of Koya religious beliefs, attitudes, self image and tribal identity". (Sachidanand, ibid. 64; also see Tyler, 1974: 23). A Koya still believes that those who still practice Podu Cultivation are participating in some thing that is an essential component of Koya life (ibid.). The Koya, the Bonda, the Kandha, the Dongoria Kandha and other tribes continue to believe that earth-mother is inhabited by unseen forces whose powers influence man's destiny. At various stages of shifting cultivation we find the invitation through various rites and rituals. These activities are closely integrated with the tribal belief and socio cultural life. (also see Mahapatra and Devi, 1973). This is one of the main reasons of continuation of this form of cultivation inspite of the efforts made to wean away the tribals from the practice of shifting cultivation.

Scarcity of Plain land

The scarcity of lands in the plains in relation to demand and their high prices put them beyond the tribals' reach. It is also not easy for them to invest large funds on bullocks, fertilisers, labour charges and other agricultural instruments required for settled cultivation. On the other hand with the ashes of natural vegetation as a manure and their own hard labour, they need to spend only a little for seeds in the system implements like hoe, digging stick and axe all of which can be manufactured by cultivators themselves excepting the iron part which are provided to them by the local black smiths in exchange of small amount of their produce.

Provides Work to all the Members of a Family

Shifting cultivation provides work to all members of a tribal family. Women take active part in cleaning Podu land, breaking clod of earth, hoeing, dibbling weeding and reaping. The children right from a tender age help their parents on all these activities. Plough cultivation in wet or dry lands involves clear division of labour which does not fit in with the traditional style of life and work of these people.

Mixed Cropping

The tribals usually follow mixed cropping on Podu lands for meeting with their different food requirement. This offers many advantages. Mixed cropping minimise the risk of complete crop failure due to vagaries of monsoon, insect and pest attacks, which are common in a primitive environment. The age old practice utilises the soil moisture in different layers of the soil profile in divergent root system of different crops and help recouping soil fertility by plantation of leguminous crops. Thus the uplands where the practice is generally confined is less prone to draught then the lower plain lands.

In this system cultivators can produce their family requirement of food, cereals, vegetables, oil seeds, pulses and few other cash crops. Thus the system is in consonance with the primitive concept of tribal self sufficiency to which they have traditional preferences. This system of cultivation has the privilege of getting varieties of crops necessary for a tribal from a single cultivation. The seeds are sown in such a manner that harvesting does not create any problem for a Swidden as different crops become ready for reaping at different points of time.

Provision of Balanced Diet

These crops together provide the tribal with a more balanced diet than those from the low land or terraced fields of permanent cultivation which yield usually only one crop. The diet is richly supplemented by roots, tubers, fish, mutton, green leaves, etc. obtained from the forest. The small amount of cash needed is secured by growing some cash crops like turmeric, ginger, oil seeds, pulses, and the like.

The Only Means of Survival for Landless Tribals

Pondu cultivation is the only means of survival for those tribals who do not possess any low lands or terraced plots of land either because of land alienation or because of pressure of population on limited plain lands. Thus Swidden cultivation has been a safety valve against pauperisation and destitution. (Mahpatara, 1990). This aspect of swidden cultivation is more true in mining and industrialisation areas where a large number of tribals are dispossessed of their lands and village which were inherited by them from their forefathers.

Thus, we may sum up that socio-cultural imperatives are responsible for tribals sticking to shifting cultivation till to day. But the other factors discussed are equally responsible to arrest the process of change from shifting cultivation to settled one" The process of change has been effectively arrested by various types of exploitation of tribals, alienation of land, lack of capital, scarcity of suitable land, lack, of knowledge of improved method of agriculture, and absence of alternative employment opportunities. The advantages of mixed cropping system which minimises the risk of complete crop failure and the attraction of getting a balanced diet are also a few important causes of continuation of this primitive practice.

Effects of Shifting Cultivation

The destruction of tropical rain forests has become a serious threat to the global environment as well as to the local communities concerned. FAO had already warned in 1957 (op.cit) that "shifting cultivation in the humid tropical countries is the greatest obstacle not only to the immediate increase of agricultural production, but also to the conservation of the production potential of the future, in the form of soils and forests". To this, the sustainability of traditional shifting cultivation has been emphasized based on many case studies (e.g. Nye & Greenland, 1960; Fukui, 1995) in which factors other than shifting cultivation, such as commercial logging or cash crop production were assumed to be the major causes of forest destruction.

As a matter of fact, economic and social impacts of shifting cultivation are viewed differently by different groups. As shifting cultivation damages forest, it has always been a bugbear to Forest Department. According to this practice "is ruinous and wasteful, dries up the spring in the hills, causes soil erosion: destroys valuable forests' affects rainfall and deprives the people the benefit of forest and forest produce'. (Dhebar Commission, 1961). It has also been held that shifting cultivation invariably upsets the accumulated natural resources by removing more from it than that it can produce. (Tripathy, 1952). Again this type of cultivation has been held to constitute a major limitation for the spread of permanent tree crops. (Hodder, 1973). Time and again these evil effects have been pointed out by various committees and commissions.

The evil effects of shifting cultivation have been admirably summed up by Mr Harries, Agency Commissions of Madras in 1918 as follows:

(i) It causes springs below the hills to dry up.

(ii) Causes the soil below the podu land to be washed away.

(iii) Ruins valuable timber for the sake of much less valuable crops of gain.

(iv) Causes the hot weather supply in these rivers to diminish and this reduces the water available for second crop cultivation.

(v) Causes very heavy floods in the rivers and endangers life and property.

(vi) It brings down heavy silt in to tanks and makes them useless on to fields and destroys crops.

Thus, the main abuses of shifting cultivation are deforestation, soil erosion diminished rainfall, silting up of the rivers, channel, stream bed and reservoirs and deterioration of the climate of a region, it is necessary to examine the effects in detail.

"Destruction of forest leads to increasing aridity, the desiccation of the soil and the impoverishment of the mankind. Gaboon in central Africa is becoming the graveyard of the dying races of that country because of the destruction of forest for cultivation purposes".(Tripathy, op cit. 17).

Koraput region had the reputation of no serious failures of rains and no experience of famine conditions. But the effects of the rapid deforestation have begun getting this felt gradually. There are many instances to show that perennial streams that were flowing few years back are extinct to day. River, channels, stream beds and reservoirs are getting silted up. It has been observed by many in the Soil Conservation Department of Orissa that the longevity of Machkund Hydro-Electricity project will be reduced because of the rate of silting now.

Others apprehend that uncontrolled felling of trees will not only exhaust the forest wealth of the region, but also produce adverse effects on rainfall, the flow of the rivers and fertility of the soil. It has been the recent experience in the Koraput region that deforestation has reduced rainfall in the region and has caused misery and suffering to the entire population. Felling of the trees in the river banks will lead to change the course of rivers and streams which may threaten the neighbouring area with floods.

The system has been criticised even from the point of view low yields. Since the soil on slopes and hill tops is of very poor quality and ploughing is usually not done under podu cultivation, only a poor harvest is possible on such tract. Moreover, ashes and sometime even seeds are washed down the hills by heavy rains. The holding off of rains for a few weeks after the seed was sown or when the ear was forming, meant the ruin of the crops and then the owner was usually compelled to subsist entirely on wild fruits, roots and tubers. (Nag, 1958, Quoted from E.P.Stebbing).

Shifting cultivation, it is alleged makes man lazy, nomadic and averse to cultural progress. A few weeks of hard labour in this system of cultivation is followed by an interval of idleness broken only by aimless wandering. A few administrators have condemned this practice as an obstacle to aboriginal social progress.

It is also argued that this primitive system of cultivation is not in keeping with the modern economic order for it is not a system which any one would adopt if he intended the product of his land to compete in the market of the world. (Report of the Partially Excluded Areas Enquiry Committee, Orissa, 1940).

DEFENCE OF THE SYSTEM

On the other hand it has been pointed out by administrators, forest and agricultural experts and anthropologists that shifting cultivation is not very harmful to the forest and land. As it is believed to be it could be improved and its evil effects could be minimised by introducing leguminous creepers and nitrogen fixing plants besides planting fruit bearing trees on the exhausted *podu* patches and by restricting *podu* in steep slopes. All aspects of the vehement criticism of shifting cultivation have been duly answered.

Bampfylde Fuller Commissioner for Settlement and Agriculture (1893-1901) had opined that the timber cut was not of great value and was situated in such remote and difficult localities that it would never pay to transport it. The Royal Commission on Indian Agriculture Opined 'we see no objection to the controlled system of shifting cultivation (as in Bengal) under which the necessary labour for replanting clear felled is obtained by allowing certain fraction of the forest area to be replaced in rotation under temporary cultivation'. (Quoted in Nag, 1958).

In 1953 Sri M.D. Chaturvedi who was then Inspector General of Forest in the Government of India made an investigation of the forestry problems in Assam and came to the conclusion that the "Notion widely held that shifting cultivation is responsible in the main for large scale soil erosion needs to be effectively dispelled. The correct approach to the problem of shifting cultivation lies in accepting it not as a necessary evil, but recognising it as a way of life, not condemning it as a evil practice, but regarding it as an agricultural practice evolved as a reflex to the physiographical character of the hand for to long jumping has been condemned out of hand as a curse to be ashamed of a vandalism to decried. This attitude engenders an inferiority complex and an unhealthy atmosphere for the launching of any development scheme seeking to improve the current practice". (Elwin Committee, 1960: 48).

Similarly, Sri M.S. Sivaraman, Adivisor to programme Administration of the Planning Commission observed in 1957 that, "it is a mistake to assume that shifting cultivation in itself is unscientific land use. Actually it is a practical approach to certain inherent difficulties in preparing a proper seed-bed in steep slopes where any disturbance of the surface by hoeing or ploughing will result in washing away of the fertile top soil. The tribal people therefore take care not to plough or disturb the soil before sowing. The destruction of weeds and improvement of tilth necessary for a proper seed bed are achieved with the help of fire... In most of the interior areas, where communication is not developed and not sufficient land suitable for terracing is available, Jhuming alone can be done for the present and as such every effort should be made to improve the fertility of the jhumed land". (Dhebar Commission Report, 1961, Volume-I, p.146). This situation is still applicable in some of the areas of Koraput region dominated.

Mr. S.H. Howard, another former Inspector General of Forests suggested that instead of discouraging this method of cultivation, a trial should be given by regulating it, which means that if a longer period of rest is given between the fellings, there is a little danger of soil erosion (Report of the Second Conference for Tribes and Tribal (Scheduled) Areas, Nov. 1953). Mr. J.P. Mills with his long experience in the tribal areas of Assam believed that, wisely regulated, the method could probably be carried on indefinitely without causing excessive deterioration. (Dhebar Commission Report, op.cit).

According to Spencer (1966), soil studies clearly indicate that shifting cultivation does not in itself ruin the soils and produce destructive erosions. In fact many shifting cultivators develop a fine sense of regional and qualitative variations in the soils they cultivate.

In recent years it has been more and more acknowledged that shifting cultivation is in fact very much suited to the tropical forest ecology. Eric Eckholm of the World Watch Institute writes that "few of the men and women who practise it have been educated in primary schools, let alone universities. Yet they usually carry in their heads an extraordinary fund of scientifically sound knowledge about plant species and soil qualities. (Eckholm, 1976 quoted by Evelyne Hong, 1994: 525-535).

THE PRACTICAL ASPECT

We have seen two opposite views on shifting cultivation. On the one hand this system of farming has been accused of being ecologically destructive and is blamed for removing the tropical forest. On the other, this practice has been acclaimed as a highly suitable and viable form of agriculture in the tropics where soils are poor.

The tribals of the region argue that the system fits in to their forest life very well. They have so much harmonised their cultivation with forest activities that one supplements the other.

Among these two extreme views the latter seems to be more applicable in Koraput region. It has been observed that the plots selected for shifting cultivation do not contain valuable trees. Tribals generally selected plots of forest growth which are less laborious to clean. If care is taken to ensure cultivation in moderate slopes, soil erosion can be reduced to a great extent. The spread of leguminous crops which is already cultivated by the tribals in the region will help to increase production in the shifting land. Hence, improvement in the methods of shifting cultivation deserves more attention than its complete eradication, at present level of tribal development[2]. The practical way of looking at the problem is that about 17.94% of the tribal population of Koraput region depend up on shifting cultivation and they cannot be deprived of their swidden land until some viable alternative means of livelihood are provided to them. The total replacement of the system is neither feasible nor desirable as it is a mixed problem connected not only with the availability of plain lands and provision of alternative means of livelihood but also with the customs, traditions and beliefs of the tribals along with the existing level of economic operation. Hence regulation, control and improvement of shifting cultivation is a practical way of looking at the problem. (Mohapatro, 1987: 144-145). However, simultaneous efforts should be made to try for other workable alternatives. The central question is not whether shifting cultivation is desirable or undesirable but how to encourage in any specific case a more rapid change over from shifting field to permanent field cultivation that brought about through the stimulus of an increasing density of population.

Thus, it is not correct to attribute shifting cultivation to the irrationality, stupidity and ignorance of the tribals. The practice is rooted in the objective situation in which tribals have been placed by the operative institutional set up and production relationship. Therefore, without changing the objective relations, it is futile to wean away the tribals from the shifting cultivation. However, the relevance of some of the measures adopted and remedial ways suggested deserve close scrutiny and analysis.

At present the shifting cycle in Koraput region had reduced to 2 to 3 years in Primitive Tribe dominated areas like Bonda Hills, Didayi Hills and hill areas of Dongaria Kandha and Lanjia Soura. In other areas mostly there is no shifting cycle. Every year the cultivation is practised which is quite uneconomic for the shifting cultivators.

The best alternative available in the district is to allow the shifting cultivators to cultivate the practice in lands lying up to 30^0 slope and give Record of Right to them for these lands. Horticultural crops like mango, guava, mahua, tamarind along with economic species like Neem and Karanj can be planted under the National Horticultural Mission being implemented in the area. Ownership right through supply of Record of Rights can give them a confidence that the property is their own.

This will help the shifting cultivators to cultivate annual crops in the lands up to 30^0 slope and after a period of 4 to 5 years the cultivators can receive the benefit from horticultural crops.

The perception of the primitive tribes in Koraput region is that the crops grown under shifting cultivation is nutritious and fits in well with their socio, cultural life. Even the rich tribal cultivators grow pulses, vegetables and oil seeds in shifting land. The tribals of the region who are closer to the main stream believe that they are following the practice due to non-availability of alternative means of livelihood. The food security measures adopted by the Government till the end of the 10th Plan did not ensure them a sustainable means of livelihood.

ENDNOTES

1. Based on Sachinanda, 1989: 63-75.
2. See Mahapatra, 1994 for an understanding of the concept of tribal development.

REFERENCES

Aparajita, Upali (1994), *Cultural Development, Dongrias of Niyamgiri.* New Delhi: Inter-India Publications, pp.126-130.

Banerjee, N.K. (1972), "An Appraisal of Shifting Cultivation in India". In M.L. Patel (Ed.), *Agro-Economic Problems of Tribal India.* Bhopal: Progress Publishers, pp.105-116.

Behuria, N.C. (1966), Final Report on Major Settlement Operations of Koraput District, 1938-64, Government of Orissa, pp. 21-24.

Bell, R.C.S. (1945), Orissa District Gazetteers, Koraput. Cuttack: Orissa Govt. Press, pp.104-106.

Bose, Saradendu (1972), "Problem of Shifting Cultivation in India" In M.L. Patel (Ed.), *Agro-economic problems of Tribal India.* Bhopal: Progress Publishers, pp. 117-122.

Bose, Saradendu (1967), "Carrying Capacity of Land Under Shifting Cultivation", *Asiatic Society Monograph series,* Vol.XII, Calcutta, pp.131-135.

Commissioner for Scheduled Castes and Scheduled Tribes (1957), Report of the Commissioner for Scheduled Castes and Scheduled Tribes for 1956-57, (Sixth Report), Govt. of India, Delhi, pp-49-51.

Commissioner for Scheduled Castes and Scheduled Tribes. 1960. Report of the Commissioner for Scheduled Castes and Scheduled Tribes for 1959-60, (Ninth Report), Govt. of India, Delhi, pp-59-60.

Commissioner for Scheduled Castes and Scheduled Tribes (1962), Report of the Commissioner for Scheduled castes and Scheduled Tribes for 1960-61,(Tenth Report), Govt. of India, New Delhi, Part-II, pp-118-119

Commissioner for Scheduled Castes and Scheduled Tribes (1976), Report of the Commissioner for Scheduled Castes and Scheduled Tribes for 1973-74, (Twenty Second Report), Govt. of India, Delhi, pp-237

Commissioner for Scheduled Castes and Scheduled Tribes (1979), Report of the Commissioner for Scheduled Castes and Scheduled Tribes for 1977-78, (Twenty Fifth Report), Govt. of India, Delhi, pp-97.

Conklin, H.C. (1961), "Study of Shifting Cultivation". *Current Antropology*, Chicago,Vol.II No.1.

Devi, Kiranbala (1964), "Kandh", *Adibasi*, Vol. No.3. Orissa: Tribal Research Bureau, pp-69-74.

Dhebar, U.N. (1961), Report of Scheduled Areas and Scheduled Tribes Commission, Vol-I, Govt. of India, New Delhi, pp.144-149.

Elwin, V. (1960), Report of the Committee on Special Multipurpose Tribal Blocks, New-Delhi: Govt. of India, pp. 48-56.

Elwin, V. (1955), *The Religion of an Indian Tribe*. Bombay: Oxford University Press.

Elwin V. (1950), *Bondo Highlander*. London: Oxford University Press.

Hong, Evelyne (1994), "Swidden as a Rational Agricultural System". Return to the good earth, Damaging effects of Modern Agriculture and the case for ecological farming, A third world Network Dosier, Malasia, pp. 525-535.

F.A.O. (1965), African Survey.

F.A.O Staff. (1957), 'Shifting Cultivation'. *Unasylva*, 11(1): p.9–11, Rome.

Fukui, K. (1995), "Permanence of the Nature-Ecological Succession and Culturation of Field fire in Shifting Cultivation and Pastoralism". In M. Kakeya(ed.), *Socialization of the Environment.*(Living on the Earth 2) Tokyo: Yuzankaku.

Govt. of Orissa (1961), *Shifting Cultivation of Orissa*. Bhubaneswar: Soil Conservation Organisation, p.2.

Gupta, Trinath and Shreekant Sambarni (1978), "Control of Shifting Cultivation–the need for a systematic approach and Systematic appraisal", *IJAE*, Vol. XXXIII, October-December, No.4. Hodder, B.W.1973. Economic Development in the Tropic, London: Methuen and Co.Ltd, pp. 44-45.

Kaith, D.C. (1958), "Shifting Cultivation Practices in India", *Review Series No. 24*.New Delhi: I.C.A.R.

Mishra, B & P.C.Mohaptro (1980), "Evaluation Report of Malkangiri I.T.D.P, Koraput District Orissa, Bhubaneswar: Utkal University, pp.17-26.

Mahapatra, K & Kiranbala Devi (1973), "Shifting Cultivation in Orissa". *Adibasi*, Vol.XIV- 1972-73, No.4. Bhubaneswar: THRTI, pp.11-24.

Mahapatra, L.K. (1953), "Shifting Cultivation in Orissa". Report of the Second Conference for Tribes and Tribal Scheduled Areas, Lohardaga, pp. 265-277.

Mahapatra, L.K. (1990), *Swidden Cultivation and Its Traditional Alternatives in Orissa*, Bhubaneswar: Nabakrushna Choudhury Centre for Development Studies.

Mahapatra, L.K. (1994), *Tribal Development in India: Myth and Reality*. New Delhi :Vikas Pub. House.

Mohaptro, P.C. (1987), "Shifting Cultivation". In P.C. Mohapatro *Economic Development of Tribal India*. New-Delhi: Ashish Publishing House. pp. 63-76.

Mahaptra, P.K. (1964), "A Short Note on Shifting Cultivation of Koya". *Adibasi*, No. 1, 1963-64, pp.21-26.

Nag, D.S. (1958), Tribal Economy- An Economic Study of the Baiga. New Delhi: Bharatiya Adim ati Sevak Sangh.

NCAER (1977), Perspective Plan of Economic Development of Orissa, 1973-74 to 1983-84, pp.155 and 193.

Nye, P. H. and D. J. Greenland (1960), *The Soil under Shifting Cultivation*. Bucks: Commonwealth Agricultural Bureaux, Farnham Royal.

Pal, B.N. (1980), "Some Economic Aspects of Tribal Agriculture". In L.P. Vidyarthi and B.N. Sahay (Eds.) *Applied Anthropology and Development in India*. New Delhi: National Publishing House.

Patnaik, N. (1977), "Shifting Cultivation in Orissa". *Adibasi*, Vol. XVI, No.4, January, Bhubaneswar: THRTI, Govt. of Orissa, pp.1-21.

Patnaik, N. (1988), "Tribes of Koraput District (Their Pre-agricultural Economic life)". *Adibasi*, Vol.XXVIII, No.1, March. Bhubaneswar: THRTI, pp.1-18.

Roy Burman, B.K & P.S. Sharma (1970), "Tribal Agriculture in India". *Indian Journal of Agricultural Economics*, Vol 25, No. 3, pp.140-148.

Sachinanda (1989), *Shifting Cultivation in India*. New Delhi: Concept.

Saha, Niranjan (1970), *Carrying Capacity of Shifting Cultivation: A Study of Assam Hills*. Jorhat: Agro-Economic Research Centre.

Sachidananda & K.N.Pathak (1983), "Swidden Cultivation in India". *Swidden Cultivaion in Asia*, Vol.II, Bankok: UNESCO Regional office for Education in Asia and the Pacific, pp.3-107.

Samal, Jagabandhu (1979), Problems of Tribal Agriculture in India. *Unpublished M.Phil dissertation* submitted to GIPE. p.79.

Senapati, N. & N.K.Sahu (1966), Orissa District Gazetteers, Koraput. Cuttack: Orissa Govt. Press, p.155.

Spencer, J.E. (1966), *Shifting Cultivation in Southeastern Asia*. Berkeley: University of California Press.

Tripathy, B. (1973), A Portrait of Population, Orissa, Census of India, 1971, Orissa Govt. Press.

Tripathy, D.P. (1952), Shifting Cultivation in Orissa-Its Cause, Effect and Remedy. Cuttack: Orissa Govt. Press, p.17.

Tyler, Stepehn A. (1974), "Fileds are for Planting: Swidden Agriculture Among the Koyas of South India". *Journal of the India Anthropological Society*, Calcutta. Vol IX (1).

7

"WE HAVE LITTLE HOPE TO SURVIVE IN FUTURE" DILEMMA OF THE BHOXA- A HIMALAYAN PRIMITIVE TRIBE IN GLOBALIZING INDIA[1]

Bina Saklani

THE TRIBAL PEOPLE AND GLOBALIZATION

Process of globalization is an inescapable reality of modern world. Its impact on the poor, marginalized and indigenous communities is a serious subject of study for the anthropological research .There is a need to investigate the nature and direction of change in those communities which seem to be incapable of handling the challenges of globalization which is wiping out the separate identities of indigenous communities and creating a homogenized socio–economic order. Tribals are dependent upon natural resources and their local environment. They belong to sustainable economies which have been their habitat. They have experience of past generations to adapt to natural resource base for subsistence. It is part of anthropological findings that tribal cultures have unique systems of concepts evolved from past experiences and its surrounding environment. (Claude Levi-Straus, referred in

Jha, 1962:190). Their sense of intellectual engagement and abstract reasoning, understanding of nature and its intricacies is different from but in no way 'inferior to that evolved in cultivated systematic thoughts.' The tribal society maintains isolation from outside world, in order to protect their cultural identity and value system. (Misra, 2009:23). But market forces are able to penetrate this shield.

In a modern industrial era, the modes of production associated with tribal communities are systematically removed, neglected and decaying under the impact of modern market based society. Moreover, their identity and culture as a different category of human existence is in peril. Sustainability for tribal communities is synonymous with the survival and inescapable reality of perilous existence. (Saklani, 2009). Peasant and tribes are affected by the poverty which is largely out come of the decay of their natural resource base. It is under threat more due to the demands of market which is consuming natural resources beyond its carrying capacity and consumes resources more then subsistence requirements of tribal economies. Traditional societies have subsisted for centuries on non- monetary exchanges in a sustainable manner (Seabrook, 2005:45-46) which is becoming untenable in a monetized economy.

MARKET, ECOLOGY AND TRIBAL COMMUNITIES

Tribal people find themselves vulnerable to global market forces which are beyond their understanding. In terms of human resource development, they have low capacity to handle its challenges. 'These are the people who resist melting into the global market economy and their presence is taken by modern economies as unprogressive and backward, as they are taken to be a hindrance in the speedy market growth. They use resources at a very low cost and with low value addition and due to it their low value economic production and consumption economies are retrograde and decelerating the corporate economic growth.' (Saklani, 2009). In the age of globalization, the cautioning of environmentalist and pro-sustainable economist is generally ignored in practice.

However, 'it has to be understood that there can be no financial assets if there are no ecological assets.'(Biswas, 2004: 134). But with emerging fear of global warming and climate change, tribal sustainable way of living has received a new relevance and significance.

The present day international and national political leadership, economists and legislators are becoming aware of threats due to consumerism- induced global warming and climate change to some extent, and also the need for conservation of forests. But they are still not adequately concerned about the welfare and fate of those communities who live within the forests and subsist on forest and other natural resources. Market is all pervading and fulfilling basic requirement of entire spectrum of human requirements and modes of subsistence. Even tribal communities are encouraged to buy daily consumption goods and industrial inputs like chemical fertilizers, pesticides, and agricultural machinery creating a new dependence on market. It has undermined the roots of rural self-sufficiency, exposing them to onslaught of market forces. (Khor, 1999: 51). Traditional economies try to maintain a symbiotic inter-relationship within the community and its surrounding environment; market does not respect their autonomy of subsistence as it hinders and restricts its uninterrupted growth and expansion.

TRIBES, FOREST AND LAND RESOURCES

In a pre-capitalist scheme of things, natural resources were available free to most of rural and tribal people. For tribes, nature was for community use, it was a common property and no part of nature was owned as personal property. Within last two centuries principles and concepts related to land tenure in India has undergone sea changes. At least 80 percent of India's natural resources were common property and only 20 per cent were privately utilized till the end of the 19th century. This extensive common property, available, free to all, was the resource base for non-cash, non-market economy in pre-modern economy. Fuels for cooking and heating, material for making houses, animal fodder, and a number of vegetables, fruits and roots as food (Singh, 1985:46) were available without restrictions. This relationship with nature went through a fundamental change with the coming of the western colonial rule in different parts of the world, which introduced concept of private ownership of property. Even under the Princely rule all property belonged to the royalty and masses had tenancy rights but not the proprietary rights over land. The concept of private property and ownership over anything available in nature was beyond the comprehension and understanding of the original tribal world view. During earlier ages forest rights were availed without any hindrance by the tribes in general in India. Human entry and presence in forests was regulated by the colonial rulers and even petty offences like collecting domestic fuel and cutting grass for fodder became punishable offence. The restriction on free use of forests resources was an atrocity and injustice in the logic of villagers and tribal forest dwellers. (Saklani, 1987:124-128). Imperial heavy boots trampled upon the common property rights; they encroached and displaced the tribal population from their ancestral lands.

HISTORIC BACKGROUND OF BHOXA POVERTY

The alienation of tribal rights over land, forests, hunting, fishing and the resultant changes in the traditional subsistence base had converted a self sufficient community of people into poverty struck dependents and labourers, who now live on the small mercies and largesse of other groups and state. This is the general state of most of the Indian primitive tribal groups. In the areas where Rayyatwari system of land tenure was adopted during British rule, the status of farmers under went change, as it was upgraded from share croppers to individual land owners. It led to large scale upward mobilization of caste status in many parts of India and particularly among hill farmers of Uttarakhand. On the contrary, forest dwelling tribal groups had to face usurpation of their traditional subsistence base in forests as they were forced to abandon their traditional life supporting subsistence practices. It led to economic degradation, pauperization, and consequent lowering of social status vis-à-vis caste Hindu farmers, who otherwise treat tribal lower then untouchables. This disruption in traditional social balance had wider negative consequences for the Tribal community in general in foot hill society of Uttarakhand Himalayas, leading to lowering of social status, poorer economic tenacity for survival, marginalization of their culture and way of life, impacting lives of foot hill tribes of Bhoxa and Tharu. Bhoxas being more primitive were worse off.

Declining relationship of Bhoxas with natural resources remained unabated in post independence decades, when these very fertile virgin forest lands of Himalayan foothills were given to Punjabi and Bengali Refugees for agricultural purposes and also to other settlers. They were traditional farmers and for them land was a coveted personal asset, where as for Bhoxa tribal- land was a common property and not a individual asset and were not emotionally attached to it as they were unaware of concept of land ownership. They had little sense of personal and private ownership and with little persuasion and inducements were ever-ready to sell off or mortgage the land. Consequently a major part of Bhoxa farmers were duped to sell off the lands. Soon a large part of their population became land-less and started working as labourers in their own ancestral lands.

Since late nineteenth century, the forest protection act dismembered the Bhoxas from the traditional forest rights by curtailing their free entry into the forests on which they were traditionally dependent for their economic subsistence. The forests were the natural resource base for supplementing economic needs like herbs, fodder, fuel, foods, and game animals, cords and fish nets. The dissociation and dislocation from nature occurred at two levels: firstly the loosing of forest rights and secondly, land alienation.

HOUSEHOLD BASE LINE SURVEY OF BHOXAS OF GARHWAL DIVISION

During 2004 and 2005 a socio-economic base line survey of each and every Bhoxa household in Garhwal division in Uttarakhand was undertaken with the help of 23 trained field investigators and research area was revisited in 2006 and 2007 for personal observation . Some of the observations based on this survey are enumerated below:

BHOXA: A PRIMITIVE TRIBAL GROUP (PTG) OF UTTARAKHAND FOOT HILLS

The primitive tribe of Bhoxa in Uttarakhand had to face this tragic past and still the future holds little hope. The Bhoxas are a primitive tribal group (PTG) inhabiting the foothills of central Himalayan region of northern India. This tribal group cohabits the Himalayan foothills and its malaria infested jungles along with the Tharu tribe in Indian Himalayas. Whereas Tharus are well spread from India to Nepal, Bhoxas are relatively a very small community confined to foothills of Uttarakhand. Their population is distributed over the Commissionaires of Kumaun and Garhwal in the province of Uttarakhand and also in the district of Bullandshahar in Uttarpradesh .This group is listed as one among 76 primitive tribal groups in India and is on the Government list of priorities for up-liftment and welfare of their lot. The total Bhoxa population in Garhwal region is given in the table1.

Table 1
Demographic Profile of Bhoxa in Garhawal: Censuss of 1991, 2001 and 2004 Survey

	Population of 1991	*Population of 2001*	*Population of 2004*
Hardwar	671	2801	3431
Dehradun	10359	14898	17831
Pauri		792	1196

Note : 1991 and 2001 Statistics are from Census Report Govt. of India
2004 Statistics are based on Household base line Survey (2005)

Despite all pervading decadence in most of tribal populations in India, all of then are marked by positive demographic trend. (Maharatna, 2005). Similarly, in Uttarakhand all its tribal population shows increase in the number. In Garhwal division Bhoxas are spread in three districts of Hardwar, Pauri and Dehradun. Like most of the Indian tribal groups, Bhoxas also show a positive demographic growth curve. The total Bhoxa households in district Dehradun, Hardwar and Pauri were found to be 3950. The total population was 20930. The total number of males was found to be 11260, and the total number of female 9658. The total male percentage was 53.75 and percentage of female was 46.14. The sex ratio was found to be 1000:857.73.

LIMITED MALE AND FEMALE WORK DISTRIBUTION OF BHOXA TRIBE IN GARHWAL REGION

There are seven types of primary occupation identified which the Bhoxa pursue. From the Table-2, it is clear that the majority of the men and women are working as manual labourers along with farming and sericulture as the main primary occupation. Even as secondary occupation, majority of both men and women have identified farming and manual labour work as secondary occupation. Very few Bhoxa men and women are employed in government and private jobs. A large number of men have identified private job as a secondary occupation. It is to be noted that all women are workers and contribute to the family economy. Traditional hunting has been almost stopped as an economic pursuit due to the forest prohibitions. Private business and retailing are now being taken up by a good number of men and women as the primary occupation to earn their living. But majority of them have little capital to expand it.

After the formation of the Uttarakhand state this area is under the spell of fast pace of industrialization as many private and state sponsored industrial estates have been established. (Saklani, 2005:23). Table-2 shows that the daily wage has become primary source of occupation and farming is relegated to secondary position for majority of population. It shows increasing requirement for monetary income and decreasing dependents on agriculture as a primary source of occupation for both male and female population. It is a clear reflection on the rootlessness due to land alienation that has taken place with this tribe and also their incapacity to take up jobs in industrial sector due to low level of skill and education.

Table 2
Male and Female Primary and Secondary Work distribution of Bhoxa Tribe

		Primary			*Secondary*		
Occupation		*Total*	*Male*	*Female*	*Total*	*Male*	*Female*
Farmer	1480	819	661	1233	944	289	
Govt. Job	93	85	8	3	3	-	
Labourer	4305	3713	592	452	365	87	
Others	357	280	77	-	-	-	
Private Job	91	82	9	37	36	1	
Retail	47	43	4	12	11	1	
Sericulture	1319	709	610	12	6	6	
Total	7693	5732	1961	1750	1365	385	

Source: Household base line Survey (2005)

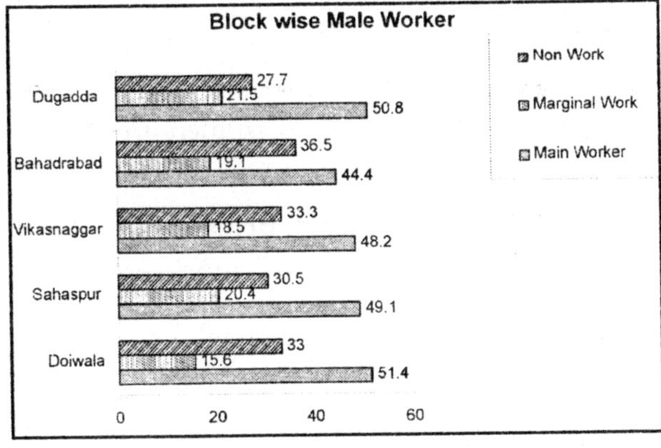

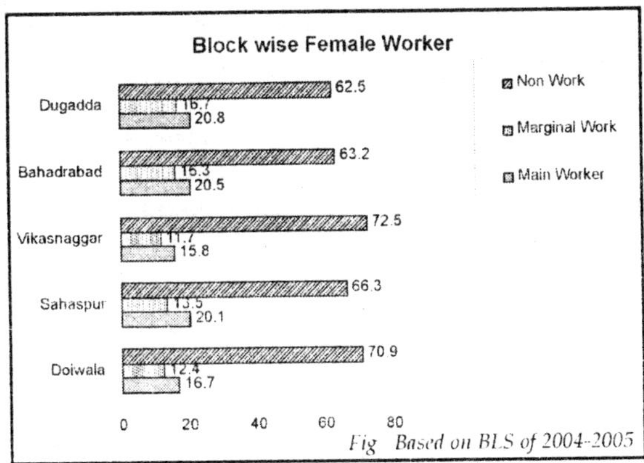

Fig. 1: Situation of Male and Female Workers Among Bhoxas in Garhwal

In a working population of about 20,000 Bhoxas in Garhwal Division, almost 43 per cent are non workers meaning thereby that they do not earn any wage or engaged in any kind of remunerative work within the family or outside .Out of these 26 per cent 0f population is marginal worker, having remunerative work less then 180 days and 32 per cent is a working population, engaged gainfully at least 180 days in a year. It shows that the 70 per cent population is almost underemployed or unemployed. It reflects a very serious situation of poverty, hunger and deprivation.

Majority of the men and women are working as labourers and fewer as farmers. Under secondary occupation, majority of both men and women have identified farming and labour work as secondary occupation. A few of Bhoxa men and women are employed in government and private jobs. A large number of men have identified private job as a secondary occupation. It is to be noted that all women are workers and contribute to the family economy.

SOCIO-ECONOMIC STATUS OF BHOXA IN GARHWAL REGION

Survey reveals a pathetic socio–economic state of Bhoxa community in Garhwal region. Majority of the Bhoxa households come under the category of poor and very poor, and very few households come under the category of rich or very rich. In District Dehradun only 11 Bhoxa households fall into the category of very rich, 49 are rich as compared to 1424 as poor and 709 as very poor. In district Hardwar only two families fall into the category of very rich, 22 as rich as against 225 as poor and 167 as very poor. In district Pauri, Dugadda block 23 families fall into the very rich, 81 is rich and 102 as poor and 44 as very poor. Overall about 50 per cent of the Bhoxa tribal can be categorized as very poor. The economic category is very rich, rich, normal, poor and very poor are subjective and based on visual assessment by the surveyors on the basis of over all land holding, visible asset value, housing quality, etc. The socio-economic status of the Bhoxa tribal in Garhwal Mandal is shown in the Pie diagram, Fig-2.

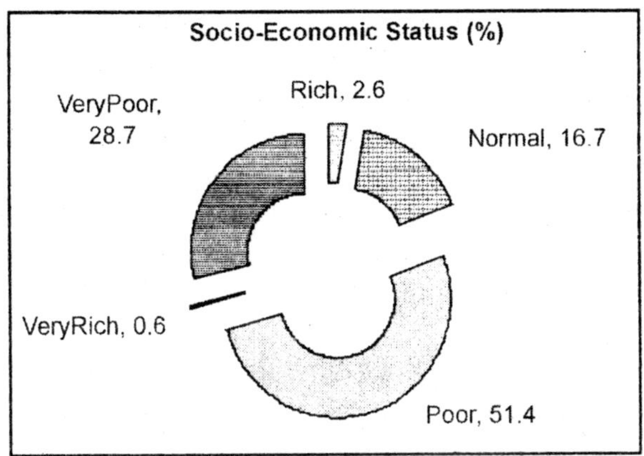

Fig. 2: Pie Chart showing Economic Status of Bhoxa Community in Garhwal

INTERNAL LEADERSHIP AND SOCIO-POLITICAL CONTROL

Today Bhoxas are almost leaderless and directionless as their traditional leadership is marginalized and forgotten. Most of the traditional Panchayats are in the process of decay and disintegration on account of the statutory panchayats set up by the State. In several Bhoxa villages of Pauri Garhwal, Bijnor and Dehradun, traditional panchayats have completely disappeared. Even where they exist, they function only for ritualistic purposes, and they are hardly effective and are able to inflict only nominal punishment like asking the guilty to hold his ears, render a public apology or blacken the face. Young generation has little regard for this institution as they feel it more profitable to align with modern panchayats, political parties and its agents, as through them they feel more empowered and useful for themselves. Majority of the Bhoxa villages are admixture of other communities and Bhoxas do not hold numerical majority. It makes difficult for their representatives to win elections with the support of their own people. Numerically a minority tribe like Bhoxa is not able to get full advantage of tribal reservations, as all the advantages are garnered by the numerous, educated and prosperous tribes like Jaunsaries, Tharus and Bhotias .Due to the lack of numbers they are politically overwhelmed by numerous neighbours; entire apparatus of local self governance is out of their reach. In a tribal community numbering 20 thousand souls only 163 are the panchayat members. Others are educated upto 5th standard and only 1 is high school pass. In Garhwal region out of 163 statutory Bhoxa leaders, a total of 108 male and 19 female had educational qualification up to high school and 4 male had above it.

The community does not have its elected representatives in Gram Panchayats, Forest Panchayats, and Kshetra Panchayat at Block level. Present legislative framework does not allow providing exclusive reservation to PTG. However, some kind of safeguards, administrative or legislative is desperately called for. Inadequate financial resources and income of Bhoxa dominated gram panchayats make them ineffective and they remain helpless in addressing the local problems. Delay in releasing of funds to gram panchayats by government till the end of the financial year, lack of co-ordination among various agencies at District, Block and Village levels make all schemes and plans ineffective. Bhoxas are feeling left out and suffocated, grudge superiority of other tribal groups and this intra- tribal comparison may go out of hand in the hands of political provocateurs.

EDUCATIONAL STATUS AND HIGH DROP-OUT RATE AMONG BHOXAS

Bhoxas have started educating themselves in present generation but majority of them drop out at class Vth standard, which they find difficult to pass. Earlier generations were averse to education is reflected from following statistics. Overall, almost 92 per cent of the aged over 60 years, 84 per cent of adults of age group of 51-60 years, over 50 per cent of 18 to 50 years are illiterates among Bhoxa. It shows that more then half of working adult population is illiterate. However, the situation shows clear improvement from 06 to 17 years of age. Low education reflects their incapability to earn living in an industrial market place.

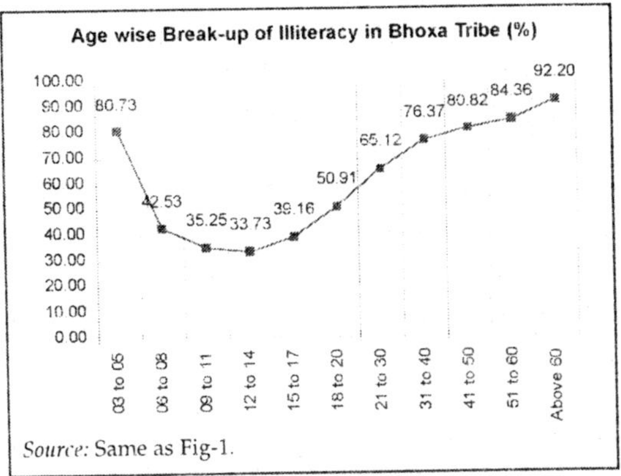

Source: Same as Fig-1.

Fig. 3: Showing Status of Illiteracy Among Bhoxas

The low social awareness and backwardness of this community can be gauged from heavy drop out rate of nearly 80 percent in the primary education. In order to minimize the psychology of dependence on Government jobs after receiving the basic education, there is no technical hands-on trainings available, so that Bhoxa youths may be trained and prepared for the open market requirements and private sector needs.

The total population of children and youth, (in the age group of 06-20 years), continuing education has been recorded for Garhwal region. It was found that only (19.07%) were continuing their education. The highest percentage of children continuing their education was in (41.4%) Vikasnagar block followed by Sahaspur block (24.16%) and Doiwala block (18.25%). In Pauri Garhwal about 34 per cent continue education and Hardwar district shows the lowest number of children continuing their education. In a population of 1340 children of educational age, only 116 (8.66%) children were found to be continuing their education above class Vth standard in Hardwar.

The drop out rate among girls is high. Main reasons for high drop out rate are the need for girls to do domestic work at home and help in looking after other children. Social insecurity and fear of sexual exploitation in school was reported reasons for dropping out of girls during the survey.

It was also found that when the agricultural work is at its peak the children do not go to schools because they help their parents in the fields as agricultural labourers. As a result, if they fail to secure promotion in one class they tend to stop going to school as they are not allowed further stipends and free rations. The inability of few educated youths to get government jobs or any other employment after managing to pass their high school or intermediate has emerged as another major factor which has proved to be a disincentive for pursuing the higher education.Some of the economically better off students showed total aversion to attend the schools as they had to face racial taunts and humiliations in the hands of students of other communities and more powerful tribal groups. Some educated youths have reported themselves as unemployed without an occupation because they do not count agricultural work as an occupation after education. A major grievance among the educated unemployed Bhoxa youths in Garhwal is that other developed tribals have total monopoly over government jobs where as not a single Bhoxa youth has received government job till 2005, after the formation of Uttarakhand. They demand special safeguards within the 4 per cent reservation quota for ST as PTG.

Some of the major problems related to education among Bhoxa tribe as observed are given below:

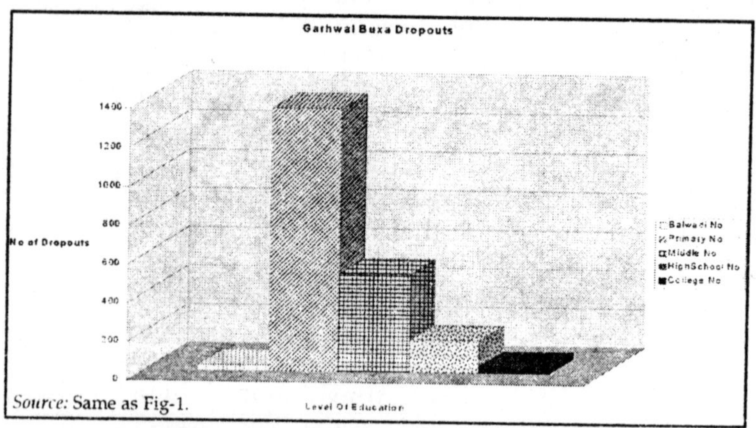

Source: Same as Fig-1.

Fig. 4: Showing Status of Drop outs Among Bhoxas

(a) high incidence of illiteracy among Bhoxa tribe especially among female population;

(b) heavy drop out rate of nearly 80% in the primary education;

(c) lack of commitment on the part of teachers, discrimination of Bhoxa students in other non-PTG tribes dominated institutions;

(d) need for participation of local community in educational activities;

(e) lack of suitable infrastructure: better school buildings, teachers, play field, etc. ;

(f) need for proper orientation of teachers and other administrators, about tribal life and culture;

(g) inadequate and untimely supply of textbooks and notebooks and inadequate provision of incentives. No role model or success story through education;

Table 3
Ailments/Disease found in Bhoxa Tribe of Garhwal Region in Numbers As Personally Reported Cases

Ailments	*Vikas nagar*	*Sahas- pur*	*Doi- wala*	*Duga- dda*	*Bahad- rabad*	*Garh- wal Mandal*
Anemia	0	3	2	2	0	7
Appendix	1	0	1	0	0	2
Asthma	1	1	0	4	0	6
Body Pain	37	12	39	12	18	118
Cancer	2	0	0	1	1	4
Chest pain	0	0	0	1	0	1
ENT & Eye Problem	32	7	17	15	12	83
Fever	187	29	62	24	29	331
Headache	24	9	26	14	10	83
Heart	6	7	6	1	3	23
Skin Disease	3	1	2	7	10	23
Stomach Disease	95	24	72	26	50	267
Stone	6	0	12	2	6	26
TB	93	12	20	4	5	134
Other	257	25	86	37	105	510

Source: Same as Table-2

(h) lack of proper medical aid and balanced diet provided to tribal students in Ashram school hostels;

(i) low quality food grains for tribal school hostels for mid day meal;

(j) lack of monitoring mechanism to motivate drop out tribal students to re-continue education;

(k) lack of suitable self-employment opportunities to the educated youth and dropouts; and

(l) no employment opportunities to educated youths. They are unable to compete with other advanced tribal groups in Uttarakhand, who are more numerous and more politically assertive and articulate.

HEALTH CONDITION OF BHOXA TRIBE

The health condition is similarly dissatisfactory and disturbing. Many of them suffer from chronic diseases but were never investigated due to fear of expenses. Drinking is a big social problem with the Bhoxas which is one of the main reasons for economic decay. The major reported ailments were body pain, E.N.T. and eye diseases, fever, headache, stomach diseases, tuberculosis and other minor health problems like cough and cold. Chronic ailments like heart disease and stone formations have been reported by those who had gone for medical diagnosis. Bhoxas are malnourished and look dispirited and famished particularly in Hardwar District.

HEALTH PREFERENCE PATTERN

The health preference trend of the Bhoxa people in the three Districts- Dehradun, Hardwar and Pauri Garhwal - shows that their first preference was for a qualified doctor followed by home remedies and treatment by a Bhagat. The histogram (Fig:5) gives the visual presentation for the preferred mode of treatment for health care among the Bhoxa population in Garhwal. However, it was the personal observation of field enumerators that Bhoxas in general preferred to go to Bhagat as the treatment of a doctor was expensive. But they have reported doctors as first choice. It also shows that they are not able to pursue their first choice because of economic hardships.

ECONOMIC CONDITION AND LAND ALIENATION

Most serious problem confronted by this tribe is the problem of land alienation. Land alienation also leads to alienation of the surrounding livelihood resources which the tribal depends on .The major causes of indebtedness are agricultural requirements, family expenses, and construction of houses or repairs, marriage, medical needs, cattle, retail business and other purposes.

A tension is visible between the old and new generation with relation to question of land alienation. The new generation accuses older generation for having alienated valuable agricultural land for petty sum of money in the past. Most of the reasons for selling the land or mortgaging were found to be marriage, medical treatment, housing, drinking, etc.

During the survey many of Bhoxa youth expressed their dissatisfaction with the policy related to the ban on selling of tribal land to non- tribal. According to them because of the ban they are forced to sell their land at low cost compared to the market value of the land to other tribal people who are not willing to or unable to pay the market price of the land they buy. The Bhoxa youths say that if the ban is lifted they can directly sell their land to outsiders and get the correct amount of value in terms of market price instead of the low price which they are able to get from tribal buyers. About 33.90 per cent of the Bhoxa households have been reported to be landless and 55.27 per cent were reported to having a land holding 0.5 to 1 hectare in size. Only 1.2 per cent of the Bhoxa have been reported to have above 2 hectares of land. The ban on selling of land to outsiders has proven to be ineffective in protecting tribal land rights. It has in effect forced needy tribal to sell it to other tribal land agents for less money who in turn sell purchased lands collected above sealing limits to outsiders for considerable profits. As per their own admission, land agents from their own tribe, their own leaders, officials of rural Bank, officials of revenue and welfare department, all are part of this unholy nexus.

The figures of alienation are only partly representative of the degree of poverty of Bhoxa households. The factor of indebtedness for medical aid, marriage, food, and other domestic purposes, drinking and lawsuits affect their expenditure. Even if some land is available with Bhoxas, they remain very poor because of their consumption pattern.

The Table No.4 shows the land alienation in various blocks in all the districts of Dehradun, Hardwar and Pauri Garhwal in Garhwal Mandal. It shows that Dehradun tops the figures in land alienation to non-scheduled tribe people. It also shows numerical comparisons of the families affected by land alienation and not the quantity of land alienated. It was found that many of the Bhoxa have admitted to selling their land but for a very small amount of money. Some of them have sold their land to outsiders i.e., non scheduled tribe.

Table 4
Land Alienation in Various Blocks of Garhwal Mandal

	No of Households				
Block	*Total*	*Sold Land*	*To Non ST*	*Non ST Not Returning Land*	*% Alienation to Non ST (Non Quantitative)*
Dehradun					
Doiwala	643	190	146	146	22.71
Sahaspur	304	86	77	77	25.33
Vikas Nagar	2034	285	153	153	7.52
Dehradun Total	2981	561	376	376	12.61
Haridwar					
Bahadarabad	465	47	21	20	4.30
Haridwar Total	465	47	21	20	4.30
Pauri Garhwal					
Dugadda	209	14	7	7	3.35
Pauri Garhwal Total	209	14	7	7	3.35
Garhwal Mandal Total	3655	622	404	403	11.03

Source: Same as Table-2

'The table of reference shows that number of households who have sold their land or mortgaged the land to non ST people, and also shows the number of households who want to reclaim their land but the non ST possessor is refusing to return their land. This table does not show those households who have no land left at all to sell in the present generation as it has already been either sold or mortgaged in the past generation by their forefathers.

ISSUE OF LAND ALIENATION AMONG BHOXA TRIBE

The Bhoxas sold their hundreds of hectares of land with free will at a very low price to new settlers. They fell in habit of selling land as their main source of income even for fulfilling their basic and urgent requirements.. Till a decade back, selling of land and receiving free Govt. grant became the main source of livelihood for the Bhoxas in Hardwar district. Within last one decade banks, cooperative societies, lending agencies and their officials along with land agents started indulging in brokerage and sale of Bhoxa lands. Bhoxas claim that their lands were taken from them by taking advantage of their ignorance and sense of honesty. Lack of education among Bhoxa became main reason for land alienation as they were easily cheated or duped.

Some of the methods adopted for land alienation noted during the field survey were following:

(i) the temporary leased lands were shown permanently sold on papers;

(ii) soft loans were given and lands were impounded in the name of non payment;

(iii) the government subsidies were given in ratio of 60% as loans and 40% as debt. Bhoxa lenders were not told about debt part and were shocked when few years after received notices for payment of interest. Many of the Bhoxas lost their land as it was confiscated for non payment of government loans;

(iv) in Bahadrabad block almost 8 families out of 10 are under the debt burden of government loan. And because of the pressure of the payments their situation is below poverty line;

(v) Land Development Banks distributed loans on land guarantee even to those who owned below 5 bigha of land. In some of the places 8 bigha of land was impounded for just Rs. 40,000;

(vi) some cooperative banks have earned a dubious reputation among the Bhoxas as they repeatedly blamed it for under hand practices;

(vii) some of the lands given on free will as lease were never returned;

(viii) some of the lands given in mortgage were never received back even after payment of heavy interest and principal;

(ix) in some of the areas like Chakmansa Bhoxa land has been taken away forcibly. State machinery was proven ineffective in stopping land alienation and exploitation of Bhoxa tribes; and

(x) Bhoxa in earlier decades were in habit of selling of lands on low rates for their household needs. Bhoxa are proud of their honesty and integrity, will not deny a word given. It is taken as major cause of getting duped by the vile out siders.

BHOXA INDEBTEDNESS

Most of the Bhoxa people are indebted for an amount of 20,000.00 or less, a few families up to Rs. 40,000.00 and three to four families for the amount up to 60,000.00. However, for the Bhoxa people these amounts are very heavy to repay which more often they are not able to do. In lieu of this small amount of money most of the Bhoxa families mortgage their agricultural lands and due to non-repayment of debts these lands are finally alienated.

Economic distress is mother of all failings and our survey noticed some of the major economic problems confronted by Bhoxa tribe in Garhwal region.

(a) problem of continuing land alienation due to inadequacy and ineffectiveness of legal safeguards;

(b) the artisans and craftsmen belonging to Bhoxa community are experiencing difficulties in collecting the raw material through forest restrictions, leading to economic hardship and decay of cultural traditions;

Table 5
Reported Cash Indebted ness of Bhoxa households of Garhwal Region

	No of persons Indebted in Range(in Rs.)						
Block	*less than 2000*	*2000 to 5000*	*5000 to 10,000*	*10,000 to 20,000*	*20,000 to 40,000*	*40,000 to 60,000*	*more than 60,000*
Dehradun							
Doiwala	34	44	38	38	16	1	2
Sahaspur	15	8	12	8	3	0	1
Vikas Nagar	67	80	86	61	16	3	0
Dehradun Total	116	132	136	107	35	4	3
Haridwar							
Bahadarabad	14	24	24	18	5	0	1
Haridwar Total	14	24	24	18	5	0	1
Pauri Garhwal							
Dugadda	9	4	5	13	6	0	0
Pauri Garhwal Total	9	4	5	13	6	0	0
Garhwal Mandal Total	139	160	165	138	46	4	4

Source: Same as Table-2

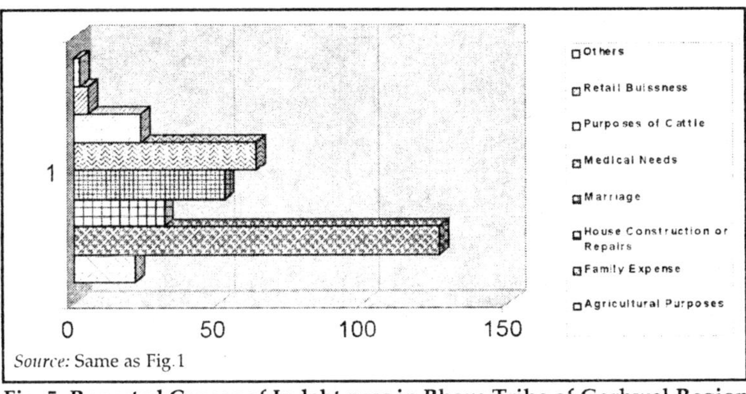

Source: Same as Fig.1

Fig. 5: Reported Causes of Indebt ness in Bhoxa Tribe of Garhwal Region

(c) non-availability of appropriate and suitable skills to supplement income. They may be trained in skills which need to supplement their primary income as has been done in Vikas nagar block by introduction of sericulture cultivation in large scale among Bhoxas;

(d) low-levels of agricultural yields due to non-adoption of improved agricultural methods and seeds. They may be introduced to new remunerative crops like Jetrofa, Olive farming; Organic farming board of Uttarakhand should adopt Bhoxa villages;

(e) poor marketing infrastructure allows tribal produce to receive short hand treatment from aggressive market, which leads to low-income levels;

(f) lack of knowledge in taking up alternative and supplementary avenues of employment other than agriculture;

(g) continued dependency on moneylenders and middle-men for financial assistance at the expanse of landed property.

(h) exploitation by various groups like, local powerful persons, tribal rich and leaders, bankers, officials, police, forest officials etc. ;

(i) supply of poor quality of seeds, pesticides and raw materials to tribal beneficiaries; and

(j) soil erosion and degradation of Bhoxa agricultural lands from flashfloods during rainy seasons.

AGRICULTURAL MARKETING

Majority of the Bhoxa interviewed were selling the agricultural surplus for money and very few who were interviewed were bartering their agricultural produce for other goods. Most of this money was in the form of repayment of debt and interest which the Bhoxas had taken earlier. It was found that a very small percentage of the actual agricultural produce is used for the domestic consumption.

ISSUE OF UPLIFTMENT OF BHOXA TRIBE: SOME SUGGESTIONS

There has not been any remarkable progress on health, or infrastructure development in PTG tribal groups, in spite of administrative interventions. After the creation of new state of Uttarakhand, there is a greater pace of industrialization and urbanization in and around the Bhoxa habitats. It has further marginalized the Bhoxas from whatever rights and resources earlier enjoyed by them. There has been no attempt to improve the skills of the tribals to compete with the mainstream communities in taking up any responsible positions in the industries set up in their areas. They have almost lost their traditional material culture and drinking is their biggest social problem.

Due to poor political representation, poverty, low education, Bhoxas are always found to be on a receiving end of the law in any kind of dispute. They are known as a peaceful and law abiding community with almost negative criminal record. Still for police, they are easy targets in any dispute and even innocents are subjected to coercion. .In view of this grim reality, law should be passed prohibiting use of force in case of disputes over resources in the PTG Bhoxa tribal villages. No industry be set up in and around the PTG area without assessing the socio –economic impact on this tribe. Along with environmental assessment a tribal impact assessment report should also be prepared.

Bhoxa youth should be encouraged and given a priority in police force, Paramilitary force, and Indian Defence forces. It will revive their self confidence and self belief. The Bhoxa community suffers most because of the lack of leadership and awareness among their community. They feel that they are not able to take the advantage of Schedule Tribe status and always feel neglected, discouraged and oppressed in comparison to other progressive and better off schedule tribe communities of Uttarakhand. They feel themselves incapable of facing the challenges and competition against other schedule tribe communities for getting government jobs or taking benefit of various government schemes.

CONCLUSIONS: FUTURE OF TRIBAL COMMUNITIES IN GLOBAL VILLAGE

Global Market economy and industrialization has undermined the self sufficiency of tribal sustenance system. A public debate needs to be initiated to safeguard the natural resources and the process of land alienation among tribal communities. It should be ensured that the tribal lands should not be procured by the state for industrial activity or for developmental projects. Since land is an ancestral heritage, it should be accounted for its ancestral value also and should not be treated as one time sale. They should be paid fixed Government rates and remaining amount equal to market rate should be given as a share money.

Due to onslaught of modern economy and market Bhoxa community is suffering from a deep sense of insecurity, a fear of loosing their identity and loosing their lands and property to others. They feel they are incapable of countering the encroachment of other dominant groups. Some feel that by the next generation there will be no Bhoxa land and culture intact. They are aware that their poor educational status is the cause for many of their socio-economic problems and exploitation. Along with other reasons, it generates a feeling of sadness in the entire community living with an inferiority complex of backwardness, of being left out from the mainstream race for all round progress. It is a case of melting identity and vanishing cultural ethos. Identity crisis has generated feeling of self depreciation and low self esteem due to their sense of failure, and incapability to adjust with the fast changing times. Sense of dejection and apathy towards manual work has accentuated habits of drinking, which has emerged as a major cause of degeneration of the tribe as a whole. Low self confidence in their capacity and culture has become real cause of concern. There is a sense of panic looming in their eyes as they find themselves helpless and incapable in coping with dominant culture and new economy which is engulfing and riding rough shod over their traditional modes of subsistence and way of life. It should not come as a surprise as has been noted " tribals as a whole in India have gained least and lost most during last six decades of democracy and development. They are even more deprived than the Dalits, simply because they have been unable to effectively articulate their grievances through the democratic and electoral processes". (Misra, 2009:40.). Poor political say and representation makes them easy target of 'contempt and condescension of state' machinery and majority communities.

Though, tribals like other Indians are free to follow their own path of progress, but in reality this path is a creation of state and international political order and this order is regressive and damaging to weak communities like Bhoxas. The issues of continuous land alienation sever unemployment, poor health and nutrition, low education, high drop out rate, lack of social leadership, poverty and drinking, are the indicators of a whole community in deep distress for survival. One of the Bhoxa community leaders is not very wrong when he says that "we have little hope to survive in future. Soon we will vanish." In a globalizing economy the fate and situation of tribal communities like Bhoxa has further relegated to the background as they are poor clients of consumer market.(Saklani, 2009:62). Increased purchasing power and consumption of commodities of Indian middle class have pushed them to lower margins of development indicators. They seem to be the last frontiers of a continuously vanishing culture and vanishing mode of living. Efforts should be made 'to evolve a civil society rather than an affluent society'. (Joshi, 2004:236)). It should cater to both rich and poor, otherwise it will invite protest, anger and strife. Globalization has not provided anticipated gains in underdeveloped communities, rather it has become instrumental in creating ethnic conflict, economic collapse and identity crisis.

No one is going to take serious note of the tribal distress in the face of present economic recession troubling middle class and industrial, capitalist class world over. But it is an ordained duty for the anthropologists to wake up the world to a grim reality that why present consumption based globalization- is finally loosing momentum. All round feel good ambience with which the global village was enjoying its enchanting music of progress, has a tragic face hidden behind a glamorous mask. Global market has to make space for the "multitude of small scale communities in which people live traditional, self-providing, and sustainable healthy life styles." Today, if poor are taught ways to get sustainable livelihood then better off class must also be trained and sensitized to live a sustainable lifestyle

ENDNOTE

1. This paper is part of a trilogy of papers on Globalization and its varied ramifications on Bhoxa tribe, based on facts observed and recorded under the base line survey, sponsored by Ministry of Social Welfare, Govt. of Uttarakhand and financed by Ministry of Tribal Affairs, Govt. of India and conducted by the author. Based on major findings of the survey, present paper is an expanded and critical version of the paper "Globalization and Marginalization of Bhoxa Tribe in Uttarakhand Himalayas", published in Tribal Development in India, ed., S.R. Padhi, 2009, Delhi, pp 43-66 .

REFERENCES

Biswas, P. K. (2004), "Indegenous People in India, A Case for reforms of Property Rights and Empowerment". In Kamal. K. Misra (ed) *Anthropology, New Global Order and Other Essays*. New Delhi: Concept.

Chomsky, Noam (1999), *Profit over People: Neoliberalism and Global Order*. Delhi: Madhyam Books.

Jha, Makhan (1962), *Anthropological Thoughts*. U.P. India: Vikas Publishing House.

Joshi, Vidyut (2004), *Tribal Situation in India*. N.Delhi: Rawat Pub.

Khor, Martin (1999), "Appropriate Development". In *International Journal of Rural Studies*, Vol. 6, No 2. Quoted in Jeremy Seabrook's *The no-nonsense Guide to World Poverty*, 2004, London/ Newyork:Verso.

Koshy, Ninan (2002), *Globalisation, The Imperial Thrust of Modernity*. Mumbai: Vikas Adhyayan Kendra.

Maharatna, Arup (2005), *Demographic Perspective on India's Tribes*. New Delhi: Oxford University Press.

Misra, S.R. (2009), "Globalization and Tribal Communities in India some Emerging Issues". In S.R. Padhy and B. M. Padhy (Eds.), *Tribal Development in India*. Delhi: Mangalam Publisher.

Saklani, Atul (1987), *History of a Himalayan Princely State - Change Conflicts and Awakening*. Delhi: Durga Pub.

Saklani, Bina (2005), *Baseline Survey of Bhoxa Tribe: A Primitive Tribal Group of Uttarakhand*. New Delhi: Ministry of Social Welfare, Government of Uttaranchal, Dehradun and Ministry of Tribal Affairs, Government of India.

Saklani, Bina (2009), "Globalization and Marginalization of Bhoxa Tribe of Uttarakhand Himalayas". In S.R. Padhy and B. M. Padhy (Eds.), *Tribal Development in India*. Delhi: Mangalam Publisher.

Seabrook, Jeremy (2006), *World Poverty*. Jaipur: Rawat Publications.

Singh, Chattrapati (1985), *Common Property and Common Poverty*. New Delhi: Oxford University Press.

Williams, G.R.C. (1992), (Re-Print). *Statistical Memoirs of Dehradun*. Dehradun: Natraj Publishers. First published in 1874, Roorkee: Thomson Civil Engineering College.

8

GINGER CULTIVATION OF ADI COMMUNITY IN LOWER DIBANG VALLEY DISTRICT OF ARUNACHAL PRADESH IN THE ERA OF GLOBALIZATION: CONSTRAINTS AND OPPORTUNITIES

Otem Moyong, Philip Mody

INTRODUCTION

It is by now almost impossible to conceive of a world without the global business and financial system. As rightly said by World Bank President Robert Zoellick at a press conference on 10th October 2008, "If you look at countries that have been able to move people out of poverty, grow, offer new opportunities, the benefits (of globalization) are enormous".

Globalization is the medium to convert local or regional things or phenomena into global one; it is a process by which the people of the world are fused into members of a single family. Infact, globalization is perceived as even-handed movements, which embrace free movements of goods and services, capital, people and information technologies, ideas, cultures, rules and regulations and politics across national boundaries. However, globalization has been understood as different things to different people as economists, business persons, political leaders and religious leaders have their own interpretation and reaction to this global phenomenon. If truth be told, globalization is an unbiased tidal wave leading to the integration of technological, economic, cultural, political, and social systems across geographical boundaries. And it is general presumption that there is free and equal participation of every nation and thereby people in race of globalization forget their national identities, racial stocks, political parties, religious background, ethnical and, cultural group. Naturally, the very objective of the globalization would get defeated if people from different countries, cultures, religions, racial stocks and political parties do not partake in this movement with equal fervour and force.

Lower Dibang valley is a district in Arunachal Pradesh with snow capped mountains and lush green hills, humming rivers and rivulets flowing down the verdant hills abruptly emerging in the plains, enchanting valleys enjoying a special climate that open up great potentials for horticulture and plantation type of agriculture. Ginger, being one of the most known emerging cash crops with high business and marketing potentiality has been under cultivation since time immemorial by the Adi community of Arunachal Pradesh. However, it is interesting to know that, at the beginning; it has been used as local spice, and was considered an inevitable ritual item. It has been widely used in different cultural and social occasions like marriage ceremony, festival, offerings and sacrifices. However, its jurisdiction of cultivation was restricted to kitchen garden only. Infact, ginger is deeply rooted in cultural fabric among the Adis of Lower Dibang Valley.

The Adis inhabit the lower part of Lower Dibang Valley district especially in Roing and Dambuk circles respectively and adopted ginger cultivation as a major source of income since early 1990s. Interestingly, about 90 per cent of Adi households undertake ginger cultivation, and on an average 40 per cent of dry cultivable land are used for it in Lower Dibang Valley District of Arunachal Pradesh. On an average every household produces about 257.5 quintals of ginger annually giving a rich annual average income of about Rs. 2,72,950 only from ginger in the three major Adi villages viz. Parbuk, Bolung and, Jia. In fact, it provides scope for self-employment to the local people and even to students pursuing education and thereby, provides economic self-dependency. Cultivation of ginger has changed the economic face and structure of Adi community of this district and has a positive and remarkable impact on socio-economic variables like annual income, per capita income, savings, investment and, employment generation, political and cultural development.

OBJECTIVES & METHODOLOGY

The main objectives of the study are:

(i) to study the effect of ginger cultivation on socio-economic life of the Adi community of Lower Dibang Valley District in the era of globlalisation;

(ii) to study the problems being faced by the people in ginger cultivation; and

(iii) to make suggestions to overcome the problems.

A field survey was conducted in the three selected villages of Lower Dibang Valley District, viz., Parbuk, Bolung and Jia by taking a total of 84 samples during the month of December'08 to January'09. During the course of survey, selection of samples was made by using Simple Random Sampling Technique and structured questionnaires were administered to all the selected samples to obtain relevant information/data. Out of the total samples, 37 samples were taken from Parbuk village and 22 samples and 15 samples from Bolung and Jia villages respectively covering the period of ginger cultivation from the year 2005 to 2008.

ANALYSIS AND INTERPRETATION OF DATA

The information/data obtained during the course of survey has been analyzed and interpreted under the following heads:

(a) Area under Ginger Cultivation: Table 1 shows the average landholdings of Adi community under ginger cultivation in Lower Dibang Valley district of Arunachal Pradesh from the

year 2005 to 2008. The information provided in the table shows an increase in area under ginger cultivation. It has been observed that quantum of land area for ginger cultivation has been doubled during the year 2007 with an average of 12 acre area per household. This implies that Adi community of the survey area is very competitive and enterprising in the field of ginger cultivation.

Table 1
Average Land holdings of the Adi Households Under Ginger Cultivation in Study Area

Year	*Average per household area under ginger cultivation(in acre)*	*%age increase/ decrease*
2005	4	-
2006	6	(+) 66.67
2007	12	(+) 100
2008	12	0

Source: Field Survey.

(b) Production of Ginger: In spite of increase in the area under ginger cultivation during the study period, proportional change in the production of ginger in some years is not in tune with the proportional changes in the area under ginger cultivation (Table 2). This is mainly due to unfavourable climatic condition and non-application of scientific cultivation of ginger by the Adi community which is being evident from

Table 2
Production of Ginger in the Study Area during Four Years

Year	*Ginger Production (in quintals)*	*%age Change*
2005	186	-
2006	240	(+) 22.5
2007	260	(+) 7.6
2008	344	(+) 24.4
Average	257.5	-

Source: Field Survey.

Table 2. However, there has been continuous increase in the production of ginger during the period of study. It has also been found that, more than 26 respondents produced favourably upto 1100 quintals of ginger which yields to them an amount of Rs. 19 lakh during peak season.

(c) Price of Ginger: It can be observed form the Table 3 that price per kilogram of ginger in the local market is very much inconsistent. Such inconsistency is due to market force where the price of the ginger ranges between Rs. 4 and 22 per kg. During the course of survey, it was found that, the price of the ginger outside the North-East crosses more than Rs. 60 per kg during harvesting season. This implies that, the ginger cultivators of the study area are unable to avail the full advantage of market due to absence of direct marketing system. Thus, the cultivators have to be content with the average bargain price of Rs 9.40 per kg.

Table 3
Price Per Kilogram of Ginger in Local Market

(in rupees)

Year	*Lowest*	*Highest*	*Average*
2005	05	10	7.5
2006	04	08	6
2007	08	22	15
2008	10	18	14
Average	6.75	12	9.4

Source: Field Survey.

(d) Income from Ginger: It can be observed from the Table 4 that the ginger cultivators earned an average income of Rs. 2, 72,950 per annum. However, the maximum annual average income of Rs. 4, 81,600 has been recorded during the year 2008.

From the analysis, it is observed that, production of commercial crops for market has touched the mindset of Adi community dwelling in the Lower Dibang Valley District of Arunachal Pradesh especially, in the field of ginger cultivation. Thus, the impact of ginger cultivation on socio-economic life of the people has been examined on the basis of information

Table 4
Annual Average Income of Ginger Cultivators

Year	*Ginger Production (in quintal)*	*Average Price per kilogram (in rupees)*	*Average Income (in rupees)*
2005	186	7.5	139500
2006	240	6	144000
2007	260	15	390000
2008	344	14	481600
Average	257.5	10.6	272950

Source: Field Survey.

obtained through survey which can be discussed under the following heads:

Income: Cultivation of ginger is a great boon for the people dwelling in Lower Dibang Valley district of Arunachal Pradesh. Especially with regard to the Adi community, ginger cultivation is considered as gold mine. By virtue of ginger, Adi community has witnessed tremendous increase in the income as evident from table 4. The reason for Lower Dibang Valley district being the district of highest per capita income[1] among the districts of the Arunachal Pradesh may be attributed to cultivation of ginger in commercial way. Infact, every member of each household (especially, the student community) earn huge income from ginger cultivation every year, due to which most of the student community enjoy economic independency in terms of money. Further, it was also observed that, the cultivators need not have to wait harvesting season to earn income especially at the time of urgency like medical treatment, marriage and festivals, etc. In this respect, the cultivators derived the value of ginger by selling the ginger plot at arbitrary future price. This implies that marketing of ginger in the study area does possess some important characteristics of derivatives/stock exchanges.

Possession of Assets and Gadgets[2]*:* Due to significant increase in income (especially from ginger) during the last one and half decades, the material comfort of the Adi community of Lower Dibang Valley has increased. This includes firstly, changing housing pattern from traditional to modern type. Today, almost all the Adi families are staying in semi to concrete RCC buildings. Even, there is improvement in the construction and structure of granaries and huts in the agricultural fields. Secondly, there has also been remarkable increase in the acquisition of motor vehicles (motor bike, public carriers, tractors etc,) and also modern amenities (T.V, telephone, Dish TV etc,). Thirdly, the rapidity of rejuvenation work related with other agriculture fields, pisciculture, horticulture, digging of cannels, etc. has significantly improved. Last but not the least, the living standard of Adi community of Lower Dibang Valley has improved to a great extent.

PROBLEMS

The brighter side of the ginger cultivation has its own darker side when ginger cultivators encounter with both foreseeable and unforeseeable problems. Some of the common problems are as below:

High Cost of Labour: It has been revealed that there has been high cost of labour, daily wages of worker engaged in ginger field normally fall within the range of Rs. 55 to 65 per day. The labour cost has been higher for ginger cultivation than other fields of agriculture because workers have to go for weeding during the peak of the summer and harvesting is executed with dusty field and workers minds are already preoccupied that ginger is a commercial crop for which they charge more to their bargaining advantage. Moreover, the owners of ginger fields have to manage their fields with unskilled labour. It is felt that there is less mobility of labour into these areas from other states and nations with greater calibres and skills owing to the enforcement of inner line permit system by the state. Therefore, in the last two years there has not been a remarkable increase in the area under ginger cultivation (Table 1) carried out by Adi tribes of this district mostly because of absolute rises in labour cost.

Inadequate Finance: The inadequacy of finance is one of the major problems being faced by the farmers. It has been revealed during the course of study that not a single respondent has taken loans or financial assistance from bank and other financial institutions for undertaking ginger cultivation. Bank and other financial institutions may not be categorically careful concerning financing and developing ginger cultivation. Therefore, there is greater scope of investment for both domestic and foreign investment companies so that domestic and foreign capitals are injected into this field.

Non-existence of Technical Assistance: It is felt that, there is non-existence of technical assistance and information from Government and other companies. There has never been a training, seminar, workshop or other equivalents on ginger cultivation, its utilities and, marketing for the Adi farmers. All ginger cultivators still follow traditional farming following either organic farming or slash cultivation or practicing follow land. There is great urgency of information and technical support including supply and availability of machines, equipments, fertilizers and, other agricultural implements into these circles from the State or Central Government or global companies enabling Adi ginger cultivators to assume cultivation of ginger on scientific lines.

Unstable Price: The behavioural pattern of local price curve of ginger is erratic in nature and quite unpredictable in these two circles ranging from Rs. 4 to 22 per kg as shown in Table 3. This is mainly due to non-existence of government support price or administered price. Thus, prices are determined by the intermediaries without being interfered by the district administration or State Government.

Lack of Pressure Group: Due to non-existence of organised pressure group among the ginger cultivators the middlemen purchase ginger at a price to their disadvantage.

Lack of Manufacturing Units: Complete non-existence of cold storage and ginger processing unit are major blockades to the development of ginger cultivation in the study area. There is neither government nor corporate owned cold storages wherein bulky production of ginger could be stored that would at least, facilitate farmers to dispose their product at and after growing seasons. In addition, governments as well as corporate entities of the nation or across the nation have not setup ginger processing unit in and around the study area in particular and district in general. Existence of manufacturing units or processing units of ginger would help in making ginger powder, medicines, pickles etc., and thereby adding value to ginger.

Monsoon Effect: As a matter of fact, Indian agriculture is a gamble of monsoon, so is the case of ginger cultivation in these areas. It is very difficult to predict the volume of ginger and productivity. Significant portion of ginger fields are damaged due to hostile climatic conditions, which is quite unpredictable. In this regard, domestic insurance companies or multinational insurance entities could have establish and expand their branches in the study areas to cover price or product risks. Unfortunately, there is complete absence of insurance companies for such matters.

Lack of Infrastructure: It is evident that, the transport and communication cost are skyrocketing day by day. Ginger is mostly carried through land (road) and water (inland) transportation. Bullock carts, tractors and trucks are the primary means of land transportation, which charge high freight. It was found that a bullock cart laden with full load of ginger is charged between Rs 50 to 60 per kilometer. The river Bramaputra (Dibang or Dihang) deserves special mention; there is still no bridge over the river Dihang connecting the study area and rest of the country. The ferry plying in this river (mostly under private ownership) via Sadiya and Dhola Ghat is still the lifeline and that to charge exorbitant fare and freight. Floods, which are frequent, disrupt the water transportation time and again.

Absence of Research and Development: Absence of in depth research regarding the cultivation of ginger in the study area in particular and state in general is also one of important phenomena posing problems to rapid growth and development of ginger cultivation carried out by Adi community. In this context, multinational research companies could invest and establish research based institutes in these areas to facilitate and promote ginger cultivation in a scientific line.

REMEDIAL MEASURES

Under the grip of globalization, to overcome above problems and to promote ginger cultivation undertaken by Adi community in Lower Dibang valley district of Arunachal Pradesh, following important aspects demand immediate attention:

There should have special inner line[3] permit for skilled and trained labours to pass through the state boundaries subject to validity at least for the time duration of ginger cultivation.

To overcome shortage of finance commercial banks, NABARD and other financial banks and development banks like ICICI, IDBI should provide financial assistance at concessional interest rate to the farmers. In addition, Government should seek assistance from international financial institutions like, World Bank, IMF, ADB etc, to meet financial need of ginger cultivation.

Improved Agricultural Implements and Tool-Kits should be supplied to the local farmers by the government at subsidized rates for better and higher productivity of ginger.

Ginger cultivators should be trained with the objective of creating and providing necessary skills and knowledge commensurate with the practice and cultivation of ginger. In this regard, establishment of training institutes having special training module for promoting ginger cultivation is expected to spearhead the cultivation of ginger.

The State government should have attractive investment incentives to retain and attract both domestic investors as well as investors beyond national boundaries for marketing, processing and packaging.

Intensified training programme should be conducted from time to time for the local farmers regarding uses of ginger, protection and cultivation of ginger on scientific lines.

Government should emphasise on vibrant transportation networks and organize cold storage facilities in the study area.

Construction of bridge over river Dibang should be started as early as possible. Introduction of shipping companies with reasonable fare and freight by the domestic or foreign companies in the river is also felt as one of imperative issue.

In order to have better bargaining power, there should be formation of cooperatives of ginger cultivators.

Domestic or foreign-based insurance companies should come forward to cover up product and price risks pertaining to the ginger produced in the area.

The Agricultural Policy of state should attempt to incorporate majestic plans, programmes to develop ginger cultivation in Lower Dibang Valley district in particular, and Arunachal Pradesh in general.

Though the study is based on the Adi cultivators, the remedial measures suggested would help cultivators of nearby districts like Dibang Valley, Lohit Upper Siang and East Siang districts.

CONCLUSION

In the age of Globalization where the world is "shrinking", the consciousness of the world is on "increase". It is the transition period where there are dramatic changes in societies and the world economy because of intensification of international trade and flow of capital, information, ideas, technologies, people and, the exchange of culture and political thoughts and diplomacies. In fact, it is a tidal wave that leads toward the integration of world economies, cultures, political states, and social systems touching lives of every people of the world, may one be a Japanese, an Indian, an American or an African; educated or uneducated; male or female; general class, Schedule Tribe, or other backward class of people. The very purpose of globalization can not be achieved in isolation and so is achieved if the ray of the light of globalization do pour upon each people, tribe, district, state, nation and, the world. It is a matter of fact that, cultivation of ginger has been the main cash crop grown by Adi community of Lower Dibang Valley since early 1990s. On contrary, ginger has been cultivated in Lower Dibang Valley in a cramped way not with a globalize format without inflow of skill labour, ideas or information, technologies, and capital.

Therefore, it is felt that, the Adi tribe of Lower Dibang Valley in particular and tribal cultivators of Arunachal Pradesh in general should rethink and spruce up their agricultural policies and practices in tune with the globalization to arrest fresh injection of skilled and trained labour, valued ideas and information, advanced technologies and, cheap and productive capital. Thus, promotion and development of ginger cultivation would go a long way in upliftment of socio-economic wellbeing of Adi community of Lower Dibang Valley in one hand and active participation of Adi community of Lower Dibang Valley in the rally of globalization in other hand.

ENDNOTES

1. Human Development Report of Arunachal Pradesh (2005), Department of Planning, Government of Arunachal Pradesh.
2. Based on field data.
3. Arunachal is a prohibited area under Inner line Regulation of 1873. Any non-Arunachalee has to obtain a valid innerline permit to enter into the territory.

9

ECONOMIC LIFE OF THE LODHAS OF WEST BENGAL: PAST, PRESENT AND FUTURE

Shyamal Kr. Jana

INTRODUCTION

One of the commitments of our national government after Independence has been to bring about all-round development of small and marginal communities who have lagged behind socially and economically in the process of national development. The basic objective therefore is to raise their standard of living at par the national average. But in the process of development, the policies and programmes of development keep on shifting and the economy of these communities do not get full benefit from development schemes. In recent years, these communities have further been exposed to globalisation through national commitments to the process.

It is under this general backdrop that Lodhas have been studied. National and state governments have made attempts after Independence to ameliorate the living standard of the Lodhas by introducing different development schemes. The schemes are concomitant to the development policies adopted by the government from time to time. When national policies have embarked upon the process of globalisation, it is but obvious that the development of Lodhas has been integrated to it. Hence, the study presents some aspects of their socio-economic development in the era of globalisation. It is to be mentioned that the aspects of development studied are not the impacts of globalisation alone. The development of Lodhas therefore has a temporal context. In other words, the process of their development has been discussed right from their exposure to modern forces of development after Independence.

FRAME OF DISCUSSION

Globalisation has its own dynamics. These are briefly integration of international market for goods, services, technology, finance and labour (Roy, 1997: 2117-2135); cultural interactions across societal boundaries-the incidence of migration and emergence of cultural diasporas bringing about intense cultural, social and economic interactions (Singh, 2000); and the worldwide dissemination of certain cultural norms and social institutions because of colonialism, trade, missionary activity, technological change, incorporation of tribal people into state and large-scale system of exchange. (Eriksen, 1995).

As the globalisation has its own dynamics, so also the traditional economy of tribal communities. The traditional economy is basically subsistence in nature and is instituted in the social process with barter mode of exchange. (see Herskovits, 1952; Piddington, 1952; Firth, 1967; Mazumdar and Madan, 1970 and Dalton, 1971 for an understanding of the nature of traditional economy and its relation with social institutions). Precisely, the traditional tribal economy happens to be basically small, non-acquisitive, simple and relatively isolated, and based on simple technology. It is normally a forest-based economy with family-based and consumption-based production, barter mode of exchange, gift and ceremonial exchanges, communal ownership of the means of production, and interdependence and periodic markets. An important aspect of traditional economy is sharing and collective use of natural resources which can be categoried on sacred or profane planes. (Durkheim, 1965).

Technology, life and livelihood strategy of a traditional community depends on the nature of habitation, environment and resources. Human being has always been dependant, to a varying extent, on fluctuating ecological balance between people and basic resources and its surrounding ecological systems. The utility of resource has constantly increased but in many cases natural resources do not increase at the same pace (Chandrasekhar, 1954:11), which results in change of techno-economic pursuits. Carrying capacity is thus basically conditioned by a stratified relation between its food resources and its cultural realities as manifested in the form of mechanism of utilisation of available resources. (Kessing, 1957:128).

It is an undeniable fact that economic conditions with existing ecological setting determine the culture of a particular group of people. However, economy is not merely an independent unit; it is a part of total socio-cultural life. Gradual changes in economic pursuits due to globalisation bring corresponding changes in the social system and allow the people to interact at varied degrees in the social and economic spheres. So wherever we find the forces of detribalisation, Hinduisation and urbanisation operating, we generally associate these with different contact situations.

The economic pursuits of a community are usually linked with the local environment, resource available and technology adopted in such a situation. The tribal people of India are exposed chiefly to forest environment and also exploit its natural resources for securing their livelihoods. Therefore, it is obvious that they possess an instinct and intimate knowledge of the 'ecological niche' (Hardesty, 1977), which is otherwise known as traditional wisdom or indigenous knowledge. With the help of this knowledge they depend on their immediate niche for their survival. In fact, these, two things, that is, physical environment and economic pursuits are closely woven with their socio-cultural fabric of relations.

The issue as discussed provides the base to understand the changing life of Lodhas, a primitive tribal group of Paschim

Medinipur district in the state of West Bengal, India, consequent upon their link with market forces and a diversified non-traditional economy right from their exposure to modern forces of development through plan programmes.

STUDY AREA

Paschim Medinipur provides an ideal ground for tribal studies not only for the simple reason that there is a substantial concentration of tribals here, but also due to the fact that the tribals here are under the grip of diverse areas of influence– local, regional, across the boundary of the state, and national. Ethnic composition of the district reveals that 16.34 per cent are Scheduled Castes and 8.28 per cent Scheduled Tribes inhabit in the area. In fact, 18 per cent of the total tribal population of West Bengal lives in this district.

From anthropological standpoint, Paschim Medinipur symbolises a 'region with unique characteristics' for the following reasons:

(i) It has the highest tribal population among all the districts of West Bengal;

(ii) There is a substantial population of the Santal, the most dominant tribe among the 38 Scheduled Tribes of the State. Other tribes include Bhumij, Munda, Kora, Oraon, Lodha, Kheria/Kharia, Mahali, etc.;

(iii) The non-tribal population represented by the Caste Hindus and the Muslims provide the contact situation for the tribals; and

(iv) In such a contact situation though each community exercises certain amount of selectiveness, tribe-peasant and tribe-caste continua are clearly discernible.

PROPOSITION

The present study is a comparative study on the economic status of the Lodha community, inhabiting in the district of Paschim Medinipur, West Bengal, at two different stages of economic development and the specific economic problems faced, which may partly be their own creation and partly imposed on them from outside. The economic status manifests itself in the form of life-style, behaviour and has to be seen against a socio-cultural matrix. The proposition is that the economic status and the consequent behaviour pattern vary because of variations at the level of economic development. It is the economy within which the people function regularly. If agriculture is taken as the reference point, the Lodha could be thought as belonging to two stages – the gathering and hunting in Nayagram and the pre–agricultural one in Narayangarh Blocks.

The present study has covered the Lodha tribal community, once treated as Criminal Tribe, later as De-notified Community and now a Primitive Tribal Group (P.T.G.) of West Bengal. The tribe reveals some degree of pre-agricultural level of technology. The group inhabits in the two Community Development Blocks, e.g., Nayagram and Narayangarh in the micro-region of western part of Paschim Medinipur, which is coterminous with the rugged terrain of Chotanagpur, in the district of Paschim Medinipur, West Bengal. Field study was conducted during Jnauary 1998 to December 2000 in 12 villages selected purposively from two CD Blocks by canvassing structures questionnaires in 150 households- 75 households from each block. Besides, data were collected from concerned line departments of the government and offices of NGOs working in the area.

The Lodhas, (see Bhowmick, 1963 for details on the life and culture of Lodhas). are significantly different in terms of physical and cultural affinities from their neighbouring communities like Santal, the Munda, the Kora, the Kharia, the Mahato and the Bhumij. The Census of India clubbed them with the Kharias.

The Lodhas of West Bengal, with a population of more then 46,000, take pride in asserting themselves as the Savara, a generic term used in ancient literature for the forest-dwelling communities. Collection of jungle produce, edible roots and tubers, small games, etc. was their main occupation, but after the enactment of the "Permanent Settlement Act", 1793, by the then British administration, the entire region of forests was given to the landlords and in this way their right over the forest produce was set at naught; ultimately, they became paupers from the level of poverty. Helpless as they are, they were flooded with all sorts of criminal activities, true or imaginary. Goaded by the pangs of hunger and tyranny of the rich belonging to varied political parties, the Lodhas practically had no other alternative than to fall back upon for a living. They were displaced both territorially and economically and could not adopt themselves to the changing situation; they were ultimately further driven to a precarious existence. The growing needs of their expanding family fixed them in a frame of narrow territory in which they could not meet their dire needs with small and irregular income. Unending frustration and lack of self-confidence brought in its train a perpetual stagnation in their collection life, which subsequently turned them into inveterate criminals.

But, now-a -days, we find some distinctiveness in the group Members of one of the groups live mainly on the southern bank of the river Subarnarekha, including the areas in Jhargram and Jamboni blocks who have categorised themselves as "Jungle Lodhas". The people of the other section, who possibly migrated to the eastern tract (less forested region), and came in contact with the agrarian communities there, gradually learnt the art of agriculture. Thus being accustomed to the techniques of agriculture, they now work as agricultural workers. Their access into the forest due to forest laws became very limited.

As has been said, main economy is gathering-hunting, collection of honey and faggots, *tusser* cocoons or gouty, from the jungles and also edible roots and tubers and small games. They sell their collections to the local people at a very low price and purchase food items and essential articles. They also hunt various poisonous and non-poisonous snakes, lizards, and sell the skins in local market. Regarding their economic activities as stated earlier, those who live near to the jungles collect firewood, put them in bundles and sell them to the nearest market or locality. Sometimes they are found to work as wage earners, working in the field of others or in road construction work or some similar activities. After the rainy season, they get some employment opportunities and they also collect various fruits, water lily, molusca for self consumption and for market. After March, however, nothing is available. They then fall on thin times and face a near famine condition.

Most of the huts of Lodhas are rectangular, thatched, mud-built and without windows. The Lodhas do not have cultivable land of their own, though they use *Khas* or government lands for doing rudimentary agriculture. A few among them have been given some land by the government for cultivation. They use earthenware for cooking. Their main equipments are bows and arrows, digging sticks, axe and spade. For cutting and felling trees, they use axe and for digging roots and tubers they use a type of digging spade with a sharp iron-blade, hafted into a wooden shaft. For hunting purpose they use bows and arrows. Fish traps, mortar and pestles are also used by the Lodhas.

The Lodhas are patriarchal and patrilineal. The whole community is divided into a few exogamous clans, which have their respective totems. Most of the Lodha families are nuclear in nature, though joint or extended families are not rare. Polygyny is also noticed among them.

They have their own tribal council, known as Panchayat, which is headed by a *Mukhia*. The messenger is called *Dakua* or *Atgharia*. His responsibility is to inform the villagers the decisions and directives of the Panchayat on village affairs. In a traditional council, personal disputes of the villagers and general problems of village administration are discussed. This council is also responsible to organise the annual worships and other celebrations. If a person is found guilty, then traditional council impose fine or ostracise him/ her as per the nature of offence. Their sacred head is known as *Dehari*, who is assisted by *Talias* while sacrificing goats. A number of sorcerers and magicians are available in different villages.

The Lodhas of Nayagram are basically food collectors and gatherers. Their economy is still in traditional form and they mainly depend upon the forest. Forest plays a vital role in the life of the Lodhas. Collection of honey and foggots, tusser cocoons or gooty, from the jungle and also edible roots and tubers and small game from the jungle are their main source of income. Now their economy may be divided into the following two categories:

(i) Traditional, and

(ii) Non-traditional or modern.

Traditional economic activities can be further divided into main and subsidiary types. The main activities are:

(i) Hunting and trapping;

(ii) Food collection;

(iii) Honey collection;

(iv) Lac collection; and

(v) Firewood collection.

Fishing is the subsidiary source of livelihood. The modern economic include;

(i) Cultivation; and

(ii) Wage Labour.

Division of labour according to one's capacity to perform any work was strictly maintained in an early traditional family. The male members used to concentrate their mind towards outdoor activities whereas the females dealt with the household works. This type of traditional division of labour is under drastic transformation overtime. For example, female are currently engaged in factories, agricultural fields, etc. i.e. they have involved themselves in all types of activities which were previously done by the males only.

The people of the study area are poverty-stricken, but in order to heal their poverty, the people are putting their earnest effort to enhance their economic conditions. They try to utilise the various forest produces in different ways giving shape to different items of handicrafts and taking them to the *hat* individually or through intermediaries for sale. Most of the people living in the studied villages are dependent on forest resources for earning their livelihood. Though agriculture or

Table 1
Economic Activities of Lodhas of Paschim Medinipur District

Occupation	*Male*	*Female*	*Children*
i. Domestic work	1. Taking care of children. 2. Collection of firewood, grazing the cattle, husking and pounding of rice and in rare cases cooking.	Sweeping or cleaning the house, bringing water for domestic use, preparing and serving food to the members, husking and pounding or rice.	Taking care of the young boys, when mother is busy with domestic work.
ii. Collection of food	Collection of fuel, silk cotton, tortoise, fish and selling them in the market.	Collection of fuel, skill-cotton, fish, tortoise, mohua fruits and selling them in the market or to neighbouring families.	Collection of Mohua flowers or fruits.
iii. Field work (in case of Narayangarh)	Ploughing, hoeing, digging, manuring, transplanting, weeding and harvesting, carrying, threshing, stacking etc.	Hoeing, transplanting, weeding, harvesting, threshing when required	Help in threshing.
iv. Other pursuits	Day labourers for road construction, herdsmen, carpenters, tusser, cocoon collection	Day labourers for road construction, helping in cattle keeping also.	

Source: Field data

incipient form of agriculture is one of the major occupations of the people of Narayangarh Block but the produce is so less that it cannot provide subsistence for even a quarter of the

Table 2

A Few Important NTFP Usually Collected by the Sample Households in Nayagram C.D. Block, Paschim Medinipur

NTFP Item	*Collection Time*	*Rate Per Unit of Product*
Sal leaf	January j March	Rs. 7.00 per paired leaves
Sal seed	April j May	Rs. 2.00 per kg.
Sabai grass	September j October	Rs. 2.50 per kg.
Need seed	June j July	Rs. 1.00 per kg.
Mohua flower	February j March	Rs. 10.00 per kg. In the form of liquor
Mohua seed	May j June	Rs. 3.00 per kg.
Mushroom	During rainy season	Rs. 6.00 - 8.00 per kg.
Cashew	April j May	Rs. 12.00 - 15.00 per kg.
Bahera	November j January	Rs. 1.00 per kg.
Haritaki	November j December	Rs. 3.00 per kg.
Amlaki	November j December	Rs. 3.00 per kg.
Kuchla (Medicinal herb)	Round the year	Rs. 4.00 per kg.
Kalmegh (Medicinal herb)	July j September	Rs. 3.00 per bundle
Kurchi (Medicinal herb)	June j July	Rs. 5.00 per bundle
Bamboo	Throughout the year	Rs. 15.00 j 20.00 per piece
Kendu leaves	November j January	Rs. 863.00 per Qntl. (low grade)Rs. 1136.00 per
Qntl. (high grade)		
Tusser cultivation on Sal, Arjun and Asan plants	Throughout the year	Rs. 500.00 per kahan Rs. 40.00 per 100 no. of coccon

Source: Same as Table-1

year. Owing to marginal land holdings, bad soil condition, primitive means of production, unavailability of water, the yield rate is not at all promising. Thus, to supplement their income people mainly depend on the vast resources of the local forest.

Table–2 shows a few important NTFP usually collected by the sample households in Nayagram C.D. Block, Paschim Medinipur.

Table–3 shows the MFP/NTFP used for households' consumption by the studied communities of Nayagram.

Table 3
MFP/NTFP used for Household Consumption in Nayagram C.D. Block, Paschim Medinipur

Plants and Plant Parts	*Mode of Consumption*
Sal leaf	Plates (dona)
Sal, Asan and others	Fuel wood
Asan	Furniture
Mohua seed	Cooking oil
Pan alu, Chun alu and other tubers, Sidha, Kend, Bahera, etc.	Food
Various herbs like Kurchi, Ishwarmul, Anantamul, Kalmegh, etc.	Medicine
Bamboo	House construction
Grass (Sabai)	Mats, Cots, Ropes

Source: Same as Table-1

Table 4
Economic Values of a Few Edible NTFP Items Available in Nayagram C.D. Block, Paschim Medinipur

Edible Items	*Price (Rs.)*	*Equivalent Units*
Chun alu	3.50 – 4.00 per kg.	
Pan alu	3.50 – 4.00 per kg.	
Baonla alu	4.00 – 5.00 per kg.	
Mata sak	4.00 per kg.	1 kg. = 4 bundles
Bon kankrol	40.00 per kg.	
Kendu fruit	1.00 per 10 pieces	
Bel	1.00 per 2 pieces	
Charkul	4.00 per kg.	1 kg. = 4 cups
Bhurur	2.00 per kg.	1 kg. = 4 cups
Mahul flower	10.00 – 11.00 per kg.	

Contd.

Edible Items	*Price (Rs.)*	*Equivalent Units*
Parab chhatu	15.00 – 20.00 per kg.	
Putka chhatu	10.00 per kg.	
Bon kundri	25.00 per kg.	
Bon pui	2.00 per kg.	
Kurol sak	2.00 per kg.	

Source: Same as Table-1

Seasonal food items like berries and plums consumed by the village children are omitted from this account because those fruits are available in scanty. This fact is also true for forest animals and birds, which are occasionally hunted by the tribals. Different types of tubers like *Pan alu, Chun alu, Kanta alu* and *Ban alu,* etc. are sold at the rate of Rs. 3.50 to 5.00 per kg. Wild mushrooms are sold at the rate of Rs. 10.00 to 20.00 per kg. Villagers sell leafy vegetables occasionally. However, *Mohua* flowers are sold almost regularly in the local *hats* (markets) and the cost varies from Rs. 8.00 to 10.00 per kg. The *Bon kankrol,* a vegetable food item is sold in the market at a rate as high as Rs. 40.00 per kg. (Table–4).

Table 5
Mean Household Annual Collection and Sale of Edible NTFPs in the Sample Villages of Nayagram C.D. Block, Paschim Medinipur (Amount in grams.)

Name of the Community	*Type of Operation*	*Leafy Vegetables*	*Flowers (Mohua)*	*Fruit*	*Tuber*	*Mushroom*
LODHA	Collection	9400	26800	13700	20700	7700
	Sale	Nil	15400	370	5000	2430

Source: Same as Table-1

Table – 5 shows the amount of collection, consumption and sale of the edible NTFP items in the sample villages of Nayagram block. Among the food items gathered by the members of the studied communities from the forests, *Mohua* flower and a variety of tubers constitute the largest portion followed by leafy vegetables, mushrooms and fruits. In all the studied villages it has been observed that the members collect and consume part of the total food items and the rest are sold in the local markets.

OCCUPATIONAL DISTRIBUTION

Occupational distribution of the people of the sample households of Nayagram shows that out of 184 persons, a large number of people are engaged in collection and selling of NWFPs – 138 (75.00%) followed by 29 (15.76%) in cultivation/ agriculture and 15 (8.15%) in agricultural labour category. Gender-wise variation in work participation exists only in case of agricultural labour where only male members of the community have engaged themselves. But occupational distribution of the people of the sample households of Narayangarh shows that out of 191 persons, 112 (58.64%) are under the category of agricultural labour followed by 46 (24.08%) in non-agricultural labour and 26 (13.61%) in cultivation or agriculture category. Collection of minor forest produce is recorded by 138 (75.00%) persons followed by 29 (15.76%) in cultivation/ agriculture and 15 (8.15%) in agricultural labour category. No gender-wise variation in work force participation exists in Narayangarh block (Table – 6).

NOTE ON MIGRATION FOR LIVELIHOOD EXPLORATION OF THE LODHAS

The foregoing account of life and livelihood matters indicates that the 'technology' is a livelihood strategy, which changes life and its conditions. Applying this to the Lodhas of Paschim Medinipur district we find that they have had a simple technology of food gatherers and hunters of small games. Usually the Lodhas of the study area collect Minor Forest Produces (MFPs) or Non-timber Forest Produces (NTFPs) and sell them to the weekly *hats* (markets). Intermediaries come to the village on alternate days and buy the collected MFPs from villagers and sell them to the nearby market centres in Orissa and Jharkhand and other parts of the districts of Paschim Medinipur. MFPs are mainly Sal leaf, Kendu leaf, various seeds, fruits, grass, medicinal plants, etc. The earning from collecting and selling of MFPs are not sufficient which divert the tribal villagers occasionally for illegal felling of timbers.

Table 6

Occupational Distribution of the Population of the Sample Households in Paschim Medinipur District, West Bengal

	Lodha Community								
	Nayagram (n = 75)			*Narayangarh (n = 75)*			*Blocks Together (n = 150)*		
Type of Occupation	*Male*	*Fe-male*	*Total*	*Male*	*Fe-male*	*Total*	*Male*	*Fe-male*	*Total*
Agril. Labour	15	00	15(8.15)	46	66	112 (58.64)	61	66	127 (33.87)
Non-agril. Labour	00	00	00(0.00)	32	14	46 (24.08)	32	14	46 (12.27)
Cultivation/ Agriculture	15	14	29(15.76)	12	14	26(13.61)	27	28	55 (14.67)
Collection and Selling of NWFPs	61	77	138(75.00)	00	00	00 (0.00)	61	77	138 (36.80)
Shop/Petty Business	00	00	00(0.00)	02	00	02 (1.05)	02	00	02 (0.53)
Govt. Service	00	01	01(0.54)	00	00	00 (0.00)	00	01	01 (0.26)
Others *	00	01	01(0.54)	04	01	05(2.62)	04	02	06 (1.60)
Total	91	93	184	96	95	191	187	188	375
	[49.46]	[50.54]	[49.07]	[50.26]	[49.74]	[50.93]	[49.87]	[50.13]	[100.00]

Source: Same as Table-1

Note : Figures in first and third brackets represent the percentages in column and row respectively.

The forest produces are processed to some extent with their traditional mechanism. Sal leaves are stitched in pairs and made in bundles for selling. Sabai grass is dried and made into ropes. Very recently tusser cocoons are reared in the forests, which are collected by the Lodhas after paying revenue to the forest departments. These activities are mainly performed by the females, though menfolk also provide assistance in bundling, selling and sometimes making of the products. These products are made in the leisure hours of the day. Most of the tribal people rear livestock. Poultry birds are found in almost all the houses. Goats are quite in large numbers in these villages.

But the Lodhas of Narayangarh Block of Paschim Medinipur district in West Bengal are dependent on agriculture, agricultural labour and non-agricultural labour for earning their livelihood. They have also engaged themselves as construction labour force in the National Highway (Golden Quadrilateral / Bharat Nirman Project) passing through this area from Howrah to Balasore in Orissa.

Besides, deforestation has compelled the Lodhas initially for seasonal migration but the process of land alienation and dispossession pushed them out to urban or industrial centres. This impact has developed acceptance of entrepreneurship among the tribals. At present, in most of the tribal dominated areas of these districts, agriculture does not provide the tribals a viable economy. The development, which took place among them after independence, shows that there has been a phenomenal shift among the tribals from agriculture to off - the farm occupations. They are inclined to accept wage-earning through road or building construction, government or private service or through agricultural labour.

The process of urbanisation, industrialization and modernization have affected the socio-economic set up, as well as day to day living of the tribal people. Thus, today there is a need for migration among them. They migrate to towns and urban centres for making a living. Similarly, often during times of crisis and disaster the tribals migrate to the nearby towns and villages. Thus, migration is a kind of crisis management protocol for the tribals. But with the coming of monsoon, most of the migrants immediately return to their place of origin. In this way, the migrant groups constitute a link between the place of migration and the place of origin.

LODHA ECONOMY AND ITS TRANSFORMATION

The whole of tribal India is, at present, going through the critical stage of transition. The tribal society today no longer gives an impression of a society based upon kinship, where social stratification of any form is absent. By and large, the Indian tribal situation today gives an altogether different picture. As Desai (1960) states,

"The study of the classification of the tribal population has also indicated another fact, viz., that even among the tribal population; a peculiar type of stratification has been progressing. On the one hand, a small privileged, property-owning, educated section has been emerging; on the other hand, the vast bulk of the tribals are being hurled into the ranks of the lowest toiling, exploited classes of contemporary Indian society. This stratification has crucial significance. This 'vocal', 'richer', 'privileged minority' will inevitable utilise the benefits on the tribals in the form of special concessions in their game of power".

Admittedly, this calls for a closer examination of the new, èmerging stratification level of the tribals.

There has been a need to define the social situation in the context of development. One has to take a total view of the social, economic, ecological, political and technological factors– a *systems approach* to the situation. Undoubtedly, vast currents of change in the form of demographic growth, adoption of urban elements, partial education, marginalisation of traditional economic activities (farming and artisanal production) and the sum total effect of coercion, conversion and the willing adoption of new ways meant the giving up of traditional ways of life sweeping the traditional tribal societies. Cultural values and norms, which are communicable only through traditional linguistic symbols, are dying out, leaving a vacuum in the life of the people. Traditional political worldview has to some extent been replaced by participant political culture and world-view. One may also like to know whether efforts at building a national identity by using the mass media, political organisations and the modern school system could narrow geographic and tribal lines of affiliation. No doubt, the tribals remain at the periphery of the mainstream culture, sometimes trying to associate with its myths, symbols and codes while denying their own individual contributions to the national culture milieu. It may be that the national policies are not culturally acceptable to the tribals. This involves examining the cultural integrity of the people and an understanding of their survival strategies. After all, it is in their culture human beings become whole.

In the economic front, the tribals are showing the same disturbing trend as has been noticed among the non-tribals. It is expected that the primary sector will employ the maximum labour force. But in the absence of any significant industrialisation, the fruits of which are yet to reach the tribals, the primary sector is incapable of employing the increasing labour force. That is why; there has been an increasing dependence on the urban centres, particularly markets. Increasing involvement with the national level party politics is another feature. Together with these, an emergent consciousness for self-identification poses a great challenge. Pan-tribal movements should no longer be dismissed as defensive gesture in the form of innocent protests. These are the positive assertions claiming the rights of the tribals. These may even mean a nostalgic desire to return to a happy past, aversion to out-sider's exploitation on them and interfering with their traditional way of living. Also implicit is a desire to determine their future.

Generally speaking, there has been an accelerated pace of change implicit in the development process that shakes up the age-old, traditional structure of the tribal culture in tribal societies in varying degrees. This accelerated change brings discontinuities and does not always allow for the evolution of existing perception to cope with and internalise change. Sometimes, the individuals experience the drift, anomie and the self-depreciation associated with ultimate adoption of negative images of self and society, and the consequent problems. The question of identity must start with an analysis of the social relation at its base. It is a social problem. But what is social may to some extent be explained in economic terms, because the specific features of any economy are mainly socially determined.

Tribal societies especially in Paschim Medinipur district of West Bengal are at different levels of development so far as their life-style is concerned. Exposure to external forces has exposed them to exploitation by the more communities, and in many cases, they have been practically dislodged from their own habitats. Few tribal households in the studied areas are able to support themselves on the basis of a single business activity (gathering and hunting, farming or non-farming) or full-time wage employment. Given limited social and economic capital and skills, a poor person's scope for developing an enterprise with ample profit margins is limited and, in any case, the risk of relying on a single business is too great. Farm incomes or wages in case of Narayangarh Block, moreover, have often fallen further and further behind the minimum required to support a family as recession and structural adjustment policies have bitten.

It seems, structurally the Lodha family has undergone a change. In early time, joint and extended family institutions contributed positively towards joint and organised endeavour in the hunting-gathering fields and it assured better stability and security to the family economy. But with a gradual recession in the hunting land as well as forest resource, the people have taken, to different non-traditional occupation including wage labour, in neighbouring areas. This shift in their occupational pursuits probably eroded the genuine necessity for joint living. Inroad of education might have added to these changing trends because of their growing individualistic attitude/personalities as well as a tendency towards maintaining more privacy in their conjugal life. Changes have occurred in the family authority too. Traditionally the eldest male member of family used to be the head of the household.

Due to increasing trend in cash earning, the earning male members are playing increased and dominant roles in the running the family. From the traditional self-sufficient and subsistence economy characterised by non-specialised roles and non-hierarchical relationships they have been turned into specialised and hierarchical relationships: employer–employee, trader–consumer, creditor–debtor, land owner peasant and overall market economy.

Owing to proximity of urban centres (in case of Narayangarh), a number of people work in non-farm activities as permanent or casual workers and also on the agricultural sector as their main occupation. This gives birth to a proliferation of occupational categories and mixed type of occupational structures consisting of agricultural activities as labourers and share-croppers, poultry farming, cattle rearing, rice-beer (*handia*) selling, tailoring, business, cycle repairing, teaching, etc. Here, it is to be noted that the tribal economy has not been fully monetised as its traditional forces of production are still operating.

However, the traditional tribal economy has changed witnessing development of new economic activities and continuous impact of new economies. Specifically, these are: development of new communication, i.e., transport, education, media and others; introduction of cash economy and changing cropping pattern from cereals to cash crops; selling of minor forest produces in local markets; emergence of tribal money – lenders; consumerism and more needs and demands for goods and services; commercialism and tribes' search for money and cash needs; development of Co-operatives and Commercial Banks; reservations in various institutions, government and semi-government establishments, panchayati raj and various development programmes; land reforms and wage legislation; and saving–investment aptitude and commercial aptitude of the tribals. The impact of these changing directions are : diversity in occupational structure, differentiation in the abilities to earn and income, higher expectations in improving the living conditions of the tribals below poverty line, development of educational opportunities, growing interactions with the non-tribals in multiplex, decline of intra-family and inter-family solidarity or joint family and the rise of a new family structure, i.e., the nuclear family, economy - determined family status rather than the order of birth and position in society, decline of intro – community and rise of intra – status solidarity, and overall de-tribalisation.

OCCUPATIONAL MOBILITY

Economic diversification and associated occupational diversification have changed the pattern of co-operation. Previously, community hunting was the main occupation and it was the only source of their income. But today's pattern of occupation is entirely different and so people move independently to various economic pursuits. Consequently, appreciable joint adventures of the people on traditional line for economic gain is out dated today.

The Table–7 shows the generation–wise occupational mobility of the people studied. It has been found from the table of reference that 60 respondents have collection and selling of NWFP as their occupation whose fathers were also in the same occupational category. Further it is also recorded that the older generations of those engaged in agriculture, or as agricultural labours or non-agricultural labours, were pursuing the same occupations. Practically, there is no such occupation mobility among the Lodhas of Nayagram.

The Table–8 shows the generation–wise occupational mobility of the Lodhas. It has been found from the table that respective fathers of 46 respondents working as agricultural labour used to pursue the same occupation. But their sons (the third generation) are in different occupational category as seen from the table. Only those who are in the 'Other' category, their respective fathers were in agricultural labours and non-agricultural labours categories. Practically, there is no such occupation mobility among the Lodhas of Narayangarh.

CONCLUSION

The present study on Lodahs throws some light on the nature and intensity of participation of small communities in the

Table 7

Generation wise Occupational Mobility of the Sample Lodhas of Studied Nayagram C.D. Block in Paschim Medinipur District, West Bengal

		Occupation of the Respondent's Father							*Occupation of the Respondent's Son*						
Occupation of the Respondent		*I*	*II*	*III*	*IV*	*V*	*VI*	*VII*	*I*	*II*	*III*	*IV*	*V*	*VI*	*VII*
I. Agril. Labour	04	01	03	-	-	-	-	-	-	-	-	-	-	-	-
II. Non-agril. Labour	03	-	03	-	-	-	-	-	-	-	-	-	-	-	-
III. Cultivation	06	06	-	-	-	-	-	-	-	-	-	-	-	-	-
IV. Selling of NWFPs	60	-	-	-	60	-	-	-	-	-	-	-	-	-	-
V. Shop/Petty Business	-	-	-	-	-	-	-	-	-	-	-	-	-	-	-
VI. Govt. Service	02	01	-	-	01	-	-	-	-	-	-	-	-	-	-
VII. Others*	-	-	-	-	-	-	-	-	-	-	-	-	-	-	-

Source: Same as Table-1

Table 8

Generation wise Occupational Mobility of the Sample Lodhas of Studied Narayangarh C.D. Block in Paschim Medinipur District, West Bengal

Occupation of the Respondent		*Occupation of the Respondent's Father*							*Occupation of the Respondent's Son*						
		I	*II*	*III*	*IV*	*V*	*VI*	*VII*	*I*	*II*	*III*	*IV*	*V*	*VI*	*VII*
I.Agril. Labour	46	01	40	05	-	-	-	-	-	02	15	-	01	-	-
II. Non-agril. Labour	12	-	02	10	-	-	-	-	-	-	03	-	-	-	-
III. Cultivation	12	10	02	-	-	-	-	-	-	-	01	-	-	-	-
IV. Selling of NWFPs	-	-	-	-	-	-	-	-	-	-	-	-	-	-	-
V. Shop/Petty Business	01	-	01	-	-	-	-	-	-	-	-	-	-	-	-
VI. Govt. Service	-	-	-	-	-	-	-	-	-	-	-	-	-	-	-
VII. Others*	04	-	03	01	-	-	-	-	-	-	-	-	-	-	-

Source: Same as Table-1

* 'Others' includes Rickshaw/Trolley pullers

process of development in general and in the era of globalisation in particular. What is viewed is that the Lodhas either remained at where they were in the previous generation or got absorbed in the fringe of the national development process. The absorption has not been able to remove their consciousness as Lodhas while situating themselves with the non-Lodhas in the development process. Their dependence on traditional resources for their livelihood strategies is giving way to resources available in development process of the nation. But their share is very much marginal when the nature of participation is recorded during field study.

Today's concept of life and its progress depend on technology and the technology improves every day. The society in general and its individual in particular should go hand in hand with technology for well-being as well human progress in the new extending horizons of civilization. The modern human's slogan of life is "Keep in touch with technology". How do we account for those who are not getting along with the pace of modern technology? Who would end up where? Time alone is a witness to human technology and consequent changes in life and livelihood matters. The effect of globalisation on culture should be seen in the long run and in multiple patterns, ranging from impact on value system to economic and management systems of the local culture. The changes are visible in management pattern of common from decentralised and diversified to centralised and utilitarian. It should also be assessed from the point of low input strategies of local culture against high cost management approach of global culture.

REFERENCES

Bhowmick, P. K. (1963), *The Lodhas of West Bengal–A Society-economic Study*. Calcutta: Punthi Pustak.

Chandrasekhar, E. (1954), *Hungary People and Empty Land*. London: George Allen and Unwin Ltd.

Dalton, George (1971), *Economic Anthropology and Development*. New York: Basic Books, pp. 89.

Desai, A. R. (1960), *Rural Sociology in India*. Mumbai: Popular Prakashan.

Durkheim, E. (1965), *The Elementary Forms of Religious Life*. New York: Free press.

Eriksen, T.H. (1995), *Small Places, Large Issues*. London: Pluto Press.

Firth, R. (1967), *Themes in Economic Anthropology*. London: Tavistock Publications Ltd.

Hardesty, Donald, L. (1977), *Ecological Anthropology*. New York: John Willey & Sons.

Herkovits, M.T. (1952), *Economic Anthropology*. New York: Albert A. Knopf.

Kessing, F.M. (1957), "Population Pattern in Stable Societies". *Proceedings of World Conference*, 1954, Vol. VI, New York: U.N.

Mazumdar, D.N. and T.N. Madan (1970), *An Introduction to Social Anthropology*. Bombay: Asia Publishing House.

Piddington, Ralph (1952), *An Introduction to Social Anthropology*. Vol. I. Edinburgh & London: Oliver & Boyd.

Roy, S. (1997), "Globalisation, Structural Change and Poverty: Some Conceptual and Policy Issues". *Economic and Political Weekly*, Vol.32 (33/34), Aug, 1997.

Singh, Y. (2000), *Culture Change in India: Identity and Globalisation*. New Delhi: Rawat Publications.

SECTION–III

Specious Dynamics

10

GLOBALISATION AND PROBLEMS OF HIV-AIDS AND CHILD TRAFFICKING IN MANIPUR

H.V. Singh

INTRODUCTION

Due to the advanced science and technological developments, the social structure of society is rapidly changing. The change is fast and touches upon every facets of life. Such changes in production, distribution and consumption patterns are affected by many technological innovations and media revolutions. The change has wider sweep and affects the socio-economic spheres across different parts of the globe. The change has its impact on health sector too. All of this totality of process is what we meant by globalisation. In a comprehensive term globalisation is the closer integration of countries and peoples of the world which has been brought about by the enormous reduction of costs of transportation and communication, and the breaking down of artificial barriers to the flows of goods, services, capital, knowledge, and (to a lesser extent) people across borders. (Stiglitz, 2002:9). It is transformation of global society ignoring territorial frontiers.

Globalization has both negative and positive impacts on society. In the health sector, due to cross border movements between states and nations, communicable diseases including HIV/AIDS get transmitted. Through globalization, many harmful products such as tobacco and other narcotic drugs have been creeping into the underdeveloped and developing countries. The notorious Golden Triangle at the border of Moreh in Manipur is such a major drug trafficking centre and a paradise of kingpins of smugglers. The invasion of drug trafficking in the early 1980s through the Indo-Myanmar border town at Moreh in Manipur and through the corridors of north-eastern states still has the impact specially in Manipur. The gloomy picture is more darkened and by the incident of ethnic clash, arms conflict, child trafficking, unemployment problems and many other factors.

Manipur, one of the states of India, on the North-Eastern region, lies between 23°50′ and 25°41′ N latitude and 93°2′ and 94°47′ E longitudes. The state is fringed by Nagaland on the North, Myanmar on the East and South, Assam on the West and North-west, and Mizoram on the South-west. In this paper, a discussion on the trend of HIV/AIDS in Manipur, child trafficking and other negative impacts of globalization is attempted.

GLOBALIZATION AND HIV/AIDS

It seems that globalization which is about open markets and trade policies has no link with health issue. But if one examines minutely, globalization and health issues such as HIV/AIDS are interlinked. For instance, the ability of African countries to respond to HIV/AIDS is dependent on their ability to better control of the terms of trade, which elicits more favourable patent policies on medication, and helps countries climbing out of poverty. (Naujakululu, 2008). Many local indigenous small-scale industries were collapsed when markets were liberalized and the products churning out of such indigenous knowledge and techniques were not the match for cheaper imported products from Europe, Asia and America. Many of the Africans lost their jobs and became incapable of meeting basic needs. How can one think or talk of HIV/AIDS, education or religion when one has no food and drink to satisfy hunger and quench thirst? Shrinking in poverty, everyday in Africa (ibid), HIV/AIDS kills 6,500 people; 9,500 people are infected with HIV; and 1,400 newborn babies are infected during childbirth or by their mother's milk.

As per reports of UNAIDS, the new global estimates on the scale of the AIDS epidemic, approximately 39.5 million people are living with HIV in 2006, 2.6 million more than in 2004. Of this, 8.6 million people are estimated to be infected with HIV in Asia. The situation is worse in India. According to the 2006 report on 'Global AIDS Epidemic', of the 8.6 million of people infected with HIV in Asia, India has 5.7 million cases of HIV by the end of December 2006, as against about 5.5 million people infected in South Africa. Earlier, India was having 3.97 million HIV infections by December 2001. The virus is spreading from little vulnerable population to vast general population. The world's first HIV Insurance Policy is opened at Banglore in India.

SCENARIO OF HIV/AIDS IN NORTH EAST INDIA

In India, Manipur occupies one of the topmost ranking positions in HIV/AIDS frequency chart. The first case of HIV was reported in February 1990. By July 2005, there are 20,524 HIV positive cases and 4012 AIDS cases have been reported out of 126,973 blood samples screened. There are also cases of 497 deaths. The frequency of prevalence of HIV among pregnant women has increased from 0.45% in 1995 to 1.66% in 2005. Surprisingly, the Ukhrul district, which is dominated by tribes, has reported HIV infection among the pregnant women in 2004. The HIV prevalence rate among CSWs (Commercial Sex Workers) is around 12.4% and among MSMs (Men Having Sex with Men) is 14.0%; among STD (Sexually Transmitted Diseases) patients, the HIV infection has increased from 3.9% in 1995 to 7.2% in 2005;among TB patients, the HIV prevalence has increased from 6.16% in 1995 to 18.75% in 2005; the HIV prevalence among the IDUs (Intravenous/Injecting Drug Users) has shown a decline from 80.7% in 1997 to 21.0% in

July 2005. (Lisham and Lisham, 2007). The significant decline among the IDUs is due to introduction of the Harm Reduction Project called Rapid Intervention and Care (RIAC) since 1998 with the help and support from NACO. (ibid. 2007). The following table shows the latest frequency of HIV/AIDS in Manipur.

Table 1
Age-Sex Proportion of HIV Positive Cases (Sero-surveilance)

Age-Group	*Males*	*Females*	*Total*	*% of Total Positives*
0-10 years	723	639	1362	6.18
11-20 years	892	370	1262	5.72
21-30 years	6465	3292	9757	44.24
31-40 years	5572	2257	7829	35.50
41 & above	1295	548	1843	8.36
Total	14947	7106	22053	100.00

Source: Epidemiological Analysis of HIV/AIDS in Manipur, October 2007

The high frequency of HIV/AIDS infection in Manipur is due to several factors. Geographical proximity is one such factor. Manipur has a border town at Moreh bordering with Myanmar (Burma). This Moreh town in Manipur and Lamphalong in Myanmar, which are walking distance apart, are the hubs of trade centers. The two are global markets exchanging goods legally and illegally. From early 1980s till date Heroin No. 4 and other narcotic drugs have been trafficking from Myanmar to Manipur via Moreh. Many drug-addicted youths who share needle syringes are responsible for rising up of the statistics of HIV infection. Moreover, there are flesh trade centers in these areas. Many tourists, businesspersons, police personnel, drivers and others who are mobile through the places are the High Risk Groups (HRGs) of HIV infection. Young people without any options for government employment or any other productive works deal in small petty business through this centre. They are also the easy targets of the dreaded virus.

The above mentioned global markets have the significance of invading products, which are cheaper and better in quality. The tribes especially those who are bordering to Myanmar and the general population of Manipur are affected by the globalization. Few of the people who can invest and who have skill of business can take the benefit of it. Majority of the population suffer because their products become comparatively inferior to the imported goods from Myanmar and China. Yesteryears handloom and handicraft products, agricultural produces, local wine, etc. are not match for the foreign items.

Arms conflict in Manipur is a very familiar and frequently happening incident. If one examines the daily local newspaper or the northeast news, the news from Manipur is almost the news of reporting on killing, kidnapping, extortion and the like. Many youths are killed through cross fire. Their young widows and small children are facing a living hell. Without any productive earning options, many of them are compelled to the flesh trade for earning two square meals a day. The frequency of widowhood and illegal earning is more cumulated by the incident of Naga-Kuki clash in which many innocent victims were butchered. Without proper awareness knowledge of HIV/AIDS and other Sexually Transmitted Diseases (STDs), they become easy prey to the disease. Besides that many of young boys and girls who are easily accessing to pornographic channels such as magazine, video, computer, internet, mobile phones etc. are easily motivated to indulge in premarital and extramarital sex. This increases the risk of HIV infection and other STDs. The situation is worse to areas where local made liquor is widely used as a part of the customary tradition. The tradition perhaps might have influenced to have a more liberal attitude towards sex and impair the sense of judgment for protecting from infectious STDs. Risky sexual behaviour of not using condoms basing on the principle of "eating toffee with cover or without cover" have spread a pool of infection.

Gay is another factor of increasing the HIV infection in Manipur. There are some pseudo-hermaphrodites who look like and behave like females. They are locally known as *Homo*. Among *Homos*, there are men having sex with men (MSMs). They are also a catalyst for HIV/AIDS infection. Through multi-channels of communication, the number of MSM in Manipur and other parts of India is increasing and amendments in the Indian Constitution are made. Art. 377 is such an act dealing with MSM.

The Tables from 2 to 11give the bird's eye view of HIV/AIDS in northeast India.

Table 2
Sero-surveillance During 1990-2005 in Assam

	1990-2005	*September 2005*
Number of persons tested	50,779	344
Number persons found HIV positive	920	13
Seropositivity rate	18.11	

Source: Lisham and Lisham, 2007

Table 3
Year-wise Number of AIDS Cases in Assam1990-2005

Year	*Male*	*Female*	*Total*
1990	1	-	1
1991-1993	-	-	-
1994	2	-	2
1995	7	-	7
1996	1	1	
1997	11	1	12
1998	10	4	14
1999	18	3	21
2000	35	6	41
2001	38	9	47
2002	15	1	16
2003	49	1	50
2004	39	12	51
2005 (September)	36	16	52
Total	262	53	315

Source : Same as Table No.2

Table 4
Routes of HIV Transmission in Assam

Routes of HIV Transmission	*Number of HIV Positives*	*Percentage*
Sexual	696	75.65
Blood and blood products	26	2.82
Sharing of needle and syringes	68	7.39
Mother to child	20	2.17
Others-not specified	110	11.95
Total	920	

Source : Same as Table No.2

Table 5
Age Group Distribution of AIDS Cases in Assam

Age Group	*Male*	*Female*	*Total*	*Percentage*
0-5 years	8	2	10	3.17
6-14 years	4	1	5	1.58
15-19 years	1	1	2	0.63
20-29 years	68	35	103	32.70
30-39 years	123	20	143	45.40
40-49 years	41	2	43	13.66
Above 49 years	9	0	9	2.86
Total			315	100.00

Source : Same as Table No.2

Table 6
Sero-surveillance During 1990-2005 (July) in Nagaland

Number of persons tested	46,985
Number persons found HIV positive	2963
Number of AIDS cases (including 293 deaths)	945
HIV prevalence among female sex workers	4.44%
HIV prevalence among pregnant women	1.28%
HIV prevalence among IDUs	2.92%
HIV prevalence among STD clinic Attendees	1.72%

Source : Same as Table No.2

Table 7
Sero-surveillance During 1990-2005 (July) in Meghalaya

Number of persons tested	17,664
Number persons found HIV positive	73
Number of AIDS cases	10

Source : Same as Table No.2

Table 8
Sero-surveillance During 1990-2005 (August) in Mizoram

Number persons found HIV positive	1253
Number of AIDS cases (including 75 deaths)	126
HIV prevalence among female sex workers	13.69%
HIV prevalence among pregnant women	1.5%
HIV prevalence among IDUs	5.3%

Source : Same as Table No.2

Table 9
HIV/AIDS Situation During 1990-2005 (July) in Sikkim

Number persons found HIV positive	41
Number of AIDS cases (including 5 deaths)	9

Source : Same as Table No.2

Table 10
HIV/AIDS Situation During 1990-2005 (July) in Arunachal Pradesh

Number of blood samples screened	1,26,973
Number persons found HIV positive	33
Number of AIDS cases (including 497deaths)	4012
The STD prevalence among the STD Clinic Attendees in Pasighat	31.2%
The STD prevalence among the STD Clinic Attendees in Naharlagun	16.14%
The STD prevalence among the STD Clinic Attendees in Tawang	7.25%
The STD prevalence among the STD Clinic Attendees in Along	6.86%
The STD prevalence among the STD Clinic Attendees in Bomdilla	2.10%
The STD prevalence among the STD Clinic Attendees in Tezu	1.50%

Source : Same as Table No.2

Table 11
HIV/AIDS Situation During 1990-2005 (31st August) in Tripura

Number persons found HIV positive	99
Number of AIDS cases (including 3 deaths)	8

Source: Same as Table No.2

GLOBALIZATION AND CHILD TRAFFICKING IN MANIPUR

Child trafficking has many forms-child prostitution, child soldier, trafficked for organ transplant, etc. Despite socio-legal hurdles, because of high profit, the illegal and inhuman acts are being carried out clandestinely. In January 2008, five young girls mostly Zeliarong tribe of Manipur (only one from Assam) were sold out to night bars at Malaysia after recruitment under the pretext of offering good jobs to them. Luckily they escaped. The case is the tip of the iceberg. Many girls might have been in hell working as prostitutes in bars and red light areas in Singapore and Malaysia and other places. Perhaps many other children have been used for organ transplants. Social workers Sobita, Secretary Women and Action Development and Pradipkumar, member, Manipur Alliance for Child Right, recently provided information on child trafficking. Recently, 62 children- 41 girls and 21 boys were trafficked but luckily they were rescued. Nagaland police and Tamilnadu government rescued them in time. These children and their parents were lured on the pretext of giving free education and job. Some network of agents have been operating and earning through such heinous crimes. The trafficked children are mostly tribals from hill districts of Manipur who are mostly from poor families.

Regarding a question on the inter linkage between the process of globalization and the issue of child trafficking in Manipur, Pradipkumar responds, "In some ways, can it be viewed as an episode that espoused certain impending negative impacts of India's Look East Policy on the threshold of region's emergence into globalization process? The total failure of capital formation, production based investments, human resource development and pro-people planning while implementing the globalization process made Manipur a fertile source for human trafficking. Inevitably few pertinent questions emerged –Should Manipur export sex tourism to the global tourists only to import AIDS, as they have no other profitable commodity to export? Should Manipuri women dance the night away, only to feed their hungry children and dying HIV positive husbands? Will the local Manipuris stand at the corner of the street only to breath in the exhaust toxic fumes, dust and smokes that will be emitted by upcoming trains or loaded trucks to be plying on Trans Asian Superhighways through Imphal, with many flyovers and dazzling neon lights?"(Kolkata Watch-XVIII, S.G. Dey, 2008).

It has been mentioned that many socio-economic factors accentuated the problem of HIV/AIDS. Displacement of families affected through the construction of dam has led hilly tribal to migrate to valleys particularly at Imphal. The families who are not properly rehabilitated and do not have the capacity to supervise and support their wards are easy preys to the human traffickers. Ethnic clash acts as added salt to injury.

Another deleterious dimension of globalization is seen in arms conflict. Recruitment of school going minor children by an insurgent group in Manipur in the late part of 2008 was big eye catching news. The model of child soldier recruitment perhaps might have been imitated from the Bangladeshis and Talibans.

GLOBALIZATION AND HIV/AIDS EDUCATION

Policy framers and planners are very much conscious and concerned of the students and young people. This is because of the fact that young people are more vulnerable than old people to HIV/AIDS. Therefore, as a means to give awareness to the students and young people, HIV/AIDS education as a part of the curricula, is designed and included in the education system. This has been incorporated after realising the importance of giving of HIV/AIDS education to the students. Education thus is a social vaccine. The evidence that education is the social vaccine is shown in one of the findings in Zambia. Studies point to the example of Zambia where HIV prevalence for young women between 15-19 years dropped from 27% in 1993 to 15% in 1998 (Lisham, 2004). This shows that the frequency percentage of infection with HIV/AIDS is more markedly found to less educated women than to young educated women. Therefore, focus on preventive education to HIV/AIDS and other infectious disease should be an inherent part of the national curriculum. The curriculum should include the learning needs like health and sex education, which is culturally acceptable to the community, life skills, and ways and means to protect from HIV/AIDS and other infectious disease, non-discrimination of people living with HIV/AIDS. Research works on people's attitude towards sex, nature of adolescent sex, cultural relativistic concept of masculinity and femininity, different channels of influencing sex, level of self esteem, awareness and attitude towards condom use and the like, should be carried out. For successful executing of such programmes, teachers both in in-service and pre-service should be properly trained. Only after that the global threat of this dreaded disease can be controlled.

SUMMARY AND CONCLUSION

The present paper has highlighted the negative impacts of globalization in the light of discussing the HIV/AIDS in Manipur. It is an undeniable fact that globalization has invaded the local culture- both tangible and intangible aspects of culture. The global culture through many agencies of social change has been slowly engulfing the local culture. In every sphere of life- socio-economy, political authority, religion, education, health sectors etc., the dominating features of global culture has been acting. Even the social crime ranging from eve teasing to forcibly injection of HIV/AIDS have been witnessing through the process of globalization. Cases of report of forcibly injection of HIV for demanding ransom after kidnapping people and threatening girls and women on matrimonial issues have been reporting in Hyderabad (The Telegraph, 2nd January, 2009). Through many agencies of globalization, the moral values of our people have been eroding. The increasing frequency of HIV/AIDS, child trafficking, child solder recruitment, problems of displacement etc. are some of the negative impacts of globalization seen in Manipur.

REFERENCES

Lisham, Khomdon Singh (2004), *HIV/AIDS and You. Indian AIDS Consortium, Palace Road, Imphal, Manipur-795001.*

Lisham, Khomdon Singh and Lisham, Suchitra (2007), Young People and AIDS (How to protect from HIV/AIDS?)., The AIDS Consortiumm B-3/141, Paschim Vihar New Delhi-110063, India.

MACS, Imphal (2007), *Epidemiological Analysis of HIV/AIDS in Manipur*, October 2007

S.G. Dey (2008), Kolkata Watch-XVIII.

Stiglitz J.E. (2002), *Globalization and its Discontents*. London: Allen Lane, the Penguine Press.

W.J. Naujakululu (2008), *The Impact of Globalization and Trade on HIV-AIDS in Africa*, mhtml:file://F:\aids\aids2.mht.

The Telegraph (2009), 2nd January.

11

THE IMPACT OF GLOBALISATION ON TRIBAL WOMEN IN THE NORTH EAST WITH SPECIAL REFERENCE TO ANGAMI WOMEN: AN OVERVIEW

Daisy Nath

Every event in the social process has a time period. For example, Industrial Revolution is identified with nineteenth century and Renaissance with sixteenth century. Similarly, colonialism normally spreads over the period from fifteenth to twentieth century. In the same way, the present millennium can be identified with globalisation. While globalization cuts across geographical, social and cultural boundaries, leading towards a larger integration of the world and facilitating interdependence and thereby moving towards a global economy, resistance to globalization is a move for preservation of tradition and identity. Apart from the political and economic debate concerning the effects of globalization, it can be presumed that globalisation is a threat to the economy and identity of women in general and tribal women in particular.

Over the last decade, countries across the world have embarked on changing existing economic models in favour of ones driven by the free market, incorporating the processes of liberalisation, privatisation and globalisation. While the market boomed, the gap between the rich and the poor increased. The other changes that took place with the advent of globalisation are depletion of natural resources and loss of traditional livelihoods, forced migration, consumerism and violence. The process of globalisation began in the 1980s. But in India the process was introduced in the late 1990s with the commitment of the Government of India to its "New Economic Policy."

The present kind of globalisation brings untold misery to the poor. It is marked by competition which takes place visibly among the unequals. Among the unequals are labourers of different skill endowments. They face unprecedented insecurities and hardships. At present people are living the most insecure life as jobs have become scarce and uncertain. Due to high inflation, the life of the common people has become miserable.

North East India is the home of various tribes or indigenous communities. About 26.77 per cent of the total population of the region is tribal. The tribal women constitute around half of the tribal population in the North East. The threat of globalisation can be more acute here as the region has already been labelled as backward. While the supporters of globalisation and liberalisation see it as a positive sign for the overall development of the tribes, the critics are vocal about the impoverishment and degradation in economy created by globalisation. In the present paper, we have tried to examine and evaluate the impact of globalisation on the tribal women in the North Eastern Region of India with special reference to Angami women. The presentation in this paper is based primarily on secondary sources, and information collected from field observations, discussion with NGO workers and feminist scholars on various formal and informal occasions.

Women face certain hardships peculiar to them as they have a special place in society and home; special demands are made on them as a result of this special position. The present situation has had very many grave implications. The women who worked in the formal sector, due to lack of their special technical skills had the most arduous, repetitive and insecure jobs. Many of those working women are now forced to give up their positions as members of the permanent staff, and to become contractual employees as many of these industries sub-contract parts of their operations to other operations to reduce their own liabilities. Female workers are also not paid wages according to their productivity. They are assigned to work under hazardous conditions causing health problems. (Kumar and Shivalkar, 2007: xii). Many women have migrated to the cities where they face tremendous problems of housing, sanitation, etc. (Sen, 1999: 24). Women have become selective victims of modernisation in industry in response to the globalisation of the market. Women working in corporations cannot form unions and they cannot fight for their rights. Very often women are subject to verbal and physical abuse. So their rights as human beings are violated in the present situation. (Yogish, 2007: 229). For the same work women are paid less but are preferred to men. Now they are increasingly being replaced by machines.

In agriculture, as in industry, women suffer as a result of the processes of globalisation. Ilina Sen (1999:25) in her article has said that the manifestations of the globalisation syndrome are to be seen in terms of increasing centralisation of market and product, shifting from food crops to cash crops, and the predominance of monocultures where once there was bio-diversity. Women have lost their recognition for the work they used to do in the agricultural field. With the changes that take place in agricultural sector, women's social and economic contribution is further devalued. Besides these, there are many other areas of life in which globalisation has adverse effects on women.

GLOBALISATION AND TRIBAL WOMEN

Tribal women are double victims of globalisation. With the massive land alienation to large scale industries by the foreign investor in the name of development, tribal women are under pressure to look after their families and to work in the field. Most of the women have lost their traditional livelihood. Moreover, due to lack of education they cannot fit in the formal sector also. With the loss of their economic status most of the tribal women are forced to lose their traditional status in their society. At the same time women are put to increasing hardship in their nurturing roles because of the scarcity of the locally grown and the locally marketed food crops. Their nutritional quality has also reduced. The women and mothers distribute the lion's share of food to the other family members first and they take the rest. So they have to manage on their empty stomachs which adversely affect their health. Tribals are the forest dwellers that have a distinctive and spiritual relation with the nature. They live in the midst of plants, trees, rocks, grass and fresh air and good sunshine. Hence their way of life is patterned according to the environment. Tribal people had access to a wide range of green vegetables and other natural harvest. Medicinal plants provided remedies for diseases. But now all the people have to depend on the western system of medicine which invariably destroys their economic condition and the medicinal plants of this region also. (Netam 2001: 3). With deforestation, fruit trees, roots, vegetable and herbal medicine are no longer available close at hand.

As Indian economy is based on agriculture, especially in the case of the Northeast, land is an important asset for the people. In this context, land rights of women are becoming an area of concern within the ideological frame of equality. The nature of land relations has had a great impact on women's status in the Northeast region. While community control is the primary principle on which tribal land relations are centred, but this has been changed with the commercialisation of land. As a result more and more lands are being brought under private ownership. Individual ownership in dry and wet fields among Dimasa and individual ownership in the terrace fields among Angamies are well established. (D'Souza, Cristina and Veronica, 2002:66). Everywhere the growth of individual land holdings has resulted in far reaching changes in the community in general and women's status in particular. These changes have major implications for women's status. In the community ownership system women play a vital role in the production. They participate in almost all aspects of production. But as the ownership of land has transferred from community to the individual *patta* holders the women are longer the beneficiaries in this process of change. This lack of control is extended also to the decision making process. Where cropping patterns have changed due to commercialisation women have been losing their hold on traditional market pattern also. With land passing from community to the individual, the trend that has emerged is that the man has become the sole individual owner and that from him the ownership right is transferred to his son. In individual ownership the community principle of sharing that served as risk coping mechanism is lacking. A woman has lost her rights of free access to community resources which she enjoyed during community ownership regime. She has no right to collect forest resources without any permission in the individual turned-community land. Many tribes are going through this process of transition because of the transformation of land ownership from the community to the individual. Now some tribes prefer to hold individual ownership of land which has led to the emergence of absentee landlords (Cristina, 2006:87).

The Northeast India is industrially backward, so commercialisation of the economy will affect the other areas of the life of the people of the Northeast. Most of the tribals of the Northeast had assured food self sufficiency by depending on *Jhum* cultivation. As *jhum* is the common practice of agriculture among the tribes, the community had control over the land. The concept of market was absent among many tribes. But things have changed with globalisation. The traditional food crops have changed to the cash crops. Due to lack of technological development the agricultural production is not rising to the expected levels. So people are looking for some alternative sources of income. As a result, many tribes of the Northeast are taking to education to find other sources of income for their sustenance. In this matter the power of taking decision gradually goes to men and the social position of women gets marginalised. Many tribes have now started producing some cash crops for sale. Cash crops are used to invest for the education of their children including the girl children. Although imparting education to the girl children is a positive impact but the educated women are equally facing some new emerging social problems. For example the educated women among Angamies are now facing serious problem because it is difficult for them to get suitable grooms. Some of them remain unmarried because the patriarchal society demands that men should be more educated than or at least as educated as women. The liberated woman is a captive of patriarchy.

Globalisation has forced the women to change their lifestyle with the changing forces of commercialisation and market. With the market becoming an important element in defining social relations, women too have had to change their position within the social system. Earlier women contributed to their economy through the agricultural produce. But today as centres of trade and exchange have come up, women have to transfer their control at all levels of the traditional domestic sphere. In this new medium of exchange men are beginning to exercise control over it including cash, even though women are responsible for nurturing livestock. Thus women are losing their position in the decision making with both buying and selling going out of women's hand. (Fernandes and Barbora, 2002: 135).

The changes mentioned above can be observed in the Dimasa tribal areas. Women from Dimasa tribes have been experiencing the transformation of agricultural technology and the land use pattern in their societies. The Dimasa villages in the N.C Hills have been converting their collective land holding into community coffee or tea gardens. The traditional barter system too does not seem to offer much by a way of sustenance because the market is under the control of outsiders. (ibid., 134). Many a times they have to sell their products to the middlemen. In some areas the lack of local market is the main reason for the existence of the middlemen. Traditionally man has dealt with matters pertaining to sale to middlemen especially in cash crops. With the commercialisation of market, this system is further strengthened thereby making it difficult for women to engage in the marketing of cash crops. Money is by and large under men's control particularly when they depend less on jhum and forest than on a job outside.

Kumar and Shivalkar, (2001:6), in their article mention that in addition to alienating tribal land and destroying their means of livelihood, rapid urbanisation has also destroyed their distinct culture, dialects and values. Migration in search of work is now disrupting their social structure. After loosing their traditional livelihood, many tribals have now become merely wage labourers. Many teenaged girls and young women are forced to become domestic helps in the middle class homes and work in exploitative conditions. Today globalisation intensifies the process of marginalisation among all the tribes. In the context of shortages of resources, their identities tend to get hardened. Various tribes become competitors and each group feels that it alone has a right over their livelihood and tend to ignore communities that are poorer. (op.cit. 212). The problem of access to resources over which neither tribe has much control has been the cause of antagonism between ethnic groups in the past and continues well in to the present.

One of the adverse effects of globalisation is forced migration. The North East is a mega-biodiversity zone as well as an important biodiversity hotspot. Many dams are going to be built in the North East. The dam sites are mainly located in tribal areas. As a result, people would not only lose their land but also their livelihood. In the past tribals have been exploited and treated as suppliers of cheap labour but after globalisation they have been pushed away from society. They have been deprived of their sustenance, impoverished and thus excluded. Another consequence of land acquisition is ecological degradation. The North East is very rich in bio-diversity and no attempt has been made to protect this. As displaced people have no other source or alternatives, they have no choice but to cut tress for sale and destroy the environment in other form. (Fernandes, 1999: 29). During the last 50 years, at least 300 lakh persons, possibly double that number, has been displaced or otherwise deprived of livelihood without their consent for development schemes.

So the force of commercialisation and modernisation in the form of globalisation has surely brought both the negative and also the positive changes in the society as a whole. The tribal women are also experiencing economic, social and political changes. But the so called "Fairly High Status" of women in the tribal society has also changed with above changes. The new status is yet to take its due place.

POSITION OF WOMEN IN THE ANGAMI SOCIETY

The Angami live mostly in the district of Kohima in Nagaland. They are the fourth largest Naga tribe. In 1991, there were 97,433 persons in Nagaland who speak Amgami language as their mother tongue .(Census of India, 1991:66). In 2001, the total population of the Angami tribe was 124,696. They constituted 6.27 percent of the population of Nagaland. The female population is higher than that of the male in Angami society. Among the Angami, females outnumbered males with a sex ratio of 1004. (Census of India, 2008).

There are four distinct groups among the Amgami, namely, the Khonoma group, the Kohima group, the Viswema group and the Chakroma group. A large section of the Angami population follows Christianity. But there are also a substantial number of families practising traditional religion.

Angami Nagas had a highly decentralised democratic village council. Their villages are generally large in size both in terms of geographical area and population size. Residential sites are usually located on mountain tops and the surrounding land is used for terrace cultivation.

The Angami have a patriarchal system of society. They have different type of ownership of property. They have individually owned property, property owned in common by the lineage, clan or villages. As they have a patriarchal system, ownership rights in common property are restricted to the males alone. However, women have the right of use in all common property. An Angami woman can inherit what her parents acquire but cannot inherit ancestral property. (Zehol, 1998:55). The unmarried daughter however can possess her ancestral property. After marriage an Angami woman acquires certain rights in the property of her husband. Divorce is permitted by the traditional Angami law. A divorced woman loses her rights in her husband's property if she leaves her husband's house. But she retains all her personal belongings. Thus in traditional Angami society women have substantial property rights. But these rights were restricted mainly to movable property and acquired property. She did not have any ownership in land but she had the full liberty to control and manage the land of her husband.

Agriculture is the main economic activity of the Angami Nagas, with settled terrace cultivation as the principal method. Women play a decisive role in agricultural operations. Women not only perform most of the agricultural operations, but also decide on the crops to be gown. They also take charge of the produce.

GLOBALISATION AND ANGAMI WOMEN

Like other tribes the Angami are now experiencing the consequences of the new era of globalisation. As compared to the other tribes Angami women have been able to cope fairly well with the process of globalisation. In the era of globalisation, they have gained greater access to education. They have developed new avenues of leadership. They have passed through a process of evolving an expanded identity and a consciousness of their rights.

As recorded by Kekhrieseno Christina (2006), Angami women enjoyed several property rights. Angami traditional law permitted the parents to give agricultural land as a gift to a daughter provided the parents had personally acquired that land. Further, the Anagami woman had unrestricted rights in the cultivation of her husband's land. Thus an Angami woman controlled the use of agricultural land. She could decide what crops to grow, and how the produce was to be dealt with. As I have mentioned above, tribal women are now producing some cash crops and investing the money for their children. Angami women are no exception to it; they have also started cultivating some cash crops. They take independent decisions in spending the income earned from the sale proceeds of the cash crops.

Some Angami women have received modern education in the last decades of the 20th century. The number of such women has grown with easier access to education. This has resulted in a large number of Angami women in securing gainful employment outside the home. It is such educated women who have been able to discover new avenues of leadership. In the traditional Angami society due to its strongly patriarchal structure, a woman could not play any leadership role. But with education, they are able to play leadership roles in the modern professions and in the churches. (op.cit. 2002: 159).

Although globalisation has opened up new avenues for the Angamies but it has some ill effects also. Due to modern education the Angami women are more aware of their rights but their society has not changed yet. They are facing the trouble of preserving their identity and bringing the economic development with gender equality. Moreover the possibility of earning some income on their own has only added greater responsibilities. They are often required to maintain the household and educate younger siblings or even members of their clans.

CONCLUSION

We can say that in the era of globalisation far reaching changes have been noticed in the traditional tribal societies in the Northeast. Such changes have seriously affected the women in tribal societies. Their traditional status and role have undergone changes and the significance of achieved status as an important part of women's identity has increased. While very few women in most of the tribal societies have been able to deal with the changes, the majority have become marginalized. However, the situation of Angami women is slightly different. In general, they have been able to cope with the situation because of some features of Angami traditional organisation, though they face new challenges. Their example can be a model for other tribal women in the age of globalisation. Hence the need is to take measures that can assist tribal women in the process of globalisation without leading to their marginalisation.

REFERENCES

Alphonsus D'Souza, Kekhrieseno *Christina and* Noqweno *Veronica* (2002), *Status of Women in North-East India: A Comparative Study of Three Ethnic Groups in North-East India, Aka, Angami and Dimasa.* Jakhama: St Joseph's College (mimeo).

Bhuimali Anil and S.Anil Kumar (eds.).(2007), *Women in the Face of Globalisation.* New Delhi: Seriels.

Census of India (2008), Nagaland-Data Highlights: The Scheduled Tribes- Census of India 2001. New Delhi: Register General of India.

Fernandes, Walter (1999), "Globalisation, Land and Displacement Private", in *Caritas India Quarterly,* 49 (1). pp 26-30.

Fernandes, Walter and Sanjoy Barbor (2002), *Modernisation and Women's Status in North-East India: A comparative Study of Six Tribes.* Guwahati: North Eastern Social Research Centre.

Kekhrieseno Christina (2006), *Changing Land Relations in an Angami Village,* Unpublished Ph.D. Thesis. Shillong: North Eastern Hill University.

Kumar, Navleen and Shilpa Shivalkar (2002), *Impact of Land Alienation on Adivasi Women and Children.* Ahmedabad: Setu Publication.

Netam, Indu (2001), *Adivasi Women and Globalisation,* Ahmedabad: Setu Publications.

Sen, Ilina (1999), "The Impact of Globalisation on Women", in *Caritas India Quarterly,* 49 (1). pp 23-25.

Yogish S.N. (2007), *"Human Rights of Women".* in Bhuimali Anil and S. Anil Kumar(eds). op cit., pp. 223-240

Zehol, Lucy (1998), *Women in Naga Society.* New Delhi: Regency Publications.

12

THE NYISHI IN THE PROCESS OF DEVELOPMENT: A NOTE

Nabam Nakha Hina

Tribal communities in Arunachal Pradesh were tradition bound before they got exposed to forces of national development after independence. They practised subsistence mode of production pursuing mainly shifting cultivation. The organisation of labour was community based with mutuality. The traditional polity controlled the social norms and resource management. The tribal people mostly depended on immediate environment for their livelihoods like all ecosystem people. In addition to production they also foraged natural resources like forests and rivers.

After independence the most spectacular agent of change introduced in the state happened to be education. It is education that not only created awareness but also developed skill of learners thereby enlarging the choices of the tribal people. As a result, economic diversification took place; industrial and tertiary sector activities emerged as organised activities. Besides education, government also introduced various development schemes for the all round development of the people. Infact, the schemes pertained to agriculture, horticulture and other sectoral economic activities. As a consequence of these schems, the mobility of the tribal people increased. They not only interacted with other tribes but also with people outside Arunachal Pradesh in general, and bureaucrats, other government functionaries, missionaries, etc. in particular. The provision of education outside the state *Bharatdarshan* tours and educational tours organised for Arunachalee students of schools and colleges were also instrumental in exposing the tribal people to the modern process of change. Precisely, people were acquainted with scientific knowledge, technology and market forces in different degrees.

In response to the above factors there are noticeable changes in various aspects of life of the tribal communities in Arunachal Pradesh. It is to be mentioned that the forces of change have not replaced the traditional way of life of the people altogether. There are modifications, additions and of course in a very limited sphere a few replacements of the traditional aspects of life. For example, the traditional political system coexists with modern panchayat raj system. The informal system of education is giving away to the formal one to a greater extent. Wet rice cultivation has been added to earlier hills cultivation. The hills cultivation is modified with the introduction of vegetable and horticultural crops.

A quantitative analysis to the magnitude of change is difficult to arrive at because the tribal people do not keep any records. Further, one aspect of life cannot be distinguished from the other aspects, and in the same aspect both traditional and modern ways have been integrated. For example, traditional food items are still popular though there are additional dishes of non-traditional items. Sometimes non-traditional items are prepared in traditional ways and traditional items in non-traditional ways. It is not surprising that the traditional clothes are made into coats and jackets in some communities. It is in this context a quantitative analysis will restrict the totality of comprehension given the limitations of a single paper. That is why, a subjective presentation of changes have been discussed with the Nyishi of Arunachal Pradesh as a case study. The researcher being a member of the community draws data from his own observation and from discussion with elderly Nyishi people. The present data are by-product of an intensive investigation for the PhD assignment. Though the data are inadequate but still they are suggestive to the nature and extent of changes in Nyishi community in the process of development.

THE NYISHI- A BRIEF INTRODUCTION

The Nyishi, one of the Thanyi group of tribes, constitutes the single largest tribe in Arunachal Pradesh with a population of about 276502 (as per census of 2001). They inhabit Upper Subansiri, Lower Subansiri, Kurung Kumey, Papumpare, East Kameng districts of Arunachal Pradesh and some pockets of Sonitpur and Lakhimpur district in Assam. In earlier records, the tribe has been designated as Chungi or Dafla. But the people call themselves Nyishi. It is to be mentioned that in 2007 the nomenclature Nyishi is included in the Constitution of India replacing the word Dafla.

The term Nyishi is derived from two words *Nyi* and *Ishi (some times from Nyia and shing or ashing). Nyi* refers to human descendants of *Aathu Nyia Thani* (son of Abhu Thanyi- the first man on earth). *Ishi* means upper source of the river,i.e upland. *Ashing* also refers to higher region or high land. Hence the English translation of Nyishi means 'human being living in highlands'. The tribe belongs to Mongoloid stock and speaks a Tibeto-Burman group of language.

The Nyishi are an eco-system people. They depend on their ecosystem for their livelihoods. They practise shifting cultivation and depend on forest resources for house construction materials and raw materials of utilitarian objects like various baskets. Even the semi-domesticated and domesticated animals of the Nyishi depend on the ecosystem. Important among the animals are *sebe* (*bos frontalis*), *pariah* (dog-*canis familiarise*), pig (*sus domesticus*), buffalo (*bubalus bublis*) and goat (*capra hircus*). The influence of ecology not only can be found in their life sustenance activities but also in their material culture. As has been said, raw materials for making baskets are obtained from the forest. Similarly for making the loin looms they depend on forest resources. Not in a very long past they collected fibres from the jungle to make clothes. As the Nyishi live in hill slopes their house is built on raised platforms. Even in plain grounds the houses are built on raised platform to avoid swampy ground. The houses are long houses called *namda* which accommodates a number of nuclear families. The houses also can be independent households of nuclear families called *namtu*. The Nyishi is not a tribe living in isolation from a known historical period. They had relations with Ahoms and British.

As has been said the Nyishis had a subsistence economy. The mode of exchange was barter inspite of their relation with outside. The society is patriarchal with polygynous families though monogamous families were not rare. They believe in *donyi polo* as the supreme god. Their staple food is boiled rice, leafy vegetables, meat and *oppo,* locally brewed liquor. The Nyishi have been exposed to outside forces from Ahom period, but still their economy was self sustained subsistence village economy. It is only after independence that market forces of development penetrated into the community in the form of development programmes and schemes.

ASPECTS OF SOCIO-ECONOMIC ACTIVITIES IN THE TRADITION

The traditional economy of the Nyishi was not a diversified one. It was based on primary sector activities such as agriculture and allied activities. Allied activities included forest activities such as hunting, collection of timbers, canes, bamboos, etc. mainly for house construction. It also included fishing and livestock rearing. Besides primary sector activities, the Nyishi also manufactured utilitarian objects at household level. There was no difference between the place of manufacturing and the place of residence. Usually they manufactured baskets of various shapes and sizes for different purposes. The baskets and the purpose for which they were used are: *eging/ aage* (carrying baskets used by women), *nyara* (haversack for male), *pakhya* (haversack for female), *dunge sing* (basket for storing rice), *hach / kathja* (basket as a unit of measurement), *opik* (mat), *pater* (cage for poultry birds), *apio* (winnowing fan), *chungchak* (small basket used by female for keeping seeds and collecting small things). Weaving, smithy works, pot making, etc. were some of the manufacturing activities in the traditional Nyishi community.

The other items which the Nyishi manufactured include *meji* (bell), *tasang* (beads), *talu* (brass plate), *hukhe* (disc), *dumping* (ornament wear in head), *rungbing* (ear ring), *cozy* (bangle), *monye* (necklace), *bopia* (head gear), *Salang* (smoking pipe). However, they used to procure daos and beads from Tibet directly or through middlemen which were a prized item having significant cultural values.

The Nyishi used to domesticate a few animals and birds. These were used for self consumption, exchange on occasions like marriage, barter exchange, compensation and fine in settling disputes, and ritual sacrifices. The main animals used for these purposes are *sebe* (*bosfrontalis*), *sabing/ yabing* (goat), *eri* (pig), *porok* (poultry) and *pajap* (duck).

As the scale and range of production was small so also the items of consumption. They consumed whatever they used to produce or forage. Their food items were simple and few in number. These include *aching* (rice), *adding/addin* (different varieties of meat), *auo* (of different varieties of vegetables), *eging, huse, halak* (different types of local potatos), *heekhung/ hiup,* (fermented bamboo shoot), *tachye/tusie/tabe* (flour from wild sago plant). The popular beverage is *opo,* locally produced liquor.

AGRICULTURE

Agriculture is the main stay of the Nyishis. The nature of agriculture is conditioned by the topography of their habitation. The Nyishi inhabit a vast tract of land spread over five districts of the state. Their habitation is full of hills and rugged terrains. However, there are few villages in plains. The Nyishi living in hills practise *rongho* (shifting cultivation, agriculture field is also called *rongho*). The *rongho* (in the sense of the field) is of different types depending on the nature of cultivation. For example, there is *balung* where vegetables and paddy are cultivated. The field in which early variety of crops are grown is called *tining rongho*. Similarly, in *rekte/ amite rongho* late varieties of crops are grown. In early time the Nyishi cultivated a field only for one year before they left it for fallow. On rare occasions they used to cultivate a field consecutively for more than one year and such a field is known as *rheewa rongho*. But usually they cultivate the fields for one year and then leave it fallow.

In *rongo* the Nyishi used to grow *aam* (rice), *tami* (millet), *topah* (maize), *taya* (bajra), *yamdik* (chilly), *taki* (ginger), *deteh* (a type of onion), *tape* (pumpkin), *mukung* (cucumber), *opum, oju, pamik* (varieties of bottle gourd), *hulak* (yam), *enging* (yam), *meek/ kali* (tabaco leaf) and *goying* (mustard leaf).

Those Nyishi who lived in plains during British time practised wet cultivation along with dry land cultivation. Paddy was the main crop in wet land cultivation.

LAND TENURE

Among the Nyishi the land belonged to the community which is a village in Nyishi sense for all practical purposes in early days. The Nyishi village used to be a single clan village and so the land belonged to the clan. In fact the Nyishi lived in *namda*, a long house accommodating father, mother and their children and married sons. It was not rare to find paternal uncle living in the same house with his children and married sons. Each married son with his wife and children usually had his separate hearth. The land belonged to the *namda* head but each married son had his separate field for cultivation. In fact he enjoyed the usufructuary rights over his field. In case of polygyny, the husband used to distribute fields to each of his wives who cultivated by herself. But the land belonged to husband as per customary practices. The field/fields cultivated by a mother was/were inherited by her sons.

The Nyishi community is a patriarchal one. The women do not have right to inherit land. In other words, a woman can not own any land. But there are some sayings which establish the ownership to both male and female.

Nyokge keyus ngw Ish ge tutung ngw or *Nyoke aat/athu or Ish Ayu*

(*aat/authu* is a honorific term used to address father, father-in-law, grandfather, etc. It also connotes to male ownership. *Ayu* is also an honorific term used to address mother, mother-in-law, grandmother, etc. It also connotes to female ownership. The sayings refer to male/female ownership of land and water).

Even *sit-sakam*, the source of drinking water, has an owner. The Nyishi used to say *sit-sakam athu*. The man who collected water from the source for the first time becomes its owner. Similarly, a field is owned by an individual or a family who cultivates it for the first time; such fields are known as *rongho pawo*, indicating the ownership of the first user.

ORGANISATION OF LABOUR AND TECHNOLOGY

In traditional Nyishi community, family and clan provided labour for economic activities. The labour was organised on the basis of age and sex and basically labour–intensive in nature. Young children looked after the siblings and the elder persons were engaged in basket making or some other works at home. They also looked after the house and infants when elder members were out for agricultural or other out side activities. Children also used to collect water and protected standing crops in the fields from animals and birds. There was relaxation for old people from hard labour. Weaving was in the domain of female folks. Similarly hunting was exclusively male activities. There was both individual and community hunting. In fishing both male and female members took part. The various methods of fishing include *tamjangnam*- poisoning the water using herbal poisons, *pesusukanem*- a method of angling without iron hook, *aker penam*- angling with the use of iron hook, *subu penam/ beltar tarnam*- diversion of rivers/ streams, *sepe monam/pucha kennam*- blocking and diverting rivers/streams, *sakam neknam/ taham*- using traps usually in big rivers and *edor gegyanam*- trapping using conical shaped traps made of bamboo in both big and small rivers and also in stagnant water bodies.

The hunting implements were bows and arrows and later they used guns. In fact the common and popular methods they have been using include killing the animals and birds through crushing, noose trapping and piercing. The traps used to crush the animals are *sogum* and *chepak*. *Sogum* is a trap with a platform on the top where stones are kept. When animal enters into it, the trigger is let off and the stones are released thereby crushing the animal. In *chepak* a wooden post/beam/plank is fixed in such a way that when the animal enters into it the lever gives away and the wooden post crushes the animal. Piercing is done in two ways: the first one is by releasing the darts/arrows/pointed shaft from an adjusted lever. The traps used are *komiya, gotak*, etc. In these traps the arrow is fixed in a way that when an animal hits the target the lever releases the arrow which hits and kills the animal. The second method is piercing the unaware animal from a hideout especially during hunting of boar. Various snares for noose traps like *murang/gorang, pochiks/gochiks*, etc. are also used. *Murang/gorang* is a bow shaped noose trap while *pochiks/gochiks* is a trap consisting of a rope and bait which remains suspended at the opening of an enclosure.

In agriculture, male members used to perform difficult tasks like cutting big trees or putting fences around fields. The female members performed almost all the tasks associated with different stages of agriculture starting from the preparation of fields, to sowing of seeds and lastly to harvesting, transporting and storing of grains. Even they used to collect the firewood from *deap rongho* (jhum fields).

The family source of labour supply is not adequate in times of house construction or in some stages of agricultural activities. So they engage the lineage or clan labour on the basis of mutual reciprocity. This type of labour exchange is called *Rye Guknam* or *Rye Angnam*. However, the family engaging such labour provides food and drinking.

As it has been mentioned, the Nyishi live in long houses called *namda*. So when there is a shortage of labour in the nuclear family, other families in the *namda* supply the required labour on mutual reciprocation. Even labour outside the *namda* or village can be appropriated on the same principle. During the construction of *namda*, all its members work together and there is no reciprocation. In case they engage labour from other *namda* it is reciprocated later on. A married son also used to live in a separate house and during its construction organisation of labour is based on mutual reciprocation.

In a polygynous family each wife cultivates her land with the help of her children and if required engaging community labour on the principle of reciprocation. The husband works usually during cleaning time.

The scale of production was small and subsistence in nature. Moreover, number of crops produced was not many. As the production was subsistence in nature, the spatial movement of such products was limited to village or neighbouring villages. This was further limited because of the use of human muscle energy in transportation. The means of transportation were a few baskets which have been mentioned in the earlier section.

Oryok (dao) was an implement of multi purpose use. They used it for cutting, slicing, digging, killing animals and for many other purposes. Besides *oryok* other implements used in economic activities include *yokchik* (knife), *ayigiks* (quiver), *eeree* (bow), *opuk* (arrow), *nangkio* (spear), *marto* (arrow points made of iron),etc.

These items were manufactured in the community. However, there was no specialisation on the basis of occupation. Any one who has the skill could make it.

THE CHANGING TREND

The traditional economy of Arunachal Pradesh in general and of the Nyishi in particular got exposed to development forces after independence through various plan programmes. But the level of exposure has not been uniform. The Nyishi villages in plains and near administrative headquarters have greater exposure as compared to remote and hilly villages. But there are changes though in different degrees in all villages. Because of these changes agriculture is no more the major source of livelihood supported by hunting, fishing and gathering and forest activities. The economy has been diversified and the Nyishi people are found in government jobs, business and contract works. Family is not the source of labour for agriculture. The mutual reciprocation of social appropriation of labour has been replaced by wage labour. There are many absentee land owners because of migration to place of work or members engaged in profitable ventures like contract works. The institution of share cropping has emerged near urban areas. Even the local products and local vegetables are sold in the markets. The economy is in the process of being monetised and integrated to the market. In many villages terrace and plains cultivation have replaced the traditional option of only jhum cultivation. In jhum fields commercial and horticultural crops are grown.

Unlike earlier situation road communication has developed and through various schemes the government supplies agricultural inputs and machinery. In terrace and plains cultivation high yielding variety of paddy are raised by applying pesticides and fertilisers. Tractors not only help in cultivation in plains but help in transportation of crops even in some hilly regions. Thus machine power is gradually replacing muscle power. Many Nyishi families face the problem of labour shortage in agriculture because,

(1) Children who used to look after siblings or work in the fields with their parents are going to schools and colleges;

(2) Members of the house hold are engaged in government jobs, business or in village panchayats;

(3) There is a decline in the incidence of polygyny which provided a source of labour to agriculture.

This has resulted in leasing out land, share cropping, wage labour, etc.

Usually in terrace and plains cultivation paddy is grown as single crop unlike mixed cropping in *rongo* fields. Nevertheless in interior villages and in plains where jhum land is available people practise *rongo* cultivation also. Though, the production is still labour intensive the capital has made in road to the production system in general.

Due to shortage of time and labour many families do not make basketry and other items. Even there is a decline in weaving in many houses. At the same time weaving has been linked to the market with certain innovations in traditional clothes. Most of the time people use non-traditional clothes available in the market. Under such a situation many producer households are in the threshold of becoming consumer households. The incidence of hunting and fishing declined. But as food habit they depend on the market for the supply of these items.

The trend of change described above is not uniform. In remote villages people still depend on cultivation though, there are incidences of changes in the cropping pattern. In those areas also reciprocal labour exchange has declined; wage labour is taking its place instead. Because of education and occupational diversification people migrate to administrative centres. No doubt, the Nyishi community has been divided along the axis of occupational mobility. One section of the population, though constitutes a smaller portion, is modern by any standard. But other section is still tradition bound. The hiatus between haves and haves not is widening. Nevertheless, the modern group is not totally beyond the tradition bound, while the traditional ones are not entirely within the limit of the tradition. There are changes in the community but the degrees vary. Individual property rights in land is emerging. This has resulted in unequal ownership of landed property. Land has become a commodity within the customary frame. In other words, a Nyishi can sell land to a Nyishi only. The land is used for surplus production of commercial crops and establishing business concerns. This is a challenge to the globalisation in that the global forces ensure efficiency through competition. But competition among unequal which have arisen in the process of development after independence does not promise a fair game.

In the process of development, not only some changes have occurred in economic life of the Nyishi, there are also some changes visible in socio-cultural life of the people. Of course all the sections of the people have not been equally affected. It is to be mentioned that different sections of people have responded to the changes differently and to different degrees.

The Nysihi were traditionally uni-lingual. But due to exposure to formal system of education and interaction with various linguistic groups an average Nyishi at least knows three languages, Nyishi, Hindi and English. On the other hand, the elite section and few others know Assamese, Nepali, Bengali and languages of few other Arunachalee tribes. Interestingly, the second generation young children of elite section in capital complex and in other administrative centres are very poor in their mother tongue. On the other hand there are efforts to document Nyishi traditions, folklores in general. There is an effort to standardise the language by introducing it in primary school curriculum in schools in Nyishi area.

With regard to food habit there is noticeable changes in the process of shift from boiled items to spiced items and fast food. Moreover, the elite section is very much accustomed with snacks, tea, coffee, beer and other varieties of foreign liquor along with South and North Indian dishes.

CONCLUSION

The Nyishi community has changed over the years in response to post- Independence development interventions. But the community has not moved forward uni-directionally along the line of progress. There has emerged classes like elites and non-elites, and haves and haves-not in otherwise an undifferentiated community prior to development interventions. Notwithstanding the inequalities within, the Nyishi community also differs from other communities of the state in terms of the level of development as can be seen by a casual observer. Inter-and intra- community inequalities in the Nyishi community in particular, and tribal communities with other communities of the country in general are serious challenges which have not been meaning fully addressed while thinking of tribal development in the context of globalisation.

13

TRIBAL SITUATION IN HIMACHAL PRADESH: AN OVERVIEW

Ajay Kumar, Himani

The Constitution has several provisions to ensure social justice for the traditionally depressed and backward classes and for weaker sections. These have important implications for administration. Special provisions are made in the Constitution regarding areas with predominantly tribal population as in Northeast India. Seats are reserved in the Parliament and the state legislatures for Scheduled Tribes. Reservation is also made for them in government employment and in admission to educational institutions. The Constitution provides them reservation in educational institutions and in government; employment can be made for educationally and socially backward classes also. Such reservation has been in force in the Southern States for a numbers of years. Following the Mandal Commission Report and the judgment of the Supreme Court on the government's decisions there on reservation, for backward is being introduced in the central government and in the northern states too. There are a number of provisions in the Constitution to safeguard the individual's human rights. Since September 1993, we also have a National Human Rights Commission to safeguard rights, relating to life, liberty, equality and dignity of the individual guaranteed by the Constitution or embodied in international covenants and enforceable by courts in India.

There is also a National Commission on Women. Secondly, state-level commissions for human rights and for women are being formed. Administration is the instrument for translating policy decision in operational term for which base is provided by the legal frame.

Even though the Sub-Plan approach envisaged appropriate administrative measures as an integral part of the new strategy, it was stated that while the sub-plans may primarily provide the economic and social inputs, the protective and administrative aspects should be taken care of under the appropriate Constitutional Provisions. It was, therefore, decided that, as far as possible, the Sub-Plan area should become co-terminus with the Scheduled areas.

The concept of single line administration was prevailing in India during the British regime when they declared some of the tribal areas as 'excluded' and some as 'partially excluded'. They adopted the policy of lightly administering these areas. The normal administration of the Provinces, in which the tribal areas were located, was not extended to them. In many regions, single line administration was established where all authority was vested in one Individual who was the chief representative of the Government in that area. Initially single line administration was introduced in one tribal tehsil of Chamba district namely Pangi tehsil which is coterminous with Community Development Block and a Sub-Division. This tribal tehsil was selected for the adoption of single line administration due to its tough geographical condition in comparison to other tribal areas of the state. It still remains a land locked-valley throughout the year as there are still no proper road facilities, which can link the valley with the outside world throughout the year. With the advent of single line administration in Himachal Pradesh, every walk of life got a new lease. Tribal areas of the state no longer remained underdeveloped. Priorities were fixed to the most needed projects and programmes in the state.

The tribal population of the country, as per the 2001) census, is 8.43 crore, constituting 8.2% of the total population. The population of tribes had grown at the rate of 24.45% during the .period 1991-2001. This is slightly more than the decadal growth rate of 22.66 for the nation as a whole. More than half of the Scheduled Tribe population is concentrated in the States of Madhya Pradesh, Chhattisgarh, Maharashtra, Orissa, Jharkhand and Gujarat.

Scheduled Tribes are those, which, are notified as such by the President of India under Article 342 of the Constitution. The first notification was issued in 1950. The President considers characteristics like primitive traits, distinctive culture, shyness with the public at large, geographical' isolation and social arid economic backwardness before notifying them as a Scheduled Tribe. Seventy-five of the 698 Scheduled Tribes are identified as Primitive Tribal Groups considering they are more backward than Scheduled Tribes. They continue to live in a economy and have very low literacy rates. Their populations are stagnant or even declining. In Himachal Pradesh there were, according to 2001 Census, 2,44,587 tribal people constituting 4.02 per cent of the total population. The Scheduled Tribes of Himachal Pradesh are the Gaddi, the Gujjar, the Jad, the Khampa and the Bhot (or Bodh), the Lahaula Pangwals, the Kannaura or Kinnaura and the Swangla. Although the Scheduled Tribes population is scattered all over the State yet three districts namely Chamba, Kinnaur and Lahaul & Spiti stand distinctly apart form other districts in terms of the concentration of tribal population.

The Tribal areas are generally characterized by undulating terrain, dense forest, difficult communication and low density of population. Each tribal group with its own social customs and dialects usually lives in a compact area. The geophysical conditions and socio-cultural background make the introduction of development schemes in the tribal areas a difficult task. The problem of development in the tribal areas are linked with various socio-economic consideration viz. improvement of infrastructure, changes in social habits and customs, creation of demand for goods and services, improvement in income and opportunities for investment. The

Kinnaur and Lahaul and Spiti districts, in their entirety, and Pangi and Bharmour (now tehsil Bharmour and sub-tehsil Holi) Sub-Division of Chamba district constitute the scheduled areas in the state, fulfilling the minimum criterion of 50% scheduled tribe population concentration in a Community Development Block. These are situated in the north and northeast of the State forming a contiguous belt in the far hinterland behind High Mountain Passes and are amongst the remotest and most inaccessible area in the State with average altitude being 3281 meter above the mean sea level. The most distinguishing mark of the tribal areas in the State is that they occupy vast land area but with thin population; as a result of which per unit cost of infrastructure activity is very exorbitant.

RURAL DEVELOPMENT IN TRIBAL AREAS OF HIMACHAL PRADESH

The tribal communities exist in a simple socio-economic situa-tion. Their needs are modest and often not clearly demarcated. The money-lender meets all of their requirements, including for consumption purposes and social ceremonies. The average size of land-holding in the tribal areas is considerably large than in other areas. But the actual utilization of land and the intensity of its use is considerably lower. The yield and productivity is also low. Marketing and credit operations in the tribal areas are subjected to numerous forms of exploitation and therefore, a large portion of gross production in the tribal economy is siphoned off, making it a net deficit economy. This results in high indebtedness and land alienation. Therefore, to tackle these problems an integrated approach to the whole socio-economic structure is essential. Tribal areas, need special attention if the benefits of the new developmental programmes, are to accrue to the tribal community. A brief description of tribal areas in Himachal Pradesh is given below.

CHAMBA DISTRICT

This district is located between 32° 10' to 33° 13' North latitude and 75°45' to 77°33' East longitude. The territory is wholly mount-ainous with altitudes varying from 2,000 feet to 21,000 feet above the mean sea level. Agriculture is the mainstay of the majority of population in the district, and maize, wheat, potato, paddy and barley are the major crops. Livestock is the main wealth of the people and every house invariably keeps a few cows or buffaloes, sheep, goats, pigs and ponies. From industrial point of view the district is more "backward but 'Chamba Chappals' and 'Rumals' are quite famous and are in great demand. According to 2001 census the area of the district is 6,528 sq. km and total population is 4.60 lakh, out of which 4.26 lakh reside in rural areas and only 0.34 lakh live in urban areas. Further out of total 76,418 families, 47,165 are living below the poverty line. (Census, 1998-99). It reveals that 61.72 percent population of Chamba district is living below the poverty line. The total cultivated area in the district was 58,381 hectares out of which only 3,550 hectares, were having the irrigation facilities.

Gaddis of Barhmaur in Chamba District with their distinctive culture and customs form an inseparable part of the cultural mosiac of Himachal Pradesh. They are is a remarkable race, a very simple and virtuous race, remarkable even among the hill people for the eminent regard for truth and natural hilarity. Many aspects of customs which have more or less worked into the various forms of Himachal survive amongst them.

In his report on the Land Settlement of Kangra district (1850), G.C. Barnes wrote that the Gaddis are the most remarkable race in the hills. In fearures, maners, dress and dialect, they differ essentially from all the rest of the population. This distinct identity they have retained over the centuries. Neither the intimate and regular economic transactions with a caste-oriented, agricultural society nor the existence of a general nation of 'Caste' within their own tribal seems to have diluted the consciousness of their separateness.

The Gaddis of Gadheran, the name they lend to their native land lying on both sides of the Dhauladhar with ill-defined boundaries, are principally found in Barhmaur area of the Chamba district in Himachal Pradesh from northern part of the Kangra Valley.

The area they inhabit is hilly and mountainous and the land for cultivation is very limited. Besides the increase in population, the pressure on land is greater by the large number of live-stock-sheep and goats accounting more than 85 per cent, which form the most important factor in their domestic economy. Gaddis are the true shepherds for the conditions of sheep-farming suit them the most. They practise trans-humance.

These people who for centuries have lived a secluded tribal life in their zeal to maintain the purity of the old tradition and customs are now set to mingle in the national mainstream.

KINNAUR DISTRICT

Kinnaur lies on both sides of the Satluj river and is located between 31°55' to 32°05' North latitude and 77°45' to 9°00 East longitude. Kinnaur is one of the most backward areas, not only of Himachal Pradesh but of India as well. The economic structure is primarily agrarian and essentially rural in character. The methods of cultivation are crude as well as primitive and sheep, goats, ponies and horses are the main livestock of the people. According to 2001 census the district has 6,401 sq. km area. The total population of the district is 0.78 lakh which lives in rural areas only. Further out of 10,899 families, 2,896 or 26.57 per cent are recorded below the poverty line. (Census, 1998-99). Moreover, there are 0.39 lakh main workers, 0.07 lakh are marginal workers and 0.30 lakh are non-workers. (Census, 2001). Despite it, only 282 sq. km area of the district is under forests and the soil of Kinnaur consists of sand, sandy loam, clayey loam and gravel, etc.

LAHAUL-SPITI DISTRICT

Lahaul-Spiti became a district of Himachal Pradesh in 1960 and it is one of the frontier districts of India. The major occupation of the people is agriculture and about 25 per cent of the total landmass is under cultivation. Peas, mustard, raddish, turnip, carrot, french bean, beat root, tomatoes and soyabean are major crops of the district and yak, cow, mule, donkey, sheep and goat are major livestock. According to 2001 census the district has 13,835 sq. km. area and its total population is 33. 224. The whole population of the district lives in rural areas. Further 37.93 per cent families are living below the poverty line in the district (1998-99). There are 0.019 lakh main workers, 0.018 lakh marginal workers and 0.12 lakh non-workers. The Centrally-Sponsored Desert Development Programme of 1978 has shown good results in generating employment opportunities to the local people. In 1990, Antodya Programme was launched to uplift the people economically who are living below the poverty line.

GROWTH OF SCHEDULED TRIBES DURING 1981-91 AND 1991-2001

The population of Scheduled Tribes was 1, 97,263 in 1981 Census which rose to 218,349 in 1991 and 244,587 in 2001, Census. The growth rate of Scheduled Tribes was 10.69 during 1981-91 which rose to 12.02 per cent in subsequent decade of 1991-2001 in the State, as a whole. The highest growth rate of 44.53 percent has been returned by Solan followed by Kinnaur where population of Tribes has grown by 42.06 per cent during 1991-2001. Bilaspur and Mandi has moderate growth rate of 14.99 and 12.18 per cent respectively. However districts of Kangra, Hamirpur, Una, Sirmaur and Shimla have negative growth of Scheduled Tribes population but these districts have small population of Scheduled Tribes which usually fluctuates from one decade to other.

DISTRIBUTION OF SCHEDULED TRIBES POPULATION

Of the total Scheduled Tribes population of the State, 48.1 per cent tribal population is distributed in Chamba district followed by Kinnaur (23.0 percent), Lahul & Spiti (9.9 percent), Kullu (4.6), Mandi (4.3), Bilaspur (3.8), Sirmaur (2.4), Shimla (1.7) and Solan (1.4). Una, Kangra and Hamirpur districts have almost negligible proportion of tribal population.

SEX RATIO OF SCHEDULED TRIBES

The sex ratio among Scheduled Tribes is still better than Scheduled Castes. The sex ratio was 981 females per 1,000 males in Scheduled Tribes population in 1991 which further rose to 996 females in 2001 Census. The tribal district of Kinnaur has highest sex ratio of 1,040 females in 2001 against 1,082 in 1991 Census and is closely followed by Lahul & Spiti with 1,022 and 1,028 in 1991 and 2001 respectively. Chamba district also has significantly high sex ratio of 983 females in 1991 which further rose to 998 females in 2001 Census slightly below the parity line. The sex ratio among tribal population is also high in Kullu (1,004) followed by Mandi (991) and has improved in both districts during 1991-2001. There is decline in the sex-ratio of Solan, Shimla and Sirmaur districts and their values are far below the equality point. The districts of Una, Hamirpur and Kangra with small tribal population reflect very low sex ratio in both Censuses.

CHILD SEX RATIO (AGE 0-6) AMONG TRIBES POPULATION

The child sex ratio of Scheduled Tribes has declined from 966 in 1991 to 955 in 2001. This decline in sex ratio has been, observed in Kullu, Bilaspur, Solan, Sirmaur and Shimla district. The highest decline in sex ratio has been found in Solan district where sex ratio decreased from 1,010 in 1991 to 870 in 2001 followed by Mandi from 1,023 to 936 and Shimla from 957 to 770 females during 1991-2001. Child sex ratio in Una and Hamirpur is equal to parity in 2001 Census while in other districts, it varies between 991 in Kinnaur and 770 in Shimla district.

LITERACY RATE OF SCHEDULED TRIBES POPULATION

The proportion of literates to total Scheduled Tribes population excluding 0-6 population was 47.1 per cent in 1991 Census which rose to 65.5 per cent yielding net change of 18.4 points during the decade in the state. This literacy rate among the Scheduled Tribes is quite low as compared to literacy rate of Scheduled Castes. All districts show increase in the proportion of Scheduled Tribes literates except Kangra where literacy rate has, declined from 78.9 to 64.0, Hamirpur from 96.2 to 60.6

and Una from 90.6 to 46.7 per cent during 1991-2001. This decline in literacy rate in these districts appears to be effected by the migration of tribal population. The literacy rate in districts varies between 46.7 per cent in Una and 87.0 per cent in Shimla district as per 2001 Census.

MALE LITERACY RATE OF SCHEDULED TRIBES

Male literacy rate has increased from 62.7 per cent in 1991 to 77.7 per cent in 2001 Census. At district level, male literacy of 2001 Census shows variation in between 91.2 in Shimla and 45.9 per cent in Una district. The pattern of change in male literacy during 1991-2001 is same as discussed in total literacy rate.

FEMALE LITERACY RATE OF SCHEDULED TRIBES

Literacy in female tribal population is very low and gender gap in literacy is still very high which comes to 24.4 points as per 2001 Census. The percentage of female literates was only 31.2 in 1991 which rose sharply to 53.3 per cent in 2001 which is still far behind the male literacy rate of 77.7 per cent. In districts, this rate varies between 40.7 per cent in Sirmaur and 81.7 per cent in Shimla district. During 1991-2001, all districts except Hamirpur reflect improvement in female literacy. The percentage of female literates in Hamirpur was 71.4 in 1991 which fell down to 46.9 per cent as per 2001 Census. But Hamirpur has very small number of tribal population and demographic features of this population by and large are influenced by migration from other areas.

WORK PARTICIPATION RATE OF SCHEDULED TRIBES POPULATION

The work participation rate of Scheduled Tribes is better than that of 48.9 per cent Workers of Scheduled Castes. The percentage of Scheduled Tribes workers has increased from 49.6 in 1991 to 54.6 per cent in 2001 Census. The proportion of Scheduled Tribes workers is highest in Una (66.7 per cent) followed by Kinnaur (60. 2), Lahul & Spiti (59.1) and Solan (58.0). The lowest percentage of 37.9 has been recorded in Kangra and 41.0 per cent each in Sirmaur and Shimla districts.

MAIN AND MARGINAL WORKERS

The proportion of main workers among tribal population works out 37.0 per cent in 2001 showing slight improvement from 36.8 percent in 1991 in the state. Main workers vary between 52.8 per cent in Lahul & Spiti and 26.2 per cent in Mandi district during 2001 Census. On the other hand, the proportion of marginal workers workout 17.6 per cent in the state which varies between 29.0 percent in Solan and only 0.06 per cent in Hamirpur district. But Hamirpur district has quite high percentage of 40.0 in main workers among the tribal population.

Eugene Linder, the author of 'Lost Tribes, Lost knowledge' says "Over the ages, the indigenous peoples have developed innumerable technologies and arts. They have devised ways to farm deserts without irrigation and produce abundance from the forest without destroying the delicate balance that maintains the eco system; they have learnt how to navigate vast distances ... using the knowledge of the currents and the feel of the waves. ..; they have explored the medicinal properties of plants; and they have acquired an understanding of the basic ecology of flora and fauna". How right he is. These communities whom we call 'tribes', are as much the sons of this land any other segment of the Indian society is; So if one tribe goes much will go from our life too. For the loss of a tribe is not loss of some 'wild people', it is a loss of enormous treasure trove of wisdom and of our cultural heritage.

Those who control the Himalayas would control the plains of India. A fuller knowledge of the Himalayan region, a clearer understanding of the people living on its borders and appreciation of their backwardness, and the problems they face, thus is strategically vital from the defence point of view as well.

REFERENCES

Census of India (2001), *Himachal Pradesh, Scheduled Caste and Scheduled Tribes*, Shimla: Directorate of Census Operations, Himachal Pradesh.

Census of India (1981, 1991& 2001), *Himachal Pradesh, Various Series*. Shimla: Directorate of Census Operations, Himachal Pradesh.

SECTION–IV

Innovation as Intervention

14

FOLKLORE AND AUDIO-CASSETTE IN TEACHING LANGUAGE EFFECTIVELY TO TRIBAL STUDENTS AT PRIMARY LEVEL- AN EXPERIMENTAL STUDY[1]

Kartikeswar Behera

INTRODUCTION

Human resource development requires quality education at all levels. Quality education, on the other hand, depends on an effective mode of delivery. At primary level, when the medium of instruction is mother tongue or teaching mother tongue warrants effective delivery, then use of educational technology becomes significant. In fact teaching learning process invariably makes use of educational technology, whether it is chalk and blackboard or the more sophisticated ICT. Use of the type of educational technology, however, depends on the development and availability of the level of technology among other things. The basic aim of such uses is to make communication between the teacher and the taught effective and meaningful.

In this era of information technology, ICT plays a very significant role in the matter of educational transmission. It facilitates effective delivery of lessons and in realising the learning outcome. No doubt, multi-media approach viz. Audio/Radio Programme, Video/Television programmes, e-learning, teleconferences have been utilized with a view to ensure quality in teaching-learning process. So far as Audio/Radio programme is concerned, because of easy accessibility, affordability and appropriateness for a wide range of teaching and learning situations a variety of audio-medium, such as audio cassettes, radio broadcast, radio vision, radio text and interactive radio is being used in education.

Teaching of prescribed lessons at primary level becomes effective, no doubt, with the use of ICT in the mode of delivery. It is to be mentioned that simply teaching the prescribed lessons does not help in the expansion of the horizon of comprehension of the learners. Some well designed supplementary lessons relating to the topic if linked to the teaching learning process with the use of technology, then the level of learning outcome is realised at a higher side. While teaching mother tongue, if topics related to lessons are selected from the culture of the students, then the level of comprehension of the students to the prescribed lessons rises. Precisely, the folklores as supplementary lessons to the prescribed ones generally capture the attention of the young minds and expand the horizon of their understanding. As a result, the learning outcome is well realised. Folklores provide the ambience which is familiar to the learners and the basis for understanding of the formal lessons.

Folklores combined with ICT in the mode of delivery becomes more effective to learners of socio-economically disadvantaged sections like tribal students. The prescribed lessons use a system of vocabulary or a level of idea presented in a style which is unfamiliar to tribal students in their home environment. The class room teaching in a formal way does not meet to the heterogeneous groups with different acceptance levels. Naturally, for the tribal students the lessons become difficult to comprehend in a right perspective. Folklores teaching by using ICT is like *enabling special coaching* for those learners who need it to come up to an expected level. Moreover, this has a demonstration orientation, and a novelty different from the normal class room situation.

Though folklores are culture specific still they have universal appealing. The animals, plants and common people as characters, and events capturing the imagination of young minds have common appealing not only to tribal students but also to rural and urban students alike. That is why stories from *Panchatantra, Jataka,* etc. are increasingly popular among the children.

With this backdrop the present paper is an experimental preliminary enquiry to test the effectiveness of folklores through audio-cassettes in facilitating the understanding level of students to the prescribed lessons with selected tribal students as case study.

METHODS AND MATERIALS

The present study is experimental in nature. Essentially, the study examines the effectiveness of the audio materials on developing the language skill of the learners in general. But specifically, it aims at verifying the fundamental premise that the audio cassette delivery of folk songs and stories as supplements to the prescribed lessons is effective in developing the level of comprehension of tribal learners.

Necessarily, in this study audio programme on folk songs and folk tales has been the focus so far as class room transaction is concerned.

For the purpose, forty five out of 52 students of Class-V constituted the sample. The sample students are the students who attended the class and subsequently the test. Swami Vivekananda Vidyamandir under Umerkote Block in the district of Nawaraangpur of Orissa state was selected for the study. It is an Upper Primary School having classes one to seven. Out of 45 students 28 were boys and 17 were girls. The sample students were divided into three groups, namely, Control Group, Experimental Group-I and Experimental Group-II on the basis of a pre-test conducted on the chosen topics of prose and poetry. Each group consisted of 15 students. Marks secured in the pre-test were arranged in order of merit and care was taken to make it heterogeneous with high achievers, partial achievers and low achievers. The Experimental Group-1 was dealt with activity based approach and audio cassettes with folk-lores. The Experimental Group-2 was dealt with the same approach but cassette was not provided to them and the Group-3 was taught in traditional manner. The first week was devoted to try out of the folk-lore (Cassetted) and in the second week intervention was extended to the Experimental Group-1 while at that time Experimental Group-2 was taught with activity based approach only without audio cassette for 10 days. The control group was taught, as has been said, in the traditional manner. The next five days were devoted for conducting post-test, evaluation and seeking of opinion of the observers.

PLANNING THE EXPERIMENT

For wider use of the folk songs and folk tales cassettes were prepared with the help of the local artists. At try out stage teachers and students were included. Then the cassettes were kept ready for class room transaction and assess the impact of folklores on the language skill of the learners at primary level.

Try-Out of the Audio Cassettes in Real Classroom situation

Two selected teachers who attended the workshop during recording of folk song were allotted classes to teach poetry in Class-V using the audio-cassettes based on Folk Songs. The audio cassettes contained the local songs of Khurda, Ganjam and Dhenkanal.

Task Analysis

- Selection of Folk tale for teaching prose topics.
- Selection of Folk lore for teaching poetry.
- Try-out the cassettes.

Stages of Try-Out

- Display of cassettes of folk songs and Folk tales at the stage of introduction

— Asking lead questions to link the folk song with the topic
— Teaching the original poems meant for the class using appropriate teaching methodology.
— Display of the selected portions of folk song for creating poetic environment.
— Clarification of the stanza through compàrison ad contrast.
— Asking questions based on poetic beauty and appreciation.
— Asking the student to sing the songs according to the time of the cassette.
— Taking feedback of the audience who were present during try-out.
— Asking the students to tell the stories with action.
— Asking them to locate specific information and tell the gist.

Enjoying the Poems

The following aspects were considered to make poem reading enjoyable to learners:

- Sound Effect and Music
- Rhyme and Rhythms
- Arrangement of words
- Poetic dictations
- Alliteration
- Beauty of poetry and poetic appreciation

There was feed back to improve audio cassettes in the way of addition and deletion in the classroom taking usability and teachability into account.

The cassette aimed at facilitating thematic clarity in view of:

- Local Comprehension
- Global Comprehension
- Inferential Comprehension

Table 1
Theme of Audio Cassettes Matched to the Topics of the Text

Topics of the text book of Class V	*Selected folk tale and folk song supplementary class room teaching*
1. Ei Mo Janama Bhumi (Poetry)	1. The Dhangda and flower.
2. Kusumo/Jatiya Pakhi(Poetry)	2. Asur Barasa Bada Baras Pani
3. Mati Debata Ra Puja (Prose)	3. Marigala Jhain
4. Guru Bhakti (Prose)	4. The flying elephant
5. Amania Jhada (Prose)	5. Budhi Asuruni O Kumbhirini Gapa.

INTERVENTION INSTRUMENTS

The questions were set from the text book as well as from out side the text based on folk-lore. The difficulty level of the pre-test was less than that of post test. Short answer type Very short answer type test items were prepared. The pre-test and post-test questions are as follows:

Pre-test Questions

8×2 ½= 20 marks

1. Are the Adibasi girls fond of flowers?
2. Which flower do they like most?
3. What they do with the flowers?
4. When are they forbidden to use flowers?
5. How do they observe their festivals?
6. Sing some songs of the Adivasis?
7. What do you make their festival interesting and enjoyable?
8. They are guided by some beliefs which a modern does not accept? Give some examples?

Post-Test Questions

20 marks

A) Answer the following Questions *(2x7) (14marks)*

   1) Why do the Adibasis worship the soil?
   2) Are they refrained from animal sacrifices?
      If no, how can it be stopped?

3) When is Parab observed?
4) In which language do they sing?
5) Write two musical instruments used by the adibasis?
6) What do they offer as gift to the *sahari* babus?
7) In return what do they want?

B) Write the following words in *desia* language? *(6 marks)*

Maze :____________

Harada :____________

Alasi :____________

Jona :____________

Kanda :____________

Devata :____________

C) Write the names of flowers in Oriya which are written in *desia* language. *(4 marks)*

Alasi phul :____________

Korei phul :____________

Rani phul :____________

Dalia phul :____________

Table 2
Pre-and Post-test Scoring

Groups	*Pre-Test Mean*	*Post-test Mean*	*Differences in Mean*
Experimental Group-1	10.61	19.76	9.15
Experimental Group-2	10.55	16.85	6.3
Control Group	10.56	12.78	2.22

Source: Computed from the scorings of the test administered to the students.

It transpires from Table-1 that the performance of the Experimental Group-1 is better than Experimental Group-2 and much better than the Control Group. The mean difference of the scoring of Group-1 is 9.15 as compared to 6.3 of Group-2 and 2.22 of Group-3 respectively. The comparative higher difference is due to comparatively better method of intervention, starting from traditional method for Group-3 to only folklore method without audio-cassette for Group -2 and to folklore with audio-cassette delivery for Gropu-1. So there is a positive correlation between the quality of intervention and scoring.

FINDINGS

All the 45 students, consisting of both who were given teaching through audio-cassettes and those who were without it, were of the opinion that the cassettes could be quite useful and enjoyable containing folk songs. The following opinions were solicited on the quality of transaction, quality of the material, sound effects, musical rhythm and clarity of language through an Opinionnaire from the students, teachers and artists involved in the present project for further improvement in the experimentation:

(i) The cassette made the teaching learning more interesting than their usual classroom.

(ii) The teachers were of the opinion that they can make the prose and poetry realistic by incorporating more local specific songs.

(iii) The artists were of the opinion that students can participate actively in voice recording.

(iv) Some teachers opined that more simple and usable songs can be collected for class room use.

(v) In respect of language and audition all the teachers exercised their positive views in the context of classroom transaction.

(vi) Sound effects like growl of tiger, hailstorm followed by rattling sound and tone of the Adibasi farmer girls were highly appreciated by the students.

(vii) As the cassettes were meant for 10 minutes display to supplement classroom teaching which was inadequate as opined by the students.

(viii)Stories from *Bana Dangara Ra Gapa* fascinated the learners and the teachers.

SUGGESTIONS

(i) Teachers and students should collect more local songs and cassettes the same for class room use.

(ii) Especially for teaching poetry, the cassettes can be duplicated and circulated among other students.

(iii) While cassettes are prepared the assistance of the artist of the nearby AIR centre may be sought.

(iv) The young talented singers of the locality can be identified and their voice may be recorded.

(v) Grants under TLM sanctioned to the primary schools may be devoted towards preparation of audio cassettes.

(vi) Two in one i.e. Radio-cum-Recorder may be supplied to the schools.

ENDNOTE

1. The paper was initially an innovative and experimental lesson plan. Later it was developed into this paper. The idea draws on the following works (books, handouts, papers): Lok Gita, (nd). Kunja Bihari, Directorate of TE & SCERT, Bhubaneswar, Orissa; B.V. Verghese 2002: Creativity in English Language Teaching. New delhi: Anmol Publictions; Asa Gai Gai Patha Sikhiba, 2001.Directorate of T.E. & SCERT, Bhubaneswar; Ama Bhasa Ama Sahitya, 2007. Department of School & Mass Education, Govt. of Orissa: Class-V; Bana Dangarara Gapa, 2007.Ranjan Pradhan. Pragyan Paramita, Niginipur, Kendrapada; and Quality Dimension of Action Research and Innovative Practice 2006. New Delhi: DEP-SSA , IGNOU.

15

ROLE OF TRIBAL FOLKLORES IN DEVELOPING THE COMMUNICATIVE SKILL OF TRIBAL CHILDREN IN ENGLISH AT ELEMENTARY LEVEL UNDER S. S. A[1]

Pradeep Kumar Mishra

"Words are the essential tools of communication"

INTRODUCTION

Language is a boon to humankind. It is not only the medium of communication rather it gives all sorts of teaching, feeling, thinking and reacting to things or situation. Language is a treasure of humankind. True learning of it makes our thoughts and actions refined and perfect, and brings desirable changes in our behaviour. Behaviour is a psycho-chemical process which is mostly expressed and manifested through language only. According to Aurundhoti Ray "Language is a skin over thoughts". One can fulfil his/her needs, aspirations and thirst of thoughts by the dint of language.

When children listen to English words or phrases some words retain in their mind and very often they use those words or phrases in their speech. At initial stage, mostly they use jumbled[2] words. But when they arrange them in right order, their speech/communication becomes meaningful.

Words and group of words are functional unit or units of language which are communicated in various situations to fulfil the needs of human beings.

Though English is a foreign language, it has penetrated in our lives so deep that without it no work can be done. This foreign flower is now blooming in our own soil with its sweet native fragrance. So, English has become an inevitable means of expressing India outside. English has become the necessity of the modern times. In the teaching of English, the teacher's rule is very crucial.

Koraput (Undivided) is dominated by a number of tribes. There are 52 tribal communities living in the region out of 62 in the state of Orissa. Its population was 3541710 of which 53.74 percent were the STs; and SCs population were 14.74 as per 2001 census. According to 1991 census 54.30 per cent of the total population of undivided Koraput district was tribals. If we add the SC population to it then 69.30 per cent or say 70 per cent would be backward population or social disadvantaged section of the society.

After Chhtishgarh, Koraput is the second tribal dominated region in the country. Another feature of the region is that nearly 88.48 per cent of the people live in villages. So, the region is rural in character. The entire region comes under K.B.K. plan and quality education is merely neglected here. Tribals are socially disadvantaged section of the society. After independence Government has lunched many programmes for upliftment of tribals, but their development is not up to our expectation yet. Being a part of Indian society they are also required to be proficient in English communication. However, the teaching learning process having average orientation does not meet the specific requirements of tribal learners (disadvantaged section of the society). Hence, a situation specific teaching learning process is assumed to be effective for them. In this paper an effort is made to realise the above objective by organizing learning activities to motivate and create interest of the tribal learners in developing listening and speaking (communicative) skills keeping in view their specific societal needs. In other words, the present paper proposes an enabling environment for the tribal students to develop communicative skills in English language.

Emphasizing the need for acceptance of English language in the country, the Radha Krishna Commission (1948) remarked:

If under sentimental urges we give up English, we would cut ourselves off from the living stream of ever growing knowledge. As a result the standard of our scholarship will deteriorate and our participation in the world movements of thought would become negligible. Its effects would be disastrous for our political life. English is our only means of preventing our evolution from the world. Our students who are getting education at school most acquire sufficient mastery of this language which will later on give them enough opportunity and access to the treasure of knowledge.

But in recent years, teaching is no more an exercise of imparting the content of text book alone, it is rather a process of facilitating the learners for self learning. The National Policy on Education (1986) lays emphasis on activity based, competency based and child centred learning process. To fit in this changing scenario a language teacher is expected to be an inspirer and a helper. He should be resourceful enough to frame activities that demand a need for the students to use the language, interact with the teacher and peer in the target language. When learning happens through active participation of students in learning activities, they develop a taste for learning and their learning becomes permanent.

In the Forward to National Curriculum Framework (NCF-2005), Prof. Yaspal, Chairman of NCF, has rightly said:

We need to give our children some taste of understanding, following which they would be able to Learn and create their own version of knowledge as they go out to meet the world of bits, images and transactions of life. Such taste would make the present of our children whole some, creative and enjoyable; they would not be traumatised by the excessive burden of information that is required merely for a short time before the hurdle race we call examination.

Understanding is given top priority in teaching-learning process. Hence in Language learning quality measures/ approaches must be taken to make classroom learning effective and joyful. If we take the right steps in this regard we can achieve UEE. Under S.S.A. their must be good coordination among right inputs and process within the classroom so that we can have best outcomes for our efforts.

VISION OF EDUCATION

Every child must get the opportunity to learn. Our vision of education encompasses the four pillars: learning to know, learning to do, learning to live together and learning to be.

The Education of Schedule Tribe

- A cursory glance at the educational status of the tribal children reveals that inspite of the best efforts of the government and NGOs, a significant number of them are out of schools and under- achievers.
- New tools, strategies and approaches should be formulated and implemented so that those currently marginalized are able to participate fully in the education across the spectrum and accept their constitutional right to education of an acceptable quality.
- Adopted strategies and modalities along with its implementations may be reviewed, modified and new innovative need-based and low-cost technology- adopted inputs may be syringed.
- In the new approach, children should learn integrated knowledge of different subjects through literature.
- This approach should motivate the children to promote school coming habit and self learning.
- New approach inculcates their own culture, value and ethos among the tribal children.
- In this way special attention should be given to primitive tribes and their children who are most educationally and economically backward.

Universal Literacy and Empowerment for Tribal Children

- Literacy empowers the mass. When the world has become a global village, every citizen should learn to upgrade his/her skill for survival. "Each one should teach one" should be the main motto of human society. In tribal area there are so many constrains and problems. Poverty, lack of communication and language problems are the major issues. Hence proper planning, systematic endeavour, and enthusiastic workers should be engaged with a missionary zeal. As tribal people are the major part of global population, special care should be taken to make them aware and link it with their life. In fact Government funding, community participation, management and conducive environment for teachers and learners, proper motivation of target tribal group, accountability should be the key to spread the light of literacy and education among tribal people. Literacy is the main instrument for empowerment.
- It should be the major objective to adopt right based approach. Right to learn, to know and right to do the item should entertain them.
- An integrated package with the help of tribal tales and lores could inspire and motivate them for better learning. This approach could upgrade their skills.

RATIONALE OF THE STUDY

In the present context of teaching learning process the traditional chalk and talk method has lost its meaning. Creative and innovative learning is gaining popularity among the students. Children tend to learn at their own according to their personal interest and potency.

Tribal children are fond of songs, riddles and stories. Any teaching learning process incorporating them in the delivery system, no doubt, would be effective means in realising the teaching-learning objectives of improving learners' communicative skill in English. It is because songs, riddles and stories would provide a familiar situation which they are accustomed with in the process of informal learning in the culture. However, the formal system does not provide such a process and tribal students ultimately lag behind in learning communicative skills. As has been mentioned, in this paper an attempt has been made to prepare a joyful learning package for tribal children to enhance their communicative skill in English.

Every language has four basic skills, such as listening, speaking, reading and writing; in brief it can be termed LSRW skills. The present researcher has taken first two basic skills of language as topic of study through an innovative approach that includes the application of rhymes, riddles and stories. Children love to recite poems and rhymes; they also like listening to the stories. Teacher must create a conducive atmosphere in which children would take utmost interest to listen the teacher. Good listening makes the child to imitate the same with voice modulation and acting. Imitation is the basic principle of learning for a child. It has been noticed that rhymes, riddles and stories are the best and suitable items of language learning. Words and sentences that contain various child-liking-tips and funs touch the hearts of the children. If we take care of these aspects of language speaking skill can be developed by listening.

The base of language learning will be the building block of the castle of charming personality. In teaching of English at Primary level, the problem is how to make the students remember and learn the use of new words or sentences taught in the class. Unless the newly introduced words are given repeated exposure, students are likely to forget them quickly. Exposure through activities with riddles, rhymes and stories can help the teacher make the newly taught words tick and stick in the tender minds of the students. This study is confined among the class four standards of Oriya Medium schools. They start enjoying learning at Class-IV.

Recent research explores a new dimension that language learning should take place in a most informal way like eating, drinking and sleeping. If any language is taught like mother tongue in a homely manner, children will take natural interest to learn them.

OBJECTIVES OF THE STUDY

The objectives of the present action research are:

(i) to design learning activities for developing the listening and speaking skill of the tribal learners at Primary level;

(ii) to provide scope for repeated learning practice of new words and related sentences through dialogue practice, recitation of poems and telling stories; and

(iii) to assess the effectiveness of the designed learning activities in developing listening and speaking.

METHODS AND MATERIALS

The present study is an action plan and experimental in nature. Essentially, the study examines the effectiveness of the folklores in developing the communicative skill of tribal children in English at elementary level under S. S. A.

For the purpose, thirty students of Class-IV were selected from Swami Vivekananda Vidyamandir under Umerkote Block in the district of Nawaraangpur of Orissa state. It is an Upper Primary School having classes one to seven. Thirty students of class IV out of 48 students were selected on the basis of regular attendance. For measuring the learning outcome and evaluating the achievement of the learner's, both pre- and post- test questionnaires were used. The study was a single group pre-test and post-test experimental design and so the sample learners were not divided on the basis of any attribute.

Task Analysis

The Researcher has taken the following task for the purpose of the study:

1. Conducting pre-test in Class-IV of Swami Vivekananda Vidya Mandir (a Govt. School) Umerkote.
2. Ascertaining the level of difficulties of the learners.
3. Selection/composition of suitable rhymes, riddles, action songs and stories according to their age and stage to develop their listening and speaking skills.

4. Extending the intervention for the selected sample.
5. Conduct of post test.
6. Analysis and interpretation of data.

TRANSACTION

(a) Listening and Speaking.

PRESENTATION MODALITY

(i) Riddles, rhymes and poems must be recited as an action song to transmit word and theme.

(ii) Acting out the story from "Story Bank" with proper gestures and postures.

TECHNIQUES FOR CLASS ROOM TRANSACTION

Group Recitation

Children like to recite a poem in group; it gives them, joy, happiness and certain message. When the poem is composed relating to the topic of the subject, it gives us the desirable results. Before group recitation, teacher should select the poem. He should give the tips how to recite the poem. If the teacher demonstrates first with proper voice modulation, the students will imitate him/her in a better manner. At last there should be question-answer session.

Bi-Group Recitation

It is another interesting method to teach a topic through poem to the tribal students. The entire class will be divided into two groups (Homogeneous or Heterogeneous) as per convince of the class. Teacher will give them the tips of rules and process. S/he will be the scorer. There will be a leader of each group to put question or answer. The leader of first group will put question to 2ndnd group for answer. Then 2nd group leader will put question to the first group. It will continue for one period at least 10 rounds. The group which will have more mark will be the winner of the day.

Recitation with Action/Action Song

Action songs are specially designed for the purpose. Students will recite the theme based action song with proper gesture and posture. It will be light exercise and will delight the students to communicate with teacher and peer groups. Teacher should give the tips of the rules and maintain discipline for better results. It is a group work in nature.

Role Plays As Per the Nature of Rhymes

It is an individual work in nature. There are certain action poems which are the best items for role play. In this approach individual development and interest can be enhanced. One small artist will talk and walk before the student audience. It is very interesting approach to develop communicative skill of tribal children.

STEPS OF RIDDLES /RHYMES / POEMS

(a) They will recite the small rhymes and riddles, one/two/ three stanza for one or two days.

(b) There will be a competition to fill up of the blank line or word of the stanza.

(c) Testing of sweet voice modulation and recitation style.

(d) Poetic questions out of the stanza.

(e) Recap of the entire poem to select 'Honey Bee'.

STEPS FOR STORY TELLING

(a) Selecting and telling the story from 'Story Bank'.

(b) Small stories from Aesop, Panchatantra, popular folk stories or collection of the same from different childrens journals.

(c) After story telling there will be recap of various portions by taking the help of students.

(d) They will be encouraged to tell the same story in their own way.

(e) One, who will tell maximum stories will be 'Story Master' and will be praised in the class.

(f) Then the questionnaire will be prepared containing of 10 marks (riddles and rhymes) and 10 marks for stories. There will be 20 marks of oral test. A score sheet will prepared accordingly. As the pre-test mark sheet which with us, we can make out clearly the difference.

Table 1

Test	*N*	*Mean*	*Mean Difference*
Pre-Test	30	15.06	10.18
Post-Test	30	25.24	-

Source: computed from the test scoring

Table-1 represents pre-test score of thirty students of Class-III. The mean of pre test score is 15.06 and that of the post score is 25.24. It clearly indicates that the average gain in score 10.18.

FINDINGS

1. Better performance at the post-test is a measure of achievement
2. The students were found reciting deeply with rhymes and riddles and more than 60 per cent students responded well towards this new innovative activities.
3. During the competition among the groups they tired to earn credit for the group in the way of winning the competition.
4. During role play they performed their role with proper modulation and acting.
5. During recapitulation of riddles/poems stories it was marked that listening and speaking capacity of the tribal students improved noticeably.

IMPLICATIONS

Folktales and suitable stories from children's journal can be collected for 'Story Bank' and used to improve their listening and speaking skills.

1. Rhymes/Riddles/Poems can be collected in a similar way from children's literature and can be composed and used as per needs of children in a creative manner.
2. Teachers can use this approach at primary level to promote the basic skill of listening and speaking at the beginning of English learning.
3. It can be used at informal way to entertain children as a joyful learning.

ENDNOTES

1. The paper was initially an innovative and experimental lesson plan. Later it was developed into a paper. The idea draws on the following works (books, handouts, papers): Kumar, Krishna 2004. The Child's Language and the Teacher: A Hand Book. New Delhi:NBT; Sinha, Sharmila 2001. Aspects of Children's Literature. New Delhi:NBT; Mohanti K.K, Mohapatra P.C., Samal J. 2006. Tribes of Koraput, Koraput: COATS;Mohapatro P.C.2009. "Rethinking Social Inclusion in Education", at the National seminar on Issues in Education on Disadvantaged Sections, organised by COATS, Koraput, Orissa,09-10, May,2009; and NCERT Journal, Jan., 2002. "The Primary Teacher (innovative issue)", New Delhi: NCERT.
2. For an example; Milk give cows (Jumbled words), becomes cows give milk. Fly birds the in air (Jumbled words) becomes birds fly in the air. Tails long have monkeys (Jumbled words) becomes monkeys have long tails.

16

BILINGUAL PRIMERS IN TRIBAL LANGUAGES IN ORISSA: INCONSISTENCY IN EFFORTS TO DEVELOP TRIBAL LANGUAGES

Ramesh C Malik

We are living in the age of globalization which has covered all the aspects of human life. The study of tribal languages, education, culture and society are interesting areas which have been demarked in the lime light of the process of globalization. On one hand, it has ruled over the domain of tribal culture, on the other, it has some of the indigenous practices and the social stigmas got out of their culture. 'Globalization is a process (or set of process) which embodies a transformation in the spatial organization of social relations and transactions–assessed in terms of their extensity, intensity, velocity, and impact generating transcontinental or interregional flows and networks of activity, interaction, and the exercise of power'. (Fairclough, 2005.16). Globalization brings people into the process and it also brings in culture: economic and political 'objects' are also culturally conditioned and embedded, so for instance, particular economical systems or forms of state depend upon and are closely connected with the particular meaning, interpretations, narratives, values, attitudes, identities and so forth (ibid). Further, the process of social constructions is inherently involved with the nature of globalization, and education and language are the most significant among them. The transaction of development, power and exercise of social life are closely related with education and medium of education. Globalization not only tenders power of capitalism, but it also emphasizes on the sociology of people and their entrepreneurship which regulates and develops through education. The medium of instruction is one of the important aspects in education. This is given more emphasis by the frame of globalization. Globalization tends to improve the language competence of people, so that the globalization thoughts can reach them and they can make use of their working skills for their survival and also to improve their economic status. In this connection, the process of globalization initiates in bringing out the permanent solution for social derivation through the education system which was/ is considered as a perquisite for equality and independency. So, education and language both have been included as the central theme of globalization. Globalization emphasizes on the linguistic aspect of textbooks and tries to improve the pedagogical tools for primary education. For instance, in Orissa it became unsuccessful as the global methodologies were misused by the Government authorities in developing of tribal education in Orissa.

In these respects, Government introduces many attractive policies towards tribal education through the agency of District Primary Education Programme (DPEP). Bilingual method of education is one of such policies which were meant for proper education of the children hailing from minority languages. This paper tries to focus on the issues of bilingual education which have been introduced by DPEP in Orissa from 2001-2005. The thrust of this discussion is to describe the bilingual teaching materials of Koya-Oriya and Kuvi-Oriya glossary which have been prepared by the DPEP. The Koya-Oriya Primer is meant to educate school going children of Koya tribe through their Mother-tongue. It is an extremely sturdy policy of DPEP towards tribal education in Orissa. It has been noticed that readability and flawlessness of the teaching materials are quite different from the genre of bilingual methods. The writers of the primer have made some fatal mistakes in these texts which have in turn lost their norms and thrusts in objective realisaton. It was carried out for educating the tribal children in using their mother tongue. Before discussing on the main topic, I would like to highlight the theoretical observations that emphasizes on bilingualism and its importance in teaching through the respective mother tongues. The discussion moves further to the central issues of Koya-Oriya primer *"dumtam timtam"* and Kuvi-Oriya glossary *"adibasi chabila sabdakosa: Kuvi-Odia"* which are being disturbed to promote bilingualism by the writers and editors.

Let us start with some of the definitions of bilingualism and it's importance in teaching of minority language students. The famous linguist, Bloomfield says '...bilingualism as native–like control of two languages' (1933:56). His idea on bilingualism is that one who maintains more than one language for his/her survival. Mackey considers bilingualism 'as the alternate use of two or more languages by the same individuals' (1957:51). Taylor's definition of bilingualism refers to one who speaks two or more languages, dialects or style of speech that involves different sounds, vocabularies and syntax (1976:239). Macnamara (1969) defined bilingualism by specifying four areas of linguistic skills (viz. understanding, speaking, reading and writing) each of which was further divided into four levels (viz. phonological/graphic, lexical, syntactic, and semantic) and suggesting that a person can be called a bilingual if he is in possession of at least one of these language skills 'even to a minimal degree'. In this context, the definition of Skutnabb-Kangas is more appropriate and he says 'someone who is able to function in two (or more) languages, either in monolingual or bilingual communities, in accordance with the socio-cultural demands made of an individual's communicative and cognitive competence by these communities or by the individual herself, at same level as native speakers, and who is able positively to identify with both (or all) language groups (and cultures) or part of them (quoted in Mohanty, 1994:12). Bilingualism is a linguistic principle which is one of the most popular methods of teaching in multilingual states. To use mother tongue as medium of instruction particularly in tribal education is emphasized by the linguists. The importance of bilingual education as pointed out by D.P. Pattanayak is 'the fundamental value of the mother tongue for education of all pupils in India. Further, he clarified that 'mother tongue education is fundamental right' (quoted in Mohanty, 1994:174) because 'it is not simply a matter of language learning: it involves the acquisition of all the knowledge and skill that identify the minority culture' (Crystal, 2003.368). It might be the reasons of introducing bilingual education programme of Government to educate the tribal children through their mother tongue.

METHODOLOGY

This study is based on the pedagogical sources which are Koya–Oriya Primer and Kuvi-Oriya visual glossary. Both the texts are prepared by DPEP for primary level student. These are the bilingual primer written in Oriya script. First text is Koya–Oriya primer which contains thirty lessons including 118 exercises and an editorial note by the Director. The language of text is both Koya and Oriya. The subject of the lessons and exercises are based on the local environment, animals, market, agricultural products, seasons, rituals and festivals, material culture, story of bravery, and educational institutions. Second text is a visual glossary of Kuvi-Oriya languages which runs around 48 pages with an introduction written by Director of DPEP. Though, both the texts have followed bilinguality, the principles of bilingualism is disturbed in both the texts. So, they have considered for reviewing and suggesting some of the perquisites for revision in further edition.

KOYA-ORIYA PRIMER: A REVIEW

Koya is one of the tribal communities of Malkanagiri district of Orissa. According to 1991 census the population of Koya speakers were 1,20,000. They are used to speaking in their own language Koya which belongs to Dravidian language group. In using their mother tongue, DPEP has introduced bilingual teaching programme during the period from 2001-2005 in primary level. The main purpose of the book has been clarified in the editorial note by the director of DPEP. He has categorically mentioned that the main aim of the book is to teach the tribal children through their mother tongue which will help them to read, write and develop their language competence. He has not only highlighted the subject of the lessons included in the text, but, he has also specified the steps of usability of this text for non-native language teacher, because the original lessons have been translated into Oriya. Ultimately, he wanted to say that the text is a bilingual. The text has followed three varieties of linguistic methods, they are: Koya-Oriya, only Oriya and only Koya. The writer and editor of the text have not maintained any language consistency in the text. Though they have claimed the text to be bilingual in nature, the whole text says that is not a bilingual or monolingual but, a kind of hybridism which is very difficult for non-native language teacher. There are many examples in each lesson and exercises are not followed bilingual methods. Methodologically, Koya–Oriya primer is very problematic and subjects of the lessons are un-systemic. The following table will show some light on the inconsistency of exercises given in the head lessons.

Table-1 shows that there are thirty lessons and 118 exercises in the text and that lesson three does not have any exercises. The ratio of exercise is inconsistent in nature which is not met with open arms in the primarily level text. Lesson three is about a village market; in this lesson only picture of village market is given. The exercise for this lesson is dropped. The same subject (the market) is repeated in lesson four instead of the exercise of lesson three. Three or four questions in an exercise do not include varieties of questions to meet the cognitive, affective and psycho-motor requirements of learners.

Table 1
Lesson and Exercise

S.l. No.	*Lesson*	*No. of Exercise*
1	01	5
2	02	4
3	03	0
4	04	4
5	05	3
6	06	3
7	07	5
8	08	1
9	09	3
10	10	2
11	11	3
12	12	5
13	13	4
14	14	4
15	15	5
16	16	4
17	17	4
18	18	5
19	19	4
20	20	5
21	21	6
22	22	5
23	23	4
24	24	5
25	25	4
26	26	4
27	27	5
28	28	3
29	29	6
30	30	3
Total Exercise		118

Source:Collected by the investigator himself from text books

PROBLEMS IN GLOSSING OR TRANSLATING

Bilingual text is a text of two languages. Though, Koya-Oriya is a bilingual text, it has not followed the same every lesson and exercise of text. Most of the lessons are not glossed or translated into Oriya. Only title of the lessons have maintained bilingual methods not all and some of them have failed to use of bilingual method in Lesson-3, Lesson-4, Exercise-1, Lesson-6, Exercise-1, Lesson-7, Exercise-1,2,4,5 Lesson-8 and etc. A serious problem has been found in Lesson -9, Exercise -1.

This exercise is on non-vertebrate animal like frog, fish, pig, rabbit and then a fish eating bird. In this exercise, first of all Koya equivalent are not written then under the fish, pig is written, in the place of pig, rabbit is written, in place of rabbit is written a fish eating bird. The entirely exercise is wrongly presented.

There are also Some Spelling Errors found in the text.

Lesson-18, Exercise-4

Example 1

Koya: *padi paisa:* (ten/ paisa)

Oriya: *dasa paisa:*

Example 2

Koya: erabai a:id pa:isa:(twenty five paisa)/

Oriya: pacisi paisa:

In the first example the Koya word *paisa:* is glossed into Oriya as *paisa:* whereas in the second example the Koya same word *paisa*: glossed as *pa:isa.*

Exapmple 3

Koya: a:rda: rupa:e (fifty/ paisa)

Oriya: pacasa paisa: (fifty/paisa)

Example 4

Koya: a:nda rupa:y (one/ rupee)

Oriya: eka tanka (one/rupee)

In example-3, the Koya word *rupa:e* glossed *paisa* whereas same word is glossed into *rupa:y* in example-4 which is a serious spelling error found in the text.

Apart from these spelling errors, there are many visual errors in the pictures which are not clear and visible.

KUVI-ORIYA VISUAL GLOSSARY

In Kuvi-Oriya visual glossary, the writers have not followed any lexicographical methods. Only they have collected some of the words related to kinship, body part, dress materials, household articles, agricultural tools, flora and fauna, food items and vegetables, musical instruments, ornaments, temples, name of the play, vehicles, and solar system, and etc. There are some serious problems in glossing as well as spelling in which the original meaning is dropped. For example, the Kuvi word "ayya" (Reddy and Mahapatra, 1995:03) is glossed as "aya" which means "mother" or "woman" in Kuvi language. Another word "buDDa" means "younger brother" ibid., 88 has been written as "buDa" which means only brother. There are some words which are not glossed whereas others are glossed in same chapter. The following words like: "pyant" (trouser), "katuri" (crow knife), "baliti" (bucket), "siala" (jackel), "citabagha" (leopard), "baragacha" (banyan tree), and many words are not glossed whereas other words are glossed. Inconsistency of bilingual method is employed in the process of glossary preparation which losses the readability of the text which is a serious issues in pedagogical level.

CONCLUSION

The question is about tribal education, especially Koya and Kuvi students. There is still not enough educated from "younger generation". Education has had 'no progresses during the last "two decades". It could have been the single tool and hope for the tribal for "saving itself from all future living warrior life" (Das, 2005.180). If the teaching material for tribal children will be prepared like this, then, how will the students of tribal communities be literate and how can they educate themselves? The policy should revise the methods of writing and preparing of the text books. This will be helpful for the education of the children. It needs thorough revision and respects the positive attitudes of globalization through the education policy. In this concern the following suggestions are forwarded for improvement of the bilingual teaching materials:

- appoint the experienced linguists
- thorough proof reading of textbooks
- consistency of lessons and exercises according to the subject

- the use of modern printing technology for the better visibility of the pictures
- constituency of bilingualism

If all these issues will be considered by the authority of DPEP, then the primer of tribal education will be more usable and meaningful for teaching and acquiring knowledge.

REFERENCES

Bloomfield, L. (1933), *Language*. New York. Rinehart and Winston.

Crystal, David (2003), *The Cambridge Encyclopedia of Language* (2nd edition). Cambridge: Cambridge University Press.

Das, Kornel. (2005), *Tribal and Their Culture Koya Tribe in Transition.* New Delhi, APH Publishing Company.

Fairclough, N. (2005), *Language and Globalization*. London. Routledge, Tylor and Francis Group.

Mackey, W.F. (1957), "The Description of Bilingualism". *Journal of Canadian Linguistic Association.*

Macnamara, J. (1969), "How can one Measure the Extent of a Person's Bilingual Proficiency". In L.G.Kelley(Ed.). *Description of Mesaurement of Bilingualism.* Toronto: Toronto University

Misra, Mahendra (ed.). (2001/2005), Adibasi Chabila Sabda Kosa(Koya-Oriya Visual Glossary). Bhubaneswar:DPEP.

Misra, Mahendra (ed.). (2001/2005), *dumtam timtam*(Koya-Oriya Primer).Bhubaneswar. DPEP.

Mohanty, A.K. (1994), *Bilingualism in a Multilingual Society*. Mysore, CIIL

Tylor, I. (1976), *Introduction to Psycolinguistics*. New York. Rinehart and Winston.

Reddy, B. and Mahapatra.B.P.1995. *Kuvi-Oriya–English Dictionary*. Mysore: Central Institute of Indian Languages.

- The use of [illegible] is necessary for the better visibility of the pictures
- [illegible] consequence of [illegible]

If all the [illegible] will be considered by the authority of DPEP, then the primers of tribal education will be more usable and meaningful for teaching and [illegible] knowledge.

REFERENCES

Bloomfield, L. (1933) Language. New York: [illegible] and Winston.

[illegible]

SECTION–V

Intervention Perspectives

17

RETHINKING TRIBE AND SCIENTIFIC KNOWLEDGE BASED POLICIES: A SOCIOLOGICAL ANALYSIS ON BAMBOO DEVELOPMENT IN NAGALAND

A. Wati Walling

AN OVERTURE

Tell me and I'll forget; show me and I may remember; involve me and I'll understand.

—*A Chinese Proverb*

The above emphasises the importance of participation. In the present context development, it is all the more important when the essence of involving-partnering with the marginalised and excluded is recognised in formulating policy and developmental schemes. To put it in the scope of this paper it refers to participation of the tribes in their development.

'Tribe' is a contentious term; referring to the most disadvantageous community who are so sparse yet so widely distributed through out the country. It occurs as an issue since a uniform evaluation could not be made basing on common criteria. Therefore, fresh consideration of tribal issues especially their policies need to be critically examined and rather than romanticization of the tribes, issues need to be viewed on the basis of how it fared in history. Formulation of developmental policy for the tribal people by bureaucrats (sans the knowledge of the tribals) in the state and implementation of the same is perceived sociologically and developmentally significant.

Privileging certain knowledge in the form of policy adoption can be looked at from Thomas Kuhn perspective of normal science. For him 'science' proceeds with an assumption that they know what the world is like, and firmly gets established on one or more past scientific achievement. (Kuhn, 1962: 5 & 10). However, there arise anomalies in the system with progressive shift to a new paradigm challenging the basic premises of the current scientific practice. For Feyerabend, The only principle that does not inhibit progress is the maxim 'anything goes'. (Feyerabend, 1975: 23). All these perspectives summing up together, Latour on the other hand echoes that, a society is an extension of laboratory. Hence, as scientific methods demand selection, evaluation and criticism for a paradigm shift, policies such as existing one that hinder tribal people to be reviewed and well researched effective policies and strategies need to be evolved to accommodate, empower and partner the down trodden tribal people. It is also imperative to examine whether there is an evaluation of knowledge for policy making shaped by social categories (which the globalization tends to enhance) a person belong to.

The nature of scientific knowledge, as discussed above, provides the background of analysis of the topic of IKS and utilisation of bamboo resource. Bamboo is an important resource throughout northeast India. Tribal inhabited area, particularly Nagaland, has umpteen indigenous ways of bamboo utilization and consumption underlining the age-old cultural practices evolved in the Naga society. Therefore, there is a need to understand the relationship between the bamboo resources that are abundantly available and the techniques behind its intrinsic utility. India stands next only to China in harbouring the most diverse species of bamboo. And the North-East India–Nagaland harbours about 2/3rd of them.

However, there is not much documentation of bamboo species and records of the age old techniques behind plantation, tending, extraction and production of bamboo. Analysis locates itself in the intricacies of the recent developmental policies of bamboo in Nagaland vis-à-vis the age old indigenous practices of the local people.

TRIBE OBSERVED

Arguably, India has the largest tribal population than any other countries in the world (Desai, 1977: 16), twenty millions as assessed by 1951 census. Out of total tribal population in the country about 5 million of population resides in the hills. India also harbours some of the most primitive tribes in the world, who are found in the southern part of India. (Aiyappan, 1977: 38). G.H Ghurye described tribals as the 'so- called aboriginals' or 'backward Hindus'. Some scholars have designated tribals as the 'submerged humanity'. (Desai, 1977: 17). Here, it is intriguing to know what prompted various scholars, administrators, authors and reformers ascribe different designations and describe differently, the categorically same group of people, the tribes in India? In the first ever all India census undertaken in 1881, the term used was not 'tribe' but 'forest tribe'. Risley and Gait, in charge of the 1901- 1911 censuses respectively added so called 'animists' in the table for caste and other. Marten followed the same classification in the 1921 census, except that he changed the heading from 'animism' to 'tribal religion'. (Xaxa, 1999: 1519). Globally, Oxford dictionary would define 'tribe' as 'a social group bound together by kin and duty and associated with a particular territory. Members of the tribe share the social cohesion associated with the family...' (Marshall, 1998: 674). "A unit of socio-political organization consisting of a number of families, clans, or other groups who share a common ancestry and culture and among whom leadership is typically neither formalized nor permanent." is what the free dictionary online would go on to define a tribe.

Juxtaposing the whole scenario on 'tribe', observations can be made quite intensely how appropriation of the term 'tribe' has differed contextually over space and time. (see Beteille, 1977, 1986 & 1998). Ever since the first inception of the 'tribe' in the 1881 Census in Indian context, the understanding and perception has been shaped and moulded differently. We do not find a tribe today as 'a self contained unit' in its ideal state (Beteille, 1977:8), but what we find is a 'tribe in transition'. (ibid.:14; Desai, 1977:15-28). It is true that the very dynamic nature of society add to difficulty in capturing 'tribe' (see Behera, 2008:143-157); however, another way to interpret would be that, most tribes differ from one other in its composition – historically, socio-culturally and ecologically. This very fact, therefore, maintains that just one overarching policy for such diverse tribal communities in India would not be in a right perspective. With current 8.2 per cent of India's population according to 2001 census, interpreting it into 82 million people (world's largest) and an odd 698 scheduled tribes exist at present in India, the diversification of policy is perceived inevitable. On the other hand, almost all the past observations, writings and analysis on Indian tribal are focused on viewing how tribes are becoming castes. Therefore, as Xaxa, would rightly point out, 'tribe' in a sense has never been studied in the right spirit in India, but described as having becoming a caste society, peasant society or a socially differentiated society. (Xaxa, op cit. 1522).

In the context of the inhabited geographical terrain, socio-cultural diversity, and political history of the tribals in India, economic endeavour needs to be located and put into perspective. However, it should be heeded that the fundamental problem of the tribal population is political with an economic face. Indian economy which is money controlled and profit oriented economy can pump in money to states. But unless, the policy formulation and implementation is corrected, underdevelopment of the marginalized will proliferate. Major issues among northeast tribals such as Nagas (cf. Anand, 1967) are acquisition of quality higher education, security of job, decent standard of living, accessibility to resource and facilities such as health care. These needs coupled with a sound socio-cultural, ecological and ideological knowledge ought to be incorporated for any policy implementation, which necessarily might not be the same with other tribal community in the other parts of India. Issue such as these however, has to be established on equality of opportunities and elimination of exploitation, which is quintessentially political in nature. Therefore, what comprises a good policy? Or on what basis certain knowledge is privileged and another left to oblivion?

PLURALISTIC METHODOLOGY AS POLICIES

Should there be only 'the policy/ the method' for a society? For both the answers, the pertinent question then would be the source and the notion of it? Paul Feyerabend in his work *Against Method* criticizes Kuhn's normal science as dogmatic, authoritative, narrow approach leading to the closure of the mind. Feyerabend advocated methodological pluralism to its logical extreme by proposing the anarchic concept of knowledge. The only principle that does not inhibit progress is the maxim 'anything goes'. Different forms of knowledge have its own benefits and limitations. The history of science does not just consist of facts and conclusions drawn from facts. It contains ideas, interpretations of facts, problems created by conflicting interpretations, mistakes etc. On further analysis we even find that science knows no 'facts' in isolation, but facts that enter our knowledge which is already viewed in a certain way and which are essentially notional. (Feyerabend, op cit: 19). Anarchism in this way helps to achieve progress in ways which one cares to choose (without any prejudice).

We find that there is not a single rule, no matter how credible, and how firmly grounded in epistemology, that is not violated at some time or other. It becomes evident that such violations are not accidental events; they are not results of insufficient knowledge or inattention which might have been avoided. But they are equally necessary for progress. Similarly, to understand the underlying logic of 'policy making' here, there isn't any 'knowledge' that needs to be privileged than the other. And the existing dominant discourse is all but, a mere manipulated ideology and stereotypical prejudice of knowledge based on social categorization.

From the theoretical, we presume that there is no such thing as 'the method'. In fact, even in the scientific realm and those scientists who carry out experiments with the so called methods are merely impostors and an opportunist who move from one to another empirical methodology. Therefore, the categorization of knowledge basing on their social categorization is perceived rather accountable in the light of absorbing policy such as the tribal development policy in question. The deliberation also asserts that openness to several knowledge bases on thorough enquiry should be adopted for policies considerations. A policy, as have seen (no matter how scientific or unscientific it is) is prone to injustice and prejudice towards people. Therefore, privileging of a kind of knowledge over the other for policy consideration should be evaluated with utmost concern in a multi cultured nation like India. The scenario of bamboo development in the northeast states (particularly Nagaland) indicates a very close encounter with the policy of government based on a biased 'knowledge' rather than the genuine of the tribal people.

BAMBOO AND THE NAGA TRIBE

India has the richest bamboo species resources next only to China. It harbours 136 species, including 11 exotic species. Nagaland, covering an area of 16,579 sq km, exclusively has 56 species of bamboo. India's Nagaland situated in the NER is home to the Nagas. The topography is full of hilly ranges which break into a wide chaos and spurs and ridges. The field area is Tuli (Under Mokokchung District of Nagaland, about 216 km away from the state capital Kohima) and is inhabited by the Ao- Nagas. Here, as per analysis of the present study the over all bamboo coverage is near about 35 per cent of the total forest area with a large proportion being privately owned. Tuli too, has a long history of bamboo culture and bamboo is a popular commodity in the vicinity. Here are four species of bamboo under observation for this exercise namely; *Bambusa balcooa* (Oti/Otu), *Bambusa tulda* (Longmi), *Dendrocalamus giganteus* (Anung), *Dendrocalamus hamiltonii* (Auo).

It is to be noted that, these four species of bamboo are the most commonly occurring species of bamboo in the Tuli area which are exclusively found in the wild except for the species *Dendrocalamus hamiltonii* (Aao in Ao-Naga dialect) which is cultivated. It grows naturally on many private plots, in an unorganized fashion. *"Both poor and rich use bamboo extensively for their basic needs. Bamboo means everything particularly to my family because of its applicability and versatility."* (Toshi, 59 M). For some, their main source of livelihoods came from bamboo, through selling of big and small products made out of it, which are in the form of handicraft and weaving. In order to understand the dynamics of the land based economy in Tuli, the following assessment was made. Firstly, distribution of land holdings among the sample population is presented in Fig-1.

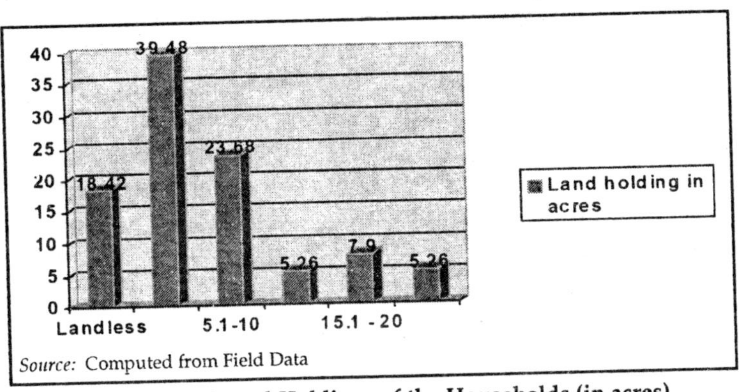

Fig. 1: Size of Land Holdings of the Households (in acres)

Among the household respondents, 39.48 per cent of them owned land up to 5 acres, followed by 23.68 per cent with land holding of up to 8 acres. And 5.26 per cent of the sample population possesses more than 20 acres of land per household. Bamboo as a naturally growing grass is recorded in 61.29 per cent of the land holdings of the households in the study (both found in the wild and cultivated). It was noted that 18.42 per cent of the households does not have any cultivable land of their own. The inheritance of landed property is so devised that the land remains under perpetual ownership of the family or lineage group even though it has to be divided amongst the successors. It can be mentioned here that the basic economic problem of Nagaland is the low yielding in jhumming and depletion of forests. Therefore, land products such as bamboo needs special attention for development.

It is found that majority (39.47 per cent) of the households' extract bamboo from their own land. Another group of households (7.89 per cent) besides extracting bamboo from their own land, purchases it for household consumption. There are also households who purchase bamboo from market and also borrow from neighbours and clan-owned land etc. (Refer Fig-2 & Table-1 & 2). In some cases, bamboo is also obtained from community owned forest or clan-owned land. About 16 per cent of the households depend on a combination of different sources such as market, forest, clan-owned land. This phenomenon of bamboo acquisition can be attributed to the culture of the Naga society where bamboo land holdings are used extensively for meeting the basic needs like food, clothing and shelter. It is rather a normal occurrence that people of this community use bamboo in so varied form and no doubt, the social vibe and social contract it creates during its course of exchanges.

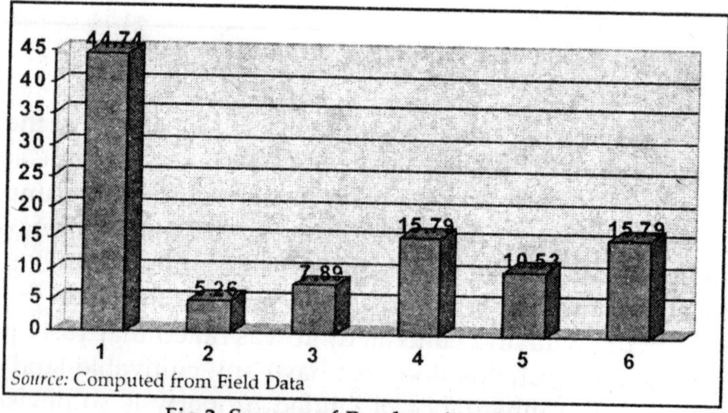

Source: Computed from Field Data

Fig.2: Sources of Bamboo Acquisition

Analysis also shows that about 40 per cent of the respondents utilize bamboo up to 25 m³ per annum (calculated by the number of bamboo poles consumed). 32 per cent uses about 38 m³ of bamboo, 11 per cent of the respondents found to be landless households; yet consumes more or less the same as others. Another 11 per cent used the highest quantity of about 113 m³ bamboo. A respondent has to say, *"almost every year my family run out of harvestable bamboo in our land, so I usually buy from the market or sometimes ask my in- laws"*. (Sashila, 45 F). The approximate overall consumption of bamboo was found to be 1758 m³ per annum and the average consumption by a household was found out to be 46.26 m³. It is worth noting from this analysis that the consumption of bamboo is independent of the land holdings.

Table 1
Sources of Bamboo Acquisition

1	Own land – 44.74%
2	Own land + Clan Owned land – 5.26
3	Own land + Purchase – 7.89
4	Purchase – 15.79
5	Own land + Forest – 10.53
6	Others – 15.79

Source: Computed from Field Data

TOWARDS 'THEIR' KNOWLEDGE AS POLICIES

If there is a perspective that today's massive development and the globalizing agent bring about, then, it is the homogenization processes that tend to diminish certain knowledge systems and privilege another in the way of policy adoption. Then question is-which kind of knowledge is absorbed as normal for a paradigm to function? Or in other words, what kind of privileged knowledge comprises the 'ideal policy'? In the words of Thomas Kuhn, no natural history can be interpreted in the absence of at least some implicit body of intertwined theoretical and methodological belief that permits selection, evaluation, and criticism. (Kuhn, op cit. : 16). He further suggests that a dominating 'science' phenomenon, tends to suppress many new researches and thus fail to rectify any mistakes. Paradigms gain status as they become seemingly more successful than their competitors in solving problems. However, the inherent problem uncontested in this kind of 'science' is first, the determination of significant fact which the paradigm guides in finding those facts. Secondly, the researchers focus on facts that can be directly predicted within the paradigmatic theory. Thirdly, researchers undertake work to articulate the paradigm theory itself which is pushed to exhaustion at times'. (ibid. : 33). Now, let us have insights on how the government policies, as 'science' would claim dominance in formulating polices over the knowledge of 'their' people.

Table 2
Land Holdings and the Quantity of Bamboo Consumption

	Utilization of Bamboo per annum.(In cubic m)m3				
Land Holdings (In acres)	*0- 25 m3*	*26- 50 m3*	*51-100 m3*	*101-125 m3*	*Total*
Landless	4	1	2		7
Upto- 5	6	3	5	1	15
5.1-10	4	3	1	1	9
10.1-15	1		1		2
15.1-20			2	1	3
20.1& above			1	1	2
Total	15	7	12	4	38

Source: Computed from Field Data

In the Naga society, particularly, in the lives of the people living in Tuli, bamboo and its products are used for an umpteen purposes chiefly including social and cultural contracts. *"In olden times, at the time of child birth, the dai (the birth attendant) would use a bamboo blade to cut the umbilical cord that connects the child and the mother in the womb. At the time of death, the dead body is wrapped in a bamboo mat (Aklep in Ao- Naga dialect) enveloping the entire lifecycle is bamboo for the Nagas."* (Imkong 87 M). In whole, bamboo unites the Nagas and enhances their solidarity among the wide spectrum of the tribal communities.

Apart form the obvious observations that bamboo is intrinsically ingrained in the socio- cultural and economic life of the Nagas, there are documentations made on some of the most common utility of bamboo among the Ao- tribal people of Nagaland which has been found absent in the policies of recent bamboo developments.

Aesthetic Dimension of Bamboo

The 'Green gold' it is considered as a unique aesthetic gift by Mother Nature for the people of Nagaland. The bamboo plant in itself is a sight of delight owing to its evergreen property and various environmental friendly features. Bamboo serves as the most authentic and easily available material for creative, artistic and sculptural works. *"For an artist in the NER, bamboo brush and paints (processed) are indispensable. In embroidery, bamboo needles were used for creating all sorts of designs."* Nuklo (45 M). Originality of any design in the Naga society ranging from buildings to ornamental and attire designs has an indication of the age-old creative tradition, aptly expressed by bamboo. Unique traditional imprints on bamboo mugs, utensils, kitchen-ware to furniture etcetera are commonly seen in modern Naga households.

Bamboo Grooves as a Buffer Zone

For demarcating village boundaries, bamboo grooves were maintained. During olden days when fire accidents were frequent, the green bamboo grooves were supposedly the sole shield from this danger. Thus, the practice has been carried out even to this day. Furthermore, bamboos species were grown in order to prevent soil erosion in land slide prone places and river sides. Bamboos are important structural components of many forest ecosystems and play a major role in ecosystem dynamics. Bamboo is held sacred in the culture and tradition of the Nagas. They regard it as their saviour as bamboo grooves safeguarded the village from other villager's invasion. It is also extensively used to make bow and arrow, spears, shields which kept them protected from enemies down the generation.

Bamboo for Constructing House

Bamboo houses shelter millions in many countries, so also the shelters the majority of the Tuli population have. It is used for pillars, post, stilts, rafters, roofing, flooring, walling, fencing scaffolding and a host of other purposes. Likewise, emergency housing in case of calamities is taken care completely with bamboo which in return facilitates the social contacts of the people. The process also saves a lot of time and money apart from being handy and cheap, because of its easy availability and proximity to inhabited areas. *"It is a far more manageable material compared to any other timber materials for construction of any kind of houses"*. (Kilem, 74 M). Another traditional usage of bamboo is construction of *Machan* (platform house). Bamboo is a useful material especially in rural areas and small towns like Tuli where almost every households rear animals. With bamboo, people construct shelter for all sorts of domesticated animals like pig sty, coop, chicken pen, stable, etcetera. Lately, modern bamboo based architectural works are also mushrooming in the region.

Bamboo for Festive

Virtually, there is no festival in which bamboo is not used. Commencing from the traditional ornaments to the eatable delicacies, bamboo is even associated with games and recreation. Festivals, which generally mark conquest of enemies and invocation of blessing for the season (sowing and harvest) involves unique ways of using bamboo. The attires of the people for the ceremonial occasion are made of bamboo. Bamboo is in fact, the essence of all colourful festivals. For example, 'Legging of split cane/bamboo' on boy's legs for festival are significant and also sight of great delight. It has been customized aesthetically in modern designs with ornamental bamboo (an exotic species).

Bamboo for food, nutrition and medicine

There are bamboo delicacies like soup, pickles, and dishes. Bamboo sauce is a well known appetizer. Bamboo shoot has a high nutritional value and low fat, and is a good source of fibre. Many specialized animal and bird species also depend upon bamboo shoots. Bamboo roots, leaves, sap and ash have been used since ancient times as a remedy for minor and major ailments. The white-papery soft layer found inside the internodes were used as haemostatic and antiseptic agent. The ashes are also used as an anti-dandruff matter. Further, the fluid-like accumulation inside the culm was traditionally used for treating urinary ailment. Taking in consideration as a nutritious and delicate wholesome food item, bamboo today finds place in menus of many airlines and restaurants.

Bamboo in Agriculture

Bamboo pipes are used to irrigate vast tracts of agricultural land in different agro-ecological settings. Bamboo is also used in making dams, gates, farm implements, props, stakes; floats in fish trap, silk cocoon trays, chicken coops, windbreak barriers and several other agricultural implements.

Bamboo in Handicraft

Bamboo's natural elegance and easy workability make it a prized material for handicrafts. The Chinese are said to have manufactured more than 8000 bamboo and rattan items from buttons to baskets, lamps to lacquer ware, mats to musical instruments, from toys to walking sticks, etcetera. Handicraft-spinning and weaving tools are made exclusively of bamboo. Bamboo is extensively used for fishing- it is used as fishing rod or for the purpose of constructing fish and animal traps of all sorts.

Bamboo in Transportation

Bamboo culms float in water as they are light-weight and the internodes are filled with air. This properly has been put to use from the time of forefathers to current time. It is used for making rafts, junks and boats, and their masts sail and outriggers. Bamboo is also used in making wagon floor, carts and their hoods, and suspension bridges traditionally.

Bamboo as an Economic Resource

The diversity of bamboo uses, as mentioned, makes bamboo an economic resource with potential for improving the quality of life of rural and urban communities. Bamboo cultivation is a low cost investment and identifying correct variety for economic extraction (longevity and hardness) could go a long way in establishment bamboo industries and even finding market for export. This also creates condition for establishing industries based on bamboo which would attract foreign exchange. Further with the natural landscape of the state, coupled with the majestic bamboo greenery, it can be developed to promote tourism in Nagaland.

Over 2.5 billion people worldwide trade in or use bamboo. Global domestic trade and subsistence use of bamboo are estimated to be worth USD 4.5 billion per annum, and export of bamboo generates another USD 2.7 billion. The world market for bamboo is USA, approximately $10 billion, of which China alone shares about 50 per cent. Demand for bamboo is expected to reach about US$ 20 billion by 2015. In the Indian context, the estimated fund requirement for the Tenth Five Year Plan is Rs. 2,608 crore for raising new bamboo in 2 million hectares of land The economic benefits of these activities have been worked out at 8.6 million jobs during the Tenth Five Year Plan. Therefore, it is an economic resource having immense potential for improving the quality of life. The people of the NER- Nagaland are important stakeholders and repositories of bamboo knowledge, which can be extremely useful for the development of the sector. For many people this activity provides a commercial, often primary vocation as well. With this enormous prospects coming, how are the policies going to be adopted indeed becomes very crucial.

CONCLUSION

Myrdal and Hirschman (quoted in Baruni, 1990:45) would echo that there is a need of the sociology of knowledge of development theory in prescribing value changes or other policy prescription. For them, it is vital that the meaning of development itself be questioned as to whether it is possible for social scientists to have an objective view of the aspirations of people in developing societies. However, there is always a middle path. And as seen from the study, despite the richness and incommensurability of bamboo utility in the Tuli area, proper knowledge of the people has not being nurtured as yet. Now the biggest challenge that lay ahead in the case of the NER particularly Nagaland is the idea of partnering with the Global market as well as partnership within the country – a vital step towards upliftment of the tribals in recognition of their knowledge which is neglected for a long time. *"Privileging other knowledge to local knowledge (for policy) should be stopped. Evidence of such failure can be seen in the case of Nagaland Pulp & Paper Company Limited (NPPC), a Government of Nagaland's joint venture with the Hindustan Corporation Limited which started in July 1982 but came to a dead end within a decade in Oct. 1992. Initiatives of the government should start from the local knowledge of the tribal people, since we cannot learn so much"* echoed Pangjung an eighty year old man. (Pangjung, 80 M).

Democratic form of government to a certain extent cannot favour tribals, where representation is based on number. Hence, we see policies 'foreign' to the tribal culture. The Government of India is quite clear that its objective is to integrate the tribal people with the rest of Indian community. On the other hand, tribes were always seen as more or less outside Hindu civilization and since the identification of tribes is also linked with political and administrative consideration, little efforts has been made to critically examine it. (Xaxa, op cit. 20). The root problem perceived among tribal community is 'diversity' (which ironically is the pride of the nation). And as far as the study here implies, the authority is far too biased against the tribal minorities living in diverse conditions across the land or is too inefficient to protect livelihood of the people. Given the ecological, cultural, political, economic variety, it is imperative to see tribe as a society in itself and not mesh and view as a caste or try to fit the conspicuously diverse tribes under one umbrella by way of implementing policies without the knowledge of the inhabitants. Now, the issue perceived here is political with an economic face rather than the vice-versa. And the heart of the matter is, to put it in Albert Einstein's words, "The significant problems we face cannot be solved at the same level of thinking we were when we created them."

REFERENCES

Aiyappan, A . (1977), "Tribes in the South", in Thapar, Romesh, (ed). 1977. *Tribes, Caste and Religion in India*. Meerut: Macmillan Company, pp.38-46.

Anand, V.K. (1967), *Nagaland in Transition*. New Delhi: Associated Publishing House.

Baruni, Tariq (1990), "Development and the Politics of Knowledge: A Critical Interpretation of the Social Role of Modernization Theories in the Development of the Third World". In Marglin, A, Frederique and Marglin, A, Stephen (eds).1990. *Dominating Knowledge: Development Culture and Resistance*, Oxford: Clarendon Press.

Behera, M.C. (2008), "Definitional Limitations in the Use of the Term Tribe: An Overview with Reference to the Padam of Arunachal Pradesh". *The Oriental Anthropologist,* Volume 8, Issue 1-2, pp. 143-157.

Beteille. A (1998), "The Idea of Indigenous People". *Current Anthropology*, Vol.39, No.2, April, pp.18-191.

——1986. "The Concept of Tribe with Special Reference to India". *Journal of European Sociology*, Vol.27, pp. 297-318.

——(1977), "The Definition of Tribe". In Thapar, Romesh, op.cit. Pp.7-14.

Desai, A.R. 1977. "Tribes in Transition". In Thapar, Romesh, op.cit. pp. 15-28.

Feyerabend, Paul. 1975. *Against Method – Outline of an anarchist theory of knowledge*. London: NLB.

Kuhn, Thomas. 1962. *The Structure of scientific revolution*. Chicago: The University of Chicago Press.

Marshall, Gordon. 1998. *A Dictionary of Sociology*. New Delhi: Oxford University Press.

Xaxa, Virginius, 1999: "Transformation of Tribes in India-Terms of Discourse". *Economic and Political Weekly,* Vol. XXXIV, No. 24, June 12, pp. 1519-1524.

Documents

Government of India. (2005), Annual Report 2004-2005, Ministry of Environment and Forests. *http://www.envfor.nic.in/report/report.html* retrieved on 10th feb. 2009

Government of India (2003), National Mission on Bamboo Technology and Trade development, Planning Commission, New Delhi.

World Commission on Environment and Development. (1989), *Our Common Future,* New Delhi: Oxford University Press, 1989 (reprint)

Government of Nagaland (2007), Statistical Hand Book of Nagaland 2007 Kohima: Directorate of Economics and Statistics. *http://www.thefreedictionary.com/tribe* , retrieved on 12th June 2009.

Persons Interviewed

1. Toshi (59 M), Extract from interview on 7th Dec. 2005, Tuli (Nagaland) at 6.30pm IST
2. Imkong (87 M), Extract from interview on 8th Dec. 2005, Tuli (Nagaland) at 5.30pm 3. IST
4. Sashila (45 F), Extract from interview on 7th Dec. 2005, Tuli (Nagaland) at 6.00pm IST
5. Nuklo (45 M), Extract from interview on 10th Dec. 2005, Tuli (Nagaland) at 6.00am IST
6. Kilem (74 M), Extract from interview on 10th Dec. 2005, Tuli (Nagaland) at 6.30pm IST
7. Pangjung (80 M), Extract from interview on 12th Dec. 2005, Tuli (Nagaland) at 4.30pm IST

18

MAUTAM FAMINE IN MIZORAM: THE POLITICS BEHIND THE CATASTROPHE

Malsawmdawngliana, C. Lalrozami

INTRODUCTION

This paper is an attempt to understand a development intervention in the northeast states of India, particularly in Mizoram. There are two parts to this intervention. One deals with the issues pertaining to the colonial rule and the other, more importantly, with the post-colonial developmental policies. The colonial state was a product of the pervasive power of the colonizers' knowledge apparatus. The British administrators gained power gradually over the local people through their knowledge in religion, medicine, education, language, etc. which nurtured the colonial supremacy and soon became deeply rooted or internalized within the individuals and society. The Mizos were left with no choice but to surrender to the British rule since the whole structure of their society had been weakened. Both the colonial state and the Christian missionaries equally participated in the process.

A new understanding of power was developed soon after the colonial rule was over. The purpose of the new government was directed towards creation of wealth and growth of population and health, rather than merely administering over territory and the subjects within it. In the meantime, the expectations from the Assam government to deal with certain problems of the region were not met. This unmet expectation was ideologically used by the local thinkers and leaders to fight against the Indian nation, particularly against the Assam Government, and instigated a feeling of ethnic nationalism among the people which started a fight for independence. The political turmoil during the period crippled the society in many ways and brought about various hardships and sufferings in the land. After several years of insurgency, the Central Government found a way to govern the people by offering the status of Union Territory to the region in 1972. Mizoram was again raised to a full-fledged State by the National Government in 1987. A close look at the political development of the region depicts the orders of knowledge applied to the peoples' mind. Several ideological apparatus has been exercised in different stages in order to integrate the people with national ethos. However, in the sphere of the state politics, development policies and plans are prepared by the government and cases have been witnessed where development is shattered by the same ruling government. The implementing work of government policies are often neglected and evaded by the policy makers themselves once they are in power. The second part of the paper deals with tension that had been built up due to the failure of implementation of the policies which finally led to the downfall of the government.

JHUM AND MIZO LIVELIHOODS

Mizo society is deeply rooted in slash and burn or jhumming cultivation which is still a popular practice in most parts of Mizoram. Out of the total population 8, 91,058 (Census 2001), 52 per cent of the population (48031 families) still depends extensively on forest resources and jhum agriculture. It was estimated that 35,000 hectares of land were put under jhum cultivation in 2001, though no systematic survey has so far been done to assess the actual areas that are subjected to shifting cultivation and its trends. Among the forest resources bamboo stands out uniquely.

It should be noted that various species of bamboo grow abundantly in Mizoram. Out of the total geographical area of 21018 sq. kms, bamboo forests cover 12.54 million hectares of the State (i.e. 57.8% of the total area). (Anonymous, 2005). The bamboo forests contribute to 14 per cent of the whole of India's bamboo area of 8.96 million ha, which further constitutes 11.71 per cent of the 74.96 million ha of the total forest area of the country.

BAMBOO AND ITS CULTURAL ATTACHMENT TO THE PEOPLE

The Mizos culture is intimately related to the utilisation of bamboo for their livelihoods. Hence, Mizoram is often described as the land of bamboos. Not surprisingly then, J.D. Baveja wrote a book *entitled The Land where the Bamboo Flowers* (1970). Professor M.P. Ranjan, Head of the Center for Bamboo Initiatives at the National Institute of Design (NID) in Ahmedabad, also vividly states that "It is a living bamboo culture. Bamboo is used for almost everything over there - their housing, their products, their livelihood supplies. ....it's so culturally tied up with the lives of the people there." (BBC World Service's Outlook Programme, 2004/10/11 16:24:09 GMT.). In addition to this, jhum agriculture areas are mainly confined to the bamboo jungles since land covered with bamboos are considered most suitable for cultivation. Folk

Table 1
Consumption of Bamboo (MT) in Mizoram

Use	*Total*	*Rural People*	*Urban People*
House building	27119	22507 (83)	4610 (17)
Agricultural implements	1196	933 (78)	263 (22)
Total Value in bracket are in percentages	28315	23442 (83)	4873 (17)

Source: Government of Mizoram (*www.mizoram.nic.in*)

agriculturists believe that bamboo-ash acts as a good fertilizer. Hence, Mizo economy is strongly based on bamboo resources.

LOCAL KNOWLEDGE OF BAMBOO FLOWERING, A PRELUDE TO FAMINE

Despite significant contributions to the local economy, bamboo flowering causes two types of famine locally called "*mautam tam*" and "*thingtam*" – their occurrence usually based on chronological sequences. In local language, *Mautam* or *thingtam* literally means bamboos withering or dying out. *Tam* meaning famine, the famine caused by bamboo is therefore called *mautam tam* and *thingtam*. According to folk tradition, the two species of bamboo (*thing* or *bambusa longispiculata* and *mautak* or *melocanna bambbasoides*) which grow in abundance in the hills flower in a cycle of 30 years and 50 years respectively. The bamboo flowers soon produce fruits which are usually brown and green in colour. The seeds contain rich protein and are the favourite food of the local rats or *Sazu*. This is followed by a sudden explosion of rat population in the bamboo hills. Local people believe that bamboo seeds increase rat fertility and that even a single female rat is able produce more than ten babies at a time if it consumes bamboo seeds. The bamboos soon die, leaving the rats without abundant food from the bamboo. C. Rokhuma says, "After eating up the bamboo fruits, rats started attacking paddy fields in the beginning of autumn season and in a matter of one night or two, such eye catching paddy fields were suddenly reduced into nothing but dead paddy straws." (Rokhuma, 1998:101).

CAUSE OF BAMBOO FLOWERING AND FAMINE

Although, bamboo flowerings and famines are also known in Myanmar, Japan, Sri Lanka, South America and Southern Africa, they seem to cause more devastation in Mizoram. Despite the numerous researches conducted by environmentalists and scientists, the cause of bamboo flowering still remains unexplained and mysterious. Various hypotheses such as the pathological, genetic, periodical, mutational, nutritional, resource matching and bamboo wildlife cycle have been drawn. However, little is known about the mechanism responsible for determining when a species of bamboo bears flowers. Mizo folk traditions provide some references on numerous signs of unnatural ecological imbalance which took place before the bamboo flowering which goes as follows:

> A host of insects locally called *thangnang* swarm the hills before and during the bamboo flowering. The Mizo elders are still able to recall the sound of the swarm of *thangnang* in the hilly skies which they said resembled that of a thunderstorm. Even the branches of tree broke off because of the numerous *thangnang* that perched on the branches. It may sound like a mere myth to scientific communities, but there is a proof that it is indeed true. In 2006, the State Agriculture Department reported that villages in the southern part of Mizoram witnessed large scale devastation of vegetables by giant snails. Folk tradition called such incidents as *tam hmahruai* or the harbinger of famine.

FOLK TRADITION AND BAMBOO FAMINE IN THE PRE BRITISH PERIOD

In the pre-British period, no written account was available regarding the nature and effect of famines. It was only through the folk tradition that we can refer to these incidents. The sub-tribe *Hmar* clans were believed to have migrated from Burma to the present Mizoram due to a famine that took place in 1500. One of the earliest known *Hmar* oral songs goes as follows:

Shan khuaah lenpur a tlakin,
Miza raza tlan their e.

"Because of the great famine that befell us in
Shan State We had to leave it behind."

The dominant sub-tribe *Lusei* was believed to have entered Mizoram sometime in the middle of the 17th century. They must have probably experienced these periodic famines even then. (Rokhuma, 1998:96). Mizo elders have recorded them on the basis of the bamboo flowerings and famine in Table-2.

Table 2
Chronology of Bamboo Flowering and Famine

Mautam	1861-1862
Thingtam	1881-1882
Mautam	1911-1912
Thingtam	1929-1930
Mautam	1959-1960
Thingtam	1977-1978
Mautam	2007-2008

Source: Field data

The politics hidden behind Mautam famine can be illustrated under two eras as mentioned, namely, the coming of the British or Colonial era and the Post colonial period.

COLONIAL ENCOUNTER AND EXPERIENCE OF FAMINE

The British, seeing no economical prospects in the initial years had no intention of interfering in the administration of the hilly rugged terrains of Mizoram. However repetitive raids, plunders and kidnaps by the Mizo chiefs had caused threats to the tea plantation of the Europeans in Cachar plains.

On the other hand, for the Mizos the British settlements in these areas were their hunting ground which they claimed to be their own. To safeguard their economic vessel, the British led a punitive expedition to the Mizo hills. Plans of expedition were made into two columns in 1871-72. The left column advanced from Cachar under the command of General. G. Bourchier, with Edgar, Deputy Commissioner, Cachar as the officer. The right column advanced from Chittagong under the command of General C.A. Brownlow, with Captain T.H Lewin, Superintendent of the Chittangong Hill Tracts, as civil officer. In addition, a contingent of Manipuris accompanied by General Nuthall, the Political Agent of Manipur, made a demonstration march across the Southern border of Manipur with the support of General Bourchier's operations. After the third Anglo Burmese war, 1885, an expedition was again held in 1889 under the command of Col. F.V.G. Tregear.

Prof. Sajal Nag argues that despite the military might, the British found it difficult to match with the guerrilla tactics of the tribal's fighting in hard mountainous terrain. It was only once that they found the people submitting- during famine when hunger forced the tribes to beg food from their staunchest enemy- the British. (Nag, 2009). As recorded by the British, Mizoram witnessed the first *Mautam* famine in the year 1862. Although Mizo inhabited areas were not under the direct rule of the British, help and assistance were provided by the colonial government of Assam and Bengal. Cachar Commissioner, Captain Steward, provided rice grain to *Suakpuilala*, one of the greatest Mizo Chiefs. Trade marts such as *Changsil*, *Sonai* and *Tipaimukh* were established at the foot hills to provide food to the starving people. A Folk phrase '*nula hmeltha tak takte pawh hian buhhum veikhat pawh an man zo lo*' which means 'the price of even the most beautiful girl could not compare to the price of a handful of rice grains.' Traditionally, the price of the brides amongst the wealthy families and the price of the beautiful girls were worth the value of the highest currency. However, during the time of famine, currencies had no value at all.

THE POLITICS WITHIN

The actors who had played the politics behind Mautam famine are the colonial and the Christian missionaries.

The initial intention of the British was to punish the tribals for their raids and keep them in the hills. But in due course of time, their imperialistic minds saw the place as experimental ground for their future colonization. Acquiring the knowledge of the land would enable them to decide the future course of action either political or military. *Mautam* famine in Mizoram opened the door for them to fulfill their aims. During *Mautam* famine, they started to introduce humanitarian actions among the starving Mizo tribes and this gesture of benevolence colonized them politically (Outside) and internally. The so-called modernization using the 'west' as a yardstick started to penetrate inside the very cultures of the Mizo society. The British Administration started to construct roads and markets to mitigate the devastation of the famine and also set up administrative machinery through which they could conquer the rest of the tribals. On the other hand, the British also advocated what Nag had termed as 'food for work' the Mizos had to render voluntary labour supply in building official quarters, residential bungalows, etc. However, the help they got from the British during the famine was required to be paid back in exchange of labour; we can say that the relief they got is not free at all.

The process of colonialization within and outside by the British had a negative impact on the minds of the Mizos. They had broken up from traditional risk coping mechanism against the famine to totally dependence on the governmental policies. As a result of this the village sufficient economy of the Mizo has been transformed into totally dependent one on the Government provisions.

The second actors, the Christian missionaries viewing this as opportunity, set foot on the hills in 1890. The missionaries J.H.Lorraine and F.W. Savidge started to propagate Christianity in the region. Their messages contradicted the traditional belief systems of the Mizos which had a close tie with their society. They found it hard to preach the gospel to the tribals in the beginning as they had to face threats from the local chiefs as they felt that their very own existence had been challenged and questioned. In due course, like the British officials, they also found an opportunity when famine crept inside the hilly region. They started to propagate that famine was the cause of their animism. To back up their ideology, they started to introduce humanitarian measures by setting up schools, medical hospitals, nursing homes, etc., Folk tradition says that the people survived by eating wild roots, jungle fruits and anything else that they could find which was edible. This resulted in widespread malnutrition, epidemics and extensive loss of life. Many of the villages became its victim and sometimes entire family succumbed to the devastating famine over the hills. "The famine, due to the growing crops being destroyed by rats, continued during 1912 in many parts of Lushais, and caused much suffering and ill-health among the people. One of the folk phrases mentions the consequences of famine on domesticated animals - *'vawkpui pawh pal nghengin a ding tlawk tlawk mai'*, which can roughly be translated as 'even a hungry pig could only stand leaning on a fence for support'. For the Mizos, in times of sickness, the local priest used to act as a doctor for all pains. This has been challenged by prayers of missionaries equipped with western medicine. The relief measures rendered at times of famine gradually won the heart of the Mizos. Therefore, they started to surrender to the colonial power both internally and externally.

POST COLONIAL PERIOD AND THE EXPERIENCE OF FAMINE

When the British left Mizo hills, the region remained isolated and underdeveloped. Moreover, this period also witnessed rapid expansion of the fear of losing cultural identity going hand in hand with social and political crisis. Politically, Mizo Hills became an autonomous district of Assam in 1952 and the institution of chieftainship was abolished with the aim of democratizing the political condition of the hills. Lack of communication from the mainland India resulted to regionalism with an uncertain future for the Mizos. Despite the growth of an educated class, majority of the people (80%) were dependent on jhum cultivation.

The post colonial period marked the new phase in the administrative structure of the Mizo Hills. The long administration of chieftainship came to an end and a new order of modern government made a new entry in the political scenario of the tribals. The period was marked by the emergence of a new class who blamed the traditional chiefs for the failure of tackling the famine. The new section of class soon transformed themselves into political party called the *Mizo Union*. The Mizo Union who represented the new modern leadership articulated the people's aspirations and demanded the abolition of the chief which was of course possible by opting Mizoram under administrative arms of the Republic of India. On the other hand, the traditional chiefs who felt that their power was being ceased sought an opportunity to strike. The famine again occurred in the year 1959. The Mizo Union who were upholding the power at the District Council lost its image dreadfully among the people due to alleged nepotism in land allotment. The Congress party hosted the Conference of EITU, which demanded the disintegration of Assam and the formation of separate tribal state. This enraged the Congress Chief Minister B.P. Chaliha. (Nag, 2001). As a result, the Assam government declared Mizo Union as Pro-Indian and bagged the entire credit of famine relief. The Mizo Cultural Society was formed in 1958 which eventually changed its name to the Mizo National Famine Front with the outbreak of Famine in 1959.

The front began as a voluntary organization offering social services to the people. At the same time, the front also started publishing a daily newspaper, *Mizo Aw* (Mizo Voice). The paper became an important means of propagating the front agenda and gained considerable popularity throughout the Mizo Hills. (Hluna, 2004:72). Laldenga, a capable leader who grabbed the sentiments of the Mizos started to promulgate his ideology. The educated middle class were frustrated because of the Assam government's indifference to the Mizo Hills. Hence, the need for a new platform pushed the Front to organize a new political party called "Mizo National Front" (MNF) on 22nd October 1961. A memorandum submitted to the Prime Minister on 30 October 1965 clearly reflected the people's perception on government relief work in the Mizo Hills; the famine left a scar on the people's psyche that the government failed to provide relief work during the previous bamboo famine. Therefore, the politics of separatism or nationalism has been instilled in the minds of the youth, blaming the Assam government for turning a deaf ear in times of crisis.

Thus, a long insurgency in the hills started to begin. The feeling of being marginalized and neglected from the government developed rapidly in the post famine period. Khondker rightly remarked, "There is a moral responsibility on the part of the government to ensure the subsistence needs of the populace. And failure to discharge this obligation is viewed as a breach of an unwritten contract raising serious questions about the effectiveness and legitimacy of the government." (Khondker, 1986: 25).

The government of India seeing this political turmoil did not sit idle and made preparation much ahead of the famine which was likely to occur again in the year 1977. It granted the status of Union Territory to Mizoram in the year 1972. The government took utmost care by setting up Rodent Control Committee and the expert teams were to investigate the situation. Even the non-governmental organizations cooperated and relief measures were taken. As a result, not much of death has been found in government records.

As predicted, after the last famine of 1977, the fear of people came true again in 2007. Interestingly, the MNF government which was born out of famine was in power to tackle the devastation of famine in Mizoram. The Government of Mizoram started preparation long before the famine actually took place. A Committee was set up under the leadership of Chief Minister Zoramthanga with C. Rokhuma as his deputy. A founder of *Tam Do Pawl* (Famine Relief Association) C. Rokhuma vividly writes, "During the Famine, no word was sufficient to express the scarcity of food and food grains". (Rokhuma, 1998:102). The Committee suggested a check to the long impending menace and that they should campaign on a mass killing of rats and store enough food grains. Experts from the Central government also supplemented with the ideas that they should grow crops like Maize which will not be eaten by the rats. To combat the famine, the Government of Mizoram set up BAFFACOS (Bamboo Flowering and Famine Combat Scheme) with financial assistance from the Central Government.

Reports of Mizoram Government noted that Government of India sanctioned Rs. 20.00 crore and Rs. 30.00 crore under one-time ACA for implementation of BAFFACOS during Annual Plan 2004-05 and 2005-06 respectively. In order to tackle and mitigate the untold miseries, severe famine and plague caused by gregarious bamboo flowering, a comprehensive action plan for a period of 5 years (2004-09) was launched covering 13 different Departments at an initial year. Two more Departments namely, Public Works Department (Roads & Bridges) and Local Administration

Department were added during Annual Plan 2005-06 as per recommendation of Twelfth Finance Commission and special priority scheme of State Government. (Anonymous, 2009). This involved various departments such as Food and Civil Supplies, Health, Agriculture, Horticulture, Rural Development and Public Works. The government's precautionary plan had five components - survey of bamboo flowering area, survey of rodent incidences and their population, publicity, awareness campaign and training, eradication by local rat-traps, purchase of rodenticides and free distribution to the needy farmers. The Government having learnt lessons from the previous effects of famine, marked by separatism and conflicts in the state did not want to commit any mistake. However, the situation of the recent famine was different from the previous experiences. Mizoram is a state where 90 per cent of the fund comes from the Central government. Large sections of the people confined themselves mainly to the urban centers, and started to cope with the white collar jobs i.e., the government jobs. Those who actually suffered the famine are at the village level, the poor farmers bore all the pains of the famine. The Action Aid International India conducted surveys between the 20th and 26th of February 2008. The report declares; "The failure of the strategy is obvious with famine conditions prevailing in large areas and the destruction of over 75 per cent of crops in the state (including the espoused cash crops like oil palms....While it has been difficult to make an accurate assessment of the needs, we can assume that there is an immediate need for food aid to a minimum 30 thousand families living with acute food shortage in the southern districts of *Lawngtlai*, *Saiha* and *Mamit*. At least 10,000 families across approximately 150 to 170 villages of *Lawngtlai* and *Saiha* districts would be on the fringe of starvation where poor communications are hampering both food delivery and the flow of information critical for making an assessment and taking decisions on the emergency." In May 2008, the government declared that food shortage had affected 630,000 people which comprised nearly 70 per cent of the population, 900,000, in Mizoram.

In the meantime, the government encouraged plantation of ginger. As a result, large quantity of ginger was produced by the farmers. However, the government was not able to find a market for the ginger products. A large amount of ginger was thrown out on the streets to rot as a kind of protests. The State Government, instead of coping with the problems started to clarify themselves through the media which created more resentment particularly among the farmers in the villages. The product of this discontentment led to the formation of Zo Kuthnathawk Pawl (Zo Farmers Association) who started to march in the street of Aizawl in April 2007. There was a collision between the policemen and the angry farmers who protested against the State Government. Their main resentment was that the government funds did not reach them. However, the MNF government in preparation for the next upcoming election in 2008 started to practise nepotism, where large amount of funds were diverted to the party workers and their beneficiaries. This was followed by maladministration and corruption. As a result the MNF party's failure of implementing its policies finally resulted to their ten year long power to decline at the general election of December 2008. The Congress' new manifesto "New Land Use Policy" on the other hand gave a chance for themselves to win the minds of the farmers. The village population comprising mostly the poor farmers and the urban middle class who felt disgusted with the false promises of the MNF government retaliated by way of vote it out of power. The reign of the MNF finally came to decline.

CONCLUSION

The colonial state was what Nicholas Dirks has called an "ethnographic state" (Dirks, 2001) and was no different from the colonial state in the region of Mizoram. The people were surveyed, classified, described and controlled which created governable subjects for the colonizers. Populations are identifiable, classifiable and describable by empirical or behavioural criteria and are amenable to statistical techniques such as censuses and sample surveys which make it possible for the government to function as an instrument for reaching large sections of the inhabitants of a country as the targets of their policies- economic policy, administrative policy, law and even political mobilization. (Chatterjee, 2004:34). The people were regarded as 'population' or 'subjects' and not as 'citizens'. The post-state Mizos expected the government to take care of them as 'citizens.' The government on the other hand, seems to see its own people as 'subjects' whom they could govern through their might and power. They neglected the fact that they were elected by the people to be their representatives, to work for them and give them their just rights. However, the citizens were denied their rights in different ways which resulted in the fall of the government.

REFERENCES

Anonymous (2005), *Bamboo Flowering and Famine Combat Schemes (BAFFACOS) (2004-2005 to 2008-2009)*. Aizwal: Planing & Programme Implementation Department, Government of Mizoram.

Anonymous (2009), *Achievements Reports on Bamboo Flowering & Famine Combat Scheme (BAFFACOS) During 2004–05 & 2005–06.* Aizwal: Government of Mizoram, India.

Dirks, Nicholas B. (2001), *Caste of Mind: Colonialism and the Making of Modern India*. Princeton: University of Princeton Press.

Chatterjee, Partha (2004), *The Politics of the Governed*. Delhi: Permanent Black.

Hluna, J.V. (2004), "The Role of the Mizo National Front in Mizoram Politics up to 1986". *Historical Journal Mizoram*, Vol 5, Aizawl: Mizo History Association.

Khondker, H.H. (1986), "Famine Policies in Pre-British India and the Question of Moral Economy in South Asia". *Journal of South Asian Studies*. Vol.9, No.2.

Lorrain, J.H. and Savidge. F.W. (1993), "Amidst Flowering Bamboos, Rats and Famine", *Report for 1912 of the BMS Mission in the South Lushai Hills, Assam, in The Annual Report of BMS on Mizoram* 1901-1938. Aizwal: The Mizoram Gospel Centenary Committee, Baptist Church of Mizoram.

Nag, S. (2001), "Tribals, Rats, Famine, State and the Nation". *Economic and Political Weekly*. 24:1029–1033.

Ranjan, M.P. (2000), "Bamboo Puts India on Famine". In: BBC World Service's Outlook programme *http://news.bbc.co.uk/go/pr/fr/-/2/hi/south_asia/3680714.stm*, (Accessed 9 May.2008.) 2004/10/11 16:24:09 GMT.

Rokhuma, C. 1998. *Tam Do Pawlin Enge a tih?* (The Secret of Famine Found). Aizawl: Mizoram, India.

19

LOOK-EAST POLICY THROUGH THE SINGPHO CORRIDOR: A STUDY IN HISTORICAL PERSEPECTIVE

Srinibash Panda, Priyanka Priyadarshini

Geographical advantage of Arunachal Pradesh as the gateway from India to South-East Asia for sharing common borderline with neighbouring countries like China and Myanmar has been well highlighted in the last one decade as the potential hot spot for booming trade and commerce in the East. Vision document of Government of India for 2020 and the Look-East policy have specially laid emphasis on developing traditional trade routes which were used in the past by the tribes to facilitate movement of trans-border trade beyond the McMahon Line and the Patkai ranges. But unfortunately so far no fast forward move has been undertaken in this direction except that of a few feasibility surveys for fear of the fact that the terrain is either inaccessible at certain stretches from freight carriage point of view, or not suitable for commercial traffic because of the operation of insurgent groups between several vantage points. Looking at the rate of globalisation achieved in the last five years and the phenomenal growth in the bilateral trade volume between India and China at the same time, it appears almost a contradiction of fact why the advantage of trans-border trade routes through Arunachal Pradesh has been turned a blind eye just for the fear of strategic brinkmanship and problem of insurgency in north-east and beyond.

Against this backdrop the development model, which was formulated at the beginning of the 21st century, calls for a review to give the Look East policy the much needed blend of local participation which was tried with a sense of great enterprise and adventure during the British rule in the Singpho frontier of Arunachal Pradesh. In the aftermath of the First Anglo-Burmese war (1824-25) although the main concern of British was to ensure the security of the Sadiya frontier in Assam to prevent the Burmese from launching renewed offensive in collusion with the Singphos,[1] still with much care it was decided to adopt a soft approach towards the Singphos so that the trouble in the frontier can be addressed with local participation. As an adjunct to this policy of involving the tribal communities in encountering the fallouts of colonial conflict with Burma in India's north eastern frontier it was also decided to promote trade and commerce in the Singpho tract so that the local community feels allured to the new enterprise and support the British as their trusted allies. Colonial interest to explore the existing trade route through the Singpho tract with Mogaung province of Burma and from thence to the Yunan province of China was given a definite go-ahead since 1825 which yielded positive result in pacifying the Singpho tract. This particular case study from the pages of history holds potential to provide enough input in sorting out the problems which the mandarins of Look-East policy often talk about as possible hindrance on the smooth travel of commercial traffic from India to Myanmar and China through the Singpho corridor of Arunachal Pradesh.

The objective of this paper is to explore how the colonial enterprise in the Singpho frontier since 1825 produced brilliant result in addressing the security needs of the British in India's north eastern frontier, and in discovering an alternate trade route to Burma and China from India's border in the land route. The findings can be best used to solve the problem of insurgency, often hyped to be a road block in the entire process, and redraw the strategy to move ahead in the Look East policy with local participation as an alternative to the trend of globalization which brings in global formulation for imposition on tribal communities with unpredictable consequences for both the sides.

POLICY SHIFT IN THE SINGPHO FRONTIER

After the fall of Rangpore (Ahom capital in Assam) in December 1825 British military operation in Assam theatre was practically over. But entrenchment of the retreating Burmese forces in collusion with the Singphos in the Sadiya frontier posed a major challenge on every serious bid to restore peace in Assam. Option was then still open to continue military operation against the Singphos. But since military operation in the Singpho frontier had the potential to commit the Government for more armed intervention in the unknown tribal frontier, permission was granted with stringent limitations. It was clearly stated that assistance was to be given for defensive purpose only, strict instructions being laid down that no advances to be made into the country undeniably held by the Singphos, and that no offensive operations should be attempted against that tribe. (Mackenzie, 1995:63). Accordingly, in his letter on 8, April 1825, David Scott, Agent to the Governor General on north-eastern frontier of Bengal, directed Neufville to engage the Singphos in the following manner:

(1) every encouragement be given to those chiefs who might be desirous of entering into an engagement upon the basis of releasing all Assamese captives taken since the capitulation of Rangpore;

(2) as security for fulfilment of the terms they might be required to give as hostages one or two persons of consequence from each clan;

(3) that occasional presents be offered to the chiefs and other persons who might prove to be useful;

(4) that endeavours be made to obtain necessary information as to the nature of the government and

political connection of the Singphos, the Khamtis and other tribes in that quarter;

(5) that annual stipends be granted to some of the influential chiefs under the pretence of employing them to defend the passes of the Patkai and to endeavour by such means to carry into effect some arrangement for the prevention of depredation in the lowlands.[2]

Neufville was also asked to gather more information on the Singpho tribe, their clan divide, territory, history and culture, so that engagements can be concluded with more chiefs on the basis of information processed earlier. Thus, Scott relied much on the information supplied by Neufville on Upper Assam to prepare his strategy on the extension of British authority up to the eastern-most part of Assam bordering the tribal frontier. Neufville on his part also maintained a regular diary recording the geographical and political features of the tract, including also the barren, desolate and jungle-covered foot hills of the present North-East Frontier Agency. (Barooah, 1970:116).

From Sadiya camp the first contact with Singpho chiefs was established by Neufville for peaceful resolution of the problems in their frontier. The first response to the overture for peace was not discouraging. Several Chiefs approached Neufville in early May 1825 soliciting their aid against the Burmese forces, still active in their frontier under the leadership of Boglee Phukan. They provided the crucial information that the discredited General, for fear of being reduced to submission, was actively engaged at Beesa in collecting men and procuring supplies to renew the offensive. Intelligence report was also received that a Burmese force under three Mogaung chiefs had entrenched themselves at a village twenty-five miles south at Nao Dihing. (Barpujari, 1970: 33). Therefore, Scott had no other option than to continue hot pursuit of the rebel chiefs in the Singpho tract which produced brilliant result in terms of liberation of slaves and acceptance of the terms of peace in that troubled frontier by the tribe.

BEGINNING OF COMMERCIAL INTERCOURSE

Military compulsions in the Sadiya frontier notwithstanding, imperial drive into the Singpho tract was also dictated by commercial compulsions in the Company's trade with China around the same time. In early 1822 the Select Committee at Canton was forced to close down their trade in China mainland because of misunderstanding over the Topaz affair. Petitions of the Select Committee were not forwarded to the Peking Authority, thus making it extremely difficult for the British to work for a compromise. This high-handed action of the Canton Authority was considered the main handicap in the smooth passage of British trade and commerce into the Chinese mainland. Therefore, the Select Committee wrote to Calcutta in 1822 to explore the possibilities of transmitting their representations over land by way of Sylhet and the province of Yunan at the time of crisis. (Lamb, 1960: 48-50). But the matter could not be taken up forthwith because of the Burmese occupation of Assam during the same period and the inability of David Scott to address the concern of the Select Committee at Canton as he was obsessed with the prime task of securing Bengal's eastern frontier bordering Assam. But the issue of exploring an alternative land route to China through Assam was raised once again by the Surveyor General, Blacker in 1824. He wrote to Lord Amherst about Assam:

> "Its interesting situation between Hindoostan and China, two names with which the civilized world has been long familiar, whilst it remains nearly unknown, is a striking fact and leaves nothing to be wished but the means and opportunity to exploring it".[3]

Military operations in Assam during the 1st Anglo-Burmese war gave Scott the first opportunity to explore Assam and its tribal frontier. Officers from the Surveyor General's department were deployed under his supervision to carry out intensive survey of Assam. Various routes were studied within, and beyond Assam, with an eye to their potential use as trade routes in future. Captain Neufville's operation in the Khamti and Singpho frontier was also fully exploited to study the commercial feasibility of the Singpho tract-Hukwang valley route to Upper Burma. Captain Bedford, Lt. Wilcox and Lt. Burlton were directed to map the area watered by the upper branches of Brahmaputra. Following the tracts of the traditional trade routes,.used by the Ahoms for carrying out trade with Hukwang Valley in Burma and Zayul Valley in Tibet, Wilcox prepared an exhaustive report of the survey work carried out in between 1825-28. (Wilcox, 1832:310, ff.). Much hope was attached to the trade route that passes through the country inhabited by the Khamptis and Mishmis to Zayul valley of Tibet and Yunan province of China through the country in the extreme north of Burma. But this route, Wilcox reported, could not be followed beyond the borders of the Khamptis as they feared it would rouse the jealousy and suspicion of the Burmese. Moreover, Wilcox and his team were discouraged by the Khamptis from entering the Mishmi tract as that tribe was reported to be hostile to receiving foreigners in their territory.(ibid.).

The second route which received much attention in the Wilcox report was the Hukwang valley route by which the Burmese had entered Assam in 1817 and in 1820. This was the same route by which the retreating Burmese forces also returned to Burma after the surrender of Rangpore in 1825. Since part of this route passes through the territory of the Beesa Gaum, it was considered very important by Scott to win over him by any means. Critical military engagements in the Singpho frontier till the signing the Treaty of Yandaboo in 1826 also made this route a strategic one for military reasons.

On the basis of detail information supplied by Neufville, Scott realized that the Singphos, like the Garos, needed to be won over to a new way of life if their predatory raids were to be stopped and if the trade route that passes through their territory is to be reused for both military and commercial purposes. (Butler, 1847: 8-10). He felt the urgent need of providing them with new outlet for their energies; involving them as middlemen in the trans-borer trade that passes through their territory. This alone, he thought would give a profitable vocation to the Singphos, thus promoting them to abandon their predatory habits in due course of time. Serious effort from the very beginning to win over Beesa Gaum was guided by this objective.

With the signing of peace treaty with sixteen Singpho chiefs in 1826, the prospects of trans-border trade through the Singpho tract appeared quiet brighter. Preliminary survey on this trans-border trade route was carried out through the Beesa Gaum territory up to Hukwang valley of Burma. In April 1826 the first credible information was received that there would be considerable demand for woollen clothes and other European manufactures like glass-wares, beads, potteries, etc. in exchange of which silver and horses of a rare breed can be procured in good quality.[4] But the arduous nature of the trade route and the continued hostility of the Singphos prevented Scott from taking a proactive stand to promote trade so early along this route. However, to explore the possibility of a profitable venture in Sadiya frontier traders from the China-Burma border were encouraged to return to Sadiya with their produce during November to December so that a trade fair could be organized during the same time at Sadiya to facilitate resumption of trans-border trade after a long time. (ibid.).

A proposal for border trade was accordingly sent to Calcutta, which received immediate approval. The first consignment comprising of silk goods, worth eight hundred rupees, were despatched from Calcutta, together with presents for the chiefs, but unfortunately the whole consignment was plundered on the way. This was the first setback for Scott in his commercial enterprise in the Sadiya frontier. Still he pursued the matter yet again in 1827 and was able to convince the Calcutta authorities about the need of a fresh investment towards the same venture. A small amount of two thousand rupees was granted no doubt, but the sheer want of a responsible officer with experience in the same field to supervise the trade led to the premature closure of Scott's adventurism in this field in the following years.[5]

EXPLORING ALTERNATE TRADE ROUTES

Cross-country trade, which continued since time immemorial between India and Tibet through the hills of north-east, was proposed to be revived again. To make a humble beginning in this direction fairs were organized with official patronage at Sadiya and Udalguri.[6] Posa was also distributed to some tribes of Arunachal Pradesh at these two places. Attempt was made to revive the Udalguri-Tawang-Lasha trade route, which once witnessed brisk trans-Himalayan trade between Assam and Tibet during the Ahom days. The role of the Bhutias (Monpas and Sherdukpens) as intermediary of trade in this route prompted the local administration in Darrang district to explore the possibility of winning over them by way of good-will gestures.(ibid.). As a first step in that direction they were allowed to hold Kuriapara Duar. Their traditional practice of collecting posa from this duar was too left untouched. (Devi, 1968: 199). Trade fair at Udalguri was organised with official support to lure the hill traders for restarting trans-border trade with Tibet. Prevailing peace in this side of the frontier and the acceptance of the Monpa tribe to become peaceful carrier of trade as an intermediary between the British in Assam and Tibet led to complete restoration of trade in the immediate aftermath of the first Anglo-Burmese war.

Meanwhile failure of Hannay's first mission (1836) in containing the Singpho menace through diplomatic contact prompted Government of India to put the blame squarely on the Burmese Government. Continued support of the Burmese Government to the rebel, Duufa Gaum and his associates, in fact, led to a serious diplomatic spat between the two countries. Burney was directed to demand from the Court of Ava peaceable behaviour from the Singphos in future. (ibid.) But the Burmese authority was not in a position to make any future commitment on this issue because of the unsettled state of the Burmese frontier in the north-west bordering Assam. Moreover, from the Burmese side every move was in the defensive mode because after testing defeat in the 1st Anglo-Burmese war, they were not in a position to take the chance of a second war with the British on a petty issue like the Singpho raid in Assam. At the same time they were not also ready to accommodate every imperialistic move from the British side on their soil on the plea of containing the Singpho menace.

Burney was quite confident from the very beginning that the response from the Court of Ava is not along positive line on the Singpho issue. Even after losing Assam to the British, the Burmese Government had not yet reconciled to giving up its last territorial claim on the Singpho tract, where its command was still operative through a trusted band of Singpho chiefs. Burney, therefore, suggested that the line of communication, opened by the 1st mission of Hannay, must be revisited from time to time, so that the diplomatic hesitation on the part of Burma to open that hidden tract in the Upper Irrawaddy region for politico-military and commercial intercourses in future can be smoothened over the passage of time.[7]

At this point of time British imperial interest was not alone confined to the Singpho tract. It was definitely centred on the Amber and Serpentine mines of Upper Burma located mostly in the Hukwang valley. For centuries the Chinese had a monopoly trade over these two minerals in Upper Burma. Imperial strategist in Calcutta and London were quite serious to make an entry into the Amber mines of Hukwang valley. The British Resident at Burma was, therefore, directed to act as facilitator in that process.(ibid.). Hannay's first mission was thus tactically used to gather information on the topography, climate, people and culture of the route traversed from Ava to Mogaung, so that in future this can be used to extend British strategic push to Upper Burma through the Singpho tract in Assam.

The Chinese, however, could smell the rot of this strategic move on the part of the British in Upper Irrawaddy region. They were quite sceptical from the very beginning that, if allowed to operate, the British would soon eat into the Chinese monopoly trade in Amber and Serpentine in that region. Therefore, the first mission of Hannay created a stir in the Sino-Burmese relations. The matter was raised by the Chinese authority in the Court of Ava when Hannay was first granted the permission to visit Mogaung in the north of Ava in 1836. At a point of time it was perceived by Hannay that even after the grant of permission, the mission may not succeed in moving out of Ava (the then capital of Burma) because of the Chinese protest. But the British Resident exerted pressure on the Ministers at Ava to override the Chinese protest on the ground that Hannay's mission is an exploratory one from Burma to Assam via the Mogaung province and the Hukwang valley route. (ibid.).

STRATEGY FOR OPENING CHINA FROM THE WEST

Yet another objective of Hannay's first mission was to get first-hand knowledge of the terrain and its connecting routes with Assam, so that in future border talks, the issue of demarcation can be argued from a sound footing.[8] Given the resistance of the Burmese to loosen their string of control on the Singphos it was even discussed to annex the whole of north-west Burma to the British-Indian Empire as a future strategy to silence every possible threat to security in India's eastern frontier.[9] From this platform the grand strategy was to enter China from the west for establishing British monopoly trade in the western province of Yunan, where French interest was seen as a threat. True to this calculation, after the second Anglo-Burmese war the advantage of victory over Burma was fully exploited by annexing Upper Burma to the British Empire in 1851.

To give the strategic planning in the Singpho frontier a definite boost, as per Burney's suggestion a second mission was planned to explore the Singpho tract from both the Burmese side and the Assam frontier. The Resident was asked to seek permission from the Court of Ava for this mission. The objective of the mission was three fold; one, release of Assamese ryots still held as captives in Burma by the Singphos, two, explore the possibility of better inland trade intercourse with Burma through the route of Sadiya-Mainkhwon-Mogaung-Baman(Bhamo) and Ava;[10] and three, boundary settlement along the Patkai. Every care was taken in the diplomatic communication to ensure that the suspicion of the Burmese is not roused on the strategic advance of British sphere of interest up to Upper Burma. It was planned that Major White would proceed from Sadiya along with Hannay through the Singpho tract to Hukwang, where he would meet G.E. Bayfield, Assistant to the Resident, proceeding from Ava through the province of Bhamo and Mogaung to the same place escorted by Burmese officials. The mission control exercise was monitored by Secretary, Government of India, Macnaghten. Initial Burmese suspicion of Chinese protest was cleared, when it was pointed out that the left-out Burmese Shans (of the retreating Burmese Army of the first Anglo-Burmese war) in Assam can return to Burma in lieu of similar safe passage for around 25000 Assamese ryots, still held as captive in places like Mainkhwon, Mogaung and Bhamo.[11] The Ministers in Burma also found merit in the second mission as they were interested to raise the border demarcation in Burma's north-west frontier, which was left unsolved in the Treaty of Yandaboo.

Dr.W.Griffith, a scientific officer, was added to the mission to get intimate knowledge of the natural history of the inner Singpho tract. The mission team left Ava and Namrup as per schedule in January 1837 and reached Mogaung on 9th March after experiencing hardship on the way because of the internecine feud between the Kakhyens and the eastern Nagas. At Mogaung Bayfield and Hannay entered into talks with the Governor of the province. Tranquillity in the Singpho frontier was demanded unconditionally from Burma. Release of the Assamese slaves too was raised in exchange of the Shans, still left in Assam since the first Anglo-Burmese war. The Mogaung chief was mainly interested on the issue of border demarcation of his province in the Assam frontier.[12] To substantiate his claim over the whole of Singpho frontier as far as Jaypore, he presented before Bayfield and Hannay the historical record dating back to the days of First Ahom ruler, Sukapha (1224), which was rejected out rightly as outrageous and baseless. The Patkai range was pointed out by the British Resident to be the natural and historical divide-line in that frontier. Unilateralism on the part of the British in border talks compelled the Burmese authority to go slow on the proposed security and commercial projects in the Singpho frontier.(ibid.). Although the Governor of Mogaung promised to cooperate in maintaining tranquillity in the Singpho frontier, the issue of containing Duffa Gaum and his associates was simply dismissed as unnecessary. Even the proposal to set up a British military post at Hukwang for operation at the time of emergency was not taken seriously by the Burmese side.

Stalemate in the informal border talks further deepened the suspicion of the Court of Ava on the British imperial strategy in the Upper Burma, and from there to Kunming of Yunan province of China, which forms the tri-junction of trade and commerce with Vietnam, Cambodia and Thailand. Therefore, Hannay's request for permission to return to Calcutta from Mainkhwon via Ava, criss-crossing the whole of Upper Irrawaddy region, was turned down on one plea or the other.(ibid.). China's silent diplomacy to keep the British out of Upper Burma cannot be ruled out as the main factor behind the reactionary move on the part of Burma this time. Moreover, since the Singphos led by Duffa, was considered trustworthy by the Mogaung chief, to keep alive his territorial agenda beyond the Patkai in the hill sections bordering Assam, no positive step was taken up by the Burmese authority since the second failed mission to restore tranquillity and trade in the volatile Singpho frontier. But with the termination of hostility in the Singpho tract in the aftermath of the abortive rebellion of the tribe in 1843 peace was restored in that volatile frontier once again which facilitated movement of commercial traffic with Upper Burma in the traditional manner.

In the years following the Second Anglo-Burmese war(1851) Upper Burma was directly annexed with India and the route of strategic trans-border trade in the east was diverted to Manipur along the Tamo-Moreh route for its advantage of accessibility and active participation from the peace loving Manipuris. Moreover the subsidiary status of the Burmese king after the second Anglo-Burmese war gave the British the opportunity to engage themselves in commercial traffic along the sea route with Burmese mainland with ease. Hence alternate option like the Sadiya-Mogaung route through the Singpho tract was allowed to gather dust in the colonial archives. But trade in traditional items carried out by the Singphos continued as before, which provides a window of opportunity for the modern planners of Look-East policy to give a fresh look to the possibility of reopening this trade route for vigorous commercial traffic in future so that the benefits of the economic boom can be shared with the indigenous population of this border state.

CONCLUSION

In this era of globalisation no set formula of the developed countries on economic development can be applied successfully in the Indian context unless and until new avenues are opened up to give the indigenous people of the border states in north-east a share of the Look-East policy, which is seen as the new vehicle of boom in our relations with the ASEAN countries. Since Arunachal Pradesh has the privilege of having the largest share of the international border with Burma and China it is highly expected that the Government of India should act decisively in developing the trans-border trade route to Burma through the Singpho corridor.

In this context a close look into the colonial history of the Singpho corridor as the link-line between India and Burma can provide the following clue to how a viable trade route can be developed on the same route.

(a) Geographical inaccessibility, which often acts as a barrier for developing an all weather trade route across high mountains and slopes from Sadiya to Mogaung in Myanmar and from there to Kunming in China (which forms the tri-junction for trade with other ASEAN countries) can be overcome by the use of latest technology, a glimpse of which is available in the colonial history.

(b) Insurgency in the area of the Kachin tribe of Burma[13] can be overcome by taking that tribe into confidence and by giving them a share of the benefit of trade in the same manner in which the British won confidence of the Singpho tribe after military pursuit failed to yield any positive result.

(c) Diplomatic engagement with Myanmar and China should be activated so that problems beyond the Indian border can be sorted out by sharing responsibilities as equitable partners of trade in the entire stretch. In this respect we must take a lesson from the Singpho's past history that both Myanmar and China keeps a hawkish watch on any unilateral move in this side of the frontier to deny India the first mover advantage in trade with ASEAN countries.

(d) Finally, we must move forward with a clear vision in this front as it involves huge investment in infrastructure development. Any policy shift or short term vision can prove to be suicidal as colonial experience in the Singpho tract leaves sufficient footprints of an ambitious project, but failed to kick start because it was botched half-way.

ENDNOTES

1. The Singphos, who are settled between the river Tengapani and Boori Dihing in the Sadiya frontier of Arunachal Pradesh, migrated to their present settlement in the 18th century from Upper Burma. For their continued trade and cultural contact with Burma they were branded by the British as the supporters of the Burmese forces during the first Anglo-Burmese war.
2. Political Consultations- Secret, 20 May, 1825, No. 25.
3. Bengal Secret Political Consultations,14 May 1824, cited in N. K. Barooah, David Scott in North-East India,New Delhi, 1970, p. 125.
4. Political consultations (Secret),19 May, 1826, No. 9.
5. Political consultations, 7 September,1827, No.17.
6. Report on the Trade Between Assam and Adjoining Countries, 1890.
7. Foreign Political Proceedings, (India), 18 July 1836, No. 42.
8. For details see Captain S.F. Hannay,1836.
9. Foreign Political Proceedings, 8 May 1837, No. 64. To Neutralize the extravagant territorial claims of Burma over Assam as far as Jaypore the Resident was directed to communicate the matter to the court of Ava that it is determined to make Patkai range the boundary between the two countries.
10. Political Proceedings (India), 27 June 1836, No. 49.
11. The First Hannay Mission gathered this information about Assamese slaves in Burma. For details see, Hannay, op cit., n. 224.

12. Foreign Political Proceedings (India), 17 April 1837, No. 48.
13. The Kachins of Burma, who shares common heritage with the Singpho tribe of Arunachal Pradesh, are leading an insurgency movement against the Burmese military junta for a share of their due rights as an indigenous group. Since their territory falls in between Mogaung and Kunming of China the proposed trade route through the Singpho tract is considered unviable at present. (Burma has been changed to Myanmar at places wherever necessary to furnish references in the Look East context).

REFERENCES

Barooah, N.K (1970), *David Scott in North East India*. New Delhi: Oriental Publishers.

Barpujari, H.K (1970), *Problem of the Hill Tribes: North East Frontier*, Vol. I. Gauhati: Lawyers' Book Stall.

Butler, J. (1847), *Sketches of Assam with Some Account of the Hill Tribes*. Calcutta: Government Press.

Devi, L. (1968) (1992), *Ahom Tribal Relations-A Political Study*. Guwahati: Lawyers' Book Stall.

Hannay, S.F. (1836), *The Journal of a route from the Capital of Ava to the Amber Mines of Hukwang Valley on the South-East Frontier of Assam*. Quoted in H.K. Barpujari, 1970. Problem of the Hill Tribes: North East Frontier, Vol. I. Gauhati: Lawyers' Book Stall, 105-114

Lamb, A. (1960), *Britain and Chinese Central Asia: the Road to Lash*. London: Routledge and Kegqan Paul.

Mackenzie, A. (1989), (reprint). *North East Frontier of India*. New Delhi: Mittal Publications.

Wilcox, R. (1832), "Memoir of a Survey of Assam and the Neighbouring Countries executed in 1825-6-7-8", Vol. XVII, *Asiatic Research*, Calcutta.

SECTION--VI

Untended Context: Challenges in Tradition

20

THE STATE OF SHAMANISTIC KNOWLEDGE SYSTEM IN THE FACE OF GLOBALIZATION: NEED FOR A POLICY DIALOGUE

Jagannath Dash, Kabiraj Behera

INTRODUCTION

Globalization is primarily conceptualized to be an economic phenomenon, which involves in the growth of the international trade, investment and capital flows. It is also identified with the rapid increase in cross boarder social, cultural and technological exchange. Globally the process of globalization is thus conceptualized as a creed, a compulsion and hyper – capitalism. It involves essentially the international movement of commodities, money, information, technology, organization, legal system and infrastructure development. Mr. Kofi Annan, U.N. Secretary General, says, "It is an irreversible process, not an option, but a positive force, it is a blind force and therefore needs to be harnessed carefully".

Globalization is basically understood as a closer global economic integration, which is most often identified with progress, development and technological advancement. With this basic goals of development both for the developing and the developed nations, the process of globalization became an essential instrument. The developing countries get into an open corridor where as the developed nations benefit by increased international trade. Beyond these country considerations there are traditional communities who also pass through such globalizing order, while enjoying better opportunities in exporting their indigenous products and accepting the outside communities as well as ideologies, face a lot of changes leading to partial and complete transformation of traditional values. We have to critically analyze whether we need such structural and functional changes in the society or not. Even though the common people or the academicians do not go in favour of it, the ultimate administration of the state or the nation needs an economic development through transformation or change or drastic change. Here comes the policy of the government and the ideologies of the people which are in clash. This is not only the critical situation for a social scientist, but a natural and spontaneous process to come obviously through man made activities Therefore it needs a policy dialogue whether we are doing right or not. We are just in an oscillating condition between yes and no. What the administration feels right, the common people may not accept. The right criticism in the field of policy mater is a basic need at the movement.

In view of the above policy problem, in the eyes of the researchers, a paradoxical situation arises; on one hand we try to introduce the economic development through globalization for the immediate progress but on the other hand we also desire for the presence of traditional ethics and values. How it would be possible is a basic question from the view point of policy matter.

For a traditional society especially tribal community like that of "Paraja" in south Orissa, the fundamental features are always in favour of the maintenance of their socio cultural tradition. Like others they also need money (In cash) for their livelihood but it should not be at the cost of their socio-cultural tradition. It is easier to lose traditional values to acquire economic development. Day-by-day due to the impact of globalization, people are tending towards new economic order which may ultimately fade away their traditional values.

Religion is the core structure of the society and essential social values are closely tied to it. The shamanistic wisdom which tells all the essential knowledge system forms the most crucial elements of the cultural tradition. Any substantial change in the structure of the society is definitely to be reflected in the state of shamanism. The shaman occupies a central place in the society and people need his service and wisdom so long as they are traditional. Therefore the persistence and continuity of Shamanistic tradition becomes an indicator of an unchanging or relatively static society. As already discussed every society desires for economic development and all the government policies favour it at the cost of the traditional values. As a result , in order to maintain both, which is extremely difficult, one needs the policy dialogue in the present administrative set up so that the paradoxical confusion will be subsided, and the due development will be achieved which may not alter the shamanistic tradition, thereby conserving the social cultural tradition in toto.

THE PARAJA SHAMANISTIC TRADITION

No doubt a traditional tribal community maintains its ideal pattern to the best extent. The shaman in tribal society becomes one of the traditional custodians of its cultural values. With his functioning on the basis of vast stock of knowledge from the natural to supernatural extension, Shaman seems to dominate most of the decision making process of the society. Economic development for the Paraja is mostly confined to the proper procurement of food clothing and shelter. Beyond such basic minimum needs, most of the tribals as well as the Paraja never desire more. But at the advent of globalization all around, the economic opportunities have attracted the tribals in the industrial sector and the intensive supply of their indigenous products / collections to the modern market have brought in automatic changes. At the same time government policy to develop the tribal communities by welfare programmes and modern technology has also added fuel to the process of transformation. Therefore the need of the hour is to appraise the policies and policy decision as regards their transformation role without making any harm to the socio-cultural tradition.

Shaman (see Eliade, 1964) in genera is a fascinating individual associated with multifarious role in the society. S/he is a part time operator as well as specialist. S/he goes into an action whether called upon and is paid for his/her services. S/he usually works alone as an individual. The shaman gets his /her power from the supernatural source individually. As a multi role specialist, the Paraja shaman, first and foremost is a healer/a doctor. S/he diagnoses the illness and intercedes with the super natural on behalf of the patient. S/he may also use other remedies as well. S/he is an intelligent performer, applies indigenous tricks through signs of hand or influential speaking. His/ her methods of diagnosis also are very much impressive and influential to the common human. S/he creates a faith and confidence among the patients. In certain hunting and gathering society, the shaman usually is the only kind of supernatural practitioner and therefore s/he is called upon in wild variety of situations. S/he performs the hunting magic, seeks to control the weather, divines the future, deals with ghosts and does whatever else needs to be done in the supernatural realm. Thus the Paraja shaman sometimes deals with the important rituals in the presence as well as absence of the priest, s/he functions like a diviner, and through trance s/he prescribes medicines and offers magico-religious treatment, and thereby mediates between the natural and super natural worlds. The policy decision to introduce the economic development through transformation in some situations, where Paraja have taken the help of modern amenities and technology, has made the state of shaman and his/her knowledge system precarious.

The term "Shaman" (see Winthrop, 1991) is derived via-Russian from Tungus "saman", it is a synonym for extraordinary individual. The Paraja shamanism in his way involves a religious complex characterized by trance, curing and ideology of cosmic flight. Following the attributes of

Siberian shamanism, the Paraja shamanism, the Paraja shaman can be also characterized by four criteria. A supernatural world to which the shaman travels; action on behalf of a social group; inspiration through familiar spirits and ecstatic or trance, experience. (Hultkrantz, 1998: 30). Although the Paraja shaman may fulfill multifarious role, the shamanic function centers on curing. Though the curing process varies from culture to culture, universally it uses magico religious procedures and sometimes prescribes herbal medicines.

According to Hunter and Whitten (1976:309), "because the shaman performance is public and important to the community as it is to the patient, much more than the effectiveness of a particular use is at stake; the shaman plays a crucial role in the maintenance of group cohesion. Thus shaman with only chance–level cure rates is maintaining in their social positions." The shaman has a great interest for the recovery of the patient as it validates his self image. Psychologically speaking the shaman desires to win the public support than just to have a high success rate in winning. As Silverman (1967), has suggested that the shamanistic experience is related to the psychological integration of the individual and the social integration of the society. He describes five stages the individual pass through in the process of curing.

Stage–I The precondition; Fear; feelings of impotence, and failure and guilt

Stage–II Pre occupation; isolation; estrangement

Stage–III Narrowing of attention; self initiated sensory deprivation

Stage–IV The fusing of higher and lower referential processes

Stage–V Cognitive reorganization

On the whole the shamanistic practice provides the mechanism to which potentially severely troubled person can re-integrate themselves cognitively and emotionally. (see Hunter and Whitten 1976 : 309 to comprehend the shaman-patient-public interrelationship).

In the Paraja society (a Dravidian Tribe) shaman is called as "Gurumain" irrespective of gender. The position of shaman /shamanin is not hereditary. They think that only the supernatural blessings can make a shaman at any age in the life time. The instructions come in the dreams from the super natural power which helps one to become a shaman. The beginner has to also work under an experienced and aged shaman to have practical experience. The knowledge system of the shaman in this way is beyond the purview of the common human. As a result of this, the shaman wins the public image through out. Because of the supernatural connectivity the shaman can explain all the life cycle problems of the people. S/he can explain the life cycle problem of the people. S/he can explain the cycle of birth, death and re birth. In majority of the village level rituals he is to assist to priest for identifying the supernatural entities to be made satisfied through ritual worship.

Gurumain is the only specialized person who can predict the state of the soul after the death. As the Gurumains says, the mortal world is under the control of *Dharanimata* where people are categorized good and bad on the basis of their deeds. The soul of the good persons soon after death go to the sky known as *'Saragpur'*, the place of sun and moon (*Jan, Bel*), where as the bad persons go to the sky in a similar manner but stay there in another part of it known as *'Jampur'* , the place of death god . In the *'Saragpur'* the good souls enjoy life till the secondary burial practice is performed and so also bad souls in the *'Jampur'* till the secondary burial right which is known as *'Khamsil'*. Both category of souls go under ground (*Patal*) and there they are known as *'Duma'*, the ancestral spirits. In the sky especially in *Jampur* the soul of the bad person has to undergo punishment (*Kilakunda*) for their bad deeds and there from they have to come to the underground only after the secondary burial rite. 'Underground' has two types of shelter, one for the benevolent spirit and the other for the malevolent spirits. Here the spirits posses the right to take rebirth. All such secret knowledge about the soul after death is the essential property of a Paraja shaman. S/he narrate the state of the soul on the basis of such knowledge system. Because of their supernatural connection in almost all major rituals they through trance enquire the reasons of dissatisfaction of the concern deities and also predict the remedies for the benefit of the village and community. Further, it is because of their knowledge system they also explain the state and typology of the souls (*Duma*) with reference to their specific deeds. As a result the public develops a special interest for the shaman because of his specialty in the treatment of the souls as per their specific state or condition. Soon after the shaman identifies the exact spirit or deity, the priest (*Pujari*) performs the ritual to satisfy them. Besides the village level major ritual in the healing process, the shaman has to worship of the concern spirit or deity for the purpose. The knowledge stock of the Paraja shaman is so vast that it is not possible to elaborate them in the form of a paper. Besides, while organizing the magico-religious and herbal methods of treatment the shaman also prescribes a lot of herbal medicines for the cure of the physical suffering. In this context a Paraja shaman also functions like a full time medicine man in the society. As already mentioned, the shaman identifies the herbal medicine by virtue of super natural instructions as well as blessings. He/ She is shown all such medicinal plants in the dream.

The state of the shamanistic wisdom is facing the challenges from the modern society to-day. The Parajas of Nandapur block head quarters are sometimes depending on the shaman for the healing process. But in the district headquarters Jeypur no Paraja is depending on the shaman today, because of the impact of the modernization, and modern health care intervention. But beyond the Nandapur block head quarters in most of the interior pockets the Parajas still strongly believe in tradition.

In this context one may feel confused with the concept of modernization and globalization. Though as definite process both are specific in their own context, they are complementary to each other. The process of modernization is rather enhanced by the incoming of globalization. When the Parajas of Jeypur, an urban center are able to send their indigenous procurements/ commodities to the exporting agencies because of their demand in the international market they no more look at the local agents or the village functionaries. They also do not depend on the supernatural instructions of the shamans, they are both modernized and connected to the globalization process on the other hand , the "ASHA KIRAN" hospital a very reputed health care centre at Lamtaput, constructed by Christian missionary is least attended by the Paraja patients of the interior villages. The simple reason is that the Parajas of these interior areas are still traditional in their ideology and value system and for them the shaman is the sole specialist for multifarious purposes.

NEED FOR A POLICY DIALOGUE

Coming to the policy dialogue, the Constitution of India pledges to secure all citizens justice, social, economic and political, bearing on which the government of India's policy is to redeem the equality of life through the quality oriented development programmes. In the field of education, economy and health care multifarious and multi level programmes have been introduced to upgrade their quality of life and to bring them into national main stream. The observations of the paper highlights that the Parajas who are comparatively more organized and literate are preferring to modern amenities, neglecting the traditional method of treatment by the shamans. In such urbanized and semi urbanized villages the shamans are no more shamans. Their own definition of shamanism has been drastically changed. The supernatural instructions they may have in the dream as before but due to no interest of the urbanized Paraja their status has been totally degenerated to the common man.

However the policy considerations of the government to bring the people to main stream are most welcome but the matter of displeasure is that how to conserve the indigenous knowledge system? The defunct shamanism may lead to degeneration of the Paraja indigenous knowledge system as maintained by the shamans. Therefore we are in the midst of a confused government approach as reflected in the policies.

The issues are broadly threefold with specific reference to economic development sector, infrastructure development sector which are specifically applied for the protection of the tribal from exploitation, improvement of their standard of living, lifting them to comparable level of development and building inner strength for over all development.

The Constitution of India was provided us the broad outlines of tribal development at the level of ideology, action and evaluation by the help of political leadership, planners, administrators and academics. In such baseline strategies in the tribal development policies further the government of India considers planning, implementation evaluation and monitoring at the centre, sate, ITDP and block levels specially coming to the policy implementation for the tribal development. The present policy–discussion has identified the location of the tribal pockets on the basis of full concentration, pockets of concentration and dispersed locations for the purpose of lifting them beyond their substance level of technology sustainable procurement of resources and their utilization and the ultimate mobility towards a better economic situation. The policy issues in this way are manifold but the purpose is one to bring them from the traditional base of backwardness to the modernized and globalised world of economic development. The academicians, social workers and researchers especially anthropologists on the other hand are not in favour of such policy issues. If the situation will continue like this one day not only the Paraja shamanism will get lost but also the whole community will loose its basic identity as a Paraja, and the shamanistic wisdom will land in a most precarious situation for ever and ever. The Paraja indigenous knowledge systems must have taken several thousand years to perceive the world around and to conceptualize the invisible entities, and ultimately have developed a precious knowledge system in equilibrium with the natural and supernatural phenomenon. But the process of globalization under the present policy set up may take only few decades for its miserable decay and destruction leading to extinction. As the authors of the paper we may not appreciate it. Economic development be continued but specific policy should be associated to keep up the shamanistic knowledge system for all time to come. This is not so easy, but not an impossible task. The official motive has to be associated with social work approach and sacrifice which may lead us to the field of success and the constructive application of the tribal policy today.

REFERENCES

Eliade, Mircea (1964), *Shamanism: Archaic Techniques of Ecstacy.* Princeton, N. J.: Princeton University press.

Hultkrantz, Ake (1978), "Ecology and Phenomenological Aspects of Shamanism", in Dioszegi and M. Hoppal (eds) *Shamanism in Siberia.* Budapest: Academiai Kiado.

Hunter, David E. & Phillip Whitten (1976), *The Study of Anthropology.* New York: Harper& Row Publishers Inc.

Silverman,William B. (1967), *Religion for Skeptics: A Theology for the Questioning Mind.* New York: Jonathan David Publishers.

Winthrop, Robert H.(1993), *Dictionary of Concept in Cultural Anthropology.* New York/Westport: Greenwood Press.

21

CONTEXTUALISING TRADITIONAL SOCIAL CAPITAL IN THE AGE OF GLOBALISATION: LOCAL RGANISATIONS AND SUSTAINABILITY AMONG THE TRIBES OF ARUNACHAL PRADESH

Tabang Mibang

The last quarter of twentieth century was a period of rapid growth in transnational linkages and flows affecting all areas of human life: economy, politics, environment, culture, society and even interpersonal relations. As transnational linkages pervade all areas of social life, national boundaries become more porous and local autonomy declines; communities and regions become increasingly interconnected and mutually dependent. Just as cutting down a forest in one place has consequence for the global environment, social, economic, cultural and political changes in a specific country are likely to affect people elsewhere. The consequence of these global processes is major social transformation throughout the world, so that old economic and cultural dichotomies such as "modern and traditional" "highly-developed and less-developed", "eastern and western", "the north and the south" lost their sharpness in the dawn of the twenty first century. Policy makers, academics, opinion leaders and the social scientists, who set out to analyze these dramatic changes in the recent years, soon came up with intense ideological and multi-dimensional debates on the nature of present world order and its historical antecedents, underlying causative forces, and future evolution. These give us a great deal of different perspectives and at the same time bring confusion and profound disagreement to the fore.

These states of confusion, multifaceted perspectives and disagreement as a result of overwhelming interaction and interdependence among the sovereign nation states is graphically described by Anthony Gidden with the metaphor of "riding the juggernaut" and compared to a bus without a driver, where everyone is a passenger, but unable to get off. Thus, these global phenomena are open ended, unpredictable and uncontrollable. The consequence of this kind of system is detraditionalisation–the receding of customs and beliefs that had given social stability and cohesion based on specific history, anchored people's lives in predictable and trans-generational practices. There are no uniformly accepted core values and norms that might provide clear guidelines for individual decisions, actions and patterns of conduct. There are no absolute moral guidelines passed on from previous generations. Modernity constantly challenges and transforms traditional values, norms and forms of conduct. (Giddens, 1994: 57). Along side this detraditionalisation goes a pluralisation of life–worlds. People now live and act in many different social settings they think of as "site" of "face to face" interaction. These particular settings and contexts for interaction are segmentalised and separated from each other. Further more, these particular segmentalised settings for action and separate life-worlds are associated with particular kinds of life-style. (Giddens, 1991: 83). This produces a world where "social bonds have effectively to be made, rather than inherited from the past–on the personal and more collective levels; this is a fraught and difficult enterprise, but one also that holds out the promise of great rewards. It is decentred in term of authorities, but re-centred in terms of opportunities and dilemmas." (Beck, Giddens and Lash, 1994: 107).

A consequence of this is that knowledge and beliefs are both contingent and contextual. Since there are numerous segmentalised settings for producing new, different forms of beliefs and culture, there are no longer any universally accepted absolute truth, so that the apparent "hero" of modernity (science) is constantly challenged by alternative forms of knowledge, by other "heroines". For instance, various alternative therapies may challenge established medical science. Ecological discourse challenges the assurance of applications of science and its associated forms of industrialism. This contingency and contextualization of knowledge and belief also extends to cultural, political and moral questions. Giddens suggests that this does not just involve a segmentation of life-worlds, but in a contradictory process, our everyday experiences, are increasingly mediated, rather than based on face to face interaction. We experience many other cultures, events, ideas through the global mass media. These highly mediated, pluralistic experiences and interaction construct new identities, and new bases for social differences. (Giddens, 1991: 86).

GLOBALISATION: ITS CONTENDING PERSPECTIVES AND SOCIAL CAPITAL

Social scientists who set out to analyse this "unique historical situation" of globalization as coined by Giddens offer a variety of perspectives and reveal considerable disagreement. The concept has been employed as a meta-concept for comprehending and explaining a diverse variety of complex and interrelated processes, structures, forces, agents, and effects. Those who use it in this manner generally try to view this phenomenon from a historical, multilevel, interdisciplinary and holistic perspective. Most theorizing and empirical research on globalization tends to be organized around five key issues or questions. (Guillen, 2001:235): Is globalization really taking place? Is it producing convergence and integration? Is it undermining the authority of nation-state? Does it characterize the present era of human history, and if so, how does this era differ from the previous era of modernity?

Is globalization producing a global culture, a global economy, a global political system, and so forth? Added to these questions is the fact put forwarded by Brazilian social scientist, Octovio Ianni who contended that the complex and multi-dimensional nature of phenomena associated with this concept has challenged the theoretical and analytical capabilities of the contemporary social sciences. (Harris, 2002:6). "The originality and complexity of globalization, in conjunction with its distinct aspects challenge the social scientists to mobilize the suggestions and conquests of diverse sciences. Globalization tends to be seen as a vast process that is not only politico-economic, but also socio-cultural, and that includes demographic, ecological, gender, religious, linguistics and other problems. Even when the investigation privileges a determined sphere of analysis, one is constantly challenged to take into account other aspects of reality, without which an economic, political, sociological, ecological, or any other kind of analysis results in abstraction that lack realism, consistency and verisimilitude.

At the most general level, globalization refers to a process of changes which affects all regions of world in a variety of sectors including the economy, technology, politics, the media, culture, and the environment. A more precise definition of globalization is:

A process (or set of processes) which embodies a transformation in the spatial organisation of social relations and transactions -assessed in terms of their extensity, intensity, velocity and impact-generating transcontinental or inter-regional flows and networks of activity, interaction, and the exercise of power. (Held et al., 1999:16).

This definition prompted many observers to call attention to the effect of this phenomenon in our sense of time and space. For example, Anthony Giddens (1990:53; 1994:57) believes that globalization has created a decoupling or "distanciation" of space and time, Samir Amin's (2000:157) contention that globalization "is an ideological discourse used to legitimize the strategies of imperialist capital". While Roland Robertson (1992:8) argues that globalization refers to both "the compression of the world and the intensification of consciousness of the world as a whole". In a similar vein, Martin Albrow (2000:88) defines globalization as the "diffusion of practices, values and technology that have an influence on people's lives world wide". Thus, the discourse on globalization has been increasingly heated between those who employ the concept as the label for what they consider to be an unfolding process of global economic, political and cultural integration that is bringing about the progressive integration of humanity and those who use the concept to describe a largely unjust and inequitable process of transnational corporate expansionism that involves the increasing exploitation of a large proportion of humanity and the increasing despoliation of the biosphere of the planet. (Harris and Seid, 2000:19). Held et al. (1999:2) categorized these varied understanding and assessment of globalization into three broad categories which they refer to as hyperglobalizers, skeptics and transformationists.

Hyperglobalizers believe that globalization represents a new epoch in human history, in which all types of relationship are becoming integrated at the global level, transcending the nation state and making it increasingly irrelevant. Hyperglobalizers include both those who celebrate these trends and those with more critical assessment. The celebratory hyperglobalizers are mainly neoliberal advocates of open and global markets who believe that these will guarantee optimal economic growth and will, in the long run, bring about improved living standards for everyone. (Castles, 2001:20-21). Critical hyperglobalizers emphasize the revolutionary character of such trends as the rapid growth in global media and global mobility, but argue that these only benefit a small elite. Globalization, they hold, is the mechanism for the rule of international investors and transnational corporations, who can no longer be controlled by ever-weaker nation-states. Trade unions and welfare systems are collapsing; unemployment and social exclusion are burgeoning, while uncontrolled growth is leading to life threatening environmental degradation. Thus globalization can lead to social fragmentation, cultural uncertainty, conflict and violence.

Perspective of the "transformationists" is very similar to the "transnational" perspective as identified by Sklair. (Harris, 2002:10). This perspective understands globalization as results of closely interlinked process of change in technology, economic activity, governance, communication, and culture. Cross border flows (of trade, investment, migrants, cultural artifacts, environmental factors, etc.) have reached unprecedented levels and now integrate virtually all countries into a global system. This brings about major social transformations at all levels. However, these trends do not necessarily lead to global convergence or the emergence of a single "world society". Rather globalization creates new forms of global stratification in which some individuals, communities, countries or regions become integrated to global networks of power and prosperity, while others are excluded and marginalized. Transfomationists argue that these new divisions cut across the old schisms of east-west and north-south. But globalization cannot be equated with a general reduction in the power of states. Rather, as nexus between territory and sovereignty is undermined by globalizing forces, new forms of governance emerge at the national, regional, and global levels, with the military and economic power of the dominant states still playing a decisive role. (Castles, 2001:21).

The sceptics focus mainly on the economic aspects of globalization. They acknowledge the high levels of cross-border flows of trade, investment, and labour, but argue that there is nothing new about this: international economic integration in the period preceding the First World War was comparable with current levels. Moreover, they point out that most world trade is between the highly developed economies, so that less-developed countries have not participated significantly in processes of economic integration. They, therefore, prefer the term "internationalization" to globalization. (Hirst and Thomson, 1996). They consider "Regionalisation" as an alternative to globalization, which allow nation state to maintain their pre-dominant position in the world system, and discount the idea that global travel and diffusion of media are giving birth to a global culture of even global civilization; rather, they see continuing hierarchy and fragmentation.

Such differences in approaches make it clear that an attempt to understand the impacts needs to look not only at general aspect of globalization, but also at the specific factors and forms that lead to varying effects and reactions at different spatial levels: the regional, the national, and the local. These should not be understood in opposition to each other, but rather as elements of complex and dynamic relationships, in which global forces have varying impacts according to differing structures. (Held et al., 1999:14-16). However, in the more recent years; for most people, the pre-eminent level for experiencing these complex and dynamic processes is the "local". This is because of the fact that the top-down methods often ignore the social situation and needs of local groups. Further, local people and their organizations are seen as obstacles to progress, to be dealt with either through public order measured or educational strategies designed to foster willingness to accept change. Thus, the changes to production and distribution systems, social relations, cultural practices and resultant transformed conditions in the local community have become the main thrust of debate at the dawn of 21st century.

The concept of social capital has come to the forefront as a crucial ingredient in achieving equitable and sustainable development, participatory democracy, empowerment from below, and effective government. It is considered as an essential element in the realm of social coherence, stability and solidarity, and work as a catalyst in containing the intrusion of social anomalies and aberrations. The current popularity of the concept had paved the way for variety of definitions. Pierre Bourdieu, a French Socialist, who is considered as pioneer in attempting a systematic analysis of social capital defined the concept as, "the aggregate of actual or potential resources, which are linked to position of a durable network of more or less institutionalized relationships of mutual acquaintance or recognition". (Bourdieu, 1985: 241). Subsequently, Coleman (1988: 98) working on the same concept, provided a more refined analysis stretching social capital to the extent of generating human capital, emphasized the importance of social capital in the society Both Bourdieu and Coleman emphasized its intangible character relative to other forms. Despite the absence of a universally agreed upon definition, growing consensus is emerging that the social capital stands for the ability of actors to secure benefits by virtue of membership in social network or other social structures. (Portes, 1998:5).

A review of literature makes it possible to distinguish three basic functions of social capital applicable in a variety of contexts: (a) as a source of social control; (b) as a source of family support; and (c) as a source of benefit through extra-familial network. Several scholars have emphasized on the importance of social capital for the social control. Even Coleman (*ibid*) has gone to the extent of lamenting over the disappearance of informal family and community structure that produce this type of social capital. Robert D. Putnam (1995:67-74), again in his endeavour gave a new dimension to the concept of social capital. He focuses on the extent to which individuals have regular contacts with others beyond the spheres of family or the markets, and notably the kind of face to face relation of relative equality associated with participation in common endeavours (*ibid*). The premise is that the social networks generated by such pattern of sociability constitute an important form of social capital. It also helps to increase the trust and fellow feeling towards others and enhance their capacity to join together in collective action to resolve the common problems. Higher levels of social capital have been associated with many outcomes ranging from prevention of crime to higher rates of economic growth as well as that of functioning of democracy. (Putnam, 1996:48). In short, this is a literature that linked relatively diffused patterns of sociability to the effectiveness of democracy.

THE CONTEXT OF ARUNACHAL PRADESH

In context of Arunachal Pradesh, which was once considered as an island of peace, traditional social capital has undergone a tremendous change in the realm of social-inter-relationship among varied ethnic groups. It is a home of about thirteen lakhs population distributed in 16 districts belonging to about 26 major tribes and several sub-tribes. Taking into account the ethnic plurality of Arunachal Pradesh, it can be truly said as a mosaic of ethnicity. Traditionally, these ethnic groups with their distinct socio-cultural patterns were enriched with intensive social networks[1], trusts, mutual reciprocity[2] and social commitment[3] within the groups. It is reflected in observance of various socio-cultural festivals and rituals[4] to that of mundane day to day affairs.

These tribal societies were almost unknown to the other parts of the country before the advent of the Britishers. There was no formal system of governance as we know to day. But they had their local system of governance, sanctioned by customs, which they evolved through ages to meet up different situation. (Elwin, 1965:174). The society was regulated through the traditional governing bodies[5], now popularly known as village councils and traditional reciprocal cooperation in solving different aspects of socio-political and economic life. Apart from the judicial decision through deliberative method and general administrations, these traditional village councils were concerned with all activities related to welfare and security of the individual to the village as a whole, thereby maintaining social stability and coherence in the society. These traditional institutions are known by different local names in different tribes and led either by local chiefs or councils of elders exercising the authority in council's deliberations or people as a whole govern themselves. (*ibid.*).The striking features of the functioning of these institutions in Arunachal Pradesh, as can be observed, are that the elders are always regarded and they enjoyed a respectable position in the society, by virtue of their experience, wisdom, command over the traditional conventions and expertise in local works such as construction of house, fencing, rituals, etc. Needless to say, in the realm of social domains, these time-tested and time-honoured institutions worked as a catalyst in maintaining the intrusion of social anomalies and aberrations. Therefore, it can be concluded that the art of good governance and local administration conductive to the welfare of the society is not alien to the tribes of Arunachal Pradesh from the very beginning.

Beside these socio-political organizations, cooperation and mutual help is an inherent trait among the tribes of Arunachal Pradesh, which inspires them to work together and find solutions to the local problems. It would not be an exaggeration to say that every tribal community has evolved traditional institutions of mutual help and cooperation during the agricultural operations, at the time of construction of house or in a work which require more labour, etc, are still functioning among the people, though in a lesser degree[6]. They have a strong social sense and believe in collective and community efforts to solve the problems. In matter of common interest like construction of village roads, bridges, clearing of forests for agricultural purposes, construction of village fencing, etc, the village council or head (in case of chieftaincy) mobilized the community labour. Each household, each clan, each hemlet used to think, live and work as a single unit. In daily life, the sorrows of one are sorrows of all. During the agricultural operations, or at the time of construction of house and other such works which require different local expertise, etc, a tribal household mobilized the labour of neighbours or clan member on the basis of reciprocity. In short, these institutions which ensure or serve as the basis of social coherence and fellow feeling are evolved spontaneously in response to the individuals used for collective action and transmitted from generation to generation among the various tribes of Arunachal Pradesh for regulating public life, managing public resources, maintaining social order and for conflicts resolution.

However, in the recent years, it is becoming more transparent that the social ties, fellow-feeling, the social trust and connectedness, and support is gradually slipping away[7] and individual's pre-occupation is making in road into social domain of Arunachal Pradesh. Besides, important societal pre-requisite of a vital democracy like voluntary and disinterested participation in various activities related to social development, strong positive values (including trust in others) and ties that bind people to one another leading to more powerful norms of generalized reciprocity and cooperation is also eroding. Several factors may be considered responsible for this type of social transition and erosion of social capital. On the one hand, while the emphasis could be made that the agents of modernization have played their crucial role, on the other, the development of the individualistic trends could be considered as responsible for these changes, the result being conflicts, frustration and social tension in different parts of the state[8].

The effect or the emerging trends is noticeable in the gradual decline of solidarity of clan[9], village and community, erosion of authority of village council[10] and the institution of reciprocative mutual cooperation among the people replacing traditional social values, ethos, etc.[11] by new social capital in the form of youth organisations, cultural associations, student unions, community based organisations, self-help groups, and NGOs pertaining to emerging issue like health, gender, environment, education, etc. Over all cohesion in societal commitment, participation in civil work and extra-familial interpersonal relationship is eroding. Thus, a distinct and discernible transition of social capital is taking place following the introduction of various agents of modernization accompanied by the development of the individualistic trend.

ENDNOTES

1. For example, social networking is evident on social occasions like marriage. See 14 papers in Section-IV, entitled Marriage and Social Relations, pp.321-464, in Mibang and Behera,2006.
2. See Riba, 2004 and Mibang, 2004 for an understanding of reciprocal labour exchange in house construction in Galo and Adi communities respectively.
3. For social commitments of the Musup (a socio-cultural institution in Adi Padam community) members see Pertin, 2009.
4. See Wangsa, 2004 to understand the nature of village solidarity in family rituals.
5. Generally there are four types of governing bodies namely, chieftaincy of Khamptis, Singphows, Noctes, etc.; gerontocracy of Sherdukpens and Apatanis; arbiter system of Tagins, Mishmis and Nyishis; and democratic village councils of Monpas and Adis.
6. Mutual cooperation on reciprocal basis in house construction, agricultural operation, etc. happens to be the characteristic of traditional

tribal communities of Arunachal Pradesh. Even, for the payment of compensation/fine relating to a crime committed by an individual member, members of the whole clan stand by. Community fencing and other works pertaining to the community are done collectively. This is evident in riglap of the Adi, rye/rik guknam/gonam or rye/rik angnam of the Nyishi, etc. The practice still exists in the village life though changes are taking place due to monetization. Also refer foot notes 1-4 in this paper.

7. In this context mention may be made of the declining role of Musup and gradual disappearance of Raseng from Adi Padam community (Pertin, op cit.) and Pa from Wancho community. (Riba, 2004a).
8. This is reflected in ever increasing incidences of ethnic conflict, divorce, drug addiction, divide on religious lines, juvenile delinquency, rape, eve-teasing, robbery, etc. which did not exist in the tribal communities of Arunachal Pradesh prior to their exposure to development forces.
9. Though riglap is a system of mutual labour exchange on reciprocal basis in Adi community, Roy (1997: 126-27) has recorded it as a system of hiring outside labour on payment of cash while he was conducting his field study in plains villages of the Adis in late 1950s. However, he has mentioned of another system of labour appropriation, enlik, which is a system of hiring labour on payment of kind.(ibid.127). In Damro village of Adi Padams enlik is a system of labour appropriation which is organised by members of Musup and Raseng as a part of their social commitment ethics. (Pertin, 2009:145-148).
10. For example, it is found that panchayat members exercise more power than traditional authorities in developmental spheres. The clan is also found divided along party lines in general elections to Lok Sabha and State Assembly. Conflicting parties prefer to go to the law court in place of traditional councils for legal redressal. The traditional mutual reciprocity in labour exchange in house construction or even in agricultural operation is being replaced by wage labours.
11. Being Buddhist, the Khamptis were averse to family planning as it amounts to killing of a life. But in recent years educated Khamptis are found adopting family planning measures. (Behera, 1994:380). It is to be mentioned that elite section twists the traditional customary laws to their benefits.(ibid.346).

REFERENCES

Albrow, Martin (2000), *The Golden Age: State and Society beyond Modernity*. Stanford, C.A.: Stanford University Press.

Amin, Samir (2000), "Capitalism, Imperialism and Globalisation". In Rolland, C. (ed.), *The Political Economy of Imperialism: Critical Appraisal*. Boulder: Rowmen and Little Field. Pp.157-168.

Beck, Ulrich, A. Giddens, and Scot Lash (1994), *Reflexive Modernization:*

Politics, Tradition and Aesthetics in modern social order. Cambridge: Polity Press.

Behera, M.C. (1994), *Planning and Socio-Economic Development of the Tribals*. New Delhi: Commonwealth Publishers.

Bourdieu, P. (1985), "The Forms of Capita". In J.G.Richardson (ed). *The Hand Book of Theory and Research of the Sociology of Education*. New York: Greenwood. pp.241-258.

Castles, S. (2001), "Sudying Social Transformation", *International Political Science Review*, 22(1), pp.13-22.

Coleman, J.S. (1988), "Social Capital in Creation of Human Capital". *AJS*, Vol.94. pp. S-95 toS-120.

Elwin,V. (1965), *Democracy in NEFA*. Shillong: NEFA Administration.

Giddens, A. (1990), The Consequence of Modernity. Cambridge: Polity Press.

——(1991), *Modernity and Self-Identity: Self and Society in the late Modern Age*. Cambridge: Polity Press.

Guillen, M. (2001), "Is Globalization Civilizing, Destructive, or Feeble? A Critique of Five Key Debates in the Social Science Literature", *Annual Review of Sociology*. 27: 235-260.

Harris, R. and M. Seid. (2000), *Critical Perspectives on Globalization and Neoliberalism in the Developing countries*. Leiden: Brill.

Harris, R.L. (2002), "Globalization and Globalism in Latin America: Contending Perspectives", in *Journal of Latin American Perspectives*, issues 127, vol.29, No.9.

Held, David, Anthony G. McGrew, David Goldblatt, Jonathan Perraton (1999), *Global Transformation, Politics, Economics and Culture*, Stanford, CA: Stanford University Press.

Hirst, P. and G.Thomson (1996), *Globalisation in Question: The International Economy and Possibilities of Governance*, Cambridge M.A: Polity.

Mibang, T. & M.C. Behera, (eds.) (2006), Marriage and Culture-Reflections from Tribal Societies of Arunachal Pradesh,Vol-II. New Delhi: Mittal Publications.

Mibang, Tabang (2004). "Riglap (Reciprocal Cooperation) in Bilat-An Adi Village". In T. Mibang, & M.C.Behera (eds). 2004. *Dynamics of Tribal Villages in Arunachal Pradesh*, New Delhi: Mittal Publications. pp.115-121.

Pertin, Otem. (2009), *Rethinking Tribal Institutions*, New Delhi: Commonwealth Publishers.

Portes, A. (1998), "Social Capital: Its Origins and Applications in Modern Sociology". *Annual Review of Sociology*, 24(1), pp.1-24.

Putnam, R.D. (1995), "Bowling Alone: America's declining Social Capital". *Journal of Democracy*, 6:65-78.

——(1996), "The Strange Disappearance of Civic America". *American Prospect*, Vol.24, pp. 34-48.

Riba, Tomo (2004), "Reciprocity during House Construction: A Bond of Solidarity Among Galo Society-A Study in Dissi Village of West Siang District, Arunachal Pradesh". In T. Mibang, & M.C.Behera (eds). 2004. *Dynamics of Tribal Villages in Arunachal Pradesh*, New Delhi: Mittal Publications. pp.87-102.

Riba. Moji (2004a), "The Re-thinking of Context (Youth Dormitories in Wancho Villages)", in T. Mibang, & M.C.Behera (eds). 2004. *Dynamics of Tribal Villages in Arunachal Pradesh*, New Delhi: Mittal Publications. pp.103-114.

Robertson, Roland (1992), *Globalization: Social Theory and Global Culture*. London: Sage.

Roy, Sachin (1997), *Aspects of Padam Minyong Culture*. Itanagar: Directorate of Research. First published in 1960.

Wangsa, Chowang (2004), "Reflections on Village Solidarity in Family Rituals-A Study of Rangtuan in Kaimai Village of the Nocte". In T.Mibang, & M.C.Behera (eds). 2004. *Dynamics of Tribal Villages in Arunachal Pradesh*, New Delhi: Mittal Publications. pp.239-246.

22

SOCIAL TRANSFORMATION OF KINNAURA TRIBE: CHANGE AND CONTINUITY IN FAMILY AND MARRIAGE

O P Monga

'The aboriginals are the real "swadeshi" products or the oldest "inhabitants" of India, in whose presence everyone is a foreigner'
—*Mamoria, C B*

Facts that are not frankly faced have a habit of stabbing us in the back.
—*Sir Harold Baowdon*

INTRODUCTION

The term 'tribal community' in general parlance connotes people living in isolated surroundings from the rest of population adhering to their age old social and cultural life. In medieval English, the word 'tribe' means 'a primary aggregate of people claiming descent from a common ancestor'. The colonialists used this term to denote 'a race of people in a 'primitive or barbarous condition'-the *aborigines.* In Indian context, terms such as, *adivasi, vanajati, janajati, etc.*, are used for aboriginals. The tribes in India form the group of people who during the period of cultural evolution took refuge in the inaccessible parts of the country, lying in the hills and forests, to escape extermination. They were cut off from the mainstream of development process and lived in isolation for centuries with their culture, tradition and beliefs. (Sinha, 1993: 217). A number of scholars perceived that backwardness, social immobility, ignorance, illiteracy, superstitions, etc. have attributed to these communities. Having been cut off from the mainstream of socio-economic life for quite a long period, the social structure of tribal communities has remained almost stable which is considered one of the chief indicators of their backwardness. (Bose, 1971; Haimendorf, 1982; Chandra, 1992).

Indian society has experienced changes in all spheres of life during the last four or five decades, especially after independence. Over the years India's social, economic, political and cultural life have undergone both quantitative and qualitative changes. The transition in Indian life is generally attributed to the extensions of benefits of advancement in the field of science and technology at the grass-roots level. Other factors of change have been urbanization and industrialization, political transformation, establishment of effective communication and transport system and socio-economic development based on the principles of equality, liberty and fraternity. The pre-independence tribal India had attracted attention of the social workers, social reformers and, to some extent, administration hierarchy. However, after colonial period, an organized concern to protect the tribals against exploitation and to improve their socio-economic life came in a big way. For the last three-four decades they have become objects of central focus in national planning.

The tribal society in India is not as stagnant as has been perceived by many anthropologists and sociologists. (Pandey and Satyapathy, 1989; Mann and Mann, 1989). In the contemporary climate of development, the configurations of traditional and modernizing milieu are bound to affect one another. Now, acculturative influence has increased in its magnitude because of the planned and non-planned forces of change. These forces and processes of change have disrupted the uniformity in socio-cultural milieu of the tribals. In this context Vyas and Mann (1980) have marked three stages of tribal living in most of the tribal communities. These are: (1) those tribals who are sufficiently changed; (2) those in the process of transition; and (3) the others, who continue to confine themselves within the framework of traditionality.

The present exploration has drawn attention to the socio-cultural institutions with special reference to family and marriage signifying the directions of continuity and change in the tribal society. How is the dynamics of development influencing the socio-cultural profile of tribal communities? There are elements of stability and change. Every group comes to terms with the multifaceted reality in its own unique manner. There is no fixed pattern of blend. For Goodluck (1981), some may live in contradictions as happy mix and others as separate compartments and still others through assimilation.

The number of tribal groups in India runs into hundreds. Himachal Pradesh has a number of tribal communities, such as, Kinnauras, Lahaulas, Pangwalas, Swanglas, Khampas, Bhots, Jads, Lambs, Guzzars and Gaddis. (Mamgain, 1971; Bajpai,1981). As per Census of India 2001, out of 60.8 lakh persons in Himachal Pradesh, 2.4 lakh (4 per cent) are tribals (Table 1). It may be seen from the table of reference (Also Fig-1) that highest concentration of tribals is in the district of Lahaul-Spiti followed by Kinnaur and Chamba.

The national average of tribals is 12.50 per cent, that is, on the whole every thirteenth person in India is a tribal. In Himachal Pradesh, the Kinnaura is the single largest Scheduled Tribe (71.8%) inhabiting the district of Kinnaur (Table 3). It is the north-eastern frontier district of Himachal Pradesh and lies on both sides of the river Satluj. It is situated between 31°05′ 55" and 32° 05′ 20" north latitude and between 77° 45′ and 79° 50" east longitude. (Census of India,1981; Chib, 1984). It is bounded on the east by western Tibet; on the southern boundary it has Uttar Kashi district of U.P. and Rohru tehsil of Shimla district; on the north its boundary lies with Spiti

Table 1
Population of Tribes in Himachal Pradesh As Per Census 2001

Name of Districts	*Total Population*	*ST Population*	*% to Total Population*	*Density*
Bilaspur	3,40,885	9180	2.69	292
Chamba	460887	117569	25.51	71
Hamirpur	412700	155	.03	369
Kangra	1339030	1597	.11	233
Kinnaur	78334	56268	71.83	12
Kullu	351478	11351	3.23	69
Ll & S	33224	24238	72.95	2
Mandi	901304	10564	1.17	228
Shimla	722506	4112	.57	141
Sirmour	458593	5960	1.30	162
Solan	500557	3542	0.71	259
Una	448273	51	0.01	291
Total	6077900	244587	4.02	109

Source: Statistical Outline of Himachal Pradesh 2006-07, Economics & Statistics Department, Government of Himachal Pradesh, Shimla.

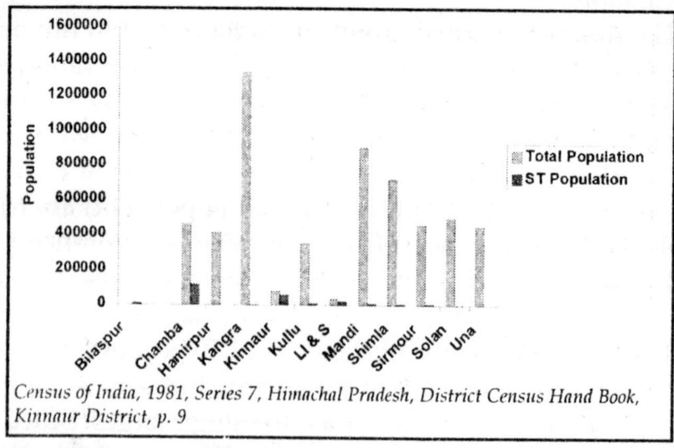

Census of India, 1981, Series 7, Himachal Pradesh, District Census Hand Book, Kinnaur District, p. 9

Fig. 1: Populatin of Tribes in Himachal Pradesh As Per Census 2001

region; and on the western boundary lie Rampur and Kullu. It is marked by precipitous sky-high mountains which are almost covered with snow most of the times. The elevation of peaks varies between 5,180 and 6,770 metres. The district has beautiful valleys, namely Sutlej Valley, Hangrang Valley, Ropa Valley and Sangla Valley. Climatically, it has long winter from

October to May and soil contains minerals such as copper, china clay, gemstones, mica, pyrites, silver, quartz, etc. It has typical flora and fauna. The forests consist of trees, such as, deodar, pine, kail, blue pine, kharsu oak, etc. The fauna of this region consists of a number of animals namely, wild sheep, goat, *goral*, musk deer, *tahr*, black bear, snow leopard, Tibetan wolf, leopard cat, *monal*, snow cock, snow pigeon, *chukor*, *koklas* pheasant, fishes, reptiles, etc.

Table 2
District-wise Literacy Rate-2001 Census

Name of Districts	*Literacy Rate (%)*	*Males*	*Females*
Bilaspur	77.8	86.0	69.5
Chamba	62.9	76.4	48.8
Hamirpur	82.5	90.2	75.7
Kangra	80.1	87.5	73.0
Kinnaur	75.2	84.3	64.4
Kullu	72.9	84.0	60.9
L & S	73.1	82.8	60.7
Mandi	75.2	85.9	64.8
Shimla	79.1	87.2	70.1
Sirmour	70.4	79.4	60.4
Solan	76.6	84.8	66.9
Una	80.4	87.7	73.2
H P Total	76.5	85.3	67.4

Source: Statistical Outline of Himachal Pradesh, 2006-07, Economics & Statistics, Department, Government of Himachal Pradesh, Shimla.

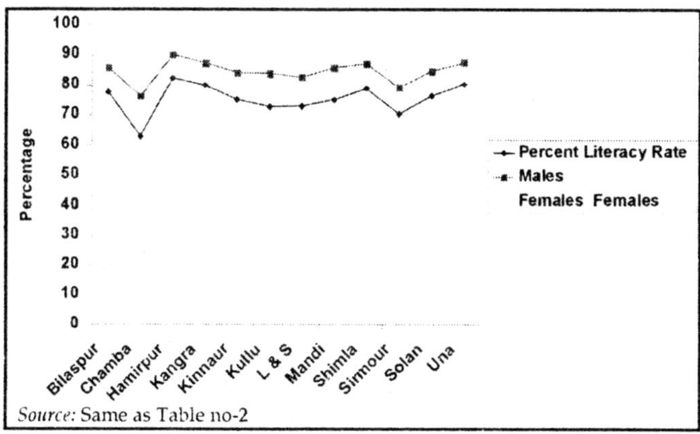

Source: Same as Table no-2

Fig. 2: District-wise Literacy Rate-2001 Census

Table 3
Tribal Districts, Population and Literacy- 2001 Census

Tribal Area	*Population*		*Literacy*		
	Persons	*Percentage to TP*	*Male*	*Female*	*Total*
Kinnaur	56,268	71.8	74.89	56.20	66.27
Lahaul & Spiti	24,238	74.2	74.60	52.35	64.67
Chamba	41,884	79.3	63.95	40.29	52.64
Total	1,22,390	04.0	71.18	50.54	61.60

Source: Statistical Booklet, Tribal Areas, Himachal Pradesh 2003, Department of Economics & Statistics, Government of Himachal Pradesh, Shimla.

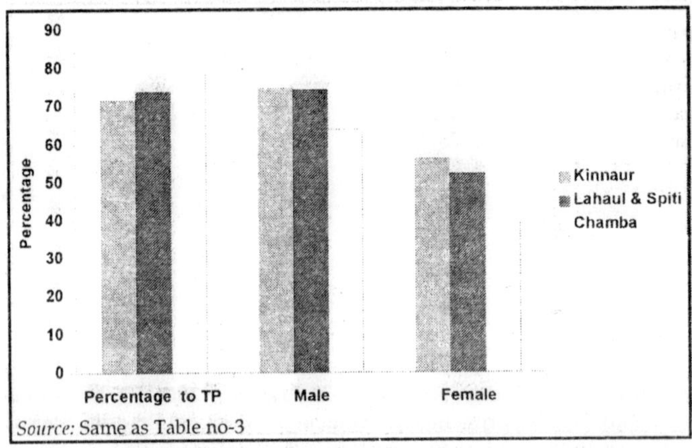

Source: Same as Table no-3

Fig. 3: Tribal Districts, Population and Literacy-2001 Census

According to the Census of India, 2001, population of Kinnaur district was 78.9 thousand persons, thus, having a density of 12 persons per sq. km. Interestingly, there is no urban population in this region. The sex-ratio (0-6 years) is 979 females per 1000 males as against 896 for the state as a whole. The general sex-ratio is 857 against 968. Literacy percentage is 75.2 (males 84.03 and females 64.4) as against the states average 76.50 (Table 3).

The entire population is categorized as Scheduled Castes or Tribes. Traditionally they have been cultivators. Their other occupations have been, such as, weaving and spinning, grazing, carpentry, silver smithy, blacksmithy and metalware manufacturing and trade. Some people are engaged in plantations and orchards. Now-a-days most of them work as labourers in different sectors of economy. Hindustan-Tibet Road is the main line of communication.

Historically, the Kinnauras are the aboriginals of Himalyan region. The socio-cultural life of people of Kinnaura is quite strong and unique as it exhibits signs of tribal, 'semi-civilized' and 'uncivilized'. The *puranas, jatakas* and other literary works referred Kinnauras as *'demigods'*. They are also said to be horse-mouthed and were known as *Hayavadana, Turangavadana, Ashwamukha, Mayu, etc.* This shows they were fond of horses. They are very hospitable and treat their guests with respect and loving care. People in general are soft spoken, peace-loving, hard working and deeply religious. All are Hindus except some who follow Buddhism. The *'shiva, vishnu* and *kali'* are the main deities of worship. Census of India, 2001 also registered some Christians, Muslims and Jains there. But Kinnauras differ from others linguistically, culturally and economically. They speak nine different dialects, but the Kinnauri called *'Homskad'* is the language of about seventy per cent of them. People of Kinnaur believe in many gods and goddesses. Temple gods knit them together in a kind of ritual relationship. They make all efforts to avoid Devta's annoyance. Through a Pujari they often seek permission and approval of *'Devta'* for their socio-cultural conduct. They celebrate fairs, festivals and *melas* with great enthusiasm and active participation. *Ukhyang, phaguli* and *dakarni* fairs are celebrated all over Kinnaur. They are fond of singing and dancing. Mask dances and other dances, such as, *jatru kayang, jubro* dance, *thar kayang, katkapa*, etc. are organized during fairs and festivals. All can participate in these dances. Due to cold climate they use woollen clothes. The gents wear shirts (*chamu-kurti*), long coats (*chhubha*) and pyjama (*suttan*) whereas ladies wear sari (*dhori*), blouse (*cholis*) and *chanali* or shawl. Both men and women wear woollen cap called *thepang*. On the occasion of joy they decorate it with flowers. Women also wear ornaments made of silver and gold. Kinnauras are mostly non-vegetarians and their staple food is wheat, *ogla*, *phafra* and barley. They use local liquor called '*ghanti*'. (Mamgain, 1971; Negi, 1976).

Kinnaura tribe is caste based community. There are four main castes which are broadly divided into upper and lower castes (see Parry, 1979). Both castes speak different languages and sing different songs. The former consists of Khaushias or Rajputs or Kanets or Negi and the latter, or the Chamangs, the Damangs and the Ores. The higher castes are further divided into a number of sub-castes. Except Rajputs, other three castes are called scheduled castes. The caste system is very rigid and Rajputs occupy top position, and followed by the Ores, the Damangs and the Chamangs. The Rajputs are a landowning caste and carries a higher social status. The Ores are carpenters, the Damangs are blacksmiths and silversmiths and the Chamangs are weavers and leather workers. There exists Jajmani system known as *Binnanas* and untouchability is widely practised. The Ores consider themselves superior to the Chamangs and the Domangs and do not enter into matrimonial alliance with them and also do not eat and drink with them. Restrictions between higher caste and lower castes with regard to dining, inter-marrying and social interaction are based on traditional Indian caste system. Interestingly, in social hierarchy the Brahmin caste is conspicuous by its absence.

Like in other parts of the state, the people of Kinnaur are also experiencing substantial changes. Inception of the Five-Year-Plans, particularly the Tribal Development Programmes, coupled with planned schemes of change, urbanization and effective network of communication, opening of educational and health institutions has created change-prone atmosphere for the tribal people of Kinnaur. As a result, there have been changes in their socio-cultural life, though there may be variations. Temporary influx of tourists, traders, and government establishments has resulted in a wider interaction with outside culture.

Literacy, which is the single effective indicator of change, has increased from 27.70 per cent in 1971 to 75.2 in 2001 (Table 2, Fig-2). Literacy among females has increased from

10.35 per cent in 1971 to 64.04 per cent during the same period. In contemporary Kinnaura community, it can be observed that educated youths no longer like to adhere to traditional occupations and aspire for white collar jobs outside Kinnaur and to a great extent have proved successful. The massive road building and power projects, government establishments and non-governmental agencies, now provide employment to Kinnauras at their native place. This has restricted their movement out of home for longer durations. Jajmani system is also changing as the artisans have started demanding cash for services. Those women and men who have moved out of Kinnaur either for education or trade, or have taken up white collar jobs seem to have imbibed new outlook of life. Some of them have married and established independent families, and have, thus, bid goodbye to polygyny and polyandry alike. Kapadia (1988) demonstrated how the institutions of marriage and family are changing in its structure and function under the impact of urbanization. Mita (1994) while commenting on the feminism, family and social change held today everyone directly or indirectly looks upon family as panacea for all social evils. Implicit in this is that social structure of any community draws its strength from healthy development of the family. Educationally, the Scheduled Tribes of Himachal Pradesh, especially in Kinnaur, Lahaul, Bharmour, Pangi and Spiti have, in that order, taken remarkable strides forward. Much of this progress is well reflected in the jobs of various kinds held by candidates from these areas (Negi, 1998). The transition in caste-system, economic life and culture is likely to influence structure of the family of Kinnauras. The character of agriculture has changed. Now vegetables, such as, potatoes, cabbage, peas and ginger are grown and marketed along with apples, pears and *chilgoza*. Mann and Mann (1989) reported transition in cultural milieu of the Indian tribal people under the influence of forces of change.

It is only after independence that processes of economic development, substantial in nature, began to make their impact and brought about changes in attitudes, values and orientations of the people. (Negi, 1998). However, Singh (1973) observed that the induction of democratic polity which is, undoubtedly, a modernizing force, the traditional features such as principle of hierarchy and charismatic elitism still dominates the tribal society and politics. Singh (1985) remarked that with the end of colonial system the relative isolation of tribal communities in India was pushed behind as they were brought into the mainstream of the new administrative set up, policy and programmes.

In this backdrop, an attempt has been made to understand change and continuity in family and marriage in Kinnaura tribals.

As described above, Kinnaura community is witnessing change in its socio-economic life under the influence of '*development forces*', therefore, to understand change and continuity in various components of social institutions of family and marriage, an exploratory study was conducted.

This paper only presents some of the preliminary observations. These are based on author's field experiences, observations and analysis of information culled through in-depth informal discussions with fifty men and women hailing from Kinnaur district and residing in Shimla due to their employment, education and business activities. These are also based on first hand experience gained from participation in family and social functions. Sharma (1984) emphasized that the dynamics of family among the tribal can be understood in terms of indicators, such as, breakdown of joint family, marriage, status of women, choice of number of children, infant and maternal mortality. This approach may help us to make a deeper understanding of dynamics of marriage and family at micro-level. Khubchandani, (1992) held that socio-cultural indicators are significant to understand directions of continuity and change in the tribal society.

FAMILY AND MARRIAGE: CONTINUITY AND CHANGE

Traditionally, the Kinnauras live in joint families. They are a patriarchal, matrilineal, patrilocal and polyandrous tribe. Socially, Kinnauras, especially women are hospitable and courteous. Women are hard working and besides domestic chores, they actively participate in agricultural and horticultural activities. The Kinnaura woman holds an important place in the family. The unity of the family depends upon her. She is generally consulted in all domestic matters and she actively participates in decision -making. To keep her happy all husbands pool their income and she in turn looks after their comforts. It is she who is a cementing force in the family. The Kinnauras have throughout been utter strangers to Purdah. In Kinnaur chastity and sexual morality were exemplarily high; there was free mixing of the opposite sexes at all ages and in all walks of life with perfect innocence being taken for granted. (Negi, 1976: 35). This shows that women enjoy an almost equal status to men except that they do not have right in inheritance.

They follow the system of arranged marriages. The custom of polyandry is attributed to Pandavas who had one common wife, Droupdi and they are believed to have lived in this area during exile. In Kinnaur free-mixing of the sexes is accepted as social norm from ancient times. The four forms of marriage pre1valent in Kinnaur are:

1. *Janetang* or *Janekang* – the socially arranged marriage or the normal and big marriage;
2. *Bennang, Damchlshish, Danatangshish, Benrabchish* or *Gashish*–the love marriage;
3. *Daroshang* or *Dab dob, Myam Shalema, Ashish* or *Huchish*–the whisking away of the intended bride or marriage by capture or when marriage is performed after elopement of the bride; and
4. *Haar* or *Harri*–enticing away someone's wife or remarriage of a divorced women.

In all these forms or methods of mate selection, negotiations start from the bridegroom's side. Negi (1976) pointed out that along with polyandry, polygyny and monogamy have also been equally accepted customs, one or other form being adopted as dictated by circumstances. Polygamous alliances have been the lowest in incidence among all these three forms of marriage.

Inheritance of property is through the male line. In case of death of one of the husbands, his share of property is inherited by the surviving husbands. In case of division of the polyandrous group the rule of *Jethang* is observed, i.e. the eldest has the right to choose the piece of agricultural land as per his choice. The ancestral house goes to the youngest. The rest of the property is equally divided among the brothers. The girls do not inherit property as the Hindu Succession Act, 1956 is not applicable to Kinnaur. People of Kinnaur follow customary laws pertaining to their social and economic matters.

The sex relations between husbands and wife are so arranged that it does not give rise to any kind of annoyance or conflict. However, exceptions may also be there. The reciprocity between wife and husbands is the binding force which keeps the family intact. Determining of parentage is also very simple. The eldest husband is known as elder father (*teg-boba*) or social father and the others as younger fathers (*gotto*). In case of division of family, the wife names the father of her different children. The eldest brother is the head (*karta*) of family. He is responsible for fulfilling economic needs of the family. The pooling of income by all, equal sharing, consumption, cohesiveness, etc., are some of the features of joint family among Kinnauras. Hence, a polyandrous family cannot exist if such arrangement at any moment of time is not acceptable to the parties or members who are the pillars of this system. It may be applicable even in such circumstances where independent households have been formed.

Over the past few decades some significant changes have occurred in Kinnaur society. These are: first, the predominant joint family structure has started breaking down towards nuclear units at an alarming rate as 27 per cent of respondents expressed this. Education and employment were cited as main reasons for this shift. Due to spread of literacy, educated persons find employment either at their native place or outside. Even a significant number of uneducated ones also find employment at local level in massive power, tele-communication, education, health and road projects. This has changed traditional outlook of life of the people especially of younger generation. There is now a growing tendency to establish independent households among them. However, those who have moved out of this region for employment, majority of them have established their independent families at their workplace. They do not pool their income with the paternal family. Easy divorce is another reason which is inherent in the system of marriage. The ties of marriage are not very permanent as it seems. In a polyandrous family, a woman who no longer wants to have relations with all her husbands and intends to move away, takes a "twig" in her hands and breaks it before her husband on a scheduled time and date in presence of the elders and becomes free from marital bonds. A male can also move out of polyandrous family and can remarry. In this case, one has to forfeit one's right in property. There have been instance of an eldest brother who was educated and employed, did not marry to avoid sharing of his wife, till all his younger brothers were married. This makes one to believe in breaking of the joint family, weakening of clan cohesion and establishment of nuclear households. But barring a few exceptions, those establishing out of traditional bonds, generally participate in all important family functions, fairs and festivals indicating they still respect their traditional socio-cultural system. Those marriages celebrated in urban areas never shun traditional singing and dancing. Community bhoj or *'dham'* is held after marriage at one's native village also in purely traditional way. This reflects continuance of some components of family and marriage.

Educated and employed youth no longer likes to adhere to the traditional custom of polyandry. Both boys and girls prefer monogamous marriages. There are instances of Kinnaura men working on good positions and remaining bachelor throughout their life. This indicates their allegiance to traditional social system and in other words, continuance of social norms. But, majority of those, who live in Kinnaur and engaged in agriculture and horticulture or traditional occupations, still adore polyandry. They consider it advantageous and in consonance to their *'dharma'*. This indicates that joint family system has started changing but persists at large in reality and in their psyche.

'Janekang' marriage is not only recognized from every angle but is also replacing all other forms of marriage in this region. In other words, *Bennang, Dabdab* and *Har* marriages are on the decline. Again this is attributed to changing socio-economic circumstances. Among the educated and employed the swing is in favour of monogamy. It is a healthy sign from point of view of social development, otherwise, due to polyandry, Kinnaura girls may have to remain unmarried or become nuns in Buddhist monasteries. The changes which are taking place in marriage rites may be significant for comprehensive perception of continuity and change in family and marriage, but these have not been covered here.

Some of us view polyandry as sexual exploitation of women and are, therefore, tempted to accord them a lower status. It may be so, but there is no single yardstick to measure status. A practice, which appears exploitative to us, may not be so to others and Kinnauras themselves. It is certainly true that present educational and employment opportunities for tribal women in Himachal Pradesh, will go a long way in ameliorating their social status in future. Kinnauras known for the cohesive and well knit family structures are now experiencing a new phenomenon. The marital conflicts have emerged in Kinnaura families. This was evident from over one hundred cases of marital conflict registered with the Family Counselling Centre, *Reckong Peo.* (Attri, 1994). Increasing marital conflict in Kinnaura community is crucial to ponder upon not only for social scientists but for all those who are directly or indirectly concerned with the welfare of tribal society. The family has been recognized as an important agency of social, political and cultural change.

In sum, it can be pointed out that over the past few decades Kinnaura society has given way to nuclearization of family structure and favourable attitude towards monogamous marriages to some extent. This has been due to extension of education, employment opportunities and other benefits of developmental programmes. But against all efforts of the state and other agencies to include Kinnaura tribe in the mainstream seem to be pushed behind in the context of their historical social-cultural milieu. Changes in Kinnauras' family structure and marriage and simultaneous persistence of important components of these two institutions attest to this fact. It seems that Kinnaura tribals persist with a parallel system, managing their lifestyles through a mix, on one hand linked with traditional family ties, and on the other hand inculcating components of modern culture.

REFERENCES

Attri, A.L. (1994), Family and Counselling: A Study of Husband-Wife Relationship. *Unpublished M.Phil Dissertation*, Shimla, H.P. University.

Bajpai, S.C. (1981), *Kinnaur in the Himalayas : Mythology and Modernity.* New Delhi: Concept Publishing Co.

Bose, N.K. (1971), *Tribal Life in India.* New Delhi: National Book Trust.

Census of India (1991), Himachal Pradesh, Series 9,Government of India.

Statistical Outline of Himachal Pradesh (1992), Department of Economics and Statistics, Government of Himachal Pradesh, Shimla.

Chandra, R. (1992), *Highlanders of North-Western Himalayas.* New Delhi: IIP.

Chib, S.S. (1984), *Kinnauras of the Trans Himalayas.* New Delhi: Ess Publication.

Haimendorf, Christoph von Fürer (1982), *Tribes of India – The Struggle for Survival.* Delhi: Oxford University Press.

Goodluck, J. (1981), "Deciding on a Development Philosophy", *Adult Education and Development, Vol.17*, Bonn, 43-46.

Kapadia, K.M. (1988), *Marriage and Family in India.* Calcutta: Oxcord University Press.

Khubchandani, L.M. (1992), *Tribal Identity: A Language and Communication Perspective.* New Delhi: Indus Publishing Company.

Mamgain, M.D. (1971), *Kinnaur District Gazetteer.* Shimla: Government of Himachal Pradesh.

Mann, R.S. and K. Mann (1989), *Tribal Culture and Change*. New Delhi: Mittal Publications.

Mamoria, C.B. (1957), *Tribal Demography in India*. Allahabad: Kitab Mahal.

Miri, Mrinal (1993), *Continuity and Change in Tribal Society*. Shimla: IIAS

Mita, Radhakrishnan (1994), "Feminism Family and Social Change: Myths and Models," *Social Action*, 44:4, pp. 34-51.

Negi, D.B. (1998), *Tribal Development and Social Change: Some Issues*. In Gupta et. al (eds), *Tribal Development: Appraisal & Alternatives*. NewDelhi: Indus Publishing Company.

Negi, T.S. (1976), *Scheduled Tribes of Himachal Pradesh : A Profile*.Shimla:Negi

——(1998), *Tribes of Himachal Pradesh: Past, Present and Future*. In Gupta et. al (eds), Tribal Development: Appraisal & Alternatives. New Delhi: Indus Publishing Company.

Pandey, K.S. and P.C. Satyapathy (1989), *Tribal India*. New Delhi: P.C. Ashish Publishing House,

Parry, Jonathan P. (1979), *Caste and Kinship in Kangra*. London: Routledge and Kegan.

Sharma, B.D. (1984), *Planning for Tribal Development*. New Delhi: Prachin Prakashan.

Singh, K.S. (1985), *Tribal Society in India: An Antrho-Historical Perspective*. New Delhi: Manohar Publishers.

Singh, Yogendra (1973), *Modernizing of Indian Tradition*. New Delhi: Thomson Press India Ltd.

Sinha, U.P. (1993), "The Demographic Situation of Tribal Population in India". In Mirnal Miri (ed.), *Continuity and Change in Tribal Society*. Shimla: IIAS.

Vyas, N.N., R.S. Mann (1980), *Indian Tribes in Transition*. Delhi: Rawat Publishers.

23

GLOBALISATION AND RICE MYTHS OF NORTH-EAST INDIA

Rabindranath Sarma

Globalisation in its literal sense is the process of transformation of local or regional phenomena into global ones. It can be described as a process by which the people of the world are unified into a single society and function together. Cultural globalisation refers to the growth in the exchange of cultural practices between nations and peoples. Although, this is a process that has undoubtedly occurred for thousands of years, economic and political globalisation has enhanced the process enormously in recent decades. In addition, many analysts point to the way new technologies and their exploitation such as commercial air travel, satellite television, mass telecommunications and the internet have created a world where billions now consume identical cultural products–such as pop music, soap opera and sporting events–and employ cultural practices they would never otherwise have encountered – such as foreign food preparations and foreign words and phrases. The discussion above gives us an idea about an important feature of globalisation, i.e. globalising the locals. This understanding pervades through the present paper that tries to locate rice myths of north-east India in the context of globalisation.

THE NORTH-EAST INDIA AND THE PEOPLE

North-East India is the home land to a number of ethnic communities and every community bears its own tradition, identity and over all, folk elements in its own culture. If North-East India happens to be 'the anthropologist's paradise'- an expression frequently used in academic circles...this region could, with equal or even greater justification, be called 'the folklorist's paradise'. (Datta 1994: 2). North-East India consists of seven states, with plains and hills, which include Assam, Meghalaya, Manipur, Mizoram, Tripura, Nagaland and Arunachal Pradesh. However, Sikkim has been included in 2002 with reference to functional coverage of NEC.

The population of Assam is made up of Assamese Hindus among whom, notwithstanding an Aryan veneer, Indo-Mongoloid elements are decidedly strong, both in terms of racial as well as cultural traits. Various tribal communities–mostly of Indo-Mongoloid Tibeto-Burman affiliation in different stages of acculturation, integration and assimilation with the Assamese-Hindu fold live in the hills and plains of the state. The more prominent among such communities are the Boros, the Rabhas, the Misings, the plain Tiwas (Lalungs), the Sonowals and the Deuris in the plains, and the Karbis, the hill Tiwas (Lalungs) and the Dimasas in the hills. While Saivism and Saktism, including Tantricism, have had strong roots here in the past, the influence of neo-Vaishnavism spearheaded by the great saint-reformer Sankaradeva (1449-1568) is deep and pervasive among the local Hindu population. The local Muslim population is also sizable in proportion and their place in and contribution to the composite socio-cultural make-up has been significant. The linguistic front presents a similar pattern of 'co-operative conglomeration'. Assamese, a modern Indo-Aryan language with a rich literary heritage, is the premier language of the state. On the one hand, it has taken on various features from the local non-Aryan speeches, and on the other, it has influenced the local tribal speeches in various ways.

Again, most of the tribal groups in the plains retain their respective own languages, a sizeable proportion of them have adopted Assamese as their mother tongue, and most others use this languages as their 'second language' with the utmost ease and naturalness. In more recent times the demographic content of the state has been considerably altered by the large-scale influx and settlement of some important ethnic groups who have adopted Assam as their homeland and who have identified themselves with the broader Assamese society. (Datta 1994: 4).

In Meghalaya, the Khasi, the Jaintia and the Garo are major tribal groups. Besides these groups some smaller groups are like the Rabha, the Boro, the Hajong, the Marngar, the Miris, the Biate, etc. are found. All these groups are Mongoloid groups and they retain their own language (/dialect), culture, tradition etc. Still some Aryan people are found for economic reasons. Christianity predominate this state except some few pockets which still adhere to the indigenous faith.

Manipur is another state where the Meitei is the dominant group. They speak Meitei-lol language. Chaitanya sect of Vaishnavism is found among them. Some Meitei have converted to Islam also. Besides Meitei people, 29 Naga-Kuki groups occupy the hill areas of Manipur.

Mizoram is another state of North-East India, where the Lushais, the Lakhers, the Kukis, the Chakmas, the Hmars, the Pawis, the Raltes, the Paites, and the Thadou inhabit. Lushai dialect is dominant and is known as Dulien. Christianity is common and Buddhism is found among the Chakmas.

Tripura, is a small state with Indo-Mongoloid and Aryan people. The Tipras, the Rheangs, the Hrangkhols, the Murasings etc. are Indo-Mongoloid people. Of the indigenous population of Tripura, the Tipras or Tripuris constitute the most prominent group and they are supposed to be the oldest inhabitants having links with some of the Bodo groups of Assam.

The inhabitants of the Nagaland are known as Nagas who are believed to be among the earliest migrants from south-east Asia to North-East India. There are more than twenty Naga groups and sub-groups, the more well-known among them are the Angamis, the Aos, the Semas, the Lhotas, the Konyaks, the Chakesangs, the Sangtams, the Changs, the Yimchungers, the Zeliangs and the Rengmas. Nagamese is a kind of pidgin Assamese that is used as lingua franca among different Naga groups. At present most of the Nagas have adopted Christianity, though as they are tradition loving people, still retaining more or less the distinctive Naga way of life.

Arunachal Pradesh is made up of over 82 groups and sub-groups of Indo-Mongoloid origin. These groups have their distinctive social and cultural identities, speaking different languages and dialects of the Tibeto-Burman family and following different beliefs, customs and traditions. Out of all groups some are the Adis, the Apatanis, the Nyishis, the Khamptis, the Shingphos, the Sherdukpens, the Monpas, the Buguns (Khowas), the Hrussos (Akas), the Dhammais (Mijis), the Wanchos, the Noctes, etc. Buddhism, Hinduism, Donyi-Poloism and Christianity are found among Arunachalee groups.

RICE CULTURE AND NORTH-EAST INDIA

Rice is life for the people of North-East India. It is the grain that has shaped the history, culture, diet, and economy of the people. Many of them sleep on rice straw, drink rice liquor and offer rice to their Gods. The growth stage of the rice crop marks the passage of time and season. For the people of this region, the day begins with morning rice and ends with evening rice. In this part of the world, rice is not just a cereal; it is the root of civilization.

Rice taken becomes the essence of life for these people. It permeates all aspects of life. Rice is in their tradition, folklore, ritual, and even language. For the people of North-East India, life without rice is unthinkable. Yet rice is almost always taken for granted.

Rice cultivation has a central role in the culture of the people of the North-East India. Here, North-East Indian culture, especially in rural areas has developed around and shaped by rice cultivation. It has always been the nucleus of their life. Its importance is celebrated by religious and secular festivals organized around the planting and harvesting seasons. Many of the cultural festivals coincide with the planting and harvesting seasons and rice plays an important symbolic role in many religious festivals. There are folk songs and dances about rice ploughing, sewing, harvesting and dehusking. The happiest time is, of course, harvesting. In the past, when machines were not available, villagers would gather together to harvest a plot of field, because harvesting was highly labour intensive, also late harvest would damage the crop Now-a-days, many traditional and cultural practices related to rice and rice cultivation still exist, although they are declining.

RICE: AN IMPORTANT ANCIENT CROP

Evidence of rice cultivation can be traced back to the period around 2960 B.C. at Thailand. This is even earlier than in China (around 2737 B.C.) and in India (around 1957 B.C.). Since then, rice cultivation has spread all over the world. Over the centuries, rice has shaped the landscape, culture and character of the Asian peoples. Any one looking behind the sweeping beauty of the hills and plains of North-East India will find societies whose customs and rituals are inextricably tied to the rice they grow. Wherever the crop has been planted, festivals, traditions, rituals, and languages celebrate its growth and harvest. Even those for whom rice is an everyday sight, something magical–more like spiritual -still radiates from the depths of the green fields.

The people of North-East India believes that they are the India's first rice cultivators, carried rice with them wherever they went during their early migrations throughout Southeast Asia, South Asia, and China. In fact their sole concern, when choosing land on which to settle, appears to have been whether or not there was enough water to plant rice. It is established by the people who seem to have a spiritual connection with the grain which is revealed in their day-to-day activities.

RICE RITUALS

Rice is the only crop that farmers arrange to give 'blessings' at every stage of its life, from planting to harvesting. It is done to boost morale and smooth over worries, with the hope that the produce will be abundant and will ultimately bring joy, happiness and stability to the farmers, their families and the community as a whole. Thus, the various rituals of rice are closely related to both the community way of life and their religious beliefs. They emphasize the need to live together in harmony and to be mutually supportive. In addition, such rituals also play an important role on the village economy that involves rice production, distribution and exchange. Some examples are the following:

Rituals for Rain Making: They aim at requesting the power that to bless the lives of the farmers so that they be free from harm and/or calamities and achieve prosperity throughout the year, and more specifically to ask for rains before they prepare the land for planting and also throughout the crop season. Varying forms of the Rain-Pleading Ceremony are practised in the villages of the plains, primarily because in the rain-fed rice area (i.e., non-irrigated area). *Bhekuli-biya* (frog marriage) is a ritual in which marriage between two frogs is performed with elaborate ceremonies, including the singing of songs, in an effort to bring down rains at the time of drought. The concerned songs are called *bhekuli-biyar geet.* Various magical activities and rituals are performed to control the weather. Bhekuli-biya or frog-marriage is such a mimic act performed by the village womenfolk when there is no rain for days together during the months of cultivation.

Rituals for Protecting the Rice Crop: These rituals mark the end of transplanting. They give offerings to ancestral and wandering spirits to ask them to protect and nurture the rice crop towards a plentiful harvest. They also pay homage to the Rice Mother like the Ka Lukhmi by the Khasi people, to the Mainao by the Boros, to Joban by the Noctes, to the Mailungma by the Tripuris, the Lijaba by the Ao Nagas, etc. to gain protection of the rice fields throughout the whole season.

Rituals for Bountiful Harvest: This is done to show respect to 'rice' in order that the harvest will be abundant and so that both farmers and their animals will be free from harm during the harvesting process. The rite is also a thanksgiving ceremony to the Rice Mother, as well as an apology if she was disturbed during plowing, planting and harvesting. In some cases, it also celebrates the completion of all the hard work for the current crop and to wish for a plentiful harvest in the next crop.

RICE GODDESSES

In most rice-growing countries of Asia, people believe the spirit of rice resides in the Rice Mother or the Rice Goddess. In Meghalaya, the Rice Goddess of the Khasis is the Ka Lukhmi. (Kharmawphlang 2002 I: 47). The Mainao of the Boros, the Joban of the Noctes, the Mailungma of the Tripuris, the Lijaba of the Ao Nagas (Kharmawphlang 2002 II: 21-22) etc. are treated in similar ways-respectful and protective. Just as mothers give food and milk to their children, so the Rice Goddess gives her body and soul to everyone. She is the goddess who protects the paddy crop and farmers, in particular, hold various rituals that demonstrate their deep respect and gratitude to her, at varying stages throughout the growing season. They believe this will bring them prosperity and wealth. The farmers believe that whoever tills and cultivates the soil ought to worship the Rice Mother, for she will endow him/her with health and wealth. Whoever does not worship her will suffer hunger, sickness and poverty. A man who is careful, whether in reaping, threshing or pounding paddy, and does not allow any grains to be scattered over the ground, will be happy and wealthy. If no care is taken and the paddy is allowed to be trodden over or disturbed by animals, or left over in a damp place, the Mother will be angry and leave the careless owner.

RICE AS FOOD

Rice has been the staple food of the people of North-East India from ancient time. People eat both glutinous and non-glutinous rice, prepared as meals, as snacks, and as drinks. Numerous ways of consuming rice have evolved over time, from the normal way of cooking rice to boiling to steaming and to grilling in bamboo. Also evolved are the many different sizes and shapes of 'rice pots,' which are dependent on the particular way that rice is cooked. Rice is generally eaten with varying kinds of 'dishes', made of meat, vegetables, and other condiments.

Snacks like *pitha* in Assamese, *spitha* in Boro, *putharo* in Khasi etc. are used in their festivals, rites and rituals. Rice beer is another important food item of the people of North-East India. It is known as *jumai-jou* among the Boros, *Horalang* and *horarak* among the Karbis, *zu* among the Tiwas and the Hmars, *apong* among the Mishings, *zonga* among the Rabhas, *ijaduijang* among the Rengma Nagas, *su* among the Garos, *sujhen* among the Deuris etc. Rice beer is more or less compulsory in every rites or ritual and festivals. Most of the people offer rice beer to their guests. Some of these people believe that rice–beer has a divine origin.

RICE IN MUSIC

Songs and music are part and parcel of people of North-East India. *Bihu* song of the Assam plains, Mishing *Bihu* song, Deuri *Bihu* song, *Krud Ksing* song of the Khasis etc. are the finest example of this. Folk songs can be related to the stages of rice farming, from the beginning of the rice growing season until after harvest. These songs are illustrative of their simplicity, nature-loving character, and way of life and over all their world view.

DOCUMENTATION OF RICE MYTHS

Though North-East India is rich in the content of Rice Myths tradition, it is observed that many elements have already disappeared from the society. But somehow, some still exist among the people and some are already documented. And in this regard, the different agencies like Tribal Research Institute of different states, the Department of Research and some academic departments like NEACTAF of Tezpur University, PROFRA of North-Eastern Hill University have collected those materials.

RICE MYTHS AND MASS MEDIA

In the present day world mass media is taking a great role to disseminate the folklore material in various ways through Radio, Television, News papers, Magazines, etc. Globalisation is the process of transformation of local phenomena into global ones. It can be described as a process by which the people of the world are unified into a single society and function together. So, mass media is giving an opportunity to make some folklore element to get its position in Global World.

CONCLUSION

The influence of rice production in the North-East India is profound. Rice fills an enormous role in the lives, livelihoods, food security and Culture of the people of North-East India and it reflects in their day-to-day activities. The continuing process concerning the culture and tradition leaves from the creative imagination and their assimilation and adaptation to produce unique performances. At present though tradition of Rice Myths is gradually disappearing, still some elements have remained which need to be documented by different academic/research organizations. Mass media has taken a great role to document and disseminate this tradition in the present day world. After all, in the context of Rice Myths of North-East India, Globalization is playing a great role.

REFERENCES

Datta, B. (1994), *Handbook of Folklore Material of North- East India.* Guwahati: ABILAC.

——(1999), *Folkloric Foragings in India's North-East.* Guwahati: ABILAC.

Kharmawphalng, D.L. (2002), *Narratives of North East India, Vol.I&II* Shillong: PROFRA Publications, NEHU.

Websites

http://en.wikipedia.org/wiki/Globalization

http://www.editiondesign.com/fgf/knowledge/article007.html

SECTION–VII

Rethinking the Context

24

ON TRIBAL ECONOMY AND SOCIETY[1]

Vinay Kumar Srivastava

I

In a seminar that the Department of Anthropology, Andhra University, Visakhapatnam (Andhra Pradesh), had organized (on 30 and 31 January 2009) on tribal development with special reference to the problems and involvement of women, one of the sessions was devoted to listening to the voices of the tribal women, some fifteen of them who had come from villages contiguous with Visakhapatnam, two of them with their breast-feeding children. This certainly was not the first time that I saw tribespersons attending anthropology seminars, the focus of which was tribal problem and its solution, but certainly the practice of inviting the *subjects* of one's study to listen to the varied deliberations on them is quite uncommon in academic circles.[2]

Not all the tribal women, who had come to attend the seminar, spoke. Six of them came to the dais, but only three addressed the well-attended gathering, one of them with exemplary eloquence.[3]

The first submission of these women was that their land (the 'tribal land'), which has since been alienated, should be returned to them. They also noted a rise in the cases of marriage between tribal women and non-tribal men, as a result of which the land that the woman gets from her parents, either as a part of inheritance or gift, or is able to buy from a co-tribal, is appropriated by her husband. In this way, land slips out of tribal control.[4] Being simple and gullible, tribal women were unable to sense the nefarious ulterior motives of their non-tribal husbands. The women categorically stated that irrespective of the circumstances of acquiring the land and the cordial relations a tribal woman might have with her husband, tribal land should never be transferred to non-tribal persons. They strongly argued in favour of women getting an equal share of their family (or father's) property, but they should always be wary of non-tribespersons, even when they happened to be their spouses.[5] A woman must keep the land under her legal control, since with this she would be able to raise her children, in the event of her husband walking out of matrimony.

The women averred that their community was perennially faced with a shortfall of cash. They frequently faced contingent as well as other situations (such as illness in family, children's education, buying agricultural equipment) for which they required instant cash.[6] Since support for these did not come from the government, they perforce had to depend upon local moneylenders, who exploited them no end, charging exorbitant interest and mortgaging their land, jewelry, and house. In many cases, these were not returned, as tribal debtors were unable to pay off the loans with interest. Tribal economy was not surplus producing; people lived hand to mouth. Debts traveled from one generation to the next, which was one of the reasons of their bondage. Through the medium of the seminar, they urged upon the government agencies (banks, particularly) to be compassionate towards them and help them in times of exigency. Their entire life, they said clearly, was an existence of insecurity.

The functionaries in tribal areas were 'self-centered', solely interested in 'devouring the grants' that came from the government. Their proclivity towards corrupt measures of amassing wealth remained the same irrespective of the social category (tribe or caste) to which they belonged. Tribal elite was as 'money-minded' as were the 'others'. Rich tribesmen exploited their poor counterparts. Knowingly, the rich tribal people often distanced themselves from their 'humble and poor brothers and sisters', whom they looked down upon.

Police came to the aid of tribes if they had received 'gifts and bribe'. Whenever tribespersons went to police station to report a matter, the answer they usually received was that they should approach their own institutions (such as the traditional council [*panchayat*]) for intervention rather than approaching the police. They were advised to solve the problem at their own local level. And, if it were a case of sexual exploitation, the patent answer was that they should not bother much about it since 'it was the culture of tribes'. What the authorities meant in this case was that since tribes were reputed to be lax about sexual mores, they should disregard (or take lightly) the instances of sexual harassment and immorality. The women unambiguously drew attention to the stereotypes that the outsiders–particularly government officials – nurtured about them.

II

My intention of succinctly describing what these tribal women shared with anthropologists and other intellectuals is that for them economy, and not culture, was a major concern. The issue of livelihood was central. One may argue that what these women said would have been what their men would have said had they been given the same opportunity to speak before the seminarians; and therefore, there is no distinct feminine perspective. Or, perhaps the patriarchal structure is so dominating that women think that when they speak in its terms and idioms only then they would be intelligible. Men talk about economy, and in order to be meaningful (and respectful), women also aim to speak about it, although it is likely that they may have their own distinct agenda and perspective, the 'true feminine view', to which they would not give vent in a predominant male congregation that a university seminar is expected to be.

For me, the issue here is not of disaggregating the gendered dimension of consciousness, but to submit that the economic condition of tribal communities has worsened to such an extent that it has cut through the gender distinction. Surely, women will have their specific charter of needs; and so would men, but where their points of view meet are the areas of economy, the issues of their basic survival. Rarely would tribespersons talk about building museums to keep their cultural artifacts; and not so often would they insist on the preservation of their dialects. Their first priority would be a survival with dignity and optimality. Like all of us, they wish to be gainfully employed, have enough for survival; they want their children to have good health, go to school, do well in studies, get a job and handsome salary, and live well.

All of us want good life, a life of satisfaction and security. Tribes are no exception to this. Development is not greed– certainly, it does not imply an excess of resources or power. For people, it means a secure existence, in which they have at their disposal what they require for their basic existence and survival. Security that thus emerges is the source of happiness. In this respect, tribal people are like all of us. The predicaments and fortitudes of humanity bind all of us, whether we are placed in one social category or the other that we have constructed. The unity of human concerns underlies all development and welfare programmes.

An aspect that makes anthropology nervous is the issue of defining the term 'tribe'. Although important, I shall bypass it, for it does not engage me here. Following Bates (1994, 1995), I shall say that those communities for which the colonial anthropologists and the authors of various compendia used the word 'tribe' came to be later known as 'scheduled tribes' with the advent of the policy of protective discrimination.[7] The students of Indian society are well aware of the continuities between tribes and non-tribes. In many cases, it will be nearly impossible to tap a person and say, 'you belong to a tribe, or you belong to a caste.'[8] Equally well known are the cases of tribes transforming into caste. There are also the cases of castes taking over the tribal characteristics or the appellation of tribe. Tribes and castes co-exist in the same geographical space, each having its own ethno-history of origin and migration. The unbroken continuity between tribes and castes in India is different from the separation one finds between the 'indigenes' (or the 'autochthones', 'minorities', 'ethnics', 'aborigines') and the 'migrants' (mostly Caucasians) who had settled down over time, as is the case of the Americas, Australia, New Zealand, and Russia.[9]

In the past quarter of a century, anthropologists and the others interested in tribal studies in India, have laid a lot of emphasis on the issues of development, exploring the contours of the 'right kind of development' for tribes and the other analogous groups. One of the consequences of this focus is that the studies of tribal economic systems have become fewer in number. Ethnographic accounts of changing tribal economies are almost out of fashion. What a survey of literature on economic anthropology yields are sketchy accounts of the processes of production, distribution, and consumption among Indian tribes. On many areas of interest–such as the household budget, response of tribes to money and market economy, impact of technological innovation on tribal economies–recent authentic information is non-existent. The theme of the autonomy of the tribal economic system and its integration with the outside (i.e., 'non-tribal') world that was investigated in mid-twentieth century and the later decades is no more a sought after and preferred area of research.[10] That economic anthropology has not attracted the attention of a number of writers in India is clear from the fact that so far only two titles with the name of this subject exist. (Rao, 2009). One is N.K. Behura's Anthropological Economics, and the other is R.K. Gupta's Essays in Economic Anthropology. Both these books were published by the Institute of Social Research and Applied Anthropology, Bidisa, Midnapur, West Bengal. Just because the detailed studies of changing economic systems do not exist in the proportion in which they should, it is unsurprising that we still carry the image of tribespersons as unmonetized, exterior to market and trade situations, having no or negligible economic considerations, and depending upon their kinspersons and neighbours for all things pertaining to their survival. The tribal economic reality is, however, far different, and needs to be studied as a separate academic specialization rather than under the general rubric of development studies.

In spite of the continuities and morphological similarities between tribes and castes, wherever tribes live, they are different from non-tribes in various social and economic features. For instance, the percentage of scheduled tribes-persons living below poverty line in 2004-05 is 47.2 in rural and 39.9 in urban areas. The corresponding figures of scheduled castes population are 36.8 and 33.3 respectively; for the other backward classes, they are 26.7 and 31.4 respectively; and for the rest, 16.1 and 16.0 respectively.[11] Take another example, this time of literacy rate among scheduled tribes: from 8.53 per cent in 1961, it has increased to 47.10 per cent in 2001; for the total population, it has increased to 64.84 in 2001 from 28.30 in 1961.[12] 47.8 per cent villages of scheduled tribes are not electrified; the corresponding percentage of scheduled caste villages is 21.4.[13]

If tribes have rolled down in these indices, in sex ratio, they are better than the overall population (933 females per 1000 males); in 2001, they had 977 women per 1000 men, and some of them have more women than men (like the Ho of Bihar and Jharkhand, who have 1026 females per 1000 males, according to Census 1981).[14] However, the studies also point out that as the interaction of tribal communities with the wider world in increasing, the patrilineal values are also finding a place among them, resulting in meting out discourteous and oppressive treatment to girls and women, thus eventually skewing the sex ratio.[15] Bridewealth, which is presumed to indicate women's high status, is found among 535 tribal communities in People of India project. (Singh, 1994: 8).[16]

In other words, whether we take the positive or the negative indices, there is no doubt that tribes are different from the non-tribes. In terms of the index of deprivation, they are at the lower rung, at places almost overlapping with lower castes. Even those tribal communities that have the reputation of being assimilated with caste Hindu people and are placed considerably higher in local social hierarchy, such as the Meena of Rajasthan who equate themselves with the Rajput, Jat, Thakur, Mahajan, and Gujar of the area, are lower in economic terms in comparison to the communities with whom they claim equality.

III

A short visit to ordinary tribal settlements or a cursory glance at them will sadden anyone with the episodes of rampant poverty. The usual sight is of dilapidated houses, emaciated people with sunken faces, becoming grizzled in young age, draped in rags and soiled clothes, bony children toiling for livelihood, sometimes in highly perilous jobs, when in fact they should have been in schools, looking for a safe, bright, and secure future, sick remaining untreated, people just squatting, waiting for some job, howsoever small, to come through, taking up any task, illegal or life-threatening, to meet two square meal. Unemployment, hunger, deprivation, illness, and stagnation loom large. The stories of exploitation one hears in tribal villages, or of terror unleashed on them, are painfully unforgettable for years. Surely, this is not the description of tribal elite or the rich people among them, but in any case they constitute a minuscule of population. The vast majority of tribespersons is in want, poor, needy, and necessitous.

The second half of the twentieth century is a witness to several qualitative and quantitative accounts that have meticulously recorded and analyzed the miseries of tribesmen. Tribal areas have been fully explored for natural resources and biodiversity. The resource richness of tribal territories has attracted the powerful outsiders, who came with the sole intention of siphoning off the local wealth, which had scant meaning for the dwellers of that area. In this context, Sahlins'

(1968: 367) following observation is relevant: '...to a hunting-and-gathering people, to Australian aborigines, say, coal is completely irrelevant: in the ground or no, it is not part of their environment; it has no selective impact on them', unless an Australian mine project found them to be 'squatting' on one of the biggest deposits of bauxite loads. And, the outcome of this was predictable: more and more outsiders came to 'search' for the resources that the aboriginal areas had, which could be useful for the 'civilized' man. Tribal world all over has witnessed its flooding by greedy and rapacious outsiders; the genesis of tribal problem lies in asymmetrical cultural contacts.

In his lecture on the future of anthropology (of 1959-60), Lévi-Strauss (1987) noted a dwindling of the 'primitive peoples' over time. Building of nuclear plants, experimental rocket ranges, and mining operations have decimated them dangerously. Their life-support systems were acutely paralyzed. These changes were so ponderous that they left an inerasable imprint on their psyche.[17] Threatened by famines and ceaseless demoralization, Lévi-Strauss estimated that between 1900 and 1950, nearly ninety tribal groups had disappeared in Brazil. Against this background, he said, the concept of *indigène* (indigenous, native) was giving place to that of *indigent* (poor, needy, destitute). The former was presented romantically, depicting the bounteous beauty and charming aesthetics of the tribespersons; the latter was its opposite. It was an account of how the tribes were losing control over their habitat, its resources, and in their own land, which they colonized decades ago and where they were lords, they were becoming serfs, to be dehumanized, displaced, and driven out to lands unknown.

The state of indigence was an outcome of the asymmetrical contact situation the indigenous and local communities had with the outsiders. Initially, these contacts were infrequent and less impetuous. Local cultures were able to withstand any shock that came in the wake of these contacts, and continued to live the way they did, carefree and happy. Thus, when anthropologists conducted studies on these communities in the first half of the nineteenth century, they did not find among them those traits that characterized the western-industrial economies.

In his famous works on economic history, Karl Polanyi identified two meanings of economy, respectively called 'formal' and 'substantive', one that rested on the principle of the 'maximization of profit' and the other, on the 'fulfillment of one's needs'. The first was based on the 'laws of mind', of reason and rationality; the second, on the 'laws of nature', that is, 'if human beings have to live, they have to eat', and what they eat comes from their processing of the habitat around them. It was the second meaning of economy that was of relevance in tribal societies, which were neither profit-oriented nor believed in individualistic hoarding. Against this backdrop can be understood a number of ethnographies on tribal economy, in which people were described as free, having no surplus motives, and subscribing to the idea that nature has plenty in her womb and they would use only that bit of it which they need for their survival.[18]

In such systems, social relations were of primary importance; so was social esteem. If a Trobriander gardener produced much more than what he could possibly consume, it was not for maximizing his economic profit, for this concept did not exist in his society. It was to compete for the title of the 'best gardener', one that brought him prestige and esteem, which his king conferred upon the person who had produced the maximum.[19] Malinowski (1922) wanted to substantiate many ideas with the case of the Trobrianders, but one of them was that the 'primitive man', like the modern, was equally interested in his well-being, increasing his life-chances of survival, and gaining a high status. So, he would make every effort to promote his interests, although they are overwhelmingly social, and not economic. In his discussion of the Kula, Malinowski described the efforts and strategies (of wooing) that Trobriand men made to acquire the best gift from their partners, since it would raise their prestige among their community people. That is the reason why Malinowski is regarded as one of the first transactional theorists.[20]

A reading of the ethnographies on 'primitive societies' brings home the point that among them economy did not exist in the form it did in modern-industrial societies. Against this backdrop, some anthropologists proposed that instead of using the terms 'economic organization' or 'economic institution' for simple, pre-literate societies, since it would imply a state of differentiation, we should use the phrase 'the economic context of social behaviour'. These societies did not have 'economic men'; they had 'social men', who wished to ceaselessly multiply their 'social gains' (reputation, veneration, esteem, prestige, networks, respect). An understanding of this reality of 'primitive societies' – the social embedding of economy – was the salient contribution of economic anthropology. But, certainly it did not imply a state of utopia, people free from the pangs of scarcity and hunger, which in fact resulted not because of an inequitable distribution of resources or from a state of 'unfreedom', but because of natural calamities, technological inefficacy, low productivity, instances of war and raiding.[21] If they recurrently faced severe famines, they resorted to a lot of sharing of food among them (Evans-Pritchard, 1940) or learnt to live with scarcity and poverty (or developed what Oscar Lewis [1966] called the 'culture of poverty'). Well known are the practices and rituals by which the chiefs or kings of tribal communities distributed among the commoners the tributes (such as the material things or items of food) they had received by virtue of their position. Not only did the occupants of political offices and the other 'big men', but also those men who produced much more than the others were expected to generously feast their kith and kin and give them gifts, or contribute a larger share to the village granary, if they had one. Against this backdrop, we can understand the significance of the feasts of merit of the Nagas, or the pig-slaughter ceremonies of the Melanesians. The practices or rituals of what Polanyi called redistribution leveled the society and restricted the emergence of class distinctions.

IV

The observers have noted that hunting and food-gathering societies have less personal effects, only those that are essential for their survival. As said previously, they collect only that much food which they need for a couple of days. Although they claim to be the first settlers of the land, they are always prepared to dismantle their houses and move to another location, if need be.

Anthropologists have never interpreted this style of living as one of poverty. Having fewer personal belongings and living least ostentatiously does not imply living like poor people. Tribespersons were not poor; they were different. Living the way they did was their culture. Initially, it was thought that hunters, foragers, horticulturists, and shifting cultivators had fewer things with them because they were constantly on move, and obviously, they could not have accumulated much, for this would have greatly thwarted their perennial physical mobility. Later, when these people started settling down, they continued with a non-hoarding practice; their accumulativeness did not increase thereafter, guiding us to the conclusion that living a life of frugality is a cultural value among them, which will continue till the time they want its continuation. Because of the way they lived, with fewer things and exemplary parsimoniousness, they were, in some cases, believed to be leading a life of austerity and asceticism.[22]

Tribes were free to choose the way they liked. They were also free to alter it. This freedom illuminated their faces, endowed them with health, gave confidence in their cultural practices and lifestyles, and made them appear before the outsiders as proud inhabitants of their land. The happiness, joyfulness, pride, and satisfaction of tribes is well captured in the ethnographies produced during the first half of the twentieth century. The attitude of anthropologists towards tribal communities had also changed, even when they were working for the colonial government. This attitude was of a 'humble learner' of tribal communities, to learn from their differences and ways of living, and look at the western life critically against the background of the values of tribal living.

With the entry of the powerful outsiders in tribal areas, the freedom of people came to be curtailed. Although Malinowski (1922) did not pay much attention to the implications of the presence of white people in Omarakana, the Trobriand village where he had pitched his tent, he did notice that with the advent of missionaries, the Trobriand institution of youth dormitory (*bakumatula*) was being greatly undermined. Trobrianders preferred to conceal its presence among them, since they thought that the mission people would not like it and lecture them to stop sending their children to dormitories. We have umpteen examples in anthropological literature where people lost freedom to live according to their culture, which gave them meaning of life, with the coming of the outsiders in their areas. The Ho institution of marriage by elopement was interpreted as 'abduction', a legal offence according to colonial masters. (Majumdar, 1944). Similarly, the Baiga man, who kept long hair, tying them as a bun on the occiput, was instructed to cut his hair, so that he looked like a 'civilized man'. (Srivastava, 1991). Bride price was seen as 'buying a woman'. And, well known is the ban the colonial administration imposed on shifting cultivation, for it thought it was the practice in which 'wild men' engaged. A shift to plough cultivation also meant a civilizing mission. (Vidyarthi and Rai, 1976). The cultural context in which these institutions needed to be understood was grossly ignored.

As the colonial rule expanded, it brought in its wake a large number of outsiders, who tacitly enjoyed the patronage of the rule. They exploited the people, ousted them from their land and other resources. Since the people were unaware of the bureaucratic rules and procedures, they did not know how to get rid of the exploiters and how to get the land legally registered in their names. Alienation of land continued unabated, first to the outsiders, and second to the state.

This process continues till date; the state is the biggest alienator of tribal land, followed by the private entrepreneurs who are building housing colonies and office complexes on tribal land.[23] When a factory comes up in tribal area, the local people are forced to work for it, and if they do not, they are subjected to various ordeals. Tribal habitat is subjected to despoliation; the people have no option but to sit and watch, unless they start their own movement or some non-governmental organizations (NGOs) takes up their cause. Poor resource base that has resulted from untrammeled exploitation, negligible capacity to borrow money to start a new venture, no skills that the emerging market needs, have led people to migrate to towns and cities, where they lead a life of extreme destitution, in which breed vagabondism, deviance and crime, and the other types of wastefulness. The story of tribes all over the world is the story of deprivation of freedom and utter powerlessness.

Unsurprisingly, it has made anthropologists voice the concerns of tribes, their problems, and suggest viable solutions. Since the beginning of tribal studies, anthropologists have time and again argued that their contribution will be enfeebled by self-silencing. They should expose the structures of exploitation of local people, trying to save them from all sorts of nefarious elements. Against this light, if one reads the idea of creating a 'national park' as a temporary solution to the problems of the Baigas, one finds that it was borne out of Elwin's (1939) profound concern for tribal communities.[24]

Notwithstanding the theoretical position, anthropologists have always been sensitive to tribal problems and have committed themselves to finding a solution to them. That is the reason why anthropologists need to be engaged as activists, aid workers, policy advisors, and consultants. This however does not imply a compromise with the basic task of anthropology, which is reaching an objective and analytical understanding of social situations. Anthropologists have always been arguing in favour of an approach of partnership and participation, in which the tribes (and other down-trodden communities) have the freedom to choose the line and the programme of development they want, the way in which they would manage their natural resources; have the freedom to choose the leaders who would govern them in a participatory way; and have the freedom to protest against unjust systems and uninformed decisions. I cannot do better than to remember Sen's (1999) famous statement: 'Development can be seen as a process of expanding the real freedoms that people enjoy.'

V

Today's economic anthropology is concerned with the changing tribal reality and the differentiation of the economic system. No more does it bask in the romanticism of the substantive approach; it also is skeptical of the fuller application of the formalist viewpoint. Tribal economies are no more unmonetized; no more are their markets of ceremonial importance; no more are they part of the domestic economy.

Tribes have become aware of the importance and power of money; they also know the ways in which they have been systematically deprived of control over their resources; they also know that their unity and leadership will help them fight inequality and unjust systems. Tribes are becoming more conscious of their identity – it is a process whereby a 'tribe *in* itself' is being transformed to a 'tribe *for* itself'. Not only are the tribes busy in creating a self-image, consolidating their culture, but also in many parts of India they have started their own movements and founded their own organizations to combat injustice. Some of these micro-movements, at the local level, are creating ripples, the effect of which cannot go unnoticed for long. For instance, the tribal villages of Surat district have a group of thirty women lawyers from different tribes who take up cases of exploitation against the members of their community.[25] In another case, in the district of Ranchi, daughters and grand daughters of women who were once branded as witches are coming forward to root out the evil.[26] And, there are several cases from the north-eastern part of India where women have started movements against the evils of alcohol consumption and drug addiction. (Narang, 2007). The Raika-Rabari have also become conscious of the fact that their contemporary state of acute debt-bondage has resulted from the custom of marriage-cum-death feast, which incurs a lot of expenditure and they have no option but to borrow money from merchants operating in their area, who charge exorbitant interest from them for the loan taken. In order to save them from indebtedness, they have started a movement to make these feasts humbler. (Srivastava, 2007).

Anthropologists have become sensitive to the gender perspective; so have they become to the problems of old people. More and more social gerontologists are now focusing on the tribal old. But what has remained largely ignored is the paediatric perspective; for instance, what happens to the children when displacement occurs, or when a disaster strikes a community? In fact, there may be some information available on people who were displaced and how they coped with the new habitat, but when it comes to the impact of development and displacement programmes on the future generation, we have very little information, since this generally has not been the focus of study. Some NGOs have compiled data on tribal children, but proper anthropological accounts have yet to be written.

One such report pointed out that after the Chenchu, a primitive tribe of Andhra Pradesh, were displaced as a consequence of the building of the 'first temple of modern India', the Nagarjunasagar dam, their children started working as bonded labourers in stone quarries and mines. Tribal children work in these quarries as apprentices from a very young age and receive exceedingly low wages. Some of these children are agricultural labourers, rickshaw-pullers, and flower-sellers. Minor Chenchu and Lambada girls work as cheap agriculture labour in chilli and tobacco farms, where they are exposed to harmful chemical pesticides. Children are most prone to sexual exploitation; there are cases of Lambada girls sold for trafficking. Local NGOs have found incidences of HIV/AIDS among the Yanadi girls living around the temple and tourist town of Srisailam. Juvenile crime, which was non-existent among tribes, is now an issue of concern. As a consequence of these factors, the children fall prey to ill health, alcoholism and other vices.[27] (See a report prepared by Samata in July 2008, pp. 67-9).

Economic anthropology is a vibrant discipline, with the potentiality to contribute a great deal to the understanding of tribal problems, and at the same time, supplementing and correcting the economist's understanding. Economic facts are inseparable from the other social and cultural facts. The impact of culture on economy is now a fact not just restricted to anthropology and sociology, but also economics has started accepting it.[28] People's decisions about resource management and distribution of gain are all influenced by their culture. Instead of disappearing or merging with the 'global culture', homogeneous and monolithic, each community's culture is able to withstand the tides of universal processes. The 'new economic anthropology', to borrow from John Clammer (1978), is concerned both with the contemporary dynamics of economic processes, the processes of class formation and conflicts, and the unremitting effect of culture on economy.

ENDNOTES

1. This paper was presented as a Keynote Address at a Seminar on Tribal Economy that the Rajiv Gandhi Chair in Contemporary Studies, Barkatullah University, Bhopal (Madhya Pradesh) had organized on 10 and 11 February 2009. I am grateful to Professor S.N. Chaudhary for giving me this honour, and to the Vice Chancellor, Barkatullah University, for presiding over the Keynote Address. Data collection for this paper was facilitated by the research grant that the University of Delhi gave me in 2008-9 under its R & D programme.
2. I attended a seminar (in 2002) on the cultural and social aspects of AIDS in which some HIV-positive patients were invited, who also took part in the discussion. Before that (in 1993), I attended a seminar in Jodhpur on pastoral communities in which their leaders also participated. On both occasions, I noted that the academicians and the members of the non-governmental organizations (NGOs) who had come to attend the seminars were more eager to speak to the 'subjects of their study', for they did not wish to lose this opportunity of collecting information.
3. What they said in Telegu (or their respective dialects) was translated into English by Professor Vijay Prakash, an anthropologist, who was also coordinating this session.
4. Although legally, land cannot be acquired by a non-tribal person, he can always enjoy its benefits. Moreover, he can always exercise political and 'money' power to keep the land in his control, although he may not be its owner. See Singh (1988), Xaxa (2004). Singh (1988:3) also noted that marriages between tribal women and non-tribal men were not stable. Xaxa (2004:362) writes: 'Often after such transactions [of land], non-tribal men have deserted tribal women. This in itself is an emotive issue among tribes in view of the long struggle that they have waged against the alienation of tribal land.'
5. In fact, as pointed out by Professor J.M. Naidu, this woman was not aware of the legal position that in Andhra Pradesh, girls have an equal right in the family property. But the important point to be noted here is

that these tribal women were drawing attention to the difference between the 'rules on paper' and the existing practices. Surely, tribal land cannot be legally taken over by the non-tribal, but in practice, the cases of alienation definitely occur.

6. In his classical study of Bisipara, Bailey (1957) noted that the people sold their land in order to meet the 'contingent expenses'. The land had already been fragmented among different brothers after the death of the head of the household. Since there were no avenues to generate cash, they had no option but to mortgage or sell their land. Land, which was not a marketable thing, became a commodity to be sold and acquired in the market.
7. See Articles 342 and 366 (25) of the Constitution of India.
8. See Béteille (1975), Pathy (1984).
9. Of 635 tribes and sub-tribes that Singh's People of India project covered, 409 (64.3 per cent) claimed to be migrants to their present habitat. Singh wrote (1994:7): 'In fact all our tribal people have been migrants. Their migration is recorded in oral history and historical accounts. About eight per cent of the tribes recall their migration in recent years.'
10. That economic anthropology has not attracted the attention of a number of writers in India is clear from the fact that so far only two titles with the name of this subject exist (Rao, 2009). One is N.K. Behura's *Anthropological Economics*, and the other is R.K. Gupta's *Essays in Economic Anthropology*. Both these books were published by the Institute of Social Research and Applied Anthropology, Bidisa, Midnapur, West Bengal.
11. *Annual Report, 2007-08*, Ministry of Tribal Affairs, Government of India, p. 32-3.
12. ibid.: 31.
13. *Report of the Task Force on Development of Scheduled Castes and Scheduled Tribes*, Planning Commission, Government of India, March 2005, p. 39.
14. See Singh (1994:404); Xaxa (2004:363).
15. See Singh, et al. (1988), Unnithan-Kumar (1997), Government of India (2000, 2001). Except in states like Andhra Pradesh, Tamil Nadu, and Uttarakhand, the scheduled tribes' sex ratio (as per Census 2001) was better than the general sex ratio (Annual Report, 2007-08, Ministry of Tribal Affairs, Government of India, p. 30).
16. Singh (1994:8) also noted that the transition from bride price to dowry was slow. Here, the generally accepted idea is that tribes are known for practicing the system of bride price (or, bride wealth), whilst castes have dowry.
17. For instance, from a Hopi Indian, Don Talayesva, six hundred dreams were collected. Their analysis pointed out that they revealed less about the individual peculiarities than about the disintegration of the subject's society (Lévi-Strauss, 1987: 18). It is well known that many of them lost the desire to live, thus suffering from what is known as thanatomania.
18. See Polanyi (1968); also see Dalton's edited volume of 1968 of the writings of Karl Polanyi; Humphreys (1969).

19. This reminds one of the distinction that Firth (1967) made between 'market mentality' and 'economic advantage'. The tribal communities definitely had the latter, but they were not market-oriented.
20. See Lewis (2003) on this point.
21. See Richards (1932, 1939). Also see Vernon (2007).
22. See Gardner (1982). He used the word 'ascribed austerity' for this.
23. Sah and Sisodia (2004:19) write: 'In contemporary India, the tribals continue to be pushed in order to acquire land–their land–for large development projects.....The demand for their resources–land, forest and water–is still forcing them out of their habitat.'
24. Elwin wrote in 1939 (p. 519): 'The gloomy future [of the Baiga] could be averted by the creation of the National Park...., or at least by the handing over to the Baiga part of the great tracts of forest that can never be exploited commercially.' Elwin's letter to Vanyajati (2[2], 1949) was: 'I am...vehemently in favour of opening communications in tribal areas. But I think that such roads should be made in the interests of the tribals and not for the benefit of those who would exploit them from the plains.' Also see Sachchidananda (2009).
25. See The Times of India, 15 March 2006; also see The Times of India(24 November 1993) for the short life sketch of C.K. Janu, a tribal girl, the president of the Southern Zone Adivasi Forum; for the role of Kalinga Nagar tribals who vowed not to vacate land for industries, see The Hindu, 11 January 2006.
26. A twenty-nine years old girl named Poonam Toppo, whose grandmother was once tortured for being a witch, has taken up cudgels to fight the crime of branding innocent people as witches.
28. Writing on teacher truancy, an economist, Kaushik Basu, writes: 'Culture is at least worth a try.' Economists today are seriously considering the importance of the concept of culture in economic analyses. See his paper in Jayaram and Deshpande, eds. (2008).

REFERENCES

Bates, Crispin (1994), 'Lost Innocents and Loss of Innocence': Interpreting *Adivasi* movements in South Asia. In R.H. Barnes, Andrew Gray, and Benedict Kingsbury (eds.), *Indigenous Peoples of Asia*. Ann Arbor: University of Michigan Press.

——(1995), "Race, Caste and Tribe in Central India". In Peter Robb (ed.), *The Concept of Race*. New Delhi: Oxford University Press.

Béteille, André (1974), *Six Essays in Comparative Sociology*. Delhi: Oxford University Press.

Clammer, John (1978), *New Economic Anthropology*. London: Macmillan.

Dalton, George (ed.). (1968), *Primitive, Archaic, and Modern Economies: Essays of Karl Polanyi*. New York: Doubleday.

Elwin, Verrier (1939), *The Baiga*. Delhi: Gyan Publishing House [Reprint 1986].

Evans-Pritchard, E.E. (1940), *The Nuer*. Oxford: Clarendon Press.

Firth, Raymond (ed.). (1967), *Themes in Economic Anthropology*. London: Routledge & Kegan Paul.

Gardner, P.M. (1982), Ascribed Austerity: A Tribal Path to Purity. *Man* (n.s.), 17: 462-9.

Government of India (2000), *Women in India (A Statistical Profile)*. New Delhi: Planning Commission.

——(2001), *Report of the Steering Committee on Empowering the Scheduled Tribes*. New Delhi: Planning Commission.

——(2005), *Report of the Task Force on Development of Scheduled Castes and Scheduled Tribes*, Planning Commission.

——(2007-8), *Annual Report*, Ministry of Tribal Affairs.

Humphreys, S.C. (1969), "History, Economics and Anthropology: The Work of Karl Polanyi". *History & Theory*, 8 (2): 165-212.

Jayaram, N. and R.S. Deshpande (eds.) (2008), *Footprints of Development and Change, Essays in Memory of Professor V.K.R.V. Rao*. New Delhi: Academic Foundation.

Lévi-Strauss, Claude (1987), *Anthropology and Myth, Lectures 1951-1982*. Oxford: Basil Blackwell.

Lewis, I.M. (2003), *Social and Cultural Anthropology in Perspective: The Relevance of Social Anthropology*. London: Transaction Publisher.

Lewis, Oscar (1966), "The Culture of Poverty". In George Gmelch and Walter Lenner (eds.), *Urban Life*. Illinois: Waveland Press.

Majumdar, D.N. (1944), *The Fortunes of Primitive Tribes*. Lucknow: Universal Publishers.

Malinowski, Bronislaw (1922), *Argonauts of the Western Pacific*. London: Routledge & Kegan Paul [Reprint 1992].

Narang, Mala (2007), Continuity and Change in an Angami Naga Village. Unpublished Ph.D. Dissertation. Department of Anthropology, University of Delhi.

Pathy, J. (1984), *Tribal Peasantry: Dynamics of Development*. Delhi: Inter-India Publishers.

Polanyi, Karl (1968), "Anthropology and Economic Theory". In Morton H. Fried (ed.), *Readings in Anthropology (Vol. II–Cultural*

Anthropology). New York: Thomas Y. Crowell Company (pp. 215-38).

Rao, P. Venkata (2009), "Economic Anthropology". *Special Assistance Programme (SAP) (of the University Grants Commission) Lecture*, Department of Anthropology, University of Delhi (19 January).

Richards, Audrey I. (1932), *Hunger and Work in a Savage Society*. London: Greenwood Press.

——(1939), *Land, Labour and Diet in Northern Rhodesia*.London: Oxford University Press.

Sachchidananda (2009), "Verrier Elwin's Anthropology". In Sachchidananda and Vinay Kumar Srivastava (eds.), *Social Anthropology in Eastern India*. New Delhi: Serials Publications (pp. 244-61).

Sah, D.C. and Yatindra Singh Sisodia (2004), Editors' Introduction. In D.C. Sah and Yatindra Singh Sisodia (eds.), *Tribal Issues in India*. Jaipur and New Delhi: Rawat Publications (pp. 15-36).

Sahlins, Marshall D. (1968), "Culture and Environment: The Study of Cultural Ecology". In Robert A. Manners and David Kaplan (eds.), *Theory in Anthropology, a Sourcebook*. London: Routledge & Kegan Paul (pp. 367-73).

Samata (2008), *A Study on the Status and Problems of Tribal Children in Andhra Pradesh*. Visakhapatnam: Samata.

Sen, Amartya (1999), *Development as Freedom*. Oxford: Oxford University Press.

Singh, J.P., N. Vyas, and R.S. Mann (eds.). *Tribal Women and Development*. Jaipur: Rawat Publications.

Singh, K.S. (1988), "Tribal Women: An Anthropological Perspective". In J.P. Singh, N. Vyas, and R.S. Mann (eds.), *Tribal Women and Development*. Jaipur: Rawat Publications, pp. 3-10.

——(1994), *The Scheduled Tribes* (*National Series Volume III*). Calcutta: Anthropological Survey of India, and Delhi: Oxford University Press.

Srivastava, Vinay Kumar (1991), "The Ethnographer and the People: Reflections on Field Work". *Economic and Political Weekly*, XXVI (22&23): 1408-11, 1413-4, and XXVI (24): 1475-81.

——(2007), "Cultural Tradition and Child Marriage in India". *The Eastern Anthropologist*, 60 (1): 45-68.

Unnithan-Kumar, Maya (1997), *Identity, Gender and Poverty: New Perspectives on Caste and Tribe in Rajasthan*. Oxford: Berghahn Books.

Vernon, James (2007), *Hunger: A Modern History*. Michigan: Harvard University Press.

Vidyarthi, L.P. and Binay Kumar Rai (1976), *The Tribal Culture of India*. New Delhi: Concept Publishing House.

Xaxa, Virginius (2004), "Women and Gender in the Study of Tribes in India". *Indian Journal of Gender Studies*, 11(3): 345-67.

25

RETHINKING SUSTAINABLE TRIBAL DEVELOPMENT IN A CULTURAL PERSPECTIVE

Jagabandhu Samal

The culture, in ordinary parlance, may be defined as the sum total of a nation's or society's thinking and living. It is the way of life based on common traditions and environment. It is the common learned way of life shared by the members of a society. It implies the behaviour of the people, their ethos, views and value system. (Amalorpavadass, 1982:92).

The culture has two aspects, i.e. material and non-material. Material aspects are the science, technology, clothing and food habits, etc. The non-material aspects of culture are the values, goals, world views, thought system, languages and symbol, status and role system, etc. Hence, the beliefs, ideas and attitudes, religious, social, political and economic organizations, science and technology are all parts of the complex net work that is called "Culture". (Aleaz, 1994: 12). Culture also means "Samskriti" which implies a process of refinement. (Amalorpavadass, op cit. : 93).

An understanding of the culture in holistic sense, as outlined above, presents development as an instituted social process. In other words, development does not happen as specialised activities within the disciplinary boundary of economics. It is a comprehensive and all encompassing process and thus embedded in culture. Over the years, the concept of development has become wider across the disciplinary understanding. With this backdrop, the present paper argues for the tribal development in a cultural perspective because the tribals are still tradition bound and culture still defines their world view at large. The paper is based on field data collected among different tribes in Koraput, Orissa over a period of time. References to a few works on the topic and the problem of backwardness of the tribes in spite of various development efforts provide logic for analysis of the research problem identified in this paper.

TRIBAL CULTURE AND TRIBAL DEVELOPMENT: ISSUES AND CONCERNS

The tribal people express their cultural identity and distinctiveness in their social and political organisations, language, rituals and festivals, as well as in their dress pattern, ornaments, technology, art and craft. Of course, there may be some traditions, customs, beliefs and faiths which generally stand on the way of tribal development[1]. These have negative impact on their life. For example, milching the cow by tribes like Koya and Kandhas in Orissa was treated as a sin. They believed that, the milk of the cow was the exclusive possession of the calf. Touching a cow or roofing a house were taboos for Kharia and Oraon women. The Todas of Nilgiri Hills do not permit their women to enter the diary area. Quite a number of tribes could not be persuaded to undertake plough cultivation as they regarded this would lacerate the breast of the "Dharti Mata" (Mother Earth). Some of them resisted the use of improved seeds, chemical fertilisers, new agricultural implements, etc. as these did not come in their religious panorama. With the spread of proper knowledge awareness and education, it is genuinely expected that those aspects of tribal faiths and beliefs, which have negative impact on their overall development, would go away. However, there are a lot of finer values in the tribal culture, which are worth mentioning and preserving and if such positive aspects of their culture are preserved, developed and encouraged the overall development of these communities will be rather easier and smoother. (Samal, 2000:73).

Most of the tribal development programmes have failed terribly both at the Planning and implementation levels. In some cases, the programmes for them were unrealistic because these did not touch the roots of their problems. In other cases, their skills, and their felt needs were not well understood. In other words, their cultural values were ignored. (Samal, 1996: 32; also see Behera,1994:325, 327, 379).

It is, therefore, realised that an anthropological approach is needed to deal with the problems of tribal development. This approach relies on creating rapport with the tribal people living in the area, understanding their life and culture, inherent skills, sentiments, their core problems and their felt needs. In tribal societies, economic development is greatly influenced by cultural life, social structure and institutional arrangement in which land and resources are owned and operated. The cultural potentials that could be the basis of enlarging the development choices of the tribes when integrated with the market forces are discussed briefly as below:

The Routine Work – An Act of Art and Joy

The tribal art, dance, song and music have greatly enriched the composite culture of Indian national life. These finer aspects of their cultural life have attracted the people from within and outside the country. These aspects of their culture have great tourists' attraction. If these things are preserved properly, developed and marketed, the tribal economy will definitely be enriched. They are the only people who can sing freely while working. They work with pleasure and peace of mind. The routine work is an act of art and joy. They sing and dance in the forests, fairs, rites and festivals and in the evening hours in the village. These performances give expression to their inner feelings, their joys and sorrows, their natural affections and passion and their sense of appreciation to beauty in nature and human.

Arts and Crafts

The tribal crafts have great artistic value. These have a demand in the national and international markets. Their sense of beauty and art is found in their wall paintings, wood carvings and weaving of clothes and garments. The beautiful wall paintings and floral designs of Sauras and Santals, the wood carving of Kondhas, indigenous loom weaving and embroiding works of Dongaria Kondhs and Bondas etc. are the best examples of tribal art[2]. The tribals in various parts of the country prepare beautiful decorative articles out of the materials available to them in their surroundings.

Tribal Way of curing Diseases

The tribals have their own way of curing diseases. They have specific herbs with high medicinal value. Research scholars from far and wide not only come to study their art, crafts and culture, but also to gather knowledge on the herbs and traditional medicines that cure diseases in tribal areas. Time has come to develop and propagate their herbal medicines and medicinal plants with recognition of patent rights.

Love for Soil and Society

A tribal loves his/her life – s/he loves his/her eco-structures or surroundings, the village, the forests, the hills, the hill streams, the countless flowers in the forests, his/her own people, songs and dances. S/he loves and respects the sky God above and Mother Earth below. In the community life of the tribal people almost everything is shared; the joy and sorrow of one becomes the joy and sorrow of the whole community. (Elwin, 1943:18). An individual never feels lonely, rootless or helpless in the vast sea of humanity. One can observe that in the tribal villages, both adult men and women go to the hills, forests and fields from morning till evening, but no house is ever locked up. There is no fear of theft and robbery. Their houses are as open as their hearts and souls.

Mutual Reciprocity in Socio-Economic Activities

An important aspect of tribal value system is the cooperative support that one finds in both economic and socio religious activities. This is a positive aspect of tribal culture, which if properly organized and managed, can go a long way in improving the level of living of these communities. It may be the thatching the roof of a house, clearing forests for agricultural purpose, preparing a field for terraced cultivation, transplantation work in paddy field and / or harvesting of crops. The tribal people in a village do these things mostly collectively and on labour exchange basis. Co-operative and collective supports are also found in various socio-religious activities in tribal communities. Collective and cooperative support is also provided in the village by members of the Youth Dormitories in socio-economic activities (A Case Study is given below while discussing the role of Youth Dormitory).

Tribals and Trees

The tribals worship trees and nature. Even in the ancient time the people in Greece and Italy were worshiping trees. The Hindus are also tree worshipers. It is not always true that forests have been destroyed by tribals. They never cut a tree unless it is badly required. In most of the tribal villages, there are "sacred groves" which are believed to be the abodes of their deities. Tribals never cut even a branch of a tree within the sacred grove. This aspect of their culture may be taken care of while planning for regeneration of forests in tribal areas. Again, this aspect of their culture would help for the development of eco-tourism in tribal areas. Development of eco-tourism in these tribal regions will go a long way to enrich tribal economy and culture.

The tribals generally do not cut fruit bearing trees. Therefore, one can find isolated trees standing in the hills and even in shifting agricultural fields. This value system of the tribals may be capitalised to encourage horticultural plantations in tribal areas. The moderately high attitude areas in tribal location in general and that of the Koraput region of Orissa in particular, offer good scope for production of horticultural crops like mango, guava, pineapple, custard, apple, banana, jackfruits, litchi, and spices like onion, garlic, chilly, ginger, turmeric and vegetables like cabbage, cauliflowers, beans, potato, tomato, brinjals, cucumber and carrot. The cashew and coffee in eastern tribal zone including Koraput region are also known for their quality. Efforts are gradually made by the Governmental and non-governmental agencies for promotion of horticultural crops including coffee and cashew production in suitable places.

Status of Women

A high status is assigned to the women in tribal culture. Women move freely with men in the hills and forests, in the fairs and festivals. In the field of economic pursuits the women have greater share than men. In the selection of a husband or in the event of divorce, the opinion of the women is given due weightage. The tribal women force is a great factor for their overall development. It is interesting to note that tribal women have proved to be better entrepreneurs when they are cooperatively organized through self help groups (SHGs).

There is no dowry system among the tribals. Rather a bride price or "Jholla" is given to the parents of the girl before accepting her in marriage. One never finds an instance of bride burning or bride torture in tribal society as sometimes we find in the case with the so-called civilised non-tribal ones.

SHG Movement and Women Empowerment–A Case Study

In the tribal dominated Koraput district of Orissa there are a total number of 9554 Women Self Help Groups (SHGs) with a membership of 1,24,223 till March, 2009. These SHGs are more or less engaged in various income generating activities. Here follows the case study of a Self Help Group (Women) named Maa Narayani Swayam Sahayak Gosti and one of its members named Smt. Daimati Kakalpadia.

Smt. Daimati Kakalpadia, a tribal woman of Pakanaguda village in Baligaon Gram Panchayat of Boipariguda Block, is an active member of the above mentioned SHG. This SHG was formed on 10th May, 2002 with the initiative taken and incentive given by the ICDS extension workers of the Block. Daimati, like other members of her group, used to deposit a sum of Rs.50/- per month. By 31st March, 2009 the total bank deposit of the group was Rs.39,940/-.

This SHG like many other SHGs in the district has been taking up various income generating activities viz. diary units, vegetable cultivation and trading and cultivation of ground nuts and mushroom, etc. At the same time the Group has also taken the responsibility of supplying rice and Kerosene, etc. to the villagers under public distribution system and also is managing the mid-day meals for school children. The members of the Group are also trying to create awareness among the villagers about immunisation of children and pregnant women, institutional delivery in the hospitals, evil effects of alcoholism and sending children to school regularly.

Smt. Daimati Kakalpadia has a family of seven members. They were very poor indeed. Before joining the group, she confesses, she and her family members were not able to get two square meals a day.

Initially she took a loan from the Group and started vegetable business mostly in the weekly Hats (markets). With her sincerity, devotion and hard work, she could earn good profit in her business. She says with great satisfaction, "I could release 0.5 acres of land which was mortgaged by my father-in-law to a local *Sahukar*[3]. I am now the owner of two milching cows. I have been able to buy one acre of agricultural land in which I am growing vegetables, and ground nuts. I have now a bank deposit of Rs.3590/-. Earlier we were mortgaging gold, land and even human labour (*Goti*) to get a loan from local money lender or *Sahukar*. Now we are not depending on them. We mostly borrow from our Groups and sometimes from banks on easy terms".

Daimati along with other members of her group had attended several meetings and workshops and got training on safe delivery practices, immunisation, diary keeping, prohibition measures, cultivation of vegetables and other crops. She is now able to give training to other women of her village and of the neighbouring villages. She is able to speak freely in public meetings. With her dynamic leadership her village has been declared as a Liquor free village[4] .

Youth Dormitories–A Powerful Source of Co-operative Labour

Youth dormitories were the core of tribal culture and reinforced the age- old traditions. These were the places of social gathering, cultural centres, entertainment and informal centres of learning positive values of life. These were the places to select life partners. Young men and women grow up in the dormitories without much inhibitions and repression to which the sophisticated communities are generally subject to. The elders of the village often assemble at the dormitory house to discuss about every important event in their corporate life.

The young members of the dormitories also provide collective and co-operative labour force in times of need either voluntarily or against some reward. About 27 years back the author (who was a Ph.D research scholar at that time) came across a helpless tribal woman, during field survey, in Upper Godala village of Dashamanthpur block in Koraput district of Orissa. Her husband had gone to some unknown destination three years ago and did not come back. She was left with two daughters, the elder one being six years old and the younger one, three years old. She was working as an agricultural labourer in the field of the village headman and was managing her family with difficulties. As the house could not be thatched due to want of money and materials it was profusely leaking during rain.

The scholar convened a meeting of the young men of the dormitory of the village and persuaded them to collect free of cost bamboo and thatching grass etc. from the villagers and thatch the house of the poor women. He also persuaded them to prepare a link road to their village from the main road (about half a kilometre), as there was no road, but a walking path to the village from the main road. The youngmen of the village agreed to take up these activities voluntarily. In the next visit to the village after two months, the scholar was overwhelmed with joy to see that the house of the poor women was thatched and a road with earth work was completed by these young people of the village. Such cooperative and collective efforts in tribal value system are potential factors of their development.

TRADITIONAL PANCHAYATS VS. STATUTORY PANCHAYAT RAJ INSTITUTIONS

All the tribal communities not only possess rich cultural heritage but also have unique traditional system of social control. The traditional Panchayats found in tribal villages exercise enormous social, moral, religious, economic, and political control over these communities. The functions and responsibilities of the traditional Panchayats include; (a) upholding social customs, traditions, mores, codes governing matrimonial alliances, divorce, family disputes, inter-personal relations; (b) safeguarding and promoting the economic interest of the members of the community in allotting community lands for cultivation, shifting cultivation, protection of common property resources; (c) religious rites and festivals; (d) political safeguards, development and encouragement of right type of leaders, administration of justice as per traditional law, hereditary rights; and (e) protection of cultural heritage-maintenance and continuity of folk dance, folk lore, traditional skills, knowledge, etc. After the introduction of statutory Panchayats elected PRI leaders have come forward to lead the villagers and put forward the problems of the village and people at different forums. Inspite of functioning of Statutory Panchayats, the tribal people have full faith in their traditional Panchayat leaders. A proper synthesis of traditional laws, ethics and customs and statutory rules have to be ensured in order to achieve sustainable development in tribal areas. Both the institutions must act as complementary to each other for better implementation of Welfare measures in tribal areas.

DIGNITY OF LABOUR

The tribals generally earn their livelihood by hard physical labour. They dislike earning by bad means. They rarely go out for begging. To them own labour is a thing of pride and honour. Persons who are worthless, lazy and shirk labour are looked down in their communities. Even they are prevented from getting married. In this respect perhaps there cannot be any comparison between them and other people.

The discipline in social life, dignity of labour, the collective and co-operative support in the filed of socio economic activities, the hospitality and friendship and above all honesty and simplicity are some of the finer values that are very much noticed in tribal culture. These have enriched and will go on enriching the great Indian culture. These human values have positive roles to play in socio-economic development of the tribal communities. (Elwin, op cit., :18-20).

Verrier Elwin, the famous Anthropologist and social worker who worked among the tribal communities in India has rightly remarked, "Mankind is one and the tribes are a very precious part of mankind" (Elwin, 1964: 246). Pandit Jawaharlal Nehru said, "The people of the tribal areas and the hills attract me greatly and deserve our very special care. I am anxious that they should advance, but I am even more anxious that they should not lose their artistry and joy of life and the culture that distinguish them in many ways".[5]

CULTURE VS. DEVELOPMENT: TRIBAL EXPERIENCES

Many of the development schemes introduced in tribal areas after independence did not take care of the cultural background of the tribal people and their traditional skills[6]. Various researchers including Vidyarthi have found that tribal people resist to changes which include introduction of modern technology and methods as they feel that these go to interfere with their respective core culture or their basic cultural adjustment[7]. (Vidyarthi, 1981:3-4). This was found true in case of various tribal groups whether they were tribes of forest hunting type, or hill cultivation type, or settle agriculture type, or simple artisan type or industrial and non industrial labour type (ibid., 4). According to Vidyarthi (ibid.,17), the tribals living in the hills and forests had developed a style of life suited to the particular natural surrounding termed as "nature-man-spirit complex", which they were not prepared to abandon under any circumstances and resisted any type of geographical rehabilitation or settlement in colonies with a quite new pattern of habitation.

The agricultural tribes who lived in the mixed villages of tribal and non-tribal population faced some negative forces like fragmentation of holdings, land alienation, excess pressure of population on land, poor agricultural technology and the traditions, lack of irrigation facilities, etc. Added to these, the tribals, because of their orientation in tradition and closed group norms have not been able to introduce many new crops, new fertilisers and other new areas of agriculture.

The tribal artisan types like basket makers, iron smelters, blacksmiths, weavers and such others in various parts of the country whose economy and culture revolve round a specific craft in which they specialise, faced serious set back with introduction of modern mill made or factory produced items of new technology. The complete negation of cultural factors and tradtional background has resulted in loss of confidence of these people. They have not been able to properly readjust themselves with the changed situation.

The tribal belt of middle India which was originally characterised by folk culture underwent large scale industrialisation in recent years without much conscious efforts to benefit the local tribals and semi tribal communities. This has resulted in loss of traditional occupation, land, house, traditional way of life, unproductive use and exhaustion of cash received by way of compensation, unemployment, keen and unfair competition with migrants in labour market, high aspiration and great frustration. (See Vidyarthi and Rai, 1985:462-471).

In this connection, it must be remembered that development implies, growth plus change which involves both material and human factors. Thus concept of development has to be defined in terms of tribals' cultural background, their values and historical experiences. There are a lot of positive aspects in tribal culture, some of which have been mentioned earlier, that can be taken care of while planning and implementing development schemes among the tribal communities and in tribal areas.

THE TRIBAL PANCHASHIL

Pandit Nehru while giving a broad frame work of tribal development emphasized on five aspects of tribal development which is known as the *Tribal Panchashil*. These are: (a) People should develop along the lines of their own genius and we should avoid imposing any thing on them. We should try to encourage in every way their own traditional arts and culture; (b) Tribal rights in land and forests should be respected; (c) We should try to train and build up a team of their own people to do the work of administration and development; (d) We should not over administer these areas or overwhelm them with multiplicity of schemes. We should rather work through, and not in rivalry to, their own social and cultural institutions; and (e) We should judge results, not by statistics or the amount of money spent, but by the quality of human character that is evolved. (Nehru 1958 in Elwin 1988 : xiii; also see Govt. of India Report, 1960:13).

These principles are very fundamental in character and have ever lasting values. The Panchayats (Extension to the Scheduled Areas) act, 1996 while clarifying the scope of the state legislation regarding extending the provisions of part IX of the Constitution to the Scheduled Areas says, "A state legislation on the Panchayats shall be in consonance with the customary law, social and religious practices and traditional management practices of community resources". It is a good thing that in the field of Panchayati Raj administration tribal culture is given weightage in the Constitutional Amendment. Tribals in various parts of the country are still revolting for their rights on land, water and forests. This point was also reflected in the *Tribal Panchashil* of Pt. Nehru. "Government in the Centre and State Governments are now coming out with various new policies or to implement existing policies sincerely relating to tribals right on land and forests, etc. The *Tribal Panchashil* rightly says that "we should rather work through their own social and cultural institutions not in rivalry to". (ibid.,13).

THE CULTURE CHANGE

Tribals no longer live alone. Contacts are there between them and their non-tribal neighbours. Modern forces are also actively moulding their way of life. As culture is dynamic, the tribals have faced and are facing changes. Factors responsible for the transformation are broadly of two types; Traditional and Modern.

The traditional process, characterised by the impact of the major neighbouring communities on the tribal group, has long been in operation and has led to the resultant concepts like Hinduization, Sanskritisation, Tribe-caste continuum, etc. The modern process includes such factors like Christianity, urbanisation and industrialisation. Tribal development schemes, community development schemes, democratic set-up of the nation through introduction of Panchayatiraj System, modernisation in education and administration and the like are of recent origin. (Vidyarthi and Rai, op cit., 454). The forces which are responsible at present to bring about significant changes may be mentioned as:

- (i) development of communication within the tribal area and with outside world;
- (ii) introduction of money economy;
- (iii) spread of formal and modern education;
- (iv) extension services by modern institutions including medical and administrative aids; and intervention of NGOs; and
- (v) introduction of advanced technology to exploit the mineral forest, power and other industrial resources.

In spite of these forces operating and changes taking place, different tribes or sections, of a tribe will continue to respond to the change differently. The tribals have also retained the principal elements of their ways of life, though these are modified to a greater or lesser extent. The identity and variety of the tribal culture, of course in a changed form, will be maintained. (ibid., 472). The aspects of the tribal culture which have survival values are to be preserved and encouraged. It is the right time to rethink sustainable tribal development through their socio-cultural background, available resources and skill endowments. Some of the positive values in tribal culture discussed above are nothing but social capital which has to be properly utilised for their sustainable development. Verrier Elwin remarked "Let us teach them that their (tribals) own culture, their own arts are precious things that we respect and need. When they feel that they can make contribution to their country, they will feel part of it. It is, therefore, an important aspect of their integration". (Elwin, 1964: 302).

ENDNOTES

1. For the Mishimis living in Lohit district of Arunachal Pradesh, the cows and bullocks did not have any use other than beef. So, when these animals were supplied to them in early 1980s either as milching animal or as draft animal they killed them and ate away. The deaths of these animals were reported as a result of the act of predatory animals. Personal communication with M.C.Behera, Arunachal Institute of Tribal Studies, Rajiv Gandhi University, Itanagar, Arunachal Pradesh.
2. Field observation.
3. Village money lender.
4. Courtesy : Pragati, 2009 Maa Sangathan Jeebika Pain (Oriya), Koraput: Pragati, Orissa. Pragati is the name of the NGO.
5. (See, Government of Orissa, Adibasi, July, 1964, Preface).
6. The Khamptis of Arunachal Pradesh had water driven rice mills. In stead of improving the existing technology the government introduced diesel driver rice hullers. As a result, the traditional rice mills of the Khamptis no more exist and except a few elderly persons no body know the technology of making and running such mills. The technology of hand made paper by the Monpas and the Khamptis was not encouraged, improved and incorporated in industrial activities during early plan periods. Personal communication with M.C.Behera, op cit.
7. Also see Behera,1994: 99, fn.18).

REFERENCES

Alez, K.P. (1994), *The Gospel of Indian Culture*. Calcutta: Punthi Pustak. Amalorpavadars, D.S. 1982. "Indian Culture in Indian Christian Spirituality". In D.S. Amalorpavadars(ed). *Indian Christian Spirituality*. Bangalore:National Biblical Catechetical and Liturgical Centre.

Behera, M.C. (1994), *Planning and Socio-EconomicDevelopment of the Tribals*. New Delhi: Commonwealth Publishers.

Elwin, Verrier (1943), *The Aboriginal*. London: Oxford University Press.

Elwin , Verrier (1964), *The Tribal World of Verrier Elwin*. London: Oxford University Press.

Elwin.V. (1988), *A Philosophy for NEFA* (reprint). Itanagar:Diretorate of Research, Government of Arunachal Pradesh.

Govt. of India (1960), *Report of Special Multipurpose Tribal Blocks Committee*. New-Delhi: Ministry of Home Affairs.

Govt. of Orissa (1964), "Jawaharlal Nehru on the Tribal People". *Adibasi* (July) Orissa: Tribal Research Bureau.

Pragati (2009), *Maa Sangathan Jeebika Pain* (Oriya), Koraput: Pragati.

Samal, J. (1996), "Socio-cultural Barriers in Tribal Development". *Parab*. Koraput: District Council of Culture, 32-35.

Samal, J. (2000), "Values in Tribal Culture". *Parab*. Koraput: District Council of Culture. 73-77.

Srivastava, K.B. (1999), *Panchayats in Scheduled Areas: An Analysis of Provisions of the Panchayats*. Hyderabad: NIRD

Vidyarthi, L.P. and B.K. Ray (1985), *The Tribal Culture of India* (reprint). New Delhi: Concept Publishing Company. First published in 1976.

Vidyarthi L.P. (1981), "The Cultural Factors in Development Process: Case Studies from Tribal Bihar". In L.P. Vidyarthi (ed) *Tribal Development and its Administration*. New Delhi: Concept Publishing Company.

26

GURJAR AGITATION IN RAJASTHAN: ISSUES AND IMPACTS

S.K. Kataria

"When the General Assembly becomes a bourgeois theatre, the bourgeois theatre must become the General Assembly."

—A Popular Slogan during Student's Agitation in France (1968)

Rajasthan, the largest state of the country is characterized by its forts, palaces, desert as well as heterogeneous socio-economic and geographical conditions. As per 2001 census there is 7.09 million (12.56%) population belonging to scheduled tribes in the state. (see appendix-1). According to the provisions of contained in Article 244(1) of the Constitution of India, South and South-East region of the state comprising five districts is declared as scheduled area where tribal communities like–Bheel, Garasiya, Saharia, Damor, Kathodi, Dhanka, Nayak etc. are living. Meena, an advanced tribe of the state has no comparison with other tribes of the country.

The Gurjar agitations of 2007 and 2008 of the state have raised new questions of law and order, political loyalty, social responsibilities, ethnicity and liberalization. The violent agitation of Gurjar community during two consecutive summers had derailed the entire politico-administrative system of the state. The Gurjars, the peasant caste of North India are demanding their inclusion in the list of Scheduled Tribes for reservation purposes. Although Gurjars are already enjoying reservation facility in OBC list, but other castes in OBC list are far advance than Gurjars. So hardly a Gurjar candidate can compete with the candidates from the communities of Jats, Malis, Khatis, Yadavas, Sunars and Kumhars, etc. Further it is to be mentioned that Gurjars are included in ST list of Himachal Pradesh and Jammu and Kashmir. Naturally, in these states hardly they face any competition. In fact, inclusion of Rajasthan's prosperous and progressive 'Jat' community in OBC list by Mr. Atal Bihari Vajpayee's government in 2003, was the turning point for Gurjar reservation seekers.

So far as representative bureaucracy is concerned the number of civil servants from Gurjar community is very marginal at various levels of government machinery. To resolve the issue, the BJP government led by Mrs. Vasundhara Raje passed a bill in the State Assembly in July, 2008 for providing 5 per cent reservation to Gurjars under a new category—SBC (Special Backward Class). The bill is still pending with the Governor. The Gurjar agitation has changed the socio-political and administrative harmony of the peaceful state and thus so many non realistic demands and subdued frustration are surfacing. Gurjars, already backward in terms of socio-economic parameters have lost public sympathy by using a violent way to avail ST status.

BACKGROUND

Although the origin of Gurjar caste is a debatable issue, yet it is assumed that the term 'Gurjar' was being used for both—a caste and a geographical area. The most popular opinion on the origin of Gurjars is given by historian *A.M.T. Jackson* and *William Brooke*. They believe that the *'Khajar'* community residing in Syria and Arminia had moved to India during Sixth Century and they inhabited in Gujrat, Rajputana and Punjab provinces of India. Since Khajars were expert in operating a weapon known as *Gurj*, so they were known as Gurjars. As per *Kalhan's Rajtarangini*, there was a king named Alkhuna from Gurjar community who was ruling Punjab during the 12th century.

As per census data of 1931 (the last census of caste) there was 4.76 per cent Gurjar population in Rajasthan. Gurjar leaders claim that at present their population is about 8 per cent in Rajasthan and 4 per cent in India. Traditionally Gurjars are earning their livelihood through farming and trading of milk. In fact, Gurjars are comparatively more illiterate, poor, backward and socially neglected. They have very marginal number in various echelons of central and state civil services. Child marriage is a major problem of Gurjar community. They are not living in the forests but residing in villages and cities.

MOVE TOWARDS S.T. STATUS

Gurjars of Rajasthan, raised their demand for ST status (see Annexure -1 for the procedure of scheduling communities and STs) first time in 1961 but no attention was paid by the government, although a revised list through SC/ST Ordinance Amendment, 1976 was issued and that is still prevalent. In 1981 Government of India sought information from state government to include various castes (including Gurjars) in SC and ST list. The government of Rajasthan replied that 'Banjara' and 'Gadia Luhar' may be included in S.T. list and other castes do not fulfil the criteria. The same exercise was done in 1999 on the basis of the reports submitted by district collectors. Meanwhile Mr. Rajesh Pilot emerged out as a national leader and ambitions of Gurjars started mounting up.

Following Mandal Commission Report Gurjars were included in state OBC list in 1994. Again in 2002 Gurjars raised their demand and presented a memorandum to Congress Party's government, but the state government opined that the matter falls under purview of Union Government. In a press conference held on May 4, 2003 four ministers of Ashok Gehlot's government said that there was no need of separate reservation for Gurjars. It was State Assembly elections of 2003, when the Gurjars put their long cherished demand to each political platform. The then BJP leader Mrs. Vasundhara Raje lured Gurjar through her *bahu* (daughter in law) who came from Gurjar community. So she sought votes from Gurjar community for being their close relatives (*Samdhan*). No doubt, Gurjars had supported BJP in these elections. In 2006, Mr. Ramgopal Guard, Chairman of district Panchayat (Zila Parishad) of Jaipur started agitation. The then Home Minister, Mr. Gulab Chand Kataria, intervened and informal meetings with Gurjar leaders were initiated. In this connection government of Rajasthan again sought views of district collectors on the status of Gurjar caste on the basis of socio-economic survey and Lokur committee parameters.

Then came May 2007, the turning point of Gurjar agitation. Ex army officer Colonel Kirori Singh Bainsla came in the light as President of "Gurjar Aarakshan Sangharsh Samiti". As soon as the meeting between government officials and Gurjar leaders ended without any result, the Gurjar Community started disobedience of all the authorities. Most parts of North and North-Western Indian were engulfed in violent agitation by the Gurjar community during May 29 to June 4, 2007. A total 26 persons were shot dead during police firing in Rajasthan. After a week long violence Colonel Bainsla withdrew the agitation and the state government constituted a judicial enquiry Commission headed by Justice Fateh Chand Bansal, to investigate police firing incidence during this agitation. Colonel Bainsla had been booked for murder and instigating violence.Meanwhile two writs were filed to Rajasthan high court by Meena community to stop state government to take any hasty decision in pressure. Facing a continuous pressure from Gurjars the state government wrote a letter to solve the issue without making a clear recommendation.

CHOPRA COMMITTEE

In accordance to the pact between state government and Gurjar leaders, the government of Rajasthan set up a Committee under Chairmanship of Justice Jasraj Chopra, which was meant primarily to look into the eligibility of Gurjars for S.T. status. It is learnt that Chopra committee toured 147 villages and received more than 40,000 representations and 35,000 affidavits. About 200 C.D. Video discs on Gurjar habitations were submitted to the district collectors, who in turn presented their own finding to the Committee. *According to Chopra Committee Gurjars did not fulfil the criteria for S.T.* In this light, Chopra Committee suggested that state government should provide a special package for underdeveloped and remote areas of the state to ensure overall development of backward communities including Gurjars. In December 2007 the state government constituted a committee under Chairmanship of Mr. Ramdas Agarwal, Member of Parliament to prepare plan of action for special package. Further, State Cabinet accepted the recommendations of Agrawal Committee and new holistic developmental programme namely 'Devnarayan Scheme' along with special package of Rs. 1000 million was announced. Similarly Rs. 1821.1 million were also especially earmarked for Gurjar development from various line departments' fund. Devnarayan Board was formed and Mr. S.S.Dungas, Retd. IAS officer of MP cadre, a close relative of Colonel Bainsla, was made its chairman.

Since Gurjars were unhappy with the recommendations of Chopra Committee, they launched a fresh agitation in May, 2008 by blocking the highways and railway lines. Destruction of State property and assault on police force by Gurjar agitators led to police firing and as a result, 37 people were shot dead and more than 300 persons were injured. Although, on next day the state government had deployed the army around the Gurjar agitators but the army was not allowed to take any action. Gurjar agitators retained all the dead bodies and refused to do funeral rituals until government declared induction of Gurjars in S.T. list. After a three weeks chaos, the state government and Sanyukt Gurjar Aarakshan Sangharsh Samiti reached to an agreement on June 18, 2008.

To implement the agreement government withdrew all the litigations against Gurjar agitators and provided Rs. 5 lac to the family of each deceased. Government had also promised to provide government job to one person from each family of deceased.

In July 2008, a special session of State Assembly was convened and "Rajasthan Scheduled Castes, Scheduled Tribes, Backward Classes, Special Backward Classes (Reservation of Seats in Educational Institutions in the state and of appointments and posts in services under the state) Bill, 2008" was passed unanimously on July 16, 2008. According to the bill a new Special Backward Class (SBC) category was made for providing reservation to Gurjars, Bunjara, Gadia Luhar and Rebari community. Similarly, 14 per cent reservation was provisioned for economically poor general castes. Apparently keeping in mind the sensitivities of the influential Meena community which enjoys the ST status in the state, the government sought to allay apprehension about the impact of the quota for Gurjars on the present reservation system.

Reservation in Rajasthan

SC	=	16%	Existing
ST	=	12%	
OBC	=	21%	
SBC	=	05%	Proposed
EBC	=	14%	
Total		68%	

Since 1997, 30 per cent seats in each category are reserved for women in Rajasthan.As a process, the bill was sent to the governor of the state for his approval but the Governor Mr. Shilendra Kumar Singh kept the bill pending. Eventually the ruling BJP party, lost the State Assembly elections in November, 2008 and Congress Party came back in the power.

Meanwhile the Governor sought expert legal opinion on the bill from various agencies. Most of the experts were with the view that state government cannot violate Articles-38 and 46 of the Constitution of India as well as the instructions given by Supreme Court to confine reservation within limit of 50 per cent. On the other hand Colonel Kirori Singh Bainsla was pressurising Governor for his consent over the bill. Governor wrote a letter to the President of India, Prime Minister, Union Home Minister and Union Law and Justice Minister regarding the controversy over the bill. In January, 2009 the leader of opposition (former Chief Minister) Mrs. Vasundhara Raje wrote a letter to the Governor and requested him to sign the bill or refer it to the President of India, while new government led by Mr. Ashok Gehlot expressed that reservation quota issue would be solved within the constitutional framework only. Mr. Gehlot has cleared his opinion. He said—"My government would not give false promise of reservation to any group."

IMPACTS OF GURJAR AGITATION

Present era of LPG (Liberalization, Privatization and Globalization) or NEO (New Economic Order) is mostly affected by information technology and international trends. So far as socio-cultural impacts of globalization are concerned, it may be characterised by following parameters:

- The concept of use and throw.
- Machiavellianism based attainment, believes that goal achievement is important, do not bother about means.
- Information technology affected behaviour tends to instant results.
- Ethnicity and its side effects.
- Needs are superseded by wants.

Impacts of Gurjar agitations can be discussed through the following points:

1. India, is the only country where time machine fails. We can observe different ages, different cultures and various unbelievable characteristics at the sametime and same place. Although regional and ethnical or cultural prejudices are dying due to globalization but this trend is leading to rootlessness and thus 'identity crisis' is emerging. Contrary to global village culture, the rise of fundamentalism has become a serious issue.

Across the globe ethnicity or inclination towards own caste, race, religion, creed and language is increasing. Raj Thakarey's *Marathi Manush* concept or Gurjar's demand for inclusion in S.T. are in the same vein proving narrow, selfish and illogical one-sided views of a community.

According to *Kurt Lewin's* force field theory there are two different types of forces working every time in each organisation and even in a society. Driving force acts as positive and motivating force to excel the society towards betterment, while restraining force blocks the progress or withdrew the achievement of any society. During Gurjar agitations of Rajasthan, force field theory of group dynamics was working and pendulum was swinging according to circumstances. It is important to learn that Meena community had filed two civil writ petitions (SB civil writ petition no. 4695/07 Shri Lakhan Singh v/s state of Rajasthan and SB civil writ petition no. 5526/07 Shri Narayan Kemala v/s state of Rajasthan) in Jaipur bench of Rajasthan high court to avoid any hasty decision by the state government under undue pressure. The Hon'ble Court had given interim order and directed to state government not to violate any legal provision or democratic process under the pressure of Gurjar agitators. It was not the government, but the Meena community who ended the first violent agitation through guerrilla method by checking supply of food and other essential material to the agitators. Even the MLAs of BJP belonging to Meena community stood against their government and entire game was fought by these two castes.

2. During first violent agitation (2007) of Gurjars, a national debate against destruction of public property by agitators was started. While hearing a public interest litigation on the issue the apex court of the country constituted two committees-one for strengthening the provisions of "Prevention of

Damage to Public Properties Act , 1984" headed by former Justice of the Supreme Court Mr. K.T.Thomas and another one was chaired by senior advocate Mr. Fali S. Nariman. Justice Thomas Committee in its Report (2009) suggested measures on the strict compliance of the Act. The Nariman committee has dealt with the issue of media coverage on strikes with specific reference to television coverage focusing on the agitation indulging in vandalism. The Nariman Committee has suggested that leaders of the agitation should be made absolutely liable for the destruction of property by their supporters and there should be self regulation on the part of the media.

3. In the history of Rajasthan, it was the first time when the state government declared a special development package (See Appendix-2) for any region or community. In terms of development of backward areas and low pace communities, the Gurjar agitation was a landmark. Even, families of Gurjars were started rethinking over their poor socio-economic status. According to an NGO after Gurjar agitations the rate of schooling of Gurjar girl child has increased remarkably.

4. A political analyst has to say: "The cost of the game played by ruling BJP government during Gurjar agitation was losing the reign." Although, there were so many factors behind the defeat of ruling party but it is clear that Gurjar factor had played a vital role. Meenas, the strongest, Schedule Tribe of the nation, were totally against the state government. Mr. Prahlad Gunjal, an MLA of BJP was expelled by the party during the agitation. Interestingly, Mr. Gunjal has lost the election held after Gurjar agitation. Perhaps, it sounds, that other castes of Gurjar dominated constituencies got united. A general conclusion of results of State Assembly elections is that no clear-cut caste factor was working in Rajasthan.

5. It is interesting to note that reservation facilities in India has removed the caste based stigmas and inferiority complexes. Even Brahmins and Rajputs have staged Dharna and organised big rallies on caste banners to seek reservation. In other words no upper caste wants to remain in general category so far as reservation in admission and recruitments is concerned. After Gurjar agitation of year 2007, at least for mega rallies have bean organised by general castes demanding inclusion of their castes in SC or ST in Rajasthan. Similarly various nomadic and semi nomadic castes or communities namely, Kalbelia, Bunjara, Sapera, Luhar, Saansi, Bawaria, Kanjar, Bhand, Bedia, Bazigar, Nat, Manganiyar, Rana and Bhopa etc. have made their federation to get reservation facilities. Though, a few of them have been included in SBC alongwith Gurjars, they are demanding to make a law.
6. As per letter of the Governor of Rajasthan to the President of India, the main hero of Gurjar agitation Colonel Bainsla says, "...I feel myself in a tight corner... in this issue I have been trapped; only you (Governor) can save me. I am at your mercy. If you do not clear the bill, I will loose all my personal and political reputation." The irony is that Gurjars have lost 63 youths and they have not gained anything. The government of Rajasthan has forwarded the Chopra Committee Report and about 4-5 letters written to the Central Government but no letter contains the recommendation or opinion of the state government.
7. Gurjar agitation has opened the new dimension and ways for political ambitions. It is the Gurjar agitation, through which Colonel Bainsla, Mr. Prahlad Singh Gunjal, Mr. Roop Singh, Mr. Avtar Singh Bhadana and Mr. Vikram Singh Gurjar were emerged on national canvas. Perhaps, keeping in mind this avenue, most notorious dacoit of Chambal (11 lac reward on head)

Mr. Jagan Gurjar surrendered to police on January 31, 2009 in presence of young congress MP Mr. Sachin Pilot. Mr. Jagan Gurjar declared that he wants to live in mainstream of the society.

8. The grey side of Gurjar agitation include Gurjar-Meena split, civil disobedience, polarization of politics, set back to tourism industry of Rajasthan as well as Agra (Taj Mahal), emergence of pressure politics, low morale of police force and destruction of public property including highways and Delhi- Mumbai railway track. The Gurjars agitators had built their huts on the railway track. Such type of vandal attitude of Gurjars not only caused grave public inconveniences but they had lost public support at large. It is very painful to state that after police firing at Peelupura in May, 2008, the state government has intimated to Mr. A.S. Gill, the Director General of Rajasthan Police to go on a long leave. In other words he was mistreated by the state government without any ground. Such type of political behaviour demoralise the police force as well as the civil servants of the state machinery.

9. This agitation has started a new debate about the criteria of determining ST status. As per the opinion of experts, the criteria laid down by the Lokur Committee are hardly relevant today, for example, a very few tribes can today be said to possess 'primitive traits'. Similarly, several ST are nomadic and they are not considered untouchable and they occupied the lowest position in social hierarchy. Munda, Orang (Oraon/Oran), Santhal are enjoying ST status in Tripura and they had been migrated to tea plantation in Assam. Now these tea and ex-tea garden communities including Munda, Oran, Gonds and Santhals from Bihar, Orissa and Madhya Pradesh are demanding ST status in Assam because they are enjoying ST status in their own states. In 2005, Assam

government submitted a report to Centre Government compiled by Assam Institute of Research for Tribals and Scheduled Castes, Guwahati recommending the inclusion of 97 tea and ex-tea tribe in ST (Plains) list. On the other hand a new debate on prosperity of existing ST community had been ignited. Even policy on tribal says –"Exclusion of the creamy layer among the ST from the benefits of reservation has never been seriously considered. As we move towards and try to ensure greater social justice, it would be necessary to give this matter more attention and work out an acceptable system."

As a conclusion we can say that the Gurjar agitations of Rajasthan have raised so many issues not only in front of policy makers of the country but to a common man too regarding rule of law, social justice, social responsibilities and equal development of all the segments of a society in a welfare state and global village. It is globalization where knowledge and information can prove their vitality to a great extent and in such a open system no issue can be solved in isolation. Perhaps the wave of globalisation has raised the level of over consciousness among all the communities across the world. Eminent anthropologist *Anthony Kohan* says, "People become more serious and conscious about their own culture when they enter to the gate of other culture" across the world.

REFERENCES

Constitution of India (2007), New Delhi: Ministry of Law and Justice, Govt. of India.

Frontline (2008), Volume 25, Issue 01, January 5-18.

Patrika Year Book, 2008, Jaipur: Rajasthan Patrika Publication.

Appendix-1
Population Growth in Rajasthan

Year	Total Population (lacs)	SC Number	SC Percentage	ST Number	ST Percentage
1951	159.71	16.90	10.58	3.36	02.04
1961	201.56	33.60	16.67	23.51	11.66
1971	257.66	40.76	15.82	31.26	12.13
1981	342.62	58.39	17.04	41.83	12.21
1991	440.66	76.08	17.29	54.75	12.44
2001	565.07	96.94	17.16	70.98	12.56

Appendix-2
Special Package for Backward Areas in Rajasthan

Name of Dept. Expenditure (Rs.millions)	*Proposed Work*	*Unit*	*Estimated*
Public Health Engineering	Handpump and Tubewells	4622	504.3
School Education	New School and Upgradation	255	301.1
Medical and Health	SC, PHC and Anganwaris	334	392.8
Dairy	Women Dairy, Co-operative Dairy and Infrastructure	820	252.3
Animal Husbandry	Hospitals and Integrated Cattle Development Centres	05	47.2
Women and Child Dev.	Anganwari Centers and Training	551	635.9
Public Works Dept.	Roads	342.12 km.	530.8
Water Resources	Minor Irrigation	29	408.7
Technical Educations	New ITIs	6	150.0
Social Justice and Empowerment	New Hostels	12	80.00
Ex Servicemen Welfare	Rest House and Hostels	6	21.4
Devasthan	Renovation of Temples	2	5.00
Rajasthan Livelihood Mission	Skill Training	5800	—
Total			2821.1

Annexture-1

PROCESS OF ENLISTING A CASTE IN ST

The Constitution of India makes following provisions for identification and enlisting of a community in the Scheduled Tribes list—

Article-342 (1) The President may with respect to any State or Union territory, and where it is a State, after consultation with the Governor thereof, by public notification, specify the tribes or tribal communities, specify the tribes or tribal communities or part of or groups within tribes or tribal communities which shall for the purposes of this constitution be deemed to be Scheduled Tribes in relation to that State or Union territory, as the case may be.

(2) Parliament may by law include in or exclude from the list of Scheduled Tribes specified in a notification issued under clause (1) any tribe or tribal community or part of or group within any tribe or tribal community, but save as aforesaid a notification issued under the said clause shall not be varied by any subsequent notification.

In June, 1965, the Government of India had constituted a committee for revision of SC and ST under chairmanship of the then home secretary. B.L. Lokur. The Lokur committee evolved the following criteria for the purpose of determing communities could be classified as ST—

1. Primitive Traits
2. Distinctive Culture
3. Geographical Isolation
4. Shyness of Contact with the Community at Large,
5. Backwardness.

The due process of enlisting a community in ST list is as following—

(i) Proposal by a state government to add or delete a caste in ST list.

(ii) Recommendation on the proposal by Registrar, General Govt. of India.

(iii) Recommendation on the proposal by National Commission of Scheduled Tribes.

(iv) Interministerial consultation on these three recommendations and its submission to cabinet.

(v) Presentation of a bill in the parliament.

(vi) Notification of the act.

It is contextual to mention here that National Policy on Tribals (2006) has also stressed upon rethinking over criteria laid down by Lokur committee for identification of ST.

27

IMPACT OF GLOBALISATION ON TRIBAL GROUPS IN INDIA: AN ANTHROPOLOGICAL STUDY ON DHANKUT OF BAHRAICH DISTRICT, U.P.)

Alok Chantia, Preeti Misra

INTRODUCTION

People around the globe are more connected to each other today than ever before in the history of humankind. Information and money flow more quickly than ever. Goods and services produced in one part of the world are increasingly available in all parts of the world. International travel is more frequent. International communication is commonplace.

We live in an intensely interdependent world in which all the people with their immense differences of culture and historical experiences are compressed together in instant communication. We face today a world of almost infinite promise which is also a world of terminal danger. This phenomenon has been titled "Globalization."

"The Era of Globalization" is fast becoming the preferred term for describing the current times. Just as the Depression, the Cold War Era, the Space Age, and the Roaring 20"s are used to describe particular periods of history; Globalization describes the political, economic, and cultural atmosphere of today. Universalisation of marriage, family is a good example of globalisation which shows the psychic unity of mind (Taylor,1871) and more than 50 cultural traits are common across the world. Universalisation of English alphabets and digits is another sphere of globalization but in present scenario globalization is defined in terms of time and space (Gidden, 2001), and is mainly concerned with different economic parameters. (Gordon, 1988:24). Importantly, globalisation has been studied as post industrial society (Castells, 1989), as a process emanating from the west and therefore another form of westernization. (Spybey, 1996). Some scholars think it as the story of homogenization. Globalisation advocates about civil society instead of society. Civil society includes the church, education, trade union and other organization which act to a lesser or greater degree independent of the state. Therefore, the civil society has been the arena of social and political protestation movements, particularly movement such as human rights, animal rights, environmentalism, trade unionism and peace movement.

In general practice it is believed that the impact of globalization on the structural changes in the society comes generally through the changes. The impact of globalization is regarded as being largely negative to India on the weaker and marginalized section of the society e.g. small and marginal farmers and agricultural labourers. There is noted adverse impact of globalization on labour and their unions. It is asserted that the new economic policy reforms in India have serious negative implications for the scheduled castes and scheduled tribes. Reforms have nothing to offer them except marginalization and displacement. Most discussion on the impact of globalization on cultural and social identity of people relate to questions such as - will globalization eventually bring about a cultural homogenization among societies which today enjoy cultural diversity? Which culture would dominate in this process? What would be the fate of local cultures? Will they face a total loss of identity? What about the cultural minority groups, religious groups and ethnicities? Will they face extinction through homoginisation? Finally is globalization of culture a new incarnation of westernization-a mark of cultural imperialism? (Hirst &Thompson, 1996a:47,1996b).

Economists the world over talk of development as the development of wealth, infrastructure, comforts, conveniences, technology, and resources possessed. They see land, oil, natural resources, buildings, roads, airport, education, etc. as development. But these are the *results* of development, not development. Again, community development, national extension service, hybrid seeds, fertilizers, and liberalization are spoken of as development. These are strategies, programmes and projects. They are the *means* to development but not development itself.

A social *energy* helps develop. Certain *will* of the society releases that energy. Sometimes that energy is *directed* to become a social force. That direction is given by the social *attitude* and social *goals*. An *organization* in the society converts that force into social power. The available social *skills* convert that social power into the social results mentioned above. The process by which the social energy is converted into social results is a social process. It is this process that is called development. (Streenten, 2001).

Development is a process and not a programme or a policy. Will, energy, direction, force, organization, power, and skill all go to accomplish development. All together they make up the development organization which incidentally includes a part known as organization too. It is this that serves as the lynch pin for development. In a sense this developmental organization is the backbone or social structure that enables the process of development to complete itself.

If we observe the pattern of social mobility and incident of poverty since independence in our country, we find that measures of social welfare, education and economic development have contributed to the reduction of poverty, but the relative social inequalities have increased. In absolute term, the standard of consumption has qualitatively improved in villages and towns; the reservation policy together with focus upon education has created a limited middle class among the weaker sections, minorities and ethnic groups; the quality and extent of participation in politics and power sharing by backward class, tribes and scheduled castes etc. has radically changed. A substantial degree of empowerment of these groups has taken place in the political realm, but in the economic and educational field the gap between them and the dominant class or class persists. The most strategic aspect of policy relate to social development of our human resource base, agriculture and infrastructure. Economic development as social development in a balanced manner holds the key to our ability to meet with the challenges of globalization and accommodate the upsurge of identities and thus lack of social development is increasing the sphere of social movements. (World Bank, 2002).

Social movements have broadly been perceived as 'organised' or collective efforts to bring about changes in the thoughts, beliefs, values, attitudes, relationships and major institutions in the society or to resist any change in the above societal arrangement. Social movement is defined as collective effort to solve a problem. (Blumer, 1951). It brings also change in certain social institutions. (Harberle, 1972 and Gusfield, 1971). But it also opposes for change. (Wilson, 1973). Social movement may be the effect of globalization which is responsible for social development.

IMPACT OF GLOBALISATION ON TRIBAL GROUPS IN INDIA

Tribals in India present a significant degree of cultural and ethnic diversity. They differ in their socio-cultural levels as well as in their behaviour patterns. Tribal situation in the country poses peculiar problems of development, not encountered in other areas. The peculiarities can be broadly summed up as geographical, demographic, socio-cultural and exploitative. Tribal development indicates serious challenges to the policy makers, administrators and development activists. The socio-economic forces of modernization and development have no doubt brought some benefits to the people of respective areas but the benefits accrued to them have been largely out weighted by the harm more to them. Development induced displacement, in voluntary migration and resettlement has also cause marginalization of tribals and presented enormous problems to them. The new economic regime has led to privatization and marketisation of economy and thus it has been treated as powerful threat to the survival of tribal communities. The socio-cultural change among the tribal communities has no doubt empowered the tribals; however, their cultural identity is under severe stress. The human development indices also demonstrate the backwardness and marginalization of tribal communities in India.

With the increase in material and moral density a new phenomenon emerged in the form of globalization for smooth survival of human being across the world. It is a well known fact that purchasing capacity of every individual on global level is not the same which generates the feeling of inequality. So far as globalization process is concerned it is reflected in different perspective with regard to different peoples. The fruits of globalization have not reached to tribal areas fully. Except facilities like roads, elementary education, primary health centre, and panchayat, no concrete change has taken place in the lives of tribal people.

Under the Indian Constitution the government can declare some specific groups as tribal groups on the fulfilment of certain conditions. The number of tribal groups have increased manifold in post Constitution India. Today we have 692 tribal groups in India and 9 per cent of the total population is tribal. Due to increase in tribal groups fruits of privileges given to them by the Government are decreasing. Some actual tribal groups are still far away from being listed as tribal groups. Anthropologically actual tribal groups are still behind the curtain and devoid of all basic facilities of life. The case of a group Dhankut living in District Bahraich of Uttar Pradesh is no different and is glaring example of violation of human rights of actual tribal people. Dhankut are living in small pocket of Dhankuttypura of District Bahraich, Uttar Pradesh and their dialect is Dhankutty in a rhythmic form. They practise cross cousin and parallel cousin marriage which is a taboo in north India and legally prohibited too under Hindu Marriage Act 1955. Even after having these tribal characteristics they are not included in the category of Scheduled Tribe. Though they are not agricultural people, cereal selling is still their main occupation. They are poor and illiterate. With 5 per cent literacy rate only three of them are in fourth class government job. No literature is available about them neither in government records nor in district gazetteer. They have full faith in their traditional panchayat and traditional God "Gullabeer." They are struggling for their tribal status since 1973 but have not succeeded so far. Dhankut want tribal status for themselves to enjoy the benefits provided by the government in the era of globalization.

METHODOLOGY

Present study was carried out between May-June 2008. It is a primary data based work with the help of participant observation and schedule based interview. Dhankut are 2687 in number (791 male and 799 female) (2001 census), 1097 (582 boys and 515 girls) are children i.e. below the age of 18 years. Therefore out of 1590 adults Dhankuts only 300 respondents above the age of 18 years have been chosen on the basis of random sampling to analyse the effect of globalization on socio-cultural life of Dhankut. The study revealed that though globalization is universal phenomenon but its effect is not homogenous at micro level as in case of Dhankut living in Bahraich district of Uttar Pradesh. The study further revealed that the impact of globalization is accelerating the process of social movement amongst Dhankut.

MEANING OF GLOBALIZATION AND AVAILABILITY OF HUMAN RIGHTS

So far as globalization is concerned it came within the comprehension of people in 1990s which not only led to overall growth and development but also opened a Pandora box leading to various socio-economic and cultural problems. One of the greatest effect of globalization was that it made the people aware of their human rights. The knowledge and awareness of human rights is essential for the formation of public opinion and the generation of public pressure for the compliance of human rights. It is thus *sine qua non* for the observance and advancement of human rights and social growth and development. Only those people who are educated about and aware of their human rights can demand that their government observe those rights. Knowledge of human rights is essential as a tool for the observance and the protection of human rights. It also creates a climate of public opinion in which gross violation of human rights are unacceptable. (Therborn, 2000:151). The term "Human Rights" came to be used after the Second World War; hence it is also not within the comprehension of each and every person.

So far as Dhankut are concerned they are not very much aware of the term "globalization and human rights". Table 1 reveals Dhankut's knowledge about globalization and human rights. It shows that majority of respondents 274(91.3%), 136(86.6%) males and 138 (96.5%) females say that they have not heard the term "globalization and human rights." Dhankut are illiterate and globalization and human right are newly launched concepts during last two decade only, that is why only those who are literate, are familiar with these terms. Only 26(8.7%) respondents, 21 (13.4%) males and 05 (3.5) females say that they have heard about the term "globalization and human rights."

Table 1
Knowledge of Globalization & Human Rights Among the Respondents

	Have you heard about Globalization & Human Rights?					
	Yes		*No*		*Total*	
Sex Ratio	*Ncs.*	*%*	*Nos.*	*%*	*Nos.*	*%*
Male	21	13.4	136	86.4	157	52.3
Female	05	3.5	138	96.5	143	47.7
Total	26	8.7	274	91.3	300	100.0

Source: Field data

A socially developed society ensures human rights for its people. Generally speaking, human rights mean those fundamental and inalienable rights which are essential for life as a human being. There is however no consensus as to what these rights should be. Human rights may be interpreted as being different according to the particular economic, social and cultural society in which they are being defined. Human rights have so far escaped a universally acceptable definition, presenting a problem to international regulation. There are four salient features of Human Rights which include citizen's rights, liberty, safety and dignity. These are nothing but natural rights necessary for the development of human life and personality.[1] (United Nations, 1995:97).

Even after the 62 years of independence, a large chunk of our population still lives below the poverty line. They do not get two square meals a day, have no access to sufficient clothing to cover their bodies and have no roof over their heads when they sleep at night. They are compelled to lead a life of semi nakedness, malnutrition, disease and drudgery. People are still illiterate and hence cannot make efforts to improve their living condition. This is nothing but great violation of the human rights of our countrymen. So far as Dhankut are concerned they are very poor, socially under developed and hence cannot afford even the basic minimum requirements of their lives. Their requirement of human rights along with socio cultural and economic life is reflected in tables from 2 to 17.

Housing Facility

Adequate housing is universally viewed as one of the most basic human needs. National as well as international laws emphasize upon the significance of a secure place to live for human dignity, physical and mental health and overall quality of life. (U.N. Pub., 2000:3).

The United Nations Centre for Human Settlements estimates that throughout the world, over one billion people live in inadequate housing, with an excess of 100 million people living in conditions classified as homelessness. (ibid.). Besides according to figures released by the World Health

Organization time to time, billions of people in developing countries do not have access to drinking water nor do they have access to adequate sanitation. (W.H.O. Report, 2000).

Table 2
Satisfaction with Housing Facility

	Are you Satisfied with Your House							
	Sufficient		*Unsatisfactory*		*Compromising*		*Total*	
Sex Ratio	*Nos.*	*%*	*Nos.*	*%*	*Nos.*	*%*	*Nos.*	*%*
Male	68	43.3	85	54.1	4	2.6	157	52.3
Female	44	30.7	76	53.1	23	16.2	143	47.3
Total	112	37.4	161	53.6	27	9.0	300	100.0

Source: Same as Table-1

In India position is no different, homelessness or inadequate housing is nothing but denial of right to live with dignity. In *Prabhakaran Nair v. State of Tamil Nadu* (AIR 1987 SC 2117) the Supreme Court admitted that there is acute shortage of housing in India. In *Shankar Banerjee v. Durgapur Projects Ltd* (AIR 1988 Cal 136), it was held that "to ask a person to live in sub-human conditions by depriving him even of the benefit of two small rooms which is the minimum requirement for a family to live and compelling him to live in one single room with his wife and children and to share the bath, toilet and kitchen with another family is nothing but animal existence". An important facet of human right is to live like a human being. Due to lack of space and over crowding in the houses people do suffer from many diseases such as pneumonia and tuberculosis. Reduced birth rate is another problem and natural consequence of over crowding due to want of privacy. Since Dhankut are living at single place Dhankuttypura, their living place has shrinked due to increase in their population over the years.

Table 2 reveals that maximum 161 (53.6%) respondents, 85 (54.1%) males and 76 (53.1%) females are not satisfied with living condition in present houses, whereas 68(43.3%) males and 44(30.7%) females or 112(37.4%) respondents are satisfied with their present abode. Only 27(9%) respondents feel that present houses are only a compromise. It is noticeable that though Dhankut have houses but it is not fit for their proper living. Maximum houses of Dhankut are non-cemented or kachcha, few houses are cemented of those Dhankut, who have acquired a good economic position. Rest of the houses are small in size. A big house is divided into many small houses according to the presence of number of families. A large number of houses (617) are without the basic amenities like water, electricity and sanitary, lavatory facility. 91 houses have a common kitchen, small veranda and one or two rooms. Most of the kachcha houses are made of clay and cow dung. The floor is non-cemented and the roofs are made of tiles (*khaparale*) and sticks (narkul).

Availability of Rooms

The clear impact of population size is reflected in the space of houses. Both are inversely proportional. The size of room is decided by financial condition. So in a limited place living is a hard task. Over crowding in houses also results in many health problems. Maximum Dhankut families are living in congested rooms. Over the years their population has grown but living area has been the same resulting in congested houses and rooms. Table 3 shows that 283 (94.4%) respondents, 148(94.3%) males and 135(94.5%) females have no separate rooms; 17(5.6%) respondents including 9(5.7%) males and 8(5.5%) females have separate rooms for everyone.

Table 3
Condition of Rooms in House

	Do you have Separate Rooms for Every One?					
	Yes		*No*		*Total*	
Sex Ratio	*Nos.*	%	*Nos.*	%	*Nos.*	%
Male	9	5.7	148	94.3	157	52.3
Female	8	5.5	135	94.5	143	47.7
Total	17	5.6	283	94.4	300	100.0

Source: Same as Table-1

Table 4
Condition of Water in House

	Do you have Water Supply in House?					
	Yes		*No*		*Total*	
Sex Ratio	*Nos.*	%	*Nos.*	%	*Nos.*	%
Male	25	15.9	132	84.1	157	52.3
Female	28	19.5	115	80.5	143	47.7
Total	53	17.6	247	82.4	300	100.0

Source: Same as Table-1

Availability of Water

Every great civilization flourished at the bank of a river because availability of water is indispensable for survival, one cannot imagine life without water. Rivers and ponds are natural resources of water and these are used to bring water for the requirement of life. The expansion of urban areas increased the requirement of water which is fulfilled by tube wells, hand pumps and tap water supply but all these devices want money. Dhankut is living in urban area and water is equally must for them, but maximum Dhankut have no water supply in their houses. In the globalised world where people are drinking mineral water, they take water from public water supply. Dhankut are poor, hence they can't afford the expenditure of water connection. The water supply available in their houses is not sufficient as is evident from the table 4, which shows that 247(82.4%) respondents,132(84.1%) males and 15(80.5%) females have no water supply. Only 53(17.6%) respondents including 25(15.9%) males and 28(19.5%) females have water supply in their houses.

Situation of Lavatory

In the very beginning human being used forest and open space and when he settled down in village he/she used open field which were utilized as natural compost. But after the increase of urban areas, no forest or open fields were left. So lavatory system came in vogue-a specific place within the house for discharge of excreta. Dhankut houses are small and they are living in urban area where lavatory system is must. But in reality majority of Dhankut are not having lavatory system in their houses.

Table 5
Situation of Lavatory in Family

	Do you have Lavatory System in your House?					
	Yes		*No*		*Total*	
Sex Ratio	*Nos.*	%	*Nos.*	%	*Nos.*	%
Male	22	14.1	135	85.9	157	52.3
Female	19	13.3	124	86.7	143	47.7
Total	41	13.7	259	86.3	300	100.0

Source: Same as Table-1

Table 5 shows that 259 (86.3%) respondents, 135(85.9%) males and 124(86.7%) females have no lavatory in their houses. Dhankut are poor and their houses are very small. A large section of population uses public drainage and open field for their routine work. They know that lavatory is must but they are helpless to have this basic requirement. Only 41(13.2%) respondents including 22(14.1%) males and 19(13.3%) females have lavatory in their houses.

Table 6
Situation of Electricity in the Family

	Do you have Electricity in your House?					
	Yes		*No*		*Total*	
Sex Ratio	*Nos.*	%	*Nos.*	%	*Nos.*	%
Male	22	14.1	13.5	85.9	157	52.3
Female	22	15.3	121	84.7	143	47.7
Total	44	14.6	256	85.4	300	100.0

Source: Same as Table-1

Facility/Availability of Electricity

In this era energy is an inevitable necessity for individual consumption and industrial production. Electricity is the main and popular source of energy and access to electricity is an indicator of development. Table 6 shows that 256 (85.4%) respondents including 135(85.9%) males and 121(84.7%) females have no electricity facility. They use lantern for this purpose. Only 22(14.1%) males and 22(15.3%) females or overall 44(14.6%) respondents have electricity. Dhankut want to avail all modern facilities but it is not so. They are very far from basic necessities even after living in urban areas.

Education Facility

Education is enlightenment. It lends dignity to a human being. Education seeks to build up the personality of the pupil by assisting his/her physical, intellectual, moral and emotional development. In *University of Delhi v. Ram Nath* (1964 2 SCR 703 at 710) it was held that human being without education is equal to animal. The notions of individual freedom, liberty and dignity of a person, which are the basic tenets of human right, are meaning less to those who are illiterate and ignorant. Education means knowledge which leads to liberation from ignorance. Without education a human being cannot make the best of him/herself and of the opportunities. That is why education is a human right[22]. But the literacy scenario for the Dhankuts provides a dismal picture.

Table 7 shows that Dhankut represent an illiterate group. Majority of respondents 158(52.7%) are illiterate. Only 79(26.4%) have studied upto 5th, 38(12.7%) up to 8th 10(3.3%) up to 10th, 10(3.3%) up to 12th 3(1.0%) up to graduation and only 2(0.6%) have studied up to post graduation. The table of reference also shows that female literacy is lower to male. 90 females are illiterates whereas only 68 males are illiterate. As we proceed towards higher education, it gets clearer. It shows that Dhankut are not very much interested in female Dhankut's education.

Availability of Occupation and Income

Poverty is inability to attain minimal standard of living and is not just absence of wealth alone but a mixture of disabilities and circumstances which breeds a culture of its own. Dr.

Table 7
Educational Qualification of Respondents

Sex Ratio	*Educational Status*														*Total*	
	Illiterate		*1-5th*		*6-8th*		*10th*		*12th*		*Graduation*		*P.G.*			
	Nos.	*%*	*Nos.*	*%*	*Nos.*	*%*	*Nos.*	*%*	*Nos.*	*%*	*Nos.*	*%*	*Nos.*	*%*	*Nos.*	*%*
Male	68	43.5	47	29.9	22	14.0	09	5.7	07	4.4	03	1.9	01	0.6	157	523
Female	90	62.9	32	22.4	16	11.2	01	06	03	2.3	?	?	01	0.6	143	47.7
Total	158	52.7	79	26.4	38	12.7	10	3.3	10	3.3	03	1.0	02	0.6	300	100.0

Source: Same as Table-1

Table 8
Occupational Description of Respondents

	Particulars of Business/Occupations													
	Labour		*Service*		*Business*		*Agriculture*		*Others*		*None*		*Total*	
Sex Ratio	*Nos.*	*%*	*Nos.*	*%*	*Nos.*	*%*	*Nos.*	*%*	*Nos.*	*%*	*Nos.*	*%*	*Nos.*	*%*
Male	60	38.2	03	1.0	62	39.4	09	5.7	-	-	23	14.6	157	52.3
Female	08	5.5	-	-	-	-	-	-	16	11.2	119	83.3	143	47.7
Total	68	22.7	03	1.0	62	20.6	09	3.0	16	5.3	142	47.4	300	100.0

Source: Same as Table-1

Ambedkar viewed equality of opportunity for all citizens as the most important right and very heart and soul of any Constitution. He regarded the Directive Principles of State Policy of Indian Constitution of great value as they lay down the ideal of economic democracy for ending the poverty, ignorance and inequality of opportunity and wipe out tears from every eye. (Constitutional Debates, 2005:494).

Poverty is a system which includes a continuous fight for survival, unemployment, low wages, unskilled labour, absence of food supplies, insufficient possibilities of privacy and child labour. (Chitkara, 1996:342).The perceptions of the poor are coloured by the complex of deprivations which make up their life and hamper their economic and social progress. So far as Dhankut are concerned they are poor and cannot afford a decent standard of living. Most of them are engaged in small time retail work of *thela* pulling, grain selling, palledari, etc. women are engaged in collection of cow dung and making of cow dung cakes. Children too are supporting family income by selling peanuts, and groundnuts etc.

Occupation enhances the status of an individual. With the change in occupation status and living standard of a community also changes. The group under study is involved in different occupations as globalization has given place to market system which took away their traditional work of grain selling. They used to sell it by going door to door but now everybody wants to purchase from the market. Since Dhankut do not have enough money to set up proper shops they have opted for retail selling of small things of every day use.

Table 8 Shows that Dhankut are engaged in different occupations. Maximum females 119(83.3%) are not involved in any occupation/business. Participant observation revealed that 16(11.2%) respondents are doing other works such as collection of cow dung and selling of wood etc. whereas only 8(5.5%) women are engaged as labourers. But males are doing different works; 62(39.4%) are engaged in betel shop, fruit shop, cereal selling, etc., 60(38.2%) are doing labour work, 23(14.6%) are unemployed, 9(5.7%) are engaged in agriculture. Dhankut is a non-agriculture community but during last decade some

Dhankut have purchased agricultural land in Meerpur village for their livelihood. In the whole community only 3(1.7%) are in government services. They are all in fourth class job.

Here it is also important to note that their traditional work was cereal selling which was given up due to emergence of new market system. Dhankut is a non-agricultural group, living in urban area. Diversity of occupation among Dhankut is due to their illiteracy and poverty.

Availability of Income

Income decides the standard of a person, group or community. Whether a person is rich or poor is decided by his/her earnings. So far as income of the Dhankut is concerned their daily/ monthly income is very meager from the occupations adopted by them. Therefore, they are considered poor by the people of adjacent communities.

Table 9 show the monthly income of respondents. Among the respondents, 142 (47.3%) do not have any income; only 84 (28%) earn only Rs. 500, 15 (5%) get Rs. 1500, 11(3.3) get up to Rs. 2000, 9 (3%) more than Rs. 4000, 6 (1.7%) up to Rs. 3000 and 5 (1.7%) are up to 2500 and only 3 (1%) respondents get an income up to Rs. 3500 per month. Thus, the table of reference shows that majority of respondents are getting Rs. 500 p.m. as Dhankut belong to a poor community. There are 119 (83.3) respondents whose occupation is domestic works.

Right to Marriage[3]

Sound and secured married life furthers social development. Marriage observes many other facets of relation between male and female besides any sexual relation. In context of man and woman, kinship plays an important role. In north India, cross-cousin marriage is prohibited, but such marriages are prevalent among tribal communities and in some parts of north India also. Children of mother's brother and father's sister can marry each other.

Among Dhankut, cross cousin and parallel cousin marriages are found to be existent. A girl may be married into that house, where her *bua* (father's sister) has got married. It is

Table 9
Monthly Income of Dhankut

	Particulars of Business/Occupations																			
	500		*1000*		*1500*		*2000*		*2500*		*3000*		*3500*		*4000*		*None*		*Total*	
Sex Ratio	*Nos.*	%	*Nos.*	%	*Nos.*	%	*Nos.*	%	*Nos.*	%	*Nos.*	%	*Nos.*	%	*Nos.*	%	*Nos.*	%	*Nos.*	%
Male	60	38.3	25	15.9	15	9.6	11	7.1	05	3.1	06	3.8	03	1.9	09	5.7	23	14.6	157	52.3
Female	24	16.7	-	-	-	-	-	-	-	-	-	-	-	-	-	-	119	83.3	143	47.7
Total	84	28	25	8.3	15	5	11	3.3	05	1.7	06	1.7	03	1.0	09	3.0	142	47.3	300	100

Source: Same as Table-1

also a notable point that when a girl gets married into one lineage (it means a group of kinsmen to trace themselves back to male or female to a common ancestor) then the girl from this lineage is not accepted as *Bahu* (daughter-in-law).

Table 10
Opinion About Cross-cousin Marriage Among Close Relatives

	Do you Practice Cross-cousin Marriage?					
	No		*Yes*		*Total*	
Sex Ratio	*Nos.*	*%*	*Nos.*	*%*	*Nos.*	*%*
Male	-	-	157	100	157	52.3
Female	-	-	143	100	143	47.7
Total	-	-	300	100	300	100.0

Source: Same as Table-1

Table 10 shows that all the respondents favour marriage between close relatives. All 300 (100%) respondents say that they are practicing such type of marriage. Why they are practicing such kind of marriage is shown in Table 11.

Table 11 shows those 141 (47%) respondents, 71 (45.2%) males and 70 (49%) females say that they practise cross cousin marriage because adjacent communities do not form endogamous partnership with the Dhankuts. Since their caste is not described in district gazetteer, people from other communities do not like to give their daughters and sons in Dhankut for marriage. A number of 135 respondents, 73 (46.5%) males and 62 (43.3%) females reports that they practise such kind of marriage to save their community's identity and existence.13 (4.3%) respondents, 6(3.8%) males and 7 (4.9%) females prefer such marriage due to their culture, whereas 11 (3.7%) respondents, 7 (4.5%) males and 4 (2.8%) females go for such marriage due to lack of mobility, which is result of their poor economic status.

Participant observation revealed that Dhankut is mainly concentrated in Dhankutty pura and their population is very small i.e. 2687. So they have no option as no girl or boy is available for marriage from outside Dhankuttypura.

Table 11
Cause of Cross Cousin Marriage

Sex Ratio	*Why do you Practice Such Marriage?*									
	Due to Culture		*To Save Community Existence/ Identity*		*Lack of Mobility*		*Non-recog-nition by Other Communities*		*Total*	
	Nos	%	*Nos*	%	*Nos*	%	*Nos*	%	*Nos*	%
Male	6	3.8	73	46.5	7	4.5	71	45.2	157	52.3
Female	7	4.9	62	43.3	4	2.8	70	49.0	143	47.7
Total	13	4.3	135	45.0	11	3.7	141	47.0	300	100.0

Source: Same as Table-1

Right to Health[4]

Good health is an indicator of healthy and developed society. There are several declarations which have a bearing on the right to health. For instance, the Declaration of the Rights of the Child, proclaimed on 29 November 1959 states (in its Principle 4) that children shall enjoy the benefits of social security, and shall be entitled to grow in health. For this, the declaration stressed that special care should be given to the child and her mother, including adequate pre-natal and post-natal care. It further stated that the child shall have right to adequate nutrition, housing and medical facilities. The International Convention on Economic, Social and Cultural Rights (ICESCR), in its Article 12 recognizes everyone's right to the enjoyment of the highest attainable standard of physical and mental health.

'The main goal of a health system is to improve the health status of the population, which is measured by indicators such as mortality, morbidity, mental health, etc. Health acts as an indicator of the level of social, economic, cultural and environmental development of a society. So far as Dhankut are concerned the situation is not good, due to lack of education and poverty they are not aware of various health schemes which play an important role in monitoring good health.

Awareness to Effect of Inbreeding

Male and female Dhankut also suffer from impotency and other reproductive problems. Infertility is a major problem among Dhankut. In different studies definite effect of consanguinity on fertility has been noted (Mukherjee and Bhaskar,1974) and various other studies also reveal that mortality rate is high among offspring of consanguineous marriages. (Kumar et al. 1967; Murty and Jamil, 1972; Rao and Reddy, 1977 and Rao, 1978). Out of 715 families of Dhankut there are 120 issueless couples, which is the direct effect of consanguineous marriages. Dhankut are illiterate so they are unable to correlate morbidity and mortality with inbreeding but participant observation revealed high rate of mortality (Table 12) and morbidity (Table 13) among Dhankut.

Table 13 shows that mortality rate is high among the offsprings of Dhankut which is a small group of 2687 people in total; in 2003, 03 children died, in 2004, 05 and in 2005, 06 children died. Present table also reveals that in the age group of 0-1 yrs, 6 children died, in 1 to 2 yrs 4, in 2-3 yrs 2 and in 3-4 yrs of age group 2 children died. Thus we notice that during the period between 2003 and 2005, 14 children died in Dhankuttypura of Baharaich.

Table 12
Rate of Mortality in the Off Spring of Consanguineous Marriages

	Year							
	2003		*2004*		*2005*		*Total*	
Age Group of Children	*Nos.*	*%*	*Nos.*	*%*	*Nos.*	*%*	*Nos.*	*%*
0-1 yrs	01	16.7	03	50.0	02	33.3	06	100.0
1-2 yrs	-	-	01	25.0	03	75.0	04	100.0
2-3 yrs	01	50.0	01	50.0	-	-	02	100.0
3-4 yrs	01	50.0	-	-	01	50.0	02	100.0
Total	03	21.4	05	35.7	06	42.9	14	100.0

Source: Same as Table-1

Table 13
Rate of Morbidity in the Offspring of Consanguineous Marriages

		Male		*Female*		*Total*	
Nature of Morbidity	*Marriage Type*	*Nos.*	*%*	*Nos.*	*%*	*Nos.*	*%*
Albinism	MBD	08	38.1	13	61.9	21	100.0
Epilepsy	MBD	02	100.0	-	-	02	100.0
Feeble Mindedness	FSD	02	66.7	01	33.3	03	100.0
Total	12	46.2	14	53.8	26	100.0	

Source: Same as Table-1
Note: MBD-Mother's brother's daughter, FSD- Father's Sister's daughter.

Participant observation revealed that consanguineous marriages among Dhankut have generated recessive genes of albinism, epilepsy and feeblemindedness due to inbreeding. (Chantia, 2001:141). Table 14 Shows that albinism is most frequent among marriage type of MBD among Dhankut. Other health problems inflicting them are epilepsy and feeble mindedness. In the present research group 21 are having albinism, 2 are inflicted with epilepsy and 3 with feeble mindedness. The table of reference also shows that rate of morbidity is higher in MBD type of marriages as compared to FSD type of marriages.

Panchayat as Guarantor of Right

Even in the age of globalization Dhankut, still believe in their traditional panchayat. Even though the civil court is at 500 yards away from their living place (Dhankutty Pura), they do not prefer going to the court as they cannot afford the expenses of the court. They go to the panchayat for the solution of their problems except in murder and other criminal matters, which are judicial matters. In the panchayat, they bring matrimonial and other social disputes. They have no land disputes due to the absence of agricultural land.

Table 14
Opinion about Panchayat

	What do you think About Panchayat							
	Easy Access for Dispute Resolution		*Inexpensive Way of Solving Dispute*		*Unavoidable for the Community*		*Total*	
Sex Ratio	*Nos.*	*%*	*Nos.*	*%*	*Nos.*	*%*	*Nos.*	*%*
Male	82	52.3	70	44.6	05	3.1	157	52.3
Female	49	34.3	90	62.9	04	2.8	143	47.7
Total	131	43.6	160	53.3	09	3.1	300	100.0

Source: Same as Table-1

Only 27 cases of separation are listed with the panchayat while the total number of families is 715 in this community. It is also very surprising that 120 families out of 715 are living without children. The span of their marriages varies from 5 to 35 years. Even after having a genuine cause the do not go to panchayat for separation because of poor economic status. They are also not in a position to afford the expenditure of remarriage. As the rules of the Panchayat are very strong with regard to remarriage, barren couples neither separate nor remarry due to poor economic condition.

What Dhankut think about the existence of Panchayat and why they do not prefer going to court is reflected in Table 14.

Table shows that 160 (53.3%) respondents, 70 (44.6%) males and 90 (62.9%) females say that it is an inexpensive system for solving disputes. 131 (43.6%) respondents, 82 (52.3%) males and 49 (34.3%) females think that it is easy to approach panchayat for dispute resolution as it is free from the technicalities and formalities of the court. 9 (3.1%) respondents, 5 (3.1%) males and 4 (2.8%) females say that it is unavoidable for the community. Participant observation revealed that Panchayat system still holds control in traditional communities. Majority of Dhankut prefer Panchayat system for solving disputes as they can not afford the expenses of court.

A smooth life is a prime requirement of everyone and an individual make effort for it but everything is not within his/her reach. In a democratic and welfare State, government is the guarantor of rights. Dhankut are living in scarcity and they want many rights for their smooth survival from the Government. Some of the rights aspired by them are depicted in Table 15.

Table shows that 135 (45%) respondents, 63 (40.1%) males and 72 (50.3%) females say that they want right to live with dignity and prestige. 37 (23.6%) males and 29 (20.3%) female or overall 66 (22%) respondents say that they want basic facilities in life i.e. right to food, water, shelter, electricity etc. 42 (14%) respondents, 25 (15.9%) males and 17 (11.9%) females say that they want their caste to be recognized by the Government. Since their caste is not recognized they are looked down upon by the members of adjacent communities and can not enjoy the right to dignity and prestige. 57 (19%) respondents, 32 (20.4%) males and 25 (17.5%) females demanded right to reservation in government jobs for their

Table 15
Required Rights in Life

Sex Ratio	*Which Rights are Necessary in your Life?*									
	Rights to Basic Facilities		*Recognition of their Caste*		*Right to Live with Dignity/ Prestige*		*Right to Reservation*		*Total*	
	Nos.	*%*	*Nos.*	*%*	*Nos.*	*%*	*Nos.*	*%*	*Nos.*	*%*
Male	37	23.6	25	15.9	63	40.1	32	20.4	157	52.3
Female	29	20.3	17	11.9	72	50.3	25	17.5	143	47.7
Total	66	22.0	42	14.0	135	45.0	57	19.0	30	100.0

Source: Same as Table-1

growth and development.

CONCLUSION

It is astonishing to note that even after the 60 years of independence and in the era of globalization, there is a group whose monthly income is very meagre, they live in congested houses, in unhealthy environment, they have no water and electricity supply in their houses. Their women have to go to open fields to answer the call of nature which is quite unhealthy and also put their safety at stake.

Dhankut is an isolated group; it has no caste identity of its own. They are not recognised by the adjacent communities of the district. Due to their poor economic position and lack of education they are looked down upon by the members of other communities. Due to living at single place, poor economy and non recognition by other communities, they are practicing cross cousin and parallel cousin marriage in order to save their lineage. They do not know the genetic effect of inbreeding- a consequence of consanguineous marriage which has led to low infertility, high mortality and to a high rate of albinism in their group. Panchayat plays an important role in their lives. Due to financial crisis they don't go to the court for the solution of their disputes which is only 500 yards away from their living place. Everyone is bound to obey the order of the panchayat. Though Dhankut are aware of their rights and want to access them like the members of other communities, but poverty, non recognition of their caste and living at single place make an environment for human right violation and deprive them of all facilities which are available around them.

Though Dhankut do not know the exact meaning of human right but they know that it is something guaranteed by the government. They want all basic facilities such as food, water, shelter, electricity, education besides recognition of their caste and reservation in jobs by the government. They want to lead a dignified life with right to equality of status with other communities.

Though Dhankut of District Bahraich are marginalized people but government consider them as of general category and therefore they are far away from all those benefits which are otherwise available to other marginalized groups such as SC/ST/OBC. Government / private job is a distant dream for them. Illiteracy and poverty has ruined their lives. Impotency, skin diseases, albinism are their main health problems. Though Civil Court is near to their living place but due to poverty they stick to their traditional Panchayat for dispute resolution. Their Children are also engaged in small time work to earn livelihood.

Their traditional system of grain selling has given place to small time retail selling of general products. In order to bring change in their living conditions a kind of social movement has arisen among Dhankut, they have started fighting for ward election after the declaration of Dhankuttypura as ward. Recently they have formed a 'Dhankut Sangharsh Samiti' to fight for their identity, status and development. A case is also pending in SC/ST Commission, U.P., Lucknow for claiming their status in society.

To reach the benefits of globalization, it is suggested that Dhankut should immediately be categorized either as Scheduled Caste, Scheduled Tribe or Other Backward Class, so as to provide them with socio-cultural identity of their own, which is very essential for enjoying basic facilities of life and social development. It is further suggested that with regard to Dhankut human rights should be developed as the way of life and should not be limited to mere slogans. They should be made aware of human rights, its significance, availability and enforcement. The government must chalk out some specific policies and programmes to enable them to strengthen their social movement to live in dignity and with respect so as to improve their moral, cultural and social values.

ENDNOTES

1. Article 25 of the United Nations Declaration on Human Rights (UNDHR) emphasises that everyone has the right to a standard of living adequate for the health and well being of himself and of his family including food, clothing, housing and medical care and necessary social services.
2. *Article 26(1) of the Universal Declaration of Human Rights (UNDHR)*- Everyone has the right to education. Education shall be free, at least in the elementary and fundamental stages. Elementary education shall be

compulsory. *Article 26(2) of the Universal Declaration of Human Rights (UNDHR)*- Education shall be directed to the full development of the human personality and to the strengthening of respect for human rights. Further, Right to education has also been recognised under Art. 13(1) of the International Covenant on Economic Social and Cultural Rights and under Article 41 of the Indian Constitution. (Jaswal & Jaswal,2001). Art. 21 A (Constitutional 86th Amendment Act 2002) and Art. 45 of Indian Constitution recognize the right to education in consonance with the commitment of international community.

3. Right to marriage is recognised under Article 21 of Indian Constitution as part of right to life and personal liberty and is judicially recognised too. Section 5(iv) of Hindu Marriage Act, 1955 also guarantees close relation marriages in the name of custom and usage which is otherwise void. It is very unhealthy practice and leads to a number of genetical problems due to inbreeding and thus devoids the person of right to health which is again a fundamental right under Article 21 of Indian Constitution. In 60 years of independence the government is not able to do away with this unhealthy practice which continues in the name of usage and custom with the sanction of the government.
4. See footnote-1. Article 24 of the United Nations Convention on the Rights of the Child, 1989, ratified by the Government of India on 11th December 1992 provides that state shall recognise the right of the child to the enjoyment of highest attainable standard of health and to facilitate for the treatment of illness and rehabilitation of health. The state parties shall strive to ensure that no child is deprived of his/her right of access to such health care services. The Alma Ata Declaration 1978 to which India is a signatory pledged "Health for all by 2000 AD". It declared health as a fundamental human right and defined it as a state of complete physical, mental and social well being (WHO,2004).

REFERENCES

Blumer, H. (1951), "Social Movements". In A.N. Lee (ed.), *New Outlines of Principles of Society*. New York: Baines D. Nolde.

Castells Manual (1989), *The Information City: Information Technology, Economic Restructuring and the Urban Regional Process*. Oxford: Blackwell .

Chantia, Alok (2001), Socio-cultural Profile of Dhankutta-An Endogamons Group of Bahraich District of U.P.,*Unpublished Thesis* ,University of Lucknow, Lucknow, P.141

Chitkara, M.G. (1996), *Human Rights: Commitment and Betrayal*, New Delhi: APH Publishing Corporation.

Constitutional Assembly Debates, Vol. III, (2004), p.494 Reprint, New Delhi: Wadhwa Publications,

Census (2001), Gazetteer of Bahraich (U.P.),Govt. Press, Lucknow

Gordon, David (1988), "The Global Economy: New Edifice or Crumbling Foundations", *New Left Review,* Vol. 168, pp. 24 – 64.

Gidden, S.A. (2001), *Sociology*. (4th Edition). London: Policy Press.

Gusfield, J.R. (1971), *Protest, Reform and Revolt, A Reader in Social Movements*. New York: John Wiley & Sons.

Harberle (1972), "Types and Functions of Social Movement", in *International Encyclopaedia of Social Sciences*. New York: Macmillan Co. Free Press.

Hirst P&G. Thompson (1996 a), "Globalisation: Ten Frequently Asked Questions and Some Surprising Answers", *Soundings*. Vol.4. U.K: Policy Press. pp 47-66.

——(1996 b), *Globalisation in Question: The International Economy*, Cambridge: Policy Press.

Jaswal, P.S. & N. Jaswal (2001), "Right to Education and Human Rights" in B.P. Singh Sehgal (ed). *Human Rights in India, Problems and Perspectives*. New Delhi: Deep & Deep Publication, pp. 124-128.

Kumar, S., R.A. Pai. & N.S. Swaminathan (1967), "Consanguineous Marriages and the Genetic Load Due to Lethal Genes in Kerala". In I.C. Verma & Auroma. (Eds.), *Reproduction in Medical Genetics in India*. Vol. 2, Pondicherry: Enterprises, pp.31:141-147.

Mukherjee, D.P. and Bhaskar (1974), *Studies on Inbreeding and Its Effects on Some Endogamous Population of Chittor District*. Andhra Pradesh. Presented at the Ist Ann. Conf., Indian Society of Human Genetics, Bombay.

Murty, J.S. & T. Jamil (1972), "Inbreeding Load in the New Born at Hyderabad". In I.C. Verma (Ed). *Reproduction in Medical Genetics in India*, Vol. 2, Pondicherry: Auroma Enterprises.

Prabhakaran Nair V. State of Tamil Nadu, AIR 1987 SC 2117.

Rao, A.P. & V. R. Reddy (1977), "Consanguineous Marriages and their Effects on Fertility and Offspring Mortality in a Rural Yadav Population of South Eastern Andhra Pradesh". In I.C. Verma (Ed.), *Medical Genetics in India*, Vol. 2. Pondicherry: Auroma Enterprises.

Rao, P.S.S. (1978), "Inbreeding in Tamil Nadu and Its Effects on Human Reproduction". In I.C. Verma (Ed.), *Medical Genetics in India*, Vol. 2, Pondicherry: Auroma Enterprises.

Shankar Banerjee v. Durgapur Projects Ltd, AIR 1988 Cal 136.

Spybey, T. (1996), *Globalisation and World Society,* Cambridge: Polity Press.

Streenten, P. (2001), *Globalisation-Threat or Opportunity,* Denmark: H. Forlong Copenhagen Business School Press.

Taylor, E.B. (1871), *Primitive Culture,* New York: Harper and Brothers (1958 Reprint).

Therborn, G. (2000), 'Globalisations, Dimensions, Historical Waves, Regional Effects, Normative Governance', *International Sociology,* Vol.XV (2), p.151.

United Nations Publication on the Human Rights to Adequate Housing, Fact Sheet (2000), No. 21. New York: United Nations Organisation, p.3.

United Nations (1995), Declaration of the World Summit For Social Development. Vol. XXI (43) WS 97-104, New York: United Nations Organisation.

University of Delhi v. Ram Nath, 1964 2 SCR 703 at 710.

Wilson, J. (1973), *Introduction to Social Movements,* New York: Basic Books.

World Bank (2002), *Globalisation, Growth and Poverty-Building an Inclusive World.* Washington DC: World Bank Publications.

World Health Organisation (2000), *Decade Assessment Report 2000.* Geneva: WHO.

——(2004), *The World Health Report.* Geneva: WHO.

28

SITUATING ASURS OF JHARKHAND IN SOCIO-ECONOMIC PERSPECTIVE

Mritunjay Kumar

A tribe like any other ethnic group, has its own self image and identity on the basis of which it considers itself historically as well as socio-culturally distinct from other groups and justifies this identity in spite of various changes taking place in their life. It is in this sense of identity which is basic for the survival of a tribal group. (Sahay, 1985:1). The tribal India lives in the forests, hills and naturally isolated regions known as a rule by different names meaning either the people of forest and hill or the original habitants, and so on. (Vidyarthi & Rai, 1985:25). These tribes, sometimes called aboriginal because of their being the earliest inhabitants of this country, not only belong to different stages of culture but they vary from area to area in regard to size of the population, language, racial types, socio-economic organization, etc. (Prasad, 1961:3). Tribal researches in India owe their beginning to the establishment of the Asiatic Society of Bengal (1774). Sir William Jones, a great Orientalist deserves the credit for defining the scope of the society in a work entitled *"Nature and Man in India"*. He also piloted a number of researches and publications on the subject. Under these influences the first Indian national, S.C. Roy, who was known as "the father of Indian Ethnology", studied tribes of present Jharkhand having very rich culture heritage. The various tribal communities living there from time immemorial has developed their own socio-economic, political and cultural pattern of life. Their love towards nature, physical labour, truthfulness, simplicity, equality, music, collectiveness and freedom make them distinct from others. There are 32 Scheduled Tribes in Jharkhand in which 9 are primitive. Criteria formulated by the Government of India for identifying primitive groups are that they must have pre-agricultural technology, a low level of literacy which is less than five per cent and a marginal or stagnant rate of growth. Dhebar Commission identified Asur, Birhor, Kharia, Korwa, Mal Paharia, Sauria Paharia and Savar as primitive groups in Bihar while the Shilu Ao team specified Asur, Korwa, Lohara, Birjia, Chik Baraik, Mahali and Paharia as backward tribal communities. On the other hand, the Commissioner for Schedule Caste and Schedule Tribes has included all the tribes mentioned by Dhebar Commission except Birhor and all the tribes identified by Shilu Ao team in the list of STs and has added Baiga, Karmali and Kisan to it. The Asurs have been identified as primitive group by all the three i.e. Dhebar Commission, Shilu Ao team and the Commissioner for Schedule Caste and Schedule tribes. They are one of the nine tribal communities in Jharkhand, who fit into this mould. Here we are trying to discuss Asur, both in historical and contemporary perspective.

Many modern German as well as Indian indologists believe the Asurs, who have a place in Vedic literature, to be the ancestors of the contemporary aboriginal tribes of the Chotanagpur, Orissa, and Central India, the Bhils and allied tribes of western India. (*ibid*, 216). In Jharkhand, the Asurs are settled in Ranchi, Gumla, lohardagga, latehar and Palamu. (Singh, 2005:250). The Asur locality is known as the Netarhat group of plateaus within Chotanagpur plateau. The modern Asur tribe is divided into three Sub-divisions, namely Bir (Kol) Asur, Birjia Asur and Agaria Asur. The Birjia are recognized as a separate Scheduled Tribe which comes under the primitive tribe groups. (Oraon, 2003: 48).

The total population of Scheduled Tribes in Jharkhand is 70, 87,068 (Seventy lakh eighty-seven thousand and sixty-eight) (GoI, 2001:192) which is 26.30 per cent (GoI, 2005:15) of total population. The total population of the tribal group of Asur is 7783. The people who belong to the Asur tribe cover only 0.13 per cent of the total population of the state,[1] out of which almost 97 per cent comes from rural areas. (Singh, 1994:71).

The word *Asura* occurs in a number of places in the Rigveda, Brahamanas, Aranyakas, Upanishadas and Epics which comprise the sacred literature of the Hindus[2]. According to Banerji-shastri (1926), the Asura was a power which claimed and received homage even from Vedic Aryans. Varuna was the principal deity of the Asura. It has been said that Asura lost their military prestige, industrial skill and their descendants were killed in great numbers. This struggle between the Aryans and the Asura is said to have dragged on for centuries. Those of the Asura who refused to be absorbed in the Neo Aryan body politic were perhaps classed along with Rakshasas or demons. Thus, we may say that the word Asura in the beginning was a synonym of god which changed later on as a synonym of demon. Other references in Vedic literature indicate that they were in Aryan times 'a distinct and mighty people' who contended with the Aryans. (Gupta, 1976:7). The meaning of Asur was 'Powerful Forest People' or 'Bir Asur'. Among the Jharkhand tribes, the Asur and the Birhor only drew their tribal name from forest (ibid.). As regards the origin of the Asurs, it is very difficult to say anything definite. In present state of our knowledge, one may try to reconstruct to a certain extent about their origin. Several theories have been put forwarded including references in Vedic literature, pre-historic evidences, etc., to account for their origin. (ibid.).

The earliest available published about the Asur is given by Forbes, Revenue Officer of Palamau, Government Estate in his report to Dalton, Commissioner of Chotanagpur Division in the year 1869. (ibid.2). Colonel Dalton was inclined to connect them with the Asurs who, according to Munda traditions, were destroyed by Sing Bonga, and it has been conjectured that they are the descendants of the original inhabitants of the plateau, who were driven out by the Mundas and of whom the only traces now to be found are a few scattered tumuli and occasional stone or copper celts. Archaeological remains indicate that Asur passed through neolithic into the megalithic period. The Kolarian speech of the Asur is shared with the Munda, Birhors, Hos, Santhals, Korkus, etc. In physical appearance too, they resemble 'Kolarian' or Proto-Australoid Tribes as do Birhor, Baiga etc., and like them are divided into exogamous totemic clans (*Killis*). (ibid.131).

The Asurs are traditionally iron-smelters and also slash burn cultivators. Iron smelting requires charcoal of green sal wood. Similarly, slash burn method of crop cultivation destroys well grown forests. Thus, they become nomadic. (Prasad, op cit., 216). But forest acts and regulations have snatched away their traditional rights over the forest. This has affected their practice of iron-smelting and shifting cultivation[3].

D.D.Koshambi suggests that the Asurs of Chotanagpur probably borrowed the Mauryan technology of iron smelting, which they surely could not have developed on their own. (Singh, 1985:63). Now they have become settled farmers and have founded their own villages. They prefer to locate their villages on sufficiently high table land for two main reasons that there may not be much land erosion during the rains and there may be enough 'Bari Land' for maize cultivation. But a village and the nearest natural sources of water supply become inconveniently separated. An Asur settlement usually consists of not more than 30 families and they prefer to be separate from others. (Prasad, op cit., 216-217). There is no set pattern of settlement except that the youth dormitory (GITI-ORA) and the dancing ground are situated in an easy accessible and central place. Generally they construct side walls of earth and different wooden frames are provided for supporting the tiled roof. Their residential house contains accommodation for their cattle too. Household goods are few cooking utensils, mat, agricultural and hunting tools and implements made of wood, bamboo and iron. (ibid).

They speak in Asuri language at home which belongs to the Austro-Asiatic family of languages, but they are also conversant with Hindi and Sadri. The script used by them is Devnagri. (Singh, 1994: 72).

The Asur society is divided into twelve *killis* i.e. clans. (Oraon, 1994:11). No matrimonial relation within the clan is allowed. Beyond the clan organisation family is most important social unit. Decent in the family goes through the male line and father is the leader of the family. (Singh, 2005, op cit.). The Asurs have a tendency to live in joint families, the nuclear family type coming next to it (Gupta, op cit., 134). Usually the most capable member acts as a family manager and guardian. (Prasad, op cit., 217).

The Asur society is guided by traditionally laid down customs. If anyone violates a custom, the matter is taken notice of by the community, which function through community panchayat, and, the office bearers are the Mahto, Baiga, Pujar, Gorait, etc. Every adult male is allowed to participate in the deliberations of the panchyat. As soon as an objectionable matter is discovered, Mahto ask Gorait to inform the whole community to assemble at the village *akhara* at a particular time. As soon as the assembly meets, the objectionable matter is brought before it and necessary evidences are produced. The judgment is immediately announced and usually honoured, but in case of inability to fulfill the decision, the defaulter leaves the village forever. Now-a-days some Asurs have adopted Christianity. So, many of the functions of the community panchyat are discharged by Christian fathers with the help of the elders. (ibid).

Marriage is considered essential for successful life. The Asurs practise a number of ways of obtaining brides like marriage by service, elopement, force and by exchange of sisters. There is the tradition of being adopted to the family of the bride, i.e. the *ghar jamai* tradition. The ways of acquiring mate in the Asur society are by bride-price, service, *raji-khushi* and *golat*. The marriage by bride price is negotiated through the fathers of the boy and the girl. At the time of negotiation, the father of the groom approaches the father of the bride. (Singh, 2005: 252).

The Asurs follow the rule of monogamy, but in case of barrenness, widower and widowhood, they follow the rule of bigamy or even trigamy. At the time of marriage they follow the rule of tribe endogamy and clan exogamy. Those who do not follow these rules are ousted from the community. However, they are allowed after they feed the community members seven times. (Oraon, 2003 op cit., 50).

In the society of Asur, divorce is allowed, but attempt is made to settle the dispute through panchayat. But if dispute is not settled, the couple is allowed for a divorce. (ibid., 51-52). Marriage life is quite stable and so divorce cases are rare. (Prasad; op cit., 218).

The woman had to leave the children to the husband at the time of divorce. The small kids are allowed to go to woman. Extramarital relation, barrenness, witchcraft, laziness and cruel behaviour become the cause of divorce. (Singh, 2005, op cit.).

Birth is treated a very pious occasion for the couple, family and community. After the birth the couple is treated fertile and the marriage is considered successful. (Oraon, 2003, op cit., 53). The Asurs welcomes more a female as the first issue, unlike in many other tribes and non-tribal communities. This is largely based on the belief that a daughter as the first issue brings all the prosperity and long life for the parents who would be able to see the marriages not only of their sons and daughters but also of their grand-sons and grand-daughters. (Gupta, op cit., 134). The occasion of birth is marked by pollution and so for certain days the whole house is considered impure and during this time no new work is done. On the sixth day the mother takes a bath and the baby's head is completely shaved. Knife is used for cutting the naval string. The name is given with the traditional ritual of dropping grains into a vessel filled with water. (Prasad, op cit. 218).

The child grows in the family and enjoys constant company of the parents. In this way s/he learns domestic works. As soon as the child becomes capable of living without his/her mother s/he begins to attend the *Dhumkuria* and sleeps there along with other unmarried girls and boys of the village. The Asurs have common dormitories in which boys and girls sleep together till they are married (ibid).

Succession in the Asur society goes through the male side. All the sons of the dead get equal share. In some cases the eldest son receives a bit more than the others. The daughters have only maintenance and marriage rights in the family. A widow also enjoys the maintenance rights but, if she leaves the house of the husband, she becomes the loser. (Singh, 2005, op cit., 252).

The *Ghar-jamai* gets the rights of manager of the properties left by his father-in-law and if he goes away to live at his own home, he does not get any right in his father-in-law's property. (Prasad, op cit., 219).

The Asurs are aware of death reality. They know well that death lays its icy hand on all living things, but a distinction is made between deaths. Natural death during old age is an acceptable truth because it provides occasion for a change of old body in the new one through death. (Oraon, op cit., 53). Disposal of dead by cremation is rare and resorted to in case of old people. They bury their dead with feet to the south. They must bathe when returning from a burial. The *Kaman* or dinner in honour of the deceased takes place in the usual way, eight days or a fortnight after the death. (Hoffmmann and Van Emelem 2008: 237). They observed the ceremony of recalling the shadow of the deceased and for this they still have the Mundari word, *umbul ader*, though the Sadri word, *Khai bhitrael* is also used. On this point Fr. Dajaegher writes as follows: "It is done, not on the burial day but on the Kaman day in a place between the ceremony and the house. They make a small *machan* which they cover with *Kher* (thatching grass). Then they bring a bit of cloth which belonged to the dead person, and with it they put fire to the whole. Then they say to the dead person's soul. "Now, run away, thy house is on fire. Go to the cemetery and never return to thy old home." (Prasad; op cit.). The dead are buried in a place known as Sasan and a stone for each one is put there. Usually such a place is situated near a water-shed but out of the settlement. (ibid.).

The Asur propitiate the Sing Bonga, Marang Bonga and certain other deities and observe festivals such as Sarhul, Sohrai, Holi, Karma and Kharwaj. Some of them have embraced Christianity though they still retain some pre-conversion practices. Their priest (*pahan*) is either from their own community or from the Kharwar, Birjia or some other communities. (Singh, 1994, op cit., 73).

Jharkhand has a long tradition of metallurgy as archaeological evidence of copper, gold and iron smelting have been found in this region. Jharkhand has been an epicenter of the growth and dispersion of a particular tool technique. It is believed that Asur had introduced the craft of iron smelting in this region (It is interesting to note that the name Asur is also associated with traditional iron technological sites of Kumaun in the Central Himalayas). How old is the Asur's association with Jharkhand is not known. There are two types of small iron smelting workshop that distinguish the iron industry of Jharkhand- the open air furnace of the nomadic blacksmith and the more numerous thatched furnace. Then, there was the larger iron-smelting workshop of the Koth-Saal type, followed by Khammar-Saal or iron refining houses. (Goyal: 2008:3)[4].

Three varieties of iron ore are recognized by Asur's at the Netarhat Plateau. One is magnetite which is called *POLA* by them. The other one is Hematite from coal measures known as *BICHI* and third one is Hematite from laterite known as *GOTA*. They were able to locate a site for the ores by observation and experience. On the basis of their family labour iron smelting was carried on by them. Green sal trees were cut by them in the neighbourhood of their furnace for preparing char coal as char coal of green sal was capable of generating sufficient heat for smelting iron ore in their furnaces which were usually located in the neighbourhood of water sources like Dari, Chua or rivulet[5].

The Asur families engaged in iron-smelting perform *SANSI-KUTASI* worship which may be called productive magic, as it is aimed at securing good iron while smelting. All the implements required for iron smelting and black smithy are collected in front of the house. A cock and a hen both of red colour are sacrificed during the worship. The offering is said to be accepted if the birds partake some of the rice from the small heap which is kept here. The cock is caught by the neck with a pair of pincers (*Sansi*) and its head is crushed with a hammer (Kutasi) by keeping it on a stone anvil. The hen is also sacrificed in the same manner. Some offerings of rice are also made to deities and ancestors to whom the worship is addressed and offered. The ritual is followed by dance and drinks and merry-makings. The peculiar feature of this festival is that musical instruments which are so essential for all social and festive occasions among the Asur are not played on this occasion when the boys and girls are engaged in dancing. Every head of a family has to don him with a new piece of cloth on this occasion which is considered important in the annual cycle of festivals of the Asur. (Gupta, op cit., 3-4).

Traditionally, at least three people work continuously for a minimum of six hours to smelt iron. The rocks-any of the three types of rocks from which iron is made-are crushed into coarse form and melted in the blast furnace. The furnace, one or one and a half meters in length, is in cylindrical shape and made of mud. Charcoal is ignited in the furnace and the crushed rocks are poured into it. The rocks are melted till the solution form starts pouring into a leather bag kept beneath the furnace. Air is pumped continuously into the furnace so that the metal does not solidify[6].

PREPARATION OF IRON SMELTING BY ASURS NEAR NETARHAT

The traditional iron working is still alive in certain remote areas of the state, where higher quality of product is made by the workers in small furnaces. But in the present context there appears a need to review the technical availability of traditional iron making due to the changing politico-culture and socio-ecological constraints. It has been said that the traditional iron making is wasteful both from the point of view of raw material as well as charcoal consumption as it plays an important role in the process of deforestation. But, if we look at their technology closely we find that these groups are tapping those ores that are neglected or rated as low grade and not considered important for smelting by modern steel mills. The other significance of their work is that they locate and exploit those small pockets of ore deposits that have not been recorded in the geological texts while listing economically viable mining zones. The delicate way of ore picking by them cannot be neglected. So if we take a holistic look, their technology is based on maximum utilization of the available ore resources. Regarding the second allegation that they are over exploiting forest resources, we find that most of the charcoal is made by them with dead trees lying in the forest. The Agaria families of Chhattishgarh and Chhota Nagpur visit forests for the collection of the sal leaves to use them as the plates for their meals, but the number of leaves per family is fixed and they do take a lot of care while plucking the leaves. Even when leaves are not plucked indiscriminately or carelessly by them, how can we accuse them of wasting trees? They show a great regard and respect towards the trees. The trees are considered as the abode of deities or ancestor spirits that take care of the welfare of the people. (Goyal, op cit., 4-5).

The indigenous iron smelting tradition is gradually losing mainly due to the following reasons:

1. This tradition is losing its grip because of the availability of better tools and implements in the market.
2. The scarcity of the raw materials forced these tribes to adopt some new ways of economic activities.
3. The work is very laborious and time consuming.
4. The other factor that is playing an important part in losing this tradition is the adoption of the western techniques. The Indian tribes have been dispossessed of their habitat and thrown into an alien world without being equipped to face the harsh world. As a result of this, they are losing their traditional techniques and are forced to adopt the new ways to eke out an existence. As we are now realizing the potential of their craft, we need to review our industrial policies after over fifty years of independence.

Indira Gandhi National Museum of Mankind, Bhopal, is trying to revive this dying tradition. This will certainly help to protect these traditional iron smelters from unemployment and thus will be able to save this traditional system of iron technology. (ibid., 5-6).

In the present ecological conditions, the traditional technology can play a vital part by saving the environment and making it pollution free. The charcoal used by them as a source of energy is proved to be a far less pollutant in comparison to the fuels used by the modern steel mills. On the one hand, coal or other fossil fuels produce a large number of carcinogenic byproducts, while on the other charcoal is not a pollutant because of its low sulphur content. The furnaces used by these communities are small and so they do not cause damage to the atmosphere. The traditional iron working is in the form of small scale household industries distributed over a large area. Resource exploitation by these communities is therefore shallow, expanding over an extensive area. So, one can say that the ore and fuel used by these communities are not affecting the environment. These data lead us to construe that these the traditional crafts of iron making have an eco-friendly economic viability in the present context. (ibid, 5).

During the last several decades due to the introduction of improved metallurgy and the forest conservation policy of the Government imposing restriction on wanton cutting of forest gave a final death blow to the industry of iron smelting in this plateau. (ibid., 4). Iron-smelting used to be the principal occupation of the Asurs, but now it has ceased to be so. Few years ago only one furnace was found working at village Ramgaria in Bishunpur police station where only two families worked and earned a very meager living (Footnote-4). Iron-smelting has now practically become a thing of the past. (ibid).

The Asurs have now become primarily agriculturist, and hunting and collecting of roots, fruits and flowers constitute the other economic bases of their traditional economy. (Prasad; op. cit). According to the 1981 census, 41.98 per cent of them are returned as workers. Of them, only 2.23 per cent are now engaged in the household industry i.e. their traditional occupation of iron smelting. They have now switched over to cultivation. Most of them (91.19%) are engaged in the primary sector of the economy (75.67% cultivators and 15.52% agricultural labourers). The remaining 6.58 per cent are engaged in iron smithy. Agriculture has become their principal means of subsistence. They also work as industrial workers and miners. Some of them are office employees and petty businessmen. (Singh, 1994, op cit.).

The Government of India has made a number of plans to protect the rights of the tribals and to integrate them into national development frame. The Minority Commission, the National Human Rights Commission, etc., are there to prevent atrocities against them and to bring their plight to national lime light. Above all, in the Constitution of India the rights of the tribals were explicitly recognized and clauses were included to permit positive discrimination in their favour.

In spite of the protection given to the tribal population by the Constitution of India (1950), tribals still remain the most backward ethnic group in India. They rate very low on the three most important indicators of development: health, education and income. The tribals are most backward not only compared with the general population, but also compared to the Scheduled Caste (Dalits), the other backward social group with constitutional protection. While examining the effects of planned developmental intervention on the tribals, it was observed that intervention has not made any significant impact in improving the conditions of the tribals. As per the Planning Commission Document 1973, "Reviewing the policies and programmes of the proceeding Five Year Plans we are of the opinion that the efforts so far made for social and economic development of the scheduled tribes have not brought an appreciable change in their condition". There can be a number of explanations for the failure of the governmental programmes for tribal development. Although, the tribals are a part of the Indian society and general problems of consciously changing or modernizing Indian society are also applicable to them. But the tribals form a special case in this wider framework and the problem is the nature and type of this special category.

Tribal development policies and programmes in India assumed that all the tribals would develop and integrate themselves with the so-called mainstream. In spite of more than sixty years of Community Development and Tribal Welfare Programmes most of them are living below subsistence level, and are leading a miserable life in isolated parts of Jharkhand. (Sandhwar, 1981:376). An Asur has to work hard nearly 20 hours a day to earn his bread and butter. This indicates that this tribal community has been deprived of the benefits meant for them as they still live in isolation (*Prabhat Khabar*, 2009:2). Although Jharkhand Government has decided to provide 35 Kg. food grains free of cost for every primitive tribe family, but result of this scheme is doubtful because the executors of the plan are generally unsympathetic to them. As a result the Asurs have been forced to migrate to various part of country such as Haryana, Punjab, U.P. etc. for their livelihood (*ibid*). It can be observed that these tribes are becoming poorer and poorer because the real fruit of the Welfare Programmes is enjoyed by the major and advanced tribal and non-tribal communities in those areas. (Sandhwar, op cit).

However, the oppression and appropriation of the tribal people by the economically and politically more powerful groups have led to tribal movements or tribal unrest. For instance, the Santal rebellion, the revolt by Birsa Bhagwan, the Praja Mandal Movement, the Tana Bhagat Movement, the Naxalbari Movement, the Jharkhand Movement etc., are all attempts by the tribal people to shake off the yoke of exploitation.

In recent times the traditional territories of the tribal people have been subjected to incursions. Their lands are taken away in the name of economic advancement of the country. But in return they become landless and face impoverishment and long term degradation of the environment on which they totally depend. For almost two centuries now, tribal communities, like many other non-tribal peasants and forest dwellers, have been witness to the collapse of their multiple relationships with the land, the forest and among themselves.

The basis of their cultural ethos, their systems of meaning have faced the collective unslaught of outsider exploiters, the disruptive impact of proselytizing Christianity, and of foreign models of economic betterment which have been conceived without their participation and implemented without their consent. Laws like Land Acquisition Act and the Indian Forest Act legitimise the continuing decline in access and control over forest resources that are the basis of their subsistence economy.

Initiatives from the Bharat-Jan-Andolan, Shosit Jan Andolan, the Indian Council of Indigenous and Tribal Peoples, Adivasi Sangamams in South India, PUCL, PUDR etc., are indicative of these modest attempts to raise - fundamental issues and define an alternative political agenda that frontally challenges the institutions and structures of our bourgeois democracy.

In the broad setting of reforms in many countries in the 1980s, India was an apparent anomaly. India was at the crossroads. She was facing a macroeconomic crisis that required immediate attention. The macroeconomic crisis provided the opportunity and the necessity to address meaningfully the inefficiencies in our policy framework that had altered our economic performance and to begin constructively the task of undertaking the necessary microeconomic or structural reforms that had long been overdue. The reform process began in India in 1991[7]. Since 1991, India has experienced rapid globalization with the opening of economy; transnational firms have been providing new opportunities to the global market. For the first time transnational consumer goods became widely available[8].

But Globalisation affects tribals differently. Urban and educated tribals may benefit from the increased opportunities for work that come with the influx of foreign companies and investments. These employment avenues are complemented by greater opportunities to receive education and training of a higher quality. The new technologies that define this era, in particular the computer and Internet may be accessible to this group of tribals. In general, the liberalization of trade and financial markets also promise benefits for this group, including a greater variety of goods at cheaper prices due to increased competition and much more attractive interest rates to undertake business ventures.

Conversely, poor, uneducated, credit-constrained, informal and agricultural sector tribals will benefit in a much less direct manner. Tribals in general benefit from long-term economic growth brought about by correcting price distortions in factor and product markets. But these changes have little effect on Asur tribe because they are almost cut off from the mainstream economic activities.

The gains from globalisation have so far accrued to those who already have education and skill advantage, easier market access and possession of assets for use as collateral to access credit. Although some tribal group such as Santhals, Oraons, Munda etc. have tested the fruit of globalization but Asur's are deprived from its taste.

However, the traditional culture of Asur passing through a challenging phase. It appears that factors like colonial rule, abrupt uncongenial development plans, land alienation, finance capital and capitalism have affected socio-cultural roots of Asur and other tribes of Jharkhand. Global economy and globalization of culture sooner or later may make the situation uncongenial. The developmental scheme should also be made in socio-cultural prospective. Element of forest economy should be encouraged. This will protect the traditional value of Asurs. Ecology and environment too would be strengthened. People's oriented planning should be given due importance. These measures may help Asurs in preserving their own value based system. Tribal identity is one of the most important parts of Indian identity. Indeed it is our responsibility to assure the plan and policies meant for these tribes.

ENDNOTES

1. http://www.mapsofindia.com/jharkhand/people-culture-festivals/asur.html.
2. Priyadarshi, Nitish (nd).
3. http://prabhat-khabar.jharkhandi.com/
4. Goyal, 2008.
5. Priyadarshi, Nitish; 2008

6. Shukla, Nityanand (nd).
7. Raj (nd) Impact of Globalization on Tribal Communities; http://www.goethals.org/globaltribal.htm
8. Derne, Steve. 2008, p 200.

REFSERENCES

Derne , Steve. (2008), *Globalization on the Ground;* New Delhi: Sage Publications.

GoI (2001), *Primary Census Abstract.* Total Population, Table A-5, Series-1. New Delhi: Registrar General & Census Commissioner, India.

GoI (2005), *India 2005.* Table1.7, Publication Department. New Delhi: Information and Broadcasting Department, India.

Goyal, Pankaj (2008), *Survival of Traditional Indian Iron Technology;* scribid.com. http://www.indianscience.org/essays/t_es_iron_technology.shtml

Gupta, Satya Prakash (1976), *The Asur Ethno-Biological Profile.* Ranchi: Bihar Tribal Research Institute, Government of Bihar.

Hoffmann, John & Arthur van Emelen (1928-78), *Encyclopedia Mundarica, Vol.I* . Patna: Government Superintendent Printing [Reprint: New Delhi: Gyan Publishing House, 1990].

Oraon, P.C. (2003), *Land and People of Jharkhand.* Ranchi: Jharkhand Tribal Welfare Research Institute, Welfare Department, Government of Jharkhand.

Prabhat Khabar (2009), Ranchi Edition, 15 February 2009, p 2 and 17 February, p 2.

Prasad, N. (1961), *Land and People of Tribal Bihar.* Ranchi: Bihar Tribal Research Institute, Government of Bihar.

Priyadarshi, Nitish (2008), *Iron Smelting by Asur Tribe- A Thing of The Past in Jharkhand State of India.* Published December 02, 2008 *http://www.americanchronicle.com/articles/view/83680*

——(nd)*The Asur Tribe and Iron smelting, http://www. magnificent jharkhand.com/more-feature.php?id=11.*

Raj, J. Felix SJ (nd).*Impact of Globalization on Tribal Communities; http://www.goethals.org/globaltribal.htm.*

Sahay, K.N. (1985), *Change of Tribal Identity in Chotanagpur.* Varanasi: Kishore Vidya Niketan.

Sandhwar, Abnindra Narayan (1981), 'Glimpses of Primitive Economy and Approaches of Development- A Case Study of Tribal Bihar'. In L.P.Vidyarthi (ed.), *Tribal Development and its Administration*. New Delhi: Concept Publishing Company.

Shukla, Nityanand (nd). *Iron smelting by Asur tribals a dying form; http://www.mail-archive.com/chhattisgarh-network@yahoogroups.com/msg00021.html*

Singh, K.S. (1985), *Tribal Society in India: An Anthropological Approach*. New Delhi: Manohar Publications.

Singh, K.S. (1994), *People of India, National Series Volume II, The Scheduled Tribes*. Delhi: Oxford University Press, p. 71.

Singh, S.K. (2005), *Inside Jharkhand*. Ranchi: Crown Publications.

Vidyarthi, L.P. & Binay Kumar Rai (1985), *The Tribal Culture of India*. New Delhi: Concept Publishing Company.

INDEX